THE WISDOM OF THE GODS

THE WISDOM OF THE GODS

VOICES OF THE DEAD: FANTASY, FRAUD OR FACT?

H. DENNIS BRADLEY

FOREWORD AND AFTERWORD

BY

MICHAEL TYMN

EXPANDED EDITION

www.whitecrowbooks.com

Wisdom of the Gods

Original Copyright © 1925 by H. Dennis Bradley.
This edition: Copyright © 2022 by White Crow Productions Ltd. All rights reserved.
Foreword and afterword copyright © 2022 by Michael Tymn

Published by White Crow Books, an imprint of White Crow Productions Ltd.

The right of the authors of this work have been asserted in accordance
with the Copyright, Design and Patents act 1988.

No part of this book maybe reproduced, copied, or used in any form
or manner whatsoever without written permission, except in the
case of brief quotations in reviews and critical articles.

A CIP catalogue record for this book is available from the British Library.

For information, contact White Crow Productions Ltd.
by e-mail: info@whitecrowbooks.com

Cover Design by Astrid@Astridpaints.com
Interior design by Velin@Perseus-Design.com

ISBN: Paperback: 978-1-78677-206-0
ISBN: eBook: 978-1-78677-207-7

Non-Fiction / Body, Mind & Spirit / Parapsychology Afterlife & Reincarnation

www.whitecrowbooks.com

To arrive at wisdom the heights and the depths of experience must be explored, and Truth must be established, not upon myth nor upon belief, but upon the solid foundation of knowledge.

CONTENTS

PREFACE 1
FOREWORD BY MICHAEL TYMN 3

BOOK ONE 15
1: THE PHYSICAL AND ELEMENTARY 17
2: HOW THE VOICES CAME THROUGH 27
   An explanation of the newest and highest form of mediumship—The first sound of a spirit voice—The lady and the trumpet—Why music helps the spirit forces to manifest themselves—The spirits manipulate the many parts of a jazz band—Mr. Caradoc Evans describes a spirit who spoke to him and Mr. Noel Jaquin his plan for a spirit imprint.

3: CONFIRMATION BY CROSS EVIDENCE 39
   In this sitting the stage is held by the spirit of Warren Clarke, who discusses Mr. Joseph De Wyckoff's charges against George Valiantine—An uncanny analysis of Mr. De Wyckoff's character—Evidential information concerning the author's son, Anthony Bradley—A spirit refutes the foolish trumpet allegation referred to in a previous chapter.

4: WITHOUT AN OUTSIDE MEDIUM 47
   The author makes his trumpet more luminous—The spirit of Lord Northcliffe speaks to Mr. Hannen Swaffer—This spirit also speaks to Miss Louise Owen—Mr. Swaffer supplies a vivid impression of this sitting—The author's sister Annie gives news of a serious illness

5: THE EVIDENCE OF LORD NORTHCLIFFE 53

Lord Northcliffe talks about certain persons on the Earth plane and makes many references of a very delicate nature—The author's startling theory of embryo children—A famous living person is severely handled—"Love is the main spring of life"—Mr. Swaffer receives advice from his former Chief—Annie delivers an urgent message, which later was confirmed

6: THE MIRACLE OF THE DIRECT VOICE 65

Among other things, this chapter records a dramatic, poignant scene between Miss Frances Carson, the famous actress, and the spirit of her dead husband—he Editor of "The Tatler" asks a question about a dog and is given a correct answer—Mr. Donald Calthrop writes: "Thank you for my first real introduction to the world beyond"—Mr. P. G. Wodehouse fails to recognize a spirit voice—The author is advised to discontinue the sittings and is given the reasons thereof—Listening to a séance behind a closed door.

7: FRAUD 73

Herein the author deals with false accusations against mediums—He tells the true story of Mr. De Wyckoff's charges against Valiantine and how he smashed them—He also tells of the strange communications between Mr. De Wyckoff and Mr. J Malcolm Bird of the "Scientific American," which account ends on a note of comedy—Captain Ben Hicks' exposure.

8: WASTE OF TIME 89

A few characteristic thoughts on fools and charlatans—The medium who bandaged her eyes and delivered "unutterable, meaningless drivel"—The investigator is indignant "with vulgar trickery designed to impress the weakly credulous."

9: THE SEARCH FOR REASONS 93

The spirit of Warren Clarke explains why the author was advised to discontinue the Dorincourt sittings, and counsels him about a proposal made by the Research Officer of the Society for Psychical Research—He is also warned of certain financial irregularities—A question about the powers of mediumship and the answer—A forecast of the great psychical upheaval—"Telepathy: the banal refuge for uneasy souls."

10: A VOICE MEDIUM SÉANCE 109

A Scottish correspondent draws the author's attention to the Sisters Moore—Arthur Brandise on Mr. DeWyckoff's estate—Unquestionable evidence obtained—The secret of obtaining mediumistic power.

CONTENTS

11: A TRANCE MEDIUM 113
Mrs. Scales, a clairvoyant and clairaudient medium—The question of control—An extraordinary transformation—Annie comes through, whereon occurred one of the most impressive and memorable experiences of the author's life.

12: THE NECESSITY FOR CRITICISM 119
Some remarks on the mediumship of Mr. Evan Powell—Miss Madeline Cohen's mother—Lord Northcliffe talks to Lord Beaverbrook—Mr. Bonar Law's faint whisper and Lord Northcliffe's reply—The late Mr. Harold Ashton's talk about Mr. A. G. Hales, the war correspondent.

13: A MIXTURE OF EMOTIONS 125
The recorder is irritated—An appointment with Mr. F. F. Craddock—The late Alfred Russell Wallace recants his theories in his book "Man's Place in the Universe"—The author's mentality on sitting with fresh mediums.

14: THE MEDIUMSHIP OF MUNNINGS 129
A discourse on Cabinet Ministers, barristers, actors, painters, poets, and newspaper proprietors as a preface to the record of a sitting with Mr. F. T. Munnings, a direct voice medium—Dan Leno sings, George R. Sims offers a Limerick—His favourite dog comes through to Mr. J. M. Dick, the sporting journalist—Animals in the spirit spheres—Dr. Ellis Powell as Mr. Munnings' guide—The psychic chord—Lord Northcliffe speaks with Mr. Swaffer and Mr. Dick.

15: THE PHILOSOPHY OF JOHANNES 137
HDB renews his acquaintance with the spirit of Johannes, the philosopher whose observations appear in "Towards the Stars" —Automatic writing—Johannes discourses on the future of spirit communication, the Northcliffe evidence, Oscar Wilde, the symbols of the Trinity, ethics and morals, energy and sloth, and attacks some of the critics of his philosophy as written in the book mentioned above.

16: A DISCUSSION ON "VOICE" POWER: THE SECOND MUNNINGS SITTING 145
Mr. Munnings' trumpet interests the investigator—Nevertheless the happenings of this sitting are recorded faithfully: how the spirit of George Herbert Lee Mallory came through, what the guide Emanuel said to Anthony, how Dr. Herbert Fullerton Ransome examined Mrs. Bradley and H.D.B. and the results of that examination.

17: A NEGATIVE EXPERIMENT 153
The private sittings are resumed, and inasmuch as the séance recorded below proved negative, the author offers his observations on his illuminated trumpet, psychic power, musical instruments, as means to confound materialists.

18: A SUCCESSFUL RESUMPTION 157
Mr. John De Forest has a dramatic experience: Theodora giving him a message to "Napper"—The spirit of T. W. H. Crosland tries to speak and fails—The author is satisfied.

19: AN IMPORTANT MATERIAL WARNING 161
The spirit of Gaston reminds Mrs. Gaston Sargeant of a social duty to her friends the Lowthers—Warren Clarke talks about his daughters—HDB's sledge-hammer tone of voice in print—Annie warns the author of financial deficiencies.

20: A WONDERFUL EVIDENTIAL SITTING 167
Lord Northcliffe gives certain evidence of the survival of his spirit—This chapter is the record of a most amazing sitting; the author regrets the expurgations relating to matters of a private nature—an attempt at materialization—Northcliffe's twenty-one statements, many of which are confirmed by Miss Louise Owen in the neat chapter.

21: ESTABLISHMENT BY EXAMINATION 177
An astounding evidential interview, in the course of which Miss Louise Owen is examined as to Lord Northcliffe's twenty-one statements.

22: THE MIRACLE OF THE "VOICES" 183
Wherein Lord Northcliffe again speaks—Warren: "I am not experienced enough to be the Chief Guide"—Confirmatory evidence of a Munnings' sitting—"Northcliffe is pleased with Queens Hall arrangements".

23: A BARREN JOURNEY 187
Concerning a pilgrimage to a simple-minded medium in the North of England—The author returns after a disappointing visit.

24: THE THIRD EXPERIMENT WITH MUNNINGS 191
The author pauses to make a few observations on Horatio Bottomley—The supernormal movements of H.D.B.'s trumpet—Spirit lights in the room.

25: DRAMATIC MATERIAL DISCOVERY 195
A thrilling experience—A sitting on the results of which many thousands of pounds depended—Spirits locate incriminating ledgers—"The fact remains, that without any outside medium, I and my wife have conversed

CONTENTS

for hours and hours with the spirits of my sister Annie and of Warren Clarke, and these spirits have talked in their own individual voices, clearly and distinctly from space"—On the threshold of the Temple of knowledge.

BOOK TWO: VALIANTINE AND THE VOICES 199

1: George Valiantine comes to England and is met by HDB—Follows a remarkable sitting, at which old friends from "Towards the Stars" come back—I know there is no death... 201

2: The author is infuriated—The negative effect of a materialistic sitter—A case of sleepy sickness is discussed and Dr. Barnet gives a prescription... 204

3: A daylight sitting at which the spirits talk with Pat, the eight-year-old son of the author—Mr. Greville Collins attends a sitting and appears to be upset and is taken out of the room—Miss Madeline Cohen's mother addresses her daughter—Evidential information—The spirit of Arthur Playfair talks with Mr. Swaffer: Miss Phyllis Monkman mentioned—The late William Archer's regrets. 207

4: A helpful passivity that made a successful sitting—Little Bobby Worrall and Pat—A spirit whistles a military tune—The Martians: their mentality and their bodies—Mrs. Helen White's testimony— "Perfectly natural." 211

5: The author enjoys a stimulating relaxation from psychics—Mrs. Bradley sits alone with Valiantine—Only a universal spiritual movement can prevent war: Dr. Barnett's solemn warning—An ideal mediumistic combination. 213

6: HDB deplores the number of ladies at this sitting: the atmosphere of a tea-party—The late Mr. Scott speaks to his widow—Spirits speak in German—The spirit of Major Dighton-Probyn on the prevention of wars—A remarkable letter. 215

7: The spirit of Bert Everett sings a duet with a gramophone record of Galli-Curci's: the comedy makes Dr. Barnett laugh—Miss Winifred Graham's father speaks to his daughter—More about the prescription for sleepy sickness—Life in the spirit spheres. 218

8: Mrs. M. I. Ellis has a private sitting with Valiantine—Two spirits speaking at the same time—Mrs. Ellis's account of talking with her daughter and Sir Ernest Shackleton. 221

9: The holding of two sittings on one day weakens the power—The question of strain and the difficulty of manifestation. 224

10: *A wait of three-quarters of an hour—A voice addresses the Countess Oeitiongham—A conversation in Chinese dialect—"Information that maybe of the utmost value"—Lord Northcliffe suggests a title for Mr. Swaffer's book.* 226

11: *HDB's hundred-guinea challenge to Captain Maskelyne—The conditions—Throwing up the sponge—Why Captain Maskelyne withdrew—An illuminating confession of ignorance tickles the author's ironic sense—"Conjurors and illusionists are dull."* 229

12: *Pat O'Brien speaks with Sir Oliver Lodge—"Pat" Raymond Lodge speaks to his father—Admiral Henderson and a strange reference to Joseph Honner—Sir Oliver discusses ether with a spirit—Dr. Barnett's sleepy sickness prescription is tried—Footnote: The victim of sleepy sickness is cured—The author unburdens his mind on the S.P.R.—Comments on "Raymond"—HDB states his spirit philosophy.* 231

13: *A sitting in an unsuitable room at 27 Trinity Street, Cambridge—'Impossible to go on,' says Dr. Barnett—HDB's address to the Heretics.* 240

14: *"Women," states the author, "are better sitters than men"—A father meets his daughter in the spirit—Miss Ida Cohen talks with her dead aunt—Seventeen voices speak.* 242

15: *A poor sitting—An untranslatable message—A persistent voice—Bert Everett tries to help but fails.* 245

16: *A spirit tries to speak to Mr. Austin Harrison—the spirit of William Archer makes an explanation—The plot of "The Green Goddess"—Feda rebuffs the anonymous Mrs. X.—Mrs. X.'s confession—The author's letter to Mr. Harrison—Photographs of Ectoplasm.* 247

17: *When publicity becomes aggravating: Valiantine's fame and the ridiculous position of the Society for Psychical Research—The S.P.R. séance room: mediaeval in conception and inquisitorial in design—The author is incensed—How the first S.P.R. test sitting was smashed—The moribund S.P.R.* 253

18: *The author emphasizes the importance of harmony—Voices speak within thirty seconds—Some remarks on bad plays and stupid people—Further advice on financial affairs—Dr. Barnett's discourse on the planet Mars—Bert Everett on the ethereal body.* 258

19: *People who make good and bad sitters—A password with a spirit—Mrs. Dawson Scott is spoken to by her grandfather—A dead friend addresses Mr.*

CONTENTS

Dennis Neilson-Terry—The late Harry Pelissier comes through to Miss Fay Compton—Pelissier plays tricks with the gramophone—Laughter the best vibration for voice phenomena—The spirit of Billie Carleton—The impressions of Miss Fay Compton and Mr. Dennis Neilson-Terry........... 263

20: Another sitting at the headquarters of the S.P.R.—A fatuous evening—The author, who is not present, attacks the conditions prevailing at the S.P.R.—Unintelligent handicapping. 275

21: The spirit of Dr. Barnett tells what is wrong with the S.P.R.—Northcliffe speaks to Mr. Gonnoske Komai, the famous Japanese poet—The Hon. Mrs. Fitzroy Stanhope receives evidence—A conversation in Japanese—Countess Ahlefeldt-Laurvig talks with a spirit in Danish and Russian......... 278

22: Mr. Hannen Swaffer's account of a successful sitting—Kokum sings his favourite song—Charles Garvice's message to his wife—Northcliffe finds a secretary for Miss Louise Owen—Dr. Barnett's new word: "hypostatic."..... 283

23: The riddle of Dr. Woolley's quest—Una, Lady Troubridge and Miss Radcliffe Hall at Dorincourt—Lady Troubridge receives evidence—Miss Radcliffe Hall's father speaks to his daughter—Mental proofs again established.. 289

24: Valiantine asks to hear the jazz band—Notes compiled from Mrs. Bradley's report—The spirit of an Italian drummer—Dr. Barnett gives news of Valiantine's family in USA—HDB's impressions outside the room—A stupendous effort. 293

25: Pat, aged eight, sits with Valiantine—He tells how his aunt spoke to him, also Bert Everett and Bobby Worrall—Attention is drawn to the perfect conditions produced by a child—Miss Constance Collier's dead mother makes a significant remark—The late Lily Hanbury speaks to Dame Clara Butt—Mrs. Hilton Philipson, M.P., is greeted by a spirit friend—Mr. Ivor Novello meets an old acquaintance who had passed out—Clara Butt's singing—The spirits compliment a great artist. 296

26: An official S.P.R. test sitting—Lady Troubridge receives an evidential communication—Dr. Woolley agrees—Lady Troubridge draws attention to a spirit speaking at the same time as Valiantine—Plain words from Dr. Barnett to Dr. Woolley... 301

27: Anthony and Valiantine experiment in the daylight—Anthony's account of Warren and Annie coming through—Mrs. Bradley's daylight experiment—A séance in a strange room without trumpets—"I regard this as a very remarkable test.".. 306

28: *The author refuses the theory of telepathy and gives his reasons for so doing—The late Albert Chevalier speaks to his widow—Sir Arthur Conan Doyle's sister—The wife of E. W. Hornung—A conversation in Japanese—Evidence which greatly impresses the author—No wars in Mars—"I know my dead husband spoke to me," says Mrs. Chevalier.* 309

29: *A sitting devoted to S.P.R.—The author confesses that his irritableness is not improved—Feda discusses a curious mistake in the identity of two ladies—Advice to psychic researchers—A second sitting on the same evening.* 313

30: *A sitting by Pat's special request—Pat makes Dr. Barnett laugh—The spirit of Camarano performs a fine drum solo—An encore performance for Pat—Bobby Worrall blows the siren—Kokum is glad to see the "little papoose in his moccasins and kimono"—A child's attitude towards death.* 318

31: *Lovers reunited—"Give my love to Vivian" in German—Miss Violet Loraine's father is proud of his daughter's career—The spirit of Minnie, Miss Loraine's maid and dresser, comes back to her mistress: "I was with you, but I am not in the grave"—Miss Loraine's impressions.* 321

32: *Miss Radclffe Hall attends a daylight sitting with Valiantine—Una, Lady Troubridge, joins the circle—"This has established Valiantine in an exceptional way."* 325

33: *A medical séance—Dr. Barnett's prescriptions for tuberculosis, cancer, syphilis—Dr. Barnett is questioned by doctors as to his formulae—The author discourses on the pros and cons of these suggested treatments.* 327

34: *An amazing development of incalculable value—Mr. Swaffer's account of a daylight sitting—No trickery possible—"We have removed the fear of death."* 342

35: *A spirit hand touches Mr. Beverley Nichols—Lord Chancellor Westbury gives advice to one of his descendants—Pat Raymond Lodge thanks Mrs. Bradley for her courtesy to his father—A spirit treats a fractured wrist—The Hon. Mrs. R. Bethell's impressions.* 344

36: *A sitting of many artists—Mr. Oliver Baldwin is spoken to by dead relative—Miss Margaret Bannerman's ring is recognized by a spirit—The author smashes a gramophone record—Mr. Oliver Baldwin's account of the sitting.* 348

CONTENTS

37: *A sitting at the request of a spirit—Health advice from Dr. Barnett—Kokum plays a joke upon the medium—Irrefutable evidence from a child spirit—The author's Uncle Michael comes through for the first time—Messages from Mars—An experience that would stagger the average psychical researcher.* 352

38: *An obstinately skeptical sitter—Dr. Barnett rebukes Mr. Allan Miller—Mrs. Gordon Craig talks with her son who was drowned—Miss Rebecca West spoken to by spirit voices—Lady Malmesbury explains a tragic delay in her journey to her dying mother.* 355

39: *The investigator invites certain members of his household to a sitting with Valiantine—The results are chronicled by his chauffeur, A. Huntley.* 359

40: *"I am a researcher and not a missionary"—The author discourses on a certain type of mentality—Miss Gladys Cooper asks for a sitting—Self-invited guests who anticipated a sensational entertainment—An unknown spirit speaks to Mr. Somerset Maugham—Mrs. Dudley Coats's sharp retort—An appallingly dull evening—"Sensitiveness is a culture of polarity."* 362

41: *S.P.R. officers at a Dorincourt daylight sitting—The first experiment: answers given by taps—The second experiment: Mr. Dingwall hears a voice through the trumpet—The third experiment: A voice saying, "Father Woolley"—A scientific advance.* 368

42: *Mr. Harry Price records this sitting—Bert Everett uses the code word—The gramophone stops for no apparent reason—An Italian conversation—The circle reproved for talking too much—Mrs. Ellis Powell speaks to her husband—Lord Northcliffe speaks to Louise Owen—The controls put the gramophone out of order—Mrs. Vlasto's impressions.* 372

43: *This experience, during which the spirit of Michael Bradley established his identity, prompts the following comment: "Such an incident shows how natural and normal spirit communication can be made in perfect conditions."* 378

44: *Miss Winifred Graham's daylight experiment—Her comment: "It seemed so marvelous and far nicer than sitting in the dark."* 380

45: *This sitting is described by Jessica Sykes, the wife of Charles Sykes, the famous artist—The whispering spirit voice that was not encouraged—My husband's aunt and father manifested their voices—A loud voice calls me by name, announcing itself as 'Mother.'* 381

46: *Five spirit voices talk with Pat in the broad daylight.* 384

47: *A sitting that stands out in vivid contrast—An illustration of the negative and positive in psychics—Leon Quartermaine, the distinguished actor, has a conversation with his brother—The spirit of a friend puzzles Mr. P. G. Wodehouse—Harry Pelissier says he will welcome Miss Fay Compton on the other side—Billie Carleton recalls her death, and her friend, Jack Marsh, recalls an incident—"No jealousy on the other side," says Dr. Barnett—Miss Compton writes her impressions.* 385

48: *Miss Winifred Graham records her impressions of her second daylight séance.* 391

49: *A poor sitting—Spirits speak to Miss Constance Collier and Mr. Ivor Novello.* 392

50: *Mr. P. H. G. Fender receives a spirit message for his father—An old servant speaks to Mrs. Arthur Bendir—Mrs. Theodore McKenna talks to her son, Justine—"You must stop these wars"—Mr. Oscar Hammerstein, the dramatist, receives valuable evidence.* 393

51: *The wonderful daylight experience of two strange ladies.* 396

52: *Countess Ahlefeldt-Laurvig joins in a conversation in French and Russian with the spirit of her brother Oscar in full daylight.* 398

53: *The author's mother, a devout Roman Catholic, speaks to the spirit of her daughter—A blue bird comes into the circle—Mr. Noel Jaquin's experiment—The imprints of a hand and of the feet of a bird—The smear of sexual perversion—HDB calls for a public exposure.* 399

54: *Three voices speak to Mrs. Gibbons Grinling—A spirit addresses Mr. Dennis Neilson-Terry—Miss Mary Glynne is reminded by her father's spirit of a visit to Penarth—The late Lord Curzon speaks to Mr. Oliver Baldwin—A message to Lord Birkenhead—Lord Curzon met by his first wife on the other side—The impressions of Mr. Denis Grinling and Mr. Oliver Baldwin.* 403

55: *Valiantine sits with two of his friends in the daylight—Bobby Worrall speaks to his grandfather.* 407

56: *Mrs. Maurice Hewlett unable to keep her appointment—The author makes a characteristic outburst—The secret of the blue bird revealed.* 408

CONTENTS

57: *Pat Bradley asks an impartial question about a boat and is given a satisfactory answer—An Alsatian wolfhound hears a spirit voice in the daylight.* 411

58: *An anonymous statesman's experience at Dorincourt—Lord Curzon says he is alive—Lord Northcliffe reminds HDB of an important omission—The statesman receives a warning.* 413

59: *A sitting for the purpose of obtaining supernormal imprints, Mr. Noel Jaquin assisting—Mr. Christopher Marlowe, M.A.—Mr. Jaquin discusses the ectoplasmic hand with Dr. Barnett—Imprints of a signature and of a butterfly—Mr. Charles Sykes' view of the butterfly—Mr. Marlowe's impression—Mr. Jaquin's analysis of the imprints—The author: "These imprints will confound the criticism of the great scientists."* 416

60: *Mr. Charles Sykes' record of a daylight sitting—He discusses the butterfly imprint with the spirit of his father—Mrs. Sykes' notes* 427

61: *The last of a wonderful series of séances—The fine friendships of this life kept intact and immeasurably strengthened in the next—The great Truth of Survival established, not upon myth or upon belief, but upon the solid foundation of knowledge.* 430

THE LAST CHAPTER 434
In which the author reviews that which he has done—Exploring the depths and climbing the heights—Defying the scientist and the Churches—The divine law of evolution—The spirit of wisdom

APPENDIX A. *MUNNINGS SÉANCES: THE 1929 EDITION* 451
APPENDIX B. THOUGHTS AND EXTRACTS FROM *AND AFTER* 461
APPENDIX C. EXPOSURE OF DENNIS BRADLEY 473
AFTERWORD 503
INDEX 517

PREFACE

According to *Wikipedia*, George Valiantine (1874 – 1947) was an American direct-voice medium who was exposed as a fraud. Since Valiantine is a key figure in this book, readers who accept *Wikipedia* and other internet sites as authoritative in their debunking of anything outside the boundaries of mainstream science should probably toss this book into the trash bin before reading beyond this point.

It is true that various researchers and intelligent observers claimed fraudulent activity by Valiantine, but it is equally true that phenomena were produced through Valiantine's mediumship that could not be explained by deception of any kind and were otherwise unexplainable without invoking influence and/or communication from spirits of the dead. As mainstream science does not recognize the existence of a spirit world, deception of some kind was and still is the only explanation for the fundamentalists of science.

"The aim of science has been for the most part a study of mechanism, the mechanism whereby results are achieved, an investigation into the physical processes which go on, and which appear to be coextensive with nature," wrote Sir Oliver Lodge, a pioneer in electricity and radio as well as president in 1913 of the British Association for the Advancement of Science. "Any theory which seems to involve the action of Higher Beings, or of any unknown entity controlling and working the mechanism, is apt to be extruded or discountenanced as a relic of primitive superstition, coming down from times when such infantile explanations were prevalent."

As Lodge, whose sitting with Valiantine is discussed in Chapter 12 of this book, saw it, such a mindset "is probably a salutary safeguard against that unbalanced and comparatively dangerous condition called 'open-mindedness,' which is ready to learn and investigate anything not manifestly self-contradictory and absurd."

Such an "open-mind" is clearly a prerequisite to reading this book. In this edition we attempt to tell the whole fascinating story.

FOREWORD

Voices of the Dead: Fantasy, Fraud or Fact?

Every renowned medium of the past was called a cheat or a fraud at one time or another, thereby raising doubts by others as to his or her credibility and otherwise significantly detracting from the weight of the evidence supporting communication with the spirit world. Subscribing to mechanistic science and obviously not familiar with the intricacies of mediumship, many modern historians and quasi-historians, especially those posting biographies on the internet, have for the most part given significantly more weight to the fraud allegations than to the evidence suggesting genuine supernormal phenomena. Therefore, the case for genuine mediumship, a spirit world, and the survival of consciousness after death has received little attention or interest since the heyday of psychical research during the late nineteenth and early twentieth centuries.

Indications are that the researchers and observers alleging fraud were applying terrestrial standards to celestial matters that were beyond human understanding. To put it another way, the debunkers were not factoring in the possibility that what they saw as cheating or deception by the medium in certain cases looked more like spirit activity – phenomena which were beyond scientific explanation. Moreover, some of the researchers who did consider spirit activity assumed, based on the teachings of various religions, that "spirits of the dead" were infallible and therefore better able to communicate than what they had experienced. By around 1880, science had impeached religion and for an intelligent person to even mention spirits was to invite guffaws from one's friends and peers in the scientific community.

Some scholars and scientific men and women concluded that at least some of the phenomena were genuine, but they rejected the spirit hypothesis, and by extension, the survival hypothesis. To remain within the boundaries of mainstream science, they preferred to see it as mind over matter in ways not yet understood by science. There were, however, some very distinguished researchers who believed the phenomena provided strong evidence of a spirit world and that human consciousness survives death and continues in other dimensions of reality.

One of the most controversial mediums in this regard was George Valiantine, an American from New York who emerges as a key figure in this book. Some of the most mind-boggling phenomena witnessed and reported by a number of esteemed scholars and researchers were repeatedly produced through Valiantine's mediumship over a number of years. Many researchers were convinced that what they had witnessed with Valiantine was beyond trickery, while others were equally certain that deception of some kind was the only explanation.

A number of other mediums, including Mina Crandon, also an American, better known as "Margery," and Rudi Schneider, of Austria, were being studied during the 1920s and early '30s, around the same time as Valiantine. The controversies surrounding Crandon, Schneider, and Valiantine all contributed to the near abandonment of psychical research in favor of parapsychology, the latter focused more on studying extrasensory perception (ESP) and psychokinetic phenomena (PK) while ignoring trance mediums, spirits and any discussion of consciousness surviving death

Perhaps the two most dedicated researchers studying Rudi Schneider at that time were Dr. Albert von Schrenck-Notzing, a German physician who conducted 88 experiments with Schneider, and Dr. Eugene Osty, a French physician who carried out 77 experiments with him. Both men were convinced that he was the real deal. "We are sure, absolutely sure, of the reality of the phenomena," Osty reported, "but we cannot say the same for our interpretation." The issue there was whether "Olga," the entity who took control of Schneider's body when he became entranced, was the spirit of a deceased human, as she claimed to be, or a "secondary personality" surfacing from Schneider's subconscious mind. It was much more "scientific" to assume the latter and thereby dismiss any suggestion of spirits of the dead, something written off by the fundamentalists of science as pure superstition.

"The phenomena were personal in the sense that there was every appearance of someone, an invisible or barely invisible 'person' acting upon the everyday world, moving objects, knotting handkerchiefs, patting sitters on the head or boxing their ears, as the case might be," British psychologist Anita Gregory explained in her book, *The Strange Case of Rudi Schneider*.

She described Olga as a "phantom person" who at times was "capable of producing tangible effects on the physical world, and of somehow or another partially clothing herself in visible and tangible substance."

Gregory references the conclusion of Dr. Alois Gatterer, a Jesuit priest and professor of physics at Innsbruck University, who reported observing a full phantom on April 12, 1926, which he described as "light, misty, and indistinct and which seemed to increase and decrease in size and luminosity." He also observed materialized hands at two different sittings with Schneider and was absolutely certain they were not Schneider's hands. "I do not hesitate to express my personal conviction on the subject of paraphysical phenomena …," he wrote.

Dr. William Brown, Wilde Reader in Mental Philosophy at Oxford University and founder of the Institute of Experimental Psychology, agreed with those supporting the genuineness of Rudi Schneider's mediumship. "I could find no evidence of fraud or trickery, and, while retaining an alert and critical attitude of mind throughout, I had a strong feeling of some mysterious power working from within the cabinet, a power for which I could imagine no mechanical or pneumatic contrivance as a cause – at least such as would be possible under the conditions of the séance," he wrote in a letter to *The Times* of London on May 7, 1932.

Brown was part of a group studying Schneider in England. The group included astronomer Christopher Clive Gregory, founder of the University of London observatory, and later, the husband of Anita Gregory, the author of the book about Schneider. According to Anita Gregory, Professor Brown was subjected to a good deal of ridicule at Oxford, notably by Professors Albert Einstein and Frederick Lindemann, both world-renowned physicists. They are said to have laughed at the phenomena reported by Brown and a number of other reputable scientists. "No way!" they must have scoffed in self-righteous indignation.

And so it also went with "'Margery," the wife of Dr. Le Roi Crandon, a prominent Boston, Massachusetts (USA) physician and surgeon.

Less than a year after she discovered her mediumistic abilities in 1923, at age 34, Margery was selected by *Scientific American* magazine to be studied by a panel of five appointed by the magazine, which was sponsoring a contest with a $2,500 prize to anyone able to satisfy the panel members that his or her abilities were genuine and not the result of deception of some kind.

Most of the phenomena produced by Margery's mediumship were physical, including levitations of a table, apports (objects floating around the room), unusual lights and breezes, the materialization of hands and arms, paraffin gloves purportedly taken from the hands of spirits, the ringing of a bell not within reach of the medium, a scale in which the weighted side went up as the unweighted side went down, and other strange happenings. However, the main attraction was the "master of ceremonies" at the Margery séances, said to be Walter Stinson, Margery's older brother, who had been killed in a railroad yard accident in 1911. Walter would speak through his entranced sister and also independently of her in a masculine voice. He would carry on conversations with the sitters, joke with them, curse at them, whistle tunes, and do automatic writing through Margery. Other "spirits" also communicated. Margery is said to have produced writing in nine different languages, including Greek and Chinese. There was, however, little in the way of veridical personal messages as associated with mental mediumship.

A verdict for Margery would have meant an indictment of mechanistic science and the philosophy of materialism. The story made front-page news in the *New York Times* and other newspapers. It included character assassinations, revenge, sexual innuendos, threatened lawsuits, suspicion that Margery's husband surgically enlarged her female anatomy to smuggle items into the séance room, and bizarre phenomena, including a table chasing a guest around the Crandon house and down a staircase.

While the Crandons were well-off and had no need for the cash prize, they agreed, at the urging of Sir Arthur Conan Doyle, the creator of Sherlock Holmes and the world's leading promoter of Spiritualism, to participate in the contest, and to give the money to charity. In the end, Margery did not get the prize, because the five panel members could not agree. One of the five found in her favor, three others sat on the fence with uncertainty and said further investigation was necessary, while the fifth member, Houdini, the great magician, called her a fraud. Although not a voting member, the mathematician in charge of the contest for the magazine, took a lead part in the panel's investigation and clearly believed that Margery deserved the prize. Other scientists, scholars, and Harvard graduate students subsequently studied her, some certain that the phenomena were real, some certain she was a fake, and others not knowing what to believe. As earlier stated, historians and internet biographers have sided with the debunkers and doubters, concluding that she was a clever trickster, probably aided by her husband.

Perhaps the most damning evidence against Margery came from Dr. Joseph B. Rhine, then a young botanist turned psychologist, who, along with his wife, Louisa, sat with her on July 1, 1926. On that one sitting only, and especially upon seeing Margery's foot move at a critical point, he concluded that Margery was a charlatan. Walter's wisecracking also contributed to his conclusion as he expected a much more solemn event. He apparently had assumed that spirits spoke only in a saintly manner.

Five days after Rhine's experience, on July 6, 1926 Dr. Robert J. Tillyard, a renowned Australian biologist and entomologist, gave a lecture at the National Laboratory of Psychical Research in London, on his sittings with Margery on April 29 and again on May 1, both at the Crandon home. He reported that Margery was tied up tightly with picture wire over rubber insulation and her neck padlocked so that she was entirely immobilized. He examined the voice machine and the scale, noting that it was made of copper and wood and that no part of it had any attraction for a magnet. Margery went into a trance after about ten minutes.

Tillyard ruled out fraud and in the August 1928 issue of *Nature*, he told of his belief in life after death based on his experiences with Margery.

During December, 1926, Dr. T. Glen Hamilton, a Canadian physician who had begun studying physical mediumship in 1921, had three sittings with Margery in Winnipeg, Canada. Two months earlier, Hamilton had attended eight sittings with Margery in Boston. He said he witnessed "brilliant phenomena" under satisfactory control in Boston. "I have no hesitancy in again stating that I am quite convinced that the Margery phenomena are not only genuine but are also among the most brilliant yet recorded in the history of metapsychic science," he wrote in his 1942 book, *Intention and Survival*.

Nevertheless, the fraud claims have been carried down over the years and often seem to outweigh the strong evidence in support of the medium. "There seems a nemesis attaching to the work of some of these investigators," wrote Dr. Mark W. Richardson, a Harvard professor of medicine who had a hundred or more sittings with Margery and was convinced that there was no trickery involved. "For a brief space they will be moved by what they witness to a point of enthusiasm which almost persuades them of reality, then as the impression fades they will fall back into that negative frame of mind in which they are no longer able to appreciate, it would seem, the reality of the occurrences, and the old, old doubts surge back upon them and leave them impotent to form any positive conclusion. And then perhaps a feeling of professional caution comes in to set the seal upon their attitude of negation."

Such also appears to have been the case with George Valiantine. While the evidence favoring Valiantine seems to be overwhelming and far beyond the abilities of the any skilled conjurer, indications are that there was obvious deception at times. The question was whether Valiantine was consciously responsible for what was seen as trickery or if devious or playful spirits were responsible. Since, according to mechanistic science, spirits don't exist, the "intelligent" answer required Valiantine to be totally responsible and a cheater. Even H. Dennis Bradley, who authored this book and a prior one, *Toward the Stars*, in which he continually praised Valiantine, eventually turned on him. This is discussed in the Afterword.

"It was fortunate that our expressions could not be seen, for my nose was tilted in scorn and my lip curled in unrestrained contempt," Bradley wrote of his initial reaction to an invitation to attend a séance with Valiantine at the country home of Joseph De Wyckoff, a retired lawyer, in Ramsey, New Jersey, not far from New York City, in *Toward the Stars*. Bradley, a playwright who lived in London, was a guest at the De Wyckoff home at the time. Although extremely skeptical, Bradley thought it might provide some amusement and agreed to it.

Also present for Bradley's first séance with Valiantine on June 16, 1923, was De Wyckoff's 20-year-old nephew, Joseph Dasher. The four men sat in a circle about five feet from each other with two aluminum trumpets in the center of the room to amplify the voices of the spirits. "The lights were turned off, when the whole affair struck me as being rather idiotic," Bradley related. "I wondered at intelligent people submitting to such infantile forms of amusement. I wondered how a shrewd mind like that of my host could be induced to waste his time on such silly exploits." It was explained to Bradley that they had to sing some hymns in order to achieve a certain passivity and harmony. Bradley's expression of "unrestrained contempt" came on after about 20 minutes into the singing, as nothing was happening. Bradley saw it as an "exceptionally dull show."

But, without warning, things started to happen. A soft and gentle woman's voice was heard. "I was called by my name, and the voice, which sounded about three feet away on my right, was full of emotion," Bradley explained. Though he then went by his middle name, his first name, Herbert, was repeated twice, and then his deceased sister, Annie, identified herself.

"Her voice on earth was soft and beautifully modulated, and her elocution in public was distinguished. In conversation she was a purist in her choice of words," Bradley recalled. "I have never met any woman who spoke in the same odd way. When she addressed me, after ten years of silence, she said sayings in her own characteristic manner. Every syllable was perfectly enunciated and every little peculiarity of intonation was reproduced …

"Then we talked, not in whispers, but in clear, audible tones, and the notes of our voices were pitched as if we might have been speaking on earth. And that which we said to each other were things of wondrous joy."

They talked for 15 minutes. "She told me that for several years she had been trying to get into communication with me, that she was always with me, and that she watched over me and accompanied me on my journeys. She knew of the books that I had written and other things that I have done since she died. …

"Throughout our talk the note of gladness was uppermost – the grateful gladness of eternity, the magnificent laughter of survival, the surety of supernatural progress, the knowledge of the inconceivable."

The cynical skeptic was suddenly a believer in spirit communication. He was certain that the information coming from his sister could not have been known by anyone else in the room. "Any suggestion of ventriloquism is ridiculous," he added, while also ruling out the possibility it was somehow coming from his subconscious mind. "No man living could imitate the clear and gentle voice which spoke, and, beyond this, no man living could talk in Annie's characteristic way, with her individual enunciation, her own choice of words, and her knowledge of the many things which she and I alone could have known."

After his sister's departure, five other spirits came though over the next two hours. "Each spirit was distinct and each spoke with an accent unlike the other," Bradley recorded. One of those spirits was unknown to anyone present and identified himself as Reverend Doctor Joseph Krauskopf of 4715 Pulaski Ave., Philadelphia. He said that he had died six days earlier. He communicated that his associates at the Hebrew Seminary were concerned that cremation would affect the life of the spirit. He asked that they be told that the spirit survives cremation.

Bradley and Dasher confirmed the prior existence of Krauskopf, although it is not stated whether they passed on the message about cremation.

On the following night, they again sat for a séance. De Wyckoff's cook and butler were invited to join with the four men. After a Dr. Barnett, one of Valiantine's "controls," spoke to the group in a loud Scottish accent, Bradley's sister again spoke. She talked for some 20 minutes about Bradley's young son, Dennis, his schooling and sensitive temperament, facts Bradley was certain Valiantine knew nothing about. "Her tones were clear and bell-like, her notes were sympathetic and understanding, and were radiant," Bradley recorded. "How can I describe the indescribable?"

Again, Bradley pointed out that his sister mentioned things that nobody else knew about or could have known about. Moreover, Bradley observed De Wyckoff talking with Valiantine at the same time Bradley's sister was communicating with him.

After his sister left, the trumpet floated in front of De Wyckoff's cook. "Anita! Anita!" the "voice' said. "Si! Si!" Anita Ripoll excitedly responded. "It is Jose! Jose!" the "voice" said. It was the cook's deceased husband. They carried on a conversation in Spanish which Bradley could not understand. However, De Wyckoff understood and described it as a mixture of Basque and corrupt Spanish, which he often heard them speak when Jose was alive and in his employment. When De Wyckoff spoke directly to Jose, Jose spoke more perfect Spanish. Jose requested De Wyckoff's assistance in bringing their children from Spain. Bradley estimated that the conversation lasted ten to twelve minutes. "To produce the scene which took place, Anita would have to be a great actress and Valiantine a magnificent actor," Bradley opined, "and having produced many plays myself, I can say with confidence that they would have had to rehearse the scene for at least three weeks."

Bradley further recorded that the butler, Percy Wheatley, then heard from his niece, who had died at age of five several years earlier. "She talked in a sweet, childish voice and her sentences were interjected with happy, childish laughter," Bradley noted. "She said that life was splendid where she was, and that she was growing up and learning, that she was so glad she was no longer a cripple." Bradley thought he saw the young girl's spirit form sitting on Wheatley's knee, referring to it as "silvery, misty, and delicate in outline," but the others did not see it.

A Canadian Indian named "Kokum," said to be one of Valiantine's spirit guides, communicated in French and broken English. De Wyckoff had communicated with him on previous occasions and asked him to sing. He then started to sing "La Paloma." "Never in my life have I heard such a colossal voice," Bradley wrote. "In all seriousness I assert that his voice could have been heard a quarter of a mile away. ..." Bradley thanked Kokum and asked him if he could touch him. He then felt fingers of a hand pat him gently on the head.

Bradley called the two séances the "most staggering event of my life," causing him to change his whole philosophy of life. "Doubt took flight when faced by an unchallengeable fact and the mind understood in a flash that what had hitherto appeared to be impossible was possible."

Perhaps the most mind-boggling experiences ever reported with any medium were those of Dr. Neville Whymant, a professor of Oriental literature and philosophy at the Universities of Tokyo and Peking and then a professor of linguistics at Oxford and London Universities. Whymant, who spoke 30 languages, was in the United States to study the languages of the American Indian. While having no interest in Spiritualism and being skeptical, Whymant felt obliged to accept an invitation to the New York Park Avenue home of Judge and Mrs. William Cannon, even after Mrs. Cannon told him that a séance would take place after the dinner. "There was no appearance or suspicion of trickery," Whymant recorded in his 1931 book, *Psychic Adventures in New York*, "but I mention these things to show that I was alert from the beginning, and I was prepared to apply all the tests possible to whatever phenomena might appear."

As soon as the lights were turned off, the group recited the Lord's Prayer and then sacred music was played on a gramophone. Voices came through for other sitters before Mrs. Whymant's father communicated in his characteristic drawl, reminiscent of the West County of England. The group then heard the "sound of an old wheezy flute not too skillfully played." It reminded Whymant of sounds he had heard in the streets of China. When the flute-like sound faded, Whymant heard a "voice" directed at him through the trumpet say in an ancient Chinese dialect: "Greeting, O son of learning and reader of strange books! This unworthy servant bows humbly before such excellence." The "voice" then identified himself by the name Confucius was known during his earth life.

Apparently, the communicating spirit recognized that Whymant was having a difficult time understanding the ancient dialect and changed to a more modern dialect. Whymant wondered how he could test the voice and remembered that there are several poems in Confucius' "Shih King" which have baffled both Chinese and Western scholars. Whymant addressed the "voice": "This stupid one would know the correct reading of the verse in "Shih King." It has been hidden from understanding for long centuries, and men look upon it with eyes that are blind. The passage begins thus: Ts'ai chüan êrh ..." Whymant recalled that line as the first line of the third ode of the first book of *Chou nan,* although he did not recall the remaining 14 lines. The 'voice' took up the poem and recited it to the end.

The "voice" put a new construction on the verses so that it made sense to Whymant. It was, the "voice" explained, a psychic poem. The mystery was solved. But Whymant had another test. He asked the "voice" if he could ask for further wisdom. "Ask not of an empty barrel much fish, O wise one! Many things which are now dark shall be light to thee, but the time is not yet ..." the "voice" answered. Whymant addressed the "voice": "...In *Lun Yü, Hsia Pien,* there is a passage that is wrongly written. Should it not read thus: ... ?

Before Whymant could finish the sentence, the "voice" carried the passage to the end and explained that the copyists were in error, as the character written as *sê* should have been *i,* and the character written as *yen* is an error for *fou.* "Again, all the winds had been taken out of my sails!" Whymant wrote, pointing out that the telepathic theory, i.e., the medium was reading his mind, would not hold up since he was unaware of the nature of the errors.

There were several additional exchanges between Whymant and Confucius before the power began to fade. Confucius closed with: "I go, my son, but I shall return ...Wouldst thou hear the melody of eternity? Keep then thy ears alert ..."

Whymant attended eleven additional sittings, dialoguing with the "voice" claiming to be Confucius in a number of them. At one sitting, another "voice" broke in speaking some strange French dialect. Whymant recognized it as Labourdin Basque. Although he was more accustomed to speaking Spanish Basque, he managed to carry on a conversation with the "voice."

"Altogether fourteen foreign languages were used in the course of the twelve sittings I attended," Whymant concluded in his short book. "They included Chinese, Hindi, Persian, Basque, Sanskrit, Arabic, Portuguese, Italian, Yiddish, (spoken with great fluency when a Yiddish- and Hebrew-speaking Jew was a member of the circle), German and modern Greek."

Whymant also recorded that at one sitting, Valiantine was carrying on a conversation in American English with the person next to him

FOREWORD

while foreign languages were coming through the trumpet. "I am assured, too, that it is impossible for anyone to 'throw his voice,' this being merely an illusion of the ventriloquist," he wrote.

Whymant consulted with various psychical researchers, including physicist Sir Oliver Lodge, and first reported the experience in the April 1928 issue of the *Journal of the American Society for Psychical Research*. Not being a Spiritualist or psychical researcher, Whymant did not initially plan to write a book about it. However, tiring of telling the story so many times, he agreed to put it in book form, asking that with the publication of the book that others not ask him to tell the story again. His experience took place in October, 1926, after this book was first published.

The reader is invited to digest the intriguing story set forth in this book and come to his or her own conclusion. An Afterword at the end of the book provides additional food for thought in this regard.

Michael Tymn
July 2022

BOOK ONE

1

THE PHYSICAL AND ELEMENTARY

The author explores an unknown territory and discovers the truth of survival—His reason for his psychic investigations and for the present book—A discourse on mediums, with special reference to Mrs. Osborne Leonard and Mr. George Valiantine—An invitation to scientists to explain even the simplest physical phenomena—The methods by which the author developed personal mediumship.

May to July, 1924
LIFE, as we know it, despite its allurements and its pains, is but the shadow of our real and ultimate existence. Before us lies a vast territory of knowledge, the outskirts of which we have barely fringed.

So: when the explorer sets forth deliberately to explore an unknown territory it is impossible for him to forecast his path or his adventures.

And as one penetrates into the vast forest of psychic research, it is impossible to know whether the adventure may lead, and what experiences may lurk in its depths. Step by step, as advances are made into the mysterious recesses, it is borne upon one with increasing certainty that the thick blacknesses are not unfathomable, that progress is not only possible, but inevitable, and that each step forward leads to amazing discoveries.

The lure of the unknown, which still drives men to the ice of the Poles and to the perils of Everest, is both explicable and understandable.

No effort of the scientist or the chemist in search of a new force or a new element, is derided in these days of materialism in excelsis, and no budding Galileo need now fear derision and persecution, as long as he adheres steadily to the material and the physical. It is only the searcher after and the student of the spiritual and the non-material who maybe called upon to endure for a while the enmity and scorn and prejudices of the mentally fossilized, the wilfully inert, and the secretly fearful.

I

It was in June, 1923, that I, a slightly bored skeptic, but amiably willing to be amused, attended my first séance. Since then my experiences have been varied and amazing and profound. Those experiences of the nine months that followed from June, 1923, to March, 1924, have been published in my book *Towards the Stars*—this narrative is a continuation and development of that work—it is necessary to recount my initiation to this great truth of survival.

I was on a visit to America and one evening, while staying with Mr. Joseph De Wyckoff at his country home, Arlena Towers, Ramsay, New Jersey, at my host's invitation, the medium, George Valiantine, gave a sitting. There were present, in addition to myself, my host and his nephew. I was in a strange country, a country in which my private and domestic affairs were utterly unknown to the three men who were in the room.

For the first twenty minutes of the sitting nothing happened.

Then the silence was broken by the gentle accents of a woman's voice. I recognized the voice of my favorite sister, Annie, who had passed over ten years since, and between whom and myself there had been a bond of affection, and an intimacy in thought and outlook that was rare indeed. She announced herself by her name and spoke to me at length with great emotion and tenderness. For over fifteen minutes we talked with each other, as only two persons of great affection and complete understanding can talk. The greater part of the conversation would have lost much of its import to an outsider, so delicate were the shades of its intimacy; and the talk was not in whispers, but in clear, audible tones. Her voice came, not through the mouth of the medium, but independently; in fact, as though she were standing some eighteen inches away from me.

I experienced no element of shock or surprise. We talked fluently and naturally, discussing intimate subjects and events which I had discussed with no one since her passing, and of which, in her lifetime, she and I alone were cognizant. She referred to incidents which occurred twenty years ago—long before I had met any of the other sitters at the séance—and of which I had never spoken, and then she, without any prompting from me, talked of events which had happened to me and affected my life since her passing over.

On the following evening my sister Annie—henceforth I shall call her Annie, because she is still alive in the spirit—again talked with me. On this occasion we spoke for about twenty minutes, and from her I gained many of the wonderful indications of the life which is to come.

During these two evenings over a dozen other spirit voices spoke to us. Each voice was distinct and individual, in accent, tone, phrasing, manner and subject of conversation.

There are, of course, many forms of mediumship, but the rarest, and the most intensely dramatic form of all is unquestionably the mediumship by means of which one is able to listen to the independent and individual spirit voice. Knowing what I do now, after two years of study and thought, I realize that I was peculiarly fortunate in receiving such astounding proofs at my first experience—an experience made, as I have stated, In the blasé, slightly contemptuous mood of the man willing to be amused, but doubtful of the quality of the amusement offered.

It was not chance that led me to this revelation; I am as certain as I am of few things in this life that it had been determined by higher intelligences than mine.

Since that night, I have seldom ceased in my study of this colossal subject. Not only have I read a great mass of the authentic literature of psychical research, but I have visited and studied almost every medium in this country—many of whom, I am sorry to say, proved to be completely disappointing.

II

I maintain deliberately that the record of my experiences, set down in many instances without any comment of mine, in *Towards the Stars* is the most staggering record of the evidence of survival ever published. This is not exaggeration; and I make the assertion in no mood of conceit.

The puny "ego," in face of the illimitable, shrinks into very proper insignificance.

At the risk of being accused of egotism, it would perhaps be as well, in order to help the reader to appreciate the value and nature of the evidence contained in that book, and in the book upon which I now embark, to indulge in a little self-revelation.

I have, I fear, naturally a cold and critical outlook on life, verging possibly upon the cynical. An adolescence in the heart of London's West End tends to remove the bloom from the peach of illusion, and in the course of my life I have met and known many rogues, male and female—some amusing, but mostly intolerably dull. Many have attempted to impose upon me; fortunately for my purse and peace of mind the majority have failed, but to the few successful ones I owe much in the experience I have gained from them. As one grows older one's critical faculties do not diminish and one's cynicism tends to harden, but I still retain sufficiency of youth to resent imposition and to despise clumsy deceit. The amusing, impecunious rogues who haunt the turf, the coulisses of the theatre, the supper-club, and the innumerable semi-smart rendezvous which the plump and desirable "pigeons" are supposed to frequent, are not unknown to me, and I do not flatter myself when I say that they pay me the compliment of leaving me alone.

In addition, I regret to say, a crudely direct appeal to the emotions has the deplorable effect of offending my artistic sense, and of leaving me uncomfortably cold.

When, therefore, with calm deliberation I decided to embark on a study of the gigantic subject which had so suddenly and so dramatically opened itself before me, I should like the reader to understand that it was no easily impressed, highly susceptible and inexperienced investigator who set himself the task, but one with a varied knowledge of the world in its amusing and unamusing phases, and possessed of that curious microcosm which is crudely labeled West End life.

Were I blessed with illusion, I should soon have lost it in the course of the investigations I undertook while writing *Towards the Stars*. The mediums in this country are few—were mediumship a well-paid trade, as assert the fanatical opponents of any revelation of an afterlife, the ranks of the profession would surely be more crowded—and even amongst that few I came across, the dull, the incompetent, and the stupidly dishonest. But as the undoubted existence of a fraudulent bank manager does not cause one to lose faith in banking, so the existence of an occasional fraudulent medium does not alter my belief in survival after death.

My considered conclusion, reached after a prolonged series of experiments and investigations, involving many failures and irritations, is that two facts of colossal importance to the human race have been established beyond cavil. First, that there is a survival of the spirit after bodily death, and second, that it is possible for living people to enter into direct communication with those who have passed over.

III

In the course of my investigations, the two most gifted mediums I came in contact with were Mrs. Osborne Leonard and George Valiantine, and the process by which they developed their power was much the same.

And here let me attempt to remove any misconception as to the properties of mediumship. A medium is simply and solely what the word implies: a medium of communication with the unseen. The possibilities for the charlatan and the impostor are obviously great, but the ingenuity necessary to deceive the experienced and scientific observer, whose sole aim is to sift the true from the false, unhampered by sentiment or prejudice, would command huge sums of money in other spheres of activity. From a material point of view, mediumship is one of the poorest paid careers open for the intelligent rogue, whose aim is easy money.

About the age of ten Mrs. Leonard was clairvoyant; at fifteen she attended her first séance, but was forbidden by her parents to attend another. At nineteen she determined to investigate the subject, and in 1909, with three other ladies, she experimented at table sittings. Twenty-seven sittings took place before anything happened, and at the twenty-eighth rappings occurred. In the case of George Valiantine, the earliest intimations that he possessed mediumistic powers came in the form of rappings when he was over forty years of age.

One result of my investigation was to convince me that mediumship is essentially a question of development; anyone, I am certain, can become mediumistic in varying degrees, that is, given the application and the study. I do not assert that it is possible for everyone to attain the high level of Mrs. Leonard or Mr. Valiantine, but I am sure that there are mediumistic powers in each of us.

As I pondered the results of my first experiments, I asked myself why,—if Mrs. Leonard and Valiantine—both perfectly normal persons—could develop this high form of mediumship starting from the simplest and crudest of beginnings,—it should not be within my power to achieve the same result, and if I could do so, why it should not be possible for my wife to do so, and why, indeed, should not everyone be capable of mediumship.

And if such a development were made, it would mean a gigantic step in the difficult task of convincing the skeptic by producing evidence not obtained through the agency of the paid medium. The paid medium is the bugbear of the fool inquirer—the inquirer who has ignorantly made up his mind "that there is nothing in it."

Frankly, I have no sympathy with the "paid" medium cry, which to some mentalities seems to faint the most wonderful results. A doctor, a barrister, or a stockbroker is not denounced as a fraud because he receives re-numeration for his work, and the fees of the most famous mediums in the world compare unfavourably with those of Harley Street, the Temple, or Throgmorton Street. But the mere fact that a medium is paid vitiates the work of that medium, and I feel that, once one could abolish the intervention of the medium and obtain direct evidence oneself, a stupendous leap forward can be made.

IV

The forms and degrees of mediumship are endless.

With regard, for example, to the extraordinary phenomenon of direct spirit voices, we know nothing as to how the spirits are enabled to materialize and produce their voices. That it is a scientific process is certain. In some unknown way it is the usage of the physical and psychical forces of the medium by the more highly developed senses of the spirit operators.

Much nonsense has been written by inexperienced people on the subject. I can now write as a medium—the proof of which will be shown later—and though the medium is but an instrument for communication, since I possess a keen intelligence, my impressions are of infinitely greater value than those of any scientist or theorist.

So far this great study has been held down by silly rules and formula: negative and unprogressive. It is the fool who tarries upon the first rung of the ladder.

The rubbish written by most of the so-termed experts of psychic phenomena is ludicrous. Their experiences are limited; most of them have concentrated their attention on some tame medium, and after observing a few of that medium's methods and conditions, they foolishly imagine that the secret powers of all mediumship are thus revealed.

Such an assumption is absurd. There are hundreds of forms of mediumship, and tens of thousands of degrees. What may apply to one is opposed to another.

It is of no use to try to determine, fix or limit the process of mediumship. It is stupid to base one's conclusions on tradition or history. It is the progress of tomorrow we look to.

Mediumship, even in the most advanced and powerful stage extant, is relatively a mere incoherent fluttering towards the knowledge we may gain in the future.

In fifty years from now, the few great mediums of today will be relegated to the position of the man who first risked the drop from the first parachute.

Educated people have a natural contempt for table rapping, a contempt which I shared. To begin with, the process is so open to ridicule that it could never appeal to me, nor do I feel, even after many successful experiments, that this form of phenomenon could be accepted alone as evidence of survival. It was only because Mrs. Leonard and George Valiantine started their experiences in this way that I was induced to make similar experiments, with the determination to use those experiments as a child masters pothooks before he can write—as steps towards a higher development.

It was in May, 1924, that I made my first experiment on my own, and except for one occasion at some ribald party in the West End, when there appeared to be much fooling, I had never before even attended a table sitting.

Circumstance played a part in deciding action, for although I had determined to pursue my investigations to the utmost, I was tired out with a year's study of psychics and with the production of *Towards the Stars*, which work was then in the press.

Although I had determined to make the endeavour to cultivate personal mediumship, I had intended first to take a thorough rest and to defer any such experiments until the autumn. To enjoy the rest and the beauties of an English spring, I took a charming little cottage on the river at Maidenhead, but for the whole of the month of May the river was a raging torrent, the rain never ceased except on the few odd occasions when in desperation I dashed to lunch or dine in London. On two or three days only could I attempt to punt a mile or so up stream, and paddle back in record time, or take the electric canoe through a few locks, and arrive home drenched.

The atmosphere of the cottage was peaceful, but rest is an illusion which my temperament can seldom create. Eternity will never appeal to me if all that it can offer is "rest in peace." To that negation of effort I would even prefer a perpetuity of existence on a plane of strife and turmoil.

One evening, tired of the dampening peace, my wife and I made our first experiment at a table sitting. It was with an ordinary small gate-leg table. We sat in the dark, waiting for anything that might happen. Quite soon a faint tapping came. Then the taps got louder. We asked who it was—mentioning names and giving a code for "yes" and "no," and we found out who it was who purported to produce the raps. The raps were said to come from the spirit of Annie and from my brother-in-law, Warren Clarke. (Warren Clarke appears in *Towards the Stars* as W.A. He has now become a famous character in literature, and it is proper that the anonymity should be shed.) Both Annie and Warren have played leading parts in my psychic studies.

There was nothing at all evidential in this experiment, but the raps were loud and distinct, and the affirmative and negative replies were intelligent. For a first experiment—compared with Mrs. Osborne Leonard's early stages of development—the distinct though insignificant results I considered to be quite good.

The next time the results were better, and by using the alphabet, simple, intelligent messages were spelt out to us. On that occasion, the table moved about the room, and in a mood of gaiety, lifted itself in the air and stood on two legs, and pushed up against us in quite an affectionate manner.

I am willing to laugh with the skeptic at the record of these feeble movements, just as I laugh at an unbalanced baby making its first few endeavors to toddle. But when I have related the progress that I have made within a few months of these attempts at mediumship, I will prove sufficient to provide the greatest scientists in the world with food for thought.

V

After one or two table sittings held by my wife and myself the circle was added to by my son, Dennis Anthony Bradley—down for vacation from Trinity College, Cambridge.[1] Then the raps became stronger and several simple messages were spelled out to us.

---

[1] My son writes under the name of Anthony Bradley. In this book he is variously referred to as "Dennis" and "Anthony."

Then one night, at Maidenhead, when my wife and son were dining out, I experimented at the table alone. I sat with my fingers lightly resting on the top of the table. I did not get any rap, but the table was taken right out of my reach. It was moved quite nine inches away from me, and was then pushed back again to me. This happened twice or three times.

We returned to my home at Dorincourt, Kingston Vale, in June, and there held a few more table sittings. On one occasion we sat in my study in the dark and used a gramophone. The music apparently increased the power very considerably. Questions we asked were readily answered by loud and distinct raps, and during the time the gramophone was playing the table vibrated enormously and was lifted into the air and pushed up against us.

Early in July Mr. Caradoc Evans, the famous Welsh novelist, and playwright, and his wife, were dining with me, and at their desire we held a sitting during the evening. The table did all manner of extraordinary! It lifted itself completely from the floor. It pushed itself against Mr. Evans' chest, and raising itself supernormally, eventually rested on his head.

Several messages were spelled out to me and to my wife from Annie and from Warren Clarke. The name of his friend, Edward Wright,[2] was spelled out to Mr. Evans and messages were given from him to Mr. Evans and his wife.

Later on, Mr. and Mrs. Charles Sykes were at a table sitting and several messages were spelled out, and the same extraordinary vibrations of the table took place.

At another sitting my brother-in-law, Edward Fry, and my sister, Gertrude Fry, sat with us. The physical phenomena on this occasion were amazing. It seems particularly curious that though Mr. and Mrs. Fry had read of my experiments, they appeared to be more impressed by this primitive method of communication than they had been by the published record of other infinitely more surprising experiences. This again demonstrates that it is the personal experience—simple as it maybe—that convinces people of the truth of survival.

During July we held a sitting at Dorincourt after dinner, with Mrs. Cory, Miss Winifred Graham, (the novelist), her husband, and Mrs. Graham (her mother). Personal messages were given to each of the sitters by the means of raps. This was, I may mention, the first experience of

---

[2] Edward Wright, whom I did not know, was a friend of Mr. and Mrs. Evans. He passed out some years ago.

the three guests of a table sitting, and as is usual with initiates, they all appeared to be astonished at the results.

Another sitting was held one night after dinner at Mrs. Cory's house at Hampton. On this occasion the table used was very heavy, and one which it was almost impossible for anyone present to lift. Several messages came through by raps, and then this heavy table was lifted up and turned completely over, so that its legs stood in the air. Such a demonstration makes no appeal to me and would never convince me of survival, but at the same time, I shall be glad if any scientist will be kind enough to explain how and why these things happen. It maybe said that if it were spirits who performed this physical act—and I am perfectly convinced it was—then this is not a very dignified manner of displaying their powers. Such demonstrations are made to convince those who are sitting that there is power beyond the human power. Physical demonstrations are given simply as first signs of that hidden power.

All this time I knew exactly what I was doing in conducting these experiments. I had used this primitive form merely to develop the psychic power in me as far as possible. My aim and my determination were to experiment in order to obtain the direct and independent voices, which I regard as the highest form of all mediumship.

How this was achieved I will show in the next chapter.

2

HOW THE VOICES CAME THROUGH

*An explanation of the newest and highest form of mediumship—
The first sound of a spirit voice—The lady and the trumpet—
Why music helps the spirit forces to manifest themselves—The
spirits manipulate the many parts of a jazz band—Mr. Caradoc
Evans describes a spirit who spoke to him and Mr. Noel Jaquin
his plan for a spirit imprint.*

I

July to September, 1924.

AMONG the many forms of mediumship, perhaps the most generally used is the so-called "automatic writing." Interesting as this form maybe, I, from personal experience and tests, should estimate that by this means any fact which can be accepted as indisputable evidence of survival emerges in barely one case in a thousand.

The objections to automatic writing are obvious, and it is perfectly possible to imagine an absolutely honest experimenter in this form of mediumship in all unconsciousness imprinting his own personality and ideas upon his messages.

By far the most wonderful and dramatic form of mediumship is the independent voice which speaks from space. It does not issue from the mouth of the medium—who may, and often does—speak simultaneously with it—a fact which enables any suggestion of ventriloquism to be dismissed as absurd. And it is with the investigation and development of this extraordinary and valuable form of mediumship that the student of psychical research must concern himself.

In the history of the subject there have been—and there still are—few direct, or independent, voice mediums. Home has been credited—somewhat loosely, I think—with being one of the greatest of all mediums, but in every record of phenomena produced by Home I fancy I am right in stating that in only one or two cases did his sitters hear even the faint whisper of a single word. At the same time, it must be borne in mind that Home did not try to get the direct voice.

The modern voice mediums, as they are called, represent the newest and highest form of mediumship.

Apart from Valiantine, who stands alone as the most remarkable medium, among those with whom I have sat include Evan Powell, the sisters Moore and F. F. Craddock.

Mr. Powell is a genuine and powerful medium, but on some occasions no voices have come through, and on other occasions the conversations have been mixed and confused and have been carried on only in a few short, ambiguous sentences. Under good conditions, conversations have been carried on for several minutes, and many evidential communications have been made.

II

The great difficulty in the way of the establishment of the fact of spirit communication is that in almost every instance, despite the inexplicable phenomena produced, and despite even the strongest evidence, allegations are invariably made against the personal character of the genuine medium.

Three times, for instance, have allegations of fraud been made against Valiantine, and on each occasion I have proved them to be scandalously untrue. Nevertheless, evil rumors will always spread like wildfire, and the great mass of loosely minded critics prefer to accept an ill-constructed lie to a solidly founded truth. It is so much easier, and such an attitude confers a sense of comic superiority.

I reasoned that if Valiantine had power to get into communication with the spirits, and if he possessed the qualities of mediumship by which the spirits were able to talk with us, there was no reason why it should not be possible for them to speak to my wife and myself without the presence of Valiantine. It was indeed Valiantine who told me on leaving England that he was sure I should be able to get the "voices."

It was towards the end of July, 1924, that I made my first effort to obtain direct and independent spirit voices.

When I suggested the experiment to my wife, she was amused, and declared that it would be absolutely impossible. So I refused to make any attempt on that evening.

Two evenings later, however, the experiment was made. There were only three sitters: my wife, her mother, and myself.

We sat in my study at Dorincourt; a trumpet—a collapsible aluminium trumpet for amplifying sounds, which Valiantine had left with me on his return to America in March last—was placed on a table in the centre of the room. We got the raps on the table as before, and after twenty minutes or so the trumpet was lifted and each of us was lightly touched.

Then a hissing sound was heard, as if someone was endeavouring, under great difficulties, to articulate something.

After a while faint voices called us by name, and two spirits communicated with us, one announcing herself as Annie, and the other as Warren.

We got only a few odd phrases, which we could not decipher. But, slight as the phenomena were, I regarded the attempt as remarkably successful.

III

During the next experiment made with the same sitters, the voices were stronger. At a sitting held under precisely the same conditions, in addition to my wife and myself, there were present Mrs. Cory (Miss Winifred Graham), her husband, and Mrs. Graham. Again the trumpet was lifted and each of the sitters was touched on the head. Again we got the faint replies to our questions in the affirmative or the negative as the case maybe, but we could not get through phrases of more than three words.

At a later sitting, when there were present only my wife, her mother, and myself, we sat at the table, placing the trumpet in the centre of the table as before. The table swiftly spelt out, by raps, the sentence: "On Saturday put the trumpet in the middle of the room." I asked: "Do you mean that we should not use the table at all?" The answer came: "No."

I said: "Shall we try without the table now?"

"Yes."

I removed the table and placed the trumpet in the middle of the room. After a while it was lifted, and floated in the air, and we got a few short phrases through.

On the following Saturday my wife and I were invited to a certain house to dinner, and included in the party were Mr. and Mrs. Osborne Leonard. I had been asked to bring the trumpet with me, and after dinner we held a sitting. In addition to Mr. and Mrs. Osborne Leonard, and my wife and myself, there were in the circle five other people: my host and hostess, a sister of the hostess, and another lady and a gentleman. I refrain from giving their names because the incident I am about to relate is of a somewhat delicate nature.

Prior to this, my mind had been working on how to overcome the handicap of the complete darkness in which direct voice séances are almost invariably held. I evolved the simple idea of having a luminous band placed on the broad end of the trumpet, so that every movement could be seen, and the exact locality of the sound of the voice determined.

For this occasion, therefore, the trumpet was luminous, and any movement could be seen by the sitters. First of all we sat at a table with the trumpet placed in the centre. There were several raps of varying character, and answers to questions. The table was lifted, and although it could easily, and would naturally, slide off, the trumpet was held in position by unseen hands. Later on we took the table away, and put the trumpet in the centre of the circle. It was lifted up, and floated in the air; everybody was touched by it, and on some occasions it actually went outside the circle. It floated over and rested itself on the hands of one of the lady guests present. We got faint answers of "yes" and "No," and at the end a voice delivered one affectionate message.

About two days afterwards to my astonishment I received a letter from my hostess, saving that we were being deceived: that during the sitting, when the trumpet had rested on her sister's hand, her sister had reached out quickly, to find a hand holding the other end of the trumpet, which, she suggested, was the hand of Mr. Osborne Leonard. It will be noticed that no charge was made at the time of the sitting. My hostess also said that she had received, through automatic writing, a message saying that Mr. Leonard was responsible for holding the trumpet and for the rest of the happenings. My correspondent's deductions were ridiculous, since the same form of phenomena had happened previously at Dorincourt, when Mr. Leonard had not been present. The lady who made the accusation had never sat before, and was extremely skeptical of séances, and it is possible that she may have felt a hand on the trumpet. If she did, it was unquestionably a materialized hand, and not that of Mr. Osborne Leonard. Anyone who knows Mr. Leonard as well as I do would laugh to scorn such an infantile allegation. This incident, however, shows how accusations of fraud are loosely thrown out by inexperienced people, and it also serves to show that a great bulk of automatic writing which comes through is coloured by the mind of the writer. Confirmation of this message could not, for various intimate reasons, possibly have cone through from the spirit from whom the writer assumed she received it. In fact, at another sitting, the spirit in question absolutely denied that the message had been given by him.

From this time onward we conducted fairly regular private sittings at home.

Many times have I been asked the reason for the practice of playing the gramophone as a preliminary to a séance, and the reason, in my case, is simple.

It has been found by experience that music of some sort, whether that of the human voice or of some instrument, is helpful in getting the minds of the sitters into harmony and also in some way, which has yet to be explained, the vibrations set up by the music are of assistance in enabling the spirit forces to manifest themselves. Moreover, I am a rotten singer, and therefore I prefer the mechanical production of music by the gramophone to my own voice.

But it must be borne in mind that music, while helpful, is by no means essential. Where there is perfect harmony between the sitters it is unnecessary; on many occasions when my wife and I have sat with Valiantine alone we have used no music whatever, and voices have come through almost immediately. On other occasions, while sitting alone with my wife, similar phenomena have taken place without music.

After the preliminary experiments, my wife and I took a rest for a few weeks, during which time we were traveling.

Towards the end of September, the sittings were resumed, and at the first there were present my wife, her mother, my son Anthony, and myself.

During the séance the voices of Annie and of Warren Clarke came through and spoke to us, and in the middle of the sitting Anthony made the suggestion that, as the spirits had the power to lift the trumpet, it should be possible for them to lift other things. He asked me whether I would mind him leaving the room and bringing in a drum and drumsticks from the dance room. I agreed to this, whereupon a drum and drumsticks were placed in the centre of the room. Whilst a jazz tune was put on the gramophone, the drumsticks were lifted and the drum was played in perfect time with the record.

The next day I went to Hamleys, and purchased a complete jazz set, and in addition to the drum, I also bought a tambourine, cymbals, triangle, siren and a set of heavy sleigh bells.

For that evening I had invited Mr. and Mrs. Caradoc Evans, Mr. Noel Jaquin—who had never sat at a séance before—and also there were present my wife, Anthony, and myself.

Mr. Noel Jaquin is one of the greatest experts in Great Britain in the study of hands and fingerprints, and he was desirous of seeing if it was possible to obtain the imprint of a spirit hand.

On this occasion all the instruments of the jazz band were played in time with the music played on the gramophone. The siren was taken up to the ceiling and blown, and during one of the melodies, the sleigh bells were played in time and harmony with the music. Before the sitting began I placed on the trumpet a vivid luminous band made by Messrs. Barratts, of Piccadilly, so that all its movements could be seen.

Here I would once more insist that physical phenomena of this kind, however extraordinary they may appear, would never appeal to me or convince me, unless I felt that there was an intelligence behind them, and unless I could also get into actual communication with those intelligences and learn from them things of value.

During that evening we had six individual spirit voices speaking to us through the trumpet, each giving his name. The spirit of Edward Wright spoke at some length to Mr. and Mrs. Evans. Mr. Jaquin was also spoken to by a spirit voice announcing itself as George Gregory. The spirit of Feda[3] came through, and laughed and talked, and seemingly walked about the room.

I should mention that Feda comes through in the independent voice. She usually interjects her remarks with a rather peculiar but happy little laugh. Feda has visited us at Dorincourt, with the peculiar characteristics

---

[3] Feda is Mrs. Osborne Leonard's control-a winsome, frolicsome spirit child.

she displayed during the Valiantine sittings in England last February. She has a personality which is recognizable immediately by any who have once heard her speak in the independent voice.

Annie and Warren Clarke also spoke to us, and towards the end of our conversation with Warren I asked him whether it had been possible to obtain a materialized fingerprint. He said it was very difficult, but in time they might be able to succeed in giving us one.

When I put on the Galli-Curci and Battistini records in operatic selections, the luminous trumpet was taken up and used as a baton, and the opera was conducted in the most professional manner. At the end of this manifestation we asked the conductor if he could give his name. We could not distinguish it at first, and Mr. Evans asked: "Are you English?"

The voice replied: "No, no."

Mr. Jaquin asked: "Are you French?" And again the voice said: "No"

My son said: "Are you Italian?"

And the voice answered: "Yes, yes, Italian."

We asked for the name, but the voice was so indistinct that we could not distinguish it.

This sitting lasted for nearly two hours, and at the finish Mr. and Mrs. Caradoc Evans and Mr. Noel Jaquin declared that they were astounded by the phenomenal results which had been obtained.

Strangely enough, after several manifestations of the trumpet acting as a music conductor, my wife one morning told me that she had had a dream in which someone told her that the name of the spirit who conducted the operatic music at our sittings was Palastrina, the great Italian composer of the sixteenth century.

At a later sitting this was confirmed by the spirit voice. It is by no means illogical that the spirit of Palastrina should manifest in this manner, for such a miraculous spiritual demonstration as this might have far-reaching effects.

I asked Mr. Caradoc Evans to write me a short record of his experience. Here it is:

"The various instruments of the small jazz band which Mr. Bradley had bought earlier in the day and which I had helped to unpack—began to move before the first gramophone record was half-way through. I had not heard jazz music previously, having no delight in that form of entertainment, but I am assured that the unseen players moved their pieces in unison with that which was played by the record. A few minutes later while a record was reproducing Madame Galli-Curci's voice in an operatic song, the trumpet rose deliberately from the floor; usually it trembles a little before rising, but on this occasion it rose as deliberately as rises a man who has made up his mind for action. In a moment it was in the air, conducting with majesty and dignity the song that came from the gramophone.

"We had been sitting about half an hour when I felt a sharp dig at the side of my left knee. I asked my neighbor, who was sitting several feet away: 'Did you stick your finger in my knee?' My neighbor answered 'No' I said: 'Somebody did.' Then I heard a laugh. It sounded in the middle of the floor. 'Is that you, Feda?' I asked, remembering Feda's tricks. Another laugh, and a voice said 'yes.'

"CE 'Look here, young woman, you mustn't play tricks. Besides, nice girls do not stick their fingers into gentlemen's knees. And I bet you don't know who I am.'

"Feda: 'I do.'

"CE: 'Well?'

"Feda: 'Carodoc Evans'

"CE: 'Come close to me. Maybe I'll be able to see you.'

"Feda came up to me, and though I could not see her, I felt her hands pressing my ankles together.

"CE: 'Sit on my lap, Feda.'

Feda's spirit sat on my lap so substantially that the spirit might have been a child of flesh and blood.

"CE: 'What about a kiss?'

"Two lips kissed my cheek several times; lips that were warm with the warmth of life and from between which came the breath that we know to be the breath of life.

"When I think of Feda now I think of her not as a spirit, but as an engaging child who was a bit spoilt in life.

"My dead friend Edward Wright made a journey to us. He spoke to my wife and to me. He did not say anything evidential,—but that which he did say he only could have said."

Here are Mr. Noel Jaquin's impressions:

"It was my privilege on the 30th September to experience for the first time a spiritualistic experiment. I had suggested to Mr. Bradley that if it were possible to obtain the imprint of a spirit hand, the materialized hand of some person whose imprint I had taken during life, then this would be concrete and incontestable proof of survival. I did not for one moment hope to be able to get these imprints at the first sitting, but

I took the precaution of preparing some smoked paper which I took with me to Dorincourt.

"Mr. and Mrs. Caradoc Evans, Mr. and Mrs. Bradley, Dennis Anthony Bradley, and myself entered the library just before nine o'clock. I assisted Anthony in erecting a jazz band set brought up from town that evening; this set comprised a drum, cymbal, triangle, swanee whistle and a hoop of small bells. These instruments were placed in the middle of the room; my case of blackened paper I placed very carefully at the side of the trumpet, and, in a semi-circle, I placed some sheets of ordinary white paper, which I had ensured being free from any marks made by contact with the human hand. All these papers I placed with forceps.

"Preparations complete, the lights were switched off, leaving us in inky darkness, the only thing visible was the end of the trumpet, which had a luminous band at one end. Unless one possessed the eyes of a cat it would have been impossible to reach the trumpet without falling over the band set or treading on some of the paper. Mr. Bradley sat opposite to me working the gramophone. During the first record nothing happened; about half-way through the second, the trumpet was suddenly lifted about eight feet into the air, and commenced to 'conduct' the operatic selection then being played.

"As the record finished Mr. Bradley asked our unknown conductor if he would endeavour to give his name. Only a hoarse, wheezing sort of whisper cane through the trumpet which we were unable to understand. Someone then asked if he were French; the reply was a faint 'No.' Everyone present heard this. Several other countries were suggested, the reply to each being 'No,' until Anthony Bradley said, 'Are you Italian?' At once the trumpet swung round and replied 'Yes.' A jazz tune was tried next, then a fox-trot; these were not conducted, but about a quarter way through the latter the drumsticks at my feet were moved. I heard the sound of one stick against the other, and in a second or two the drum was tapped, in time with the music. It was suggested that if there were other spirits present they might be good enough to assist in playing the band. Immediately the swanee whistle was played away on my right, and the hoop of bells towards the middle of the room, both high in the air.

"The unknown conductor was performing again later, when Mr. Evans asked in rather a sharp, startled voice, 'Who is touching me?' We all assured him that it was not any of us. I personally could not have reached Mr. Evans without falling over some of the apparatus on the floor. It was found to be Feda, who, with a materialized hand, was touching Mr. Evans's knee. This being my first experience, I was naturally in a critical, but not hostile, frame of mind. I asked that Feda should come over and touch me. At once my right hand was touched by a soft warm finger. I then asked if she would touch my left hand. This I at once moved down to my side, it was touched in the same way.

"A little later—half-way through a record—the trumpet was seen to rise. Mr. Bradley stopped the gramophone, and asked if the spirit would touch the person it wanted to speak to. The trumpet came gently over to me, as though the person holding it was afraid of dropping it, and very gently tapped the side of my head; this was not so much a tap as a caress. It was then held in front of my face, the luminous end being about two inches from me. Very faintly through it came 'Hullo, Bill.'

'Who are you, friend? Tell me who you are.'

'George.' This was much stronger and louder.'

'George who?' (I had guessed who it might be, but did not intend to be hasty.)

'George Gregory.'

"I then became convinced that this was my old school friend and brother-in-law actually talking to me. I told him of the experiment we were trying, and of the idea in getting the imprint of a spirit hand, and whose hands I wished to get. He promised to help me all he could. The trumpet was quivering by this time, as though the person holding it was becoming tired, so I said goodnight. It then came towards me again and caressed the side of my head. At the same moment I felt a hand gently patting m my shoulder. The trumpet was then replaced exactly in the position that it first occupied. My brother-in-law was precise to a fault, and it always was a habit of his, as we parted, for him to pat my shoulder gently. No person in the room knew that I had a brother-in-law; they certainly could not have imitated those personal traits of precision and gentle sympathy. Later during the evening I felt a hand gently patting my head in an encouraging sympathetic manner. This hand was warm and soft, like warm putty, but certainly a hand. Other spirits spoke, people whom I did not know—a relative of Mr. Evans, Mr. Bradley's sister, and Warren Clarke.

"Warren Clarke was the last one to speak. He spoke to Mr. Bradley, and then came over and spoke to Anthony Bradley. Just as he was moving away from Anthony, I said, 'Good evening, Mr. Warren, I am very pleased to meet you, and I should like to ask what you think of the imprint idea? Do you think it's any good?'

'Jolly good idea, I will help all I can.'

'Has the paper been touched at all this evening?'

'No-very difficult.'

Mr. Bradley then asked if Warren would take the trumpet up to the ceiling and tap it twice. At once the trumpet was carried quickly round the room, and spiraled up to the ceiling, which was tapped twice quite clearly. We then said goodnight, and the lights were switched on. The papers were untouched, except for a faint smudge that had been caused by the end of the trumpet falling on it.

"The height of the room would prevent anyone being able to lift the trumpet up and tap the ceiling, even had they stood on the bookcase, or the desk—which was impossible; the bookcase top having a lot of books, etc., standing on it, and the desk was behind my chair. This was a point that I particularly noticed.

"Before the sitting began, Mr. Evans and myself, at the invitation of Mr. Bradley, examined the trumpet and found that the inside was quite dry. At the end of the sitting we again examined it and found that there was a slight condensation of moisture on the inside, but the outer edges were quite dry. If materialized breath is used, it must cause precisely the same condensation of moisture as ordinary breath, but it would not moisten the outer edge of the trumpet with saliva, as in the case of a human agency.

When I 'read' the hand of Mr. Bradley I warned him against placing too great a strain upon the nervous system, as it would affect the heart, which was 'nervy.' He frankly told me that I was wrong in one thing, and that was the point about the heart."

3

CONFIRMATION BY CROSS EVIDENCE

In this sitting the stage is held by the spirit of Warren Clarke, who discusses Mr. Joseph De Wyckoff's charges against George Valiantine—An uncanny analysis of Mr. De Wyckoff's character—Evidential information concerning the author's son, Anthony Bradley—A spirit refutes the foolish trumpet allegation referred to in a previous chapter.

~

September 21, 1924.

ON September 21, 1924, took place my first sitting under the mediumship of Mrs. Osborne Leonard in her cottage in Hertfordshire since the one of January 6, 1923, recorded in my book *Towards the Stars*.

The interval of time between the two sittings I looked upon as important, as I desired to check and discuss matters referred to at recent sittings at Dorincourt, and also to probe an allegation of fraud—which had had somewhat serious consequences made against George Valiantine by Mr. Joseph De Wyckoff on April 20, 1924, the details of which, and the rebuttal of the charge, appear in another chapter.

There were present at the sitting with Mrs. Leonard, my wife, Anthony, and myself.

It must be understood that Mrs. Leonard knew nothing whatever of the various incidents referred to by Warren Clarke as regards Mr. De Wyckoff's character or of an event which had taken place in New York, and which is related in this book. I should state that whenever sitting with Mrs. Leonard a small red light is used so that one can record all that is said. Mrs. Leonard, it must be understood, is a clairvoyant and clairaudient trance medium. The "communications" are made through her lips. This is an entirely different form of mediumship to the "independent voice" séances, during which the voices come from space, and apart from the medium or any of the sitters.

Mrs. Leonard was two minutes going into her trance, and Feda came through and spoke.

It must also be understood that when the Christian name of Dennis comes through it refers to my son, Dennis Anthony Bradley, and that when the name of Herbert comes through it refers to me—Herbert Dennis Bradley.

The following is a verbatim account:

FEDA: Good morning! I spoke to Dennis through the trumpet.[4] I shall be able to help him. Annie and Warren are here and they both send their love. There are great times ahead and many important things to do. Later on we shall be able to draw out more power from the voices through the trumpet. Annie, Warren, and Bob[5] were so glad to find that they were able to materialize their voices.

WARREN ("W.A."): I know that you will be able to get very great power at your sittings, but you must be very careful whom you sit with. Winnie and Alice[6] appear to be all right. I am always with Herbert. The mediumship you have developed is a combination between the two of you, although I think that Mabel[7] could get it alone.

You must be careful of conditions. I was very pleased that you had developed this power, because it is going to be a very great help to the

---

[4] This refers to the sittings at Dorincourt.
[5] The spirit of Mr. Robert Graham.
[6] The names volunteered refer to Winifred Graham and her mother, Mrs. Alice Graham.
[7] My wife.

book[8] and to your future writings. There are important people whom I shall bring there.[9]

The Bradley clan is to afford the nucleus of a strong body of new spiritualists. Not just ordinary people who have never been interested in it before. This will be part of the important work. We are all on this side prepared, but you must be careful to find the right sitters and the right conditions to establish the power.

Later on we shall be able to draw the voices more away from you—right, outside the circle. You know Valiantine was extremely useful. We have all been able to develop through these experiments, and we should all be very grateful to the poor old chap.

Can you understand that under poor conditions, or in an undeveloped state, it is more like an elongated control? It is sometimes difficult for us to manifest our voices because we have to rely upon the ethereal more than on the purely physical.

HDB: What did you think of the sitting last night?

WARREN: Last night we managed fairly well, but things were not quite right. There was something left over from another time.

HDB: Do you think it would be possible, a little later on, to hold these sittings with a small amount of light?

WARREN: I should advise you to keep on with the dark for the present. Later on, when the power gets stronger, you might be able to introduce a little red light. You must remember that this is the birth of the development of this new power in you. It is as if we, on our side, were endeavouring to grow something and if you take the roots up from under the Earth and expose them, you are going to kill the plant. It is germination.

HDB: Since you told us to put the trumpet on the floor the voices have been very much better.

WARREN: Yes! It is easier for us to draw the power from this position. That woman affected you badly. She took it out of you. She had a paralysing effect. It also made it very difficult for us, as we could not get the power out. She is not the type for you to sit with. I am referring

---

[8] At this time, although I had kept notes I had no intention of writing another book on psychics. I was engaged on other literary work and was only impelled to commence this book towards the end of November.

[9] This is confirmed later, as the spirit of Lord Northcliffe and other important people—if they maybe so called—have come through at subsequent sittings.

to Evelyn,[10] and ——[11] could be quite a good sitter, but he must get a different point of view.

HDB: Can you tell us anything about Valiantine?

WARREN: I like him and I am grateful to him. I know that he has great power and that he is really genuine. It would be good to have him here again.

HDB: You know that De Wyckoff made allegations against him, because of one action, when he just placed the trumpet back in position, and this is being used in evidence against him.

WARREN: That was nothing. Valiantine is a good man, but if you invite him to this country again, you should give him the opportunity of getting into touch with other people. As far as the last allegation made against him is concerned, Herbert, you will be able to make mincemeat of his critics, and of your critics also. Already they have put their feet into things very badly—you will be able to jump on them. You are protected. Stick to your guns and they will never be able to bowl you over. They are the powers of ignorance.[12]

We are anxious to get certain people whom we can trust when he comes over here again. People one can vouch for Raymond's father[13] and other people of stability.

(Here Warren gave a most intimate and remarkable analysis of Mr. De Wyckoff's character and of certain personal affairs connected with him. For five minutes Warren volunteered exceptional evidence of his personal knowledge of events that had recently taken place in America. He referred in detail to Mr. De Wyckoff's attitude regarding *Towards the Stars*, and his subsequent action, details of which appear in Chapter 7.)

HDB: Do you remember, Warren, that when Valiantine was last here Dr. Barnett was discussing the matter of giving formulae for the treatments of tuberculosis, cancer, and syphilis? That is one of the experiments I should like to make with him.

WARREN: Yes—it would be right to make the attempt. You ought to bring him over, if only to make this endeavour.

---

[10] This name refers to my hostess's sister, who sat in the circle recorded earlier, and who afterwards made the assertion that one of the sitters was moving the trumpet and holding it.

[11] The name was given, but it would be indelicate to print it.

[12] This apparently refers to my controversy in the Press with Mr. Malcolm Bird, the Scientific American Committee and Mr. De Wyckoff.

[13] Presumably Sir Oliver Lodge

CONFIRMATION BY CROSS EVIDENCE

(To Mrs. Bradley) Mabel, didn't Joe look ill when you met him in New York? There were bags under his eyes, and deep lines.[14]

MRS. BRADLEY: Yes—he did. Warren, have you seen Bob[15] lately?

WARREN: Yes—he is a beautiful and simple character. He has the heart of a child. To be quite frank, he had to bring himself down to material things.

HDB: I want to ask you, Warren, whether you have ever met the spirit of Lord Northcliffe, and whether it would be possible for you to bring him through to me. I have a particular reason for asking.

WARREN: I have met Northcliffe. In a way he has been connected with me here. When he was on Earth he was a militarist, but before he passed over he was beginning to think of things in a different light.

That caused an extraordinary confusion of ideas in his mind, but it was too late for him to alter. Previously he had set ideas and strong views, formed so strongly in vivid colours. Towards the end, although these view, changed he was not strong enough to pronounce them. The effect of that was to produce disharmony in his mind and spiritual warfare. It was best that he passed over when he did; everything on Earth was getting too painful for him.[16]

HDB: Could you bring him into touch with us?

WARREN: I will try. I feel that you will have to get a sitting specially for this. I had better get hold of him and arrange it well beforehand. You know now that Northcliffe is most anxious to prevent future wars. You see I have had to take up so much time to clear up many trivial things, but I can tell you that now is the beginning of a great development in you, and Northcliffe is going to work with us, and with Louise and Swaffer.[17]

With regard to your home sittings you may get strangers but only occasionally. You, Dennis, will be able to develop considerably. You will be able to write and speak both on the political and on the social side. By the way, you are going to Cambridge soon; you need not worry

---

[14] This is correct. When Mrs. Bradley last saw De Wyckoff in New York in April last he seemed ill.

[15] The spirit of Robert Graham

[16] 1 Lord Northcliffe suffered considerable mental agony towards the end.

[17] All these names were volunteered. Miss Louise Owen was Lord Northcliffe's secretary, and Hannen Swaffer, at this time Editor of *The People*, was formerly intimately connected with Northcliffe in an editorial capacity on his newspapers.

about your rooms. I can tell you now that you are not going to live in those rooms very long. You will change them soon.[18]

(Here Warren gave me some important advice regarding a certain person who had the handling of my financial matters. He mentioned the person by his full name, and the warning was proved later to be of the utmost value to me. Here Feda announced the spirit of Robert Graham, who, she said, wished to speak, through her.)

ROBERT: Will you please give this message to Alice? First of all my fondest love. Tell her I saw her looking at some old writing of mine which she came across unexpectedly just recently. This was written some long time ago. She was not looking for it purposely.

It was something with a sort of embroidered design. I put my arms round her and said, "Alice, I am here just the same."

FEDA: Bob is very happy and it has been a great comfort to him both in writing[19] and speaking.[20] He hopes to do more wonderful things soon.

He says he did not mind Alice changing the room; her room is always his room. He is there every night when she goes to bed. Will you give his love to Winnie and say that he has much more to do through her in the way of writing? She is having a play produced quite soon.[21]

WARREN (to Mrs. Bradley): Thank you for all you have done, much of which has been working in the dark, in more senses than one.

FEDA:——[22] says he does not know what they are talking about.

WARREN: I am referring to mental colouring: the using of the trumpet.

---

[18] Anthony was going up to Cambridge in October and during the previous week had gone there to inspect his rooms, with which he was very displeased. The remarkable thing of this is that on the day after he took up residence in these rooms his tutor informed him that by a strange chance another and very excellent set of rooms at 27 Trinity Street was available, to which he moved the next day. This occurred three weeks after the sitting.

[19] Automatic writing.

[20] Through the voices at our sittings.

[21] This evidence is verified by Mrs. Graham and Miss Winifred Graham.

[22] The name was given.

CONFIRMATION BY CROSS EVIDENCE

A Spirit:[23] The trumpet, of course, is held. I hold it. The position I have to control it into is to get the power right. It is exteriorized control. The message that came through regarding this in writing[24] got through wrongly. Another mind had left its mark first.

The personal evidence volunteered throughout this sitting was quite remarkable. The various subjects were discussed at length and the information was given with intelligence and knowledge.

In addition an incident, not recorded here, was referred to by Warren, which was known only to my wife. I do not consider it desirable to publish the details, which are purely personal, but I will vouch that the information volunteered by Warren came as a complete and absolute surprise to both my son and myself.

---

[23] The name of this spirit was given and is the same as the one which manifested when the accusation was made that Mr. Leonard was holding the trumpet. It is important to mention that neither Mr. nor Mrs. Leonard knew that this accusation had been made.

[24] See chapter on Automatic writing.

4

WITHOUT AN OUTSIDE MEDIUM

The author makes his trumpet more luminous—The spirit of Lord Northcliffe speaks to Mr. Hannen Swaffer—This spirit also speaks to Miss Louise Owen—Mr. Swaffer supplies a vivid impression of this sitting—The author's sister Annie gives news of a serious illness.

I

October 7, 1924.

I INVITED Mr. Hannen Swaffer, Miss Louise Owen, and Miss Madeleine Cohen to attend a private sitting at Dorincourt, the only others present being my wife, Anthony, and myself.

In addition to the luminous band round the broad end, I had the trumpet painted up from the bottom with two half-inch stripes of luminous paint, in order that any movement of it could easily be seen and the exact angle observed. At this point I may mention that all such attempts to render the movements of the trumpet visible are as yet in the nature of experiments; the exact effect of light of any nature on the success of the phenomena is a matter of conjecture.

During the sitting the jazz band, the parts of which had been placed in the centre of the circle, was played in syncopated time when suitable music was put on the gramophone, and it was only when operatic music was played that the trumpet was taken up and used as a baton.

After a time, a spirit voice addressed Miss Madeleine Cohen. The trumpet was taken up close to Miss Cohen's face. The voice announced itself to be her mother, but only a few phrases were exchanged and the voice was very indistinct.

This was evidently the first time that the spirit of Mrs. Cohen had spoken through to the Earth plane. I have found that an inexperienced spirit usually has considerable difficulty in materializing the voice on the first occasion. Spirits have to learn and practise the usage of certain powers to master the method of speaking before they can become distinct and fluent, precisely as we have to learn how best to communicate with them.

Then Feda carne through, her voice being particularly good and distinct. The luminous trumpet was taken all round the room, and Feda chatted to each of the sitters, in her own characteristic manner. I asked her whether she thought it would be possible for Lord Northcliffe to speak to us, and she replied that she would try.

Some little time later a voice announced itself as "The Chief "—the name by which Lord Northcliffe was invariably known by his staff—and, addressing Mr. Swaffer, said: "I am so glad to see you, Swaff." and then continued speaking in a somewhat quick and excited manner to Mr. Swaffer and Miss Owen.

The spirit of Annie talked with my wife, my son, and myself and also to Mr. Swaffer. Warren spoke for same time to all of us.

HDB (to Warren): Can you take the trumpet up to the ceiling and hit it?

"That's easy!" Warren replied in an amused tone, and immediately the trumpet rose to the ceiling—which, by the way, is some twelve feet from the ground—and struck it several times.

This sitting lasted nearly two hours.

We adjourned, and as we chatted over the experiments, Mr. Swaffer turned to me, saying:

"It is marvelous. For the first time in my life, I am now absolutely convinced of survival, and of the actuality of communication with spirits."

WITHOUT AN OUTSIDE MEDIUM

II

In the next issue of *The People* (Sunday, October 12) Mr. Swaffer wrote an account of his experience, which occupied the space of two columns. I quote some extracts in order that the impressions of an outside and unprejudiced observer maybe recorded.

"In recording exactly what happened, I want to mention that all the five people present with me on that occasion were intimate friends, whom I have known for many years, that no outside medium was employed, and that it was just an experiment made by six friends in a private house.

"After placing on the ground an aluminium trumpet, the broad end of which was marked with luminous pant, we sat in the darkness, while a gramophone reproduced the voices of Galli-Curci and Battistini. Then the trumpet was seen to be lifted in the air, and, after a few seconds, it was waved, as though conducting the music, in broad, vigorous movements.

"After a time we could see the trumpet, which had fallen to the ground, again move straight towards Miss Cohen, who was seated opposite me. A loud whisper came from the trumpet, which we could not hear, although it seemed to say the word 'Mother.'

'Speak louder, said Mr. Bradley. It repeated the word 'Mother' more clearly, then said 'Madeleine' and 'Darling,' and then said something about 'kisses.'

"Miss Cohen, who had never attended a séance before, lost her mother nine years ago.

"Then the trumpet was raised in the air again, and we heard the name 'Feda.'

Feda is said to be an Indian girl, who died a century ago, and who is well known at Mrs. Leonard's séances.

"After a few friendly greetings, Mr. Bradley said "Feda, can you get Lord Northcliffe to speak? Do try."

"I will do my best," said Feda.

"Shortly afterwards, the trumpet fell to the ground again. Then, after a pause—when nothing happened, we turned the gramophone on, each time—the trumpet was lifted again. The music was stopped and the luminous trumpet came right over to me, within a few inches of my left arm, and said, 'The Chief. The Chief. I am so glad to see you, Swaff.'

"Lord Northcliffe was known as 'The Chief' by all his associates, and, although he always called me 'The Poet,' 'Swaff' is my usual nickname.

'I am so glad to see you,' went on the voice when I had answered. Then it moved directly along to Miss Owen, who was next to me on my right. It greeted her, too. And then, moving back to me, and then back to her several times, we heard, 'I have a great work for you to do for God and the world. Goodnight.'

"Afterwards, another voice, which Mr. Bradley recognized as that of Warren Clarke, his brother-in-law, and still another, that which he said was his sister Annie, held conversations with the three Bradleys.

"In the case of the voice that spoke to Miss Cohen, only she was addressed, although the trumpet, before it fell, came over and touched me on the arm. In the case of the Northcliffe voice, only Miss Owen and I were addressed. In the case of the two other voices, the Bradley family were spoken to first, and, afterwards, we three visitors were addressed. The method of approach, when the Northcliffe voice was heard through the trumpet, was that of a dominant personality. When 'Feda' spoke, it seemed that a joyous, youthful thing was using the trumpet; for it moved about quickly. When the 'Mother' voice was heard, it was all very serious. But when the Warren and Annie voices broke the silence, the trumpet moved about as though it were used to being in the circle.

"That the voices were not those of anyone in the room was beyond all doubt.

"We were all close friends, who would not trick each other, even if we had been clever enough to be ventriloquists, conjurors, and people who could move about in the dark easily, without being detected.

"To imagine, for instance, that one of the other five people would insult the sacredness of Miss Cohen's memory of her mother by pretending that her dead parent was speaking to her is, of course, beyond all possibility. Nor do intelligent people sit in the dark for two hours, playing tricks on their friends."

III

Thursday. October 9, 1924.
My wife and I sat alone, and with the trumpet only.

My sister Gertrude was very dangerously ill; and Annie came through and at once commenced to speak about her illness.

"Herbert," she began, "it was so good of you to send the car to Bath for Gertrude."

As a matter of fact, the doctors had decided that the only possible chance of saving my sister's life was to get her out to Switzerland, although, they admitted, it was doubtful whether she could, in her exhausted condition, stand the journey . But it was a last desperate chance, and they advise the risk. I therefore had sent my car down to Bath that day to take her by road to Dover, so as to save the discomfort of the train journey.

The previous year she had wintered in Switzerland and her lung had been patched up, but the trouble had again broken out—this time with dangerous complications and as a last resource the doctor decided to send her to Montana, although we were warned that even the journey might have fatal consequences.

Gertrude was so ill that she was unable to speak more than a sentence or two, so, at her request, none of her relatives, except my aged father, saw her and her husband off. My father returned from Dover, where she was carried on to the boat, and told me that he very greatly feared that she could not survive the journey.

The conversation with Annie was carried on easily and fluently, and her voice was natural and wonderfully distinct. On this occasion we did not use the gramophone, nor sing, nor indulge in any sort of preparation. We sat in silence, and Annie spoke to us almost immediately after we had sat down.

5

THE EVIDENCE OF LORD NORTHCLIFFE

Lord Northcliffe talks about certain persons on the Earth plane and makes many references of a very delicate nature—The author's startling theory of embryo children—A famous living person is severely handled—"Love is the main spring of life"— Mr. Swaffer receives advice from his former Chief—Annie delivers an urgent message, which later was confirmed.

11am. Sunday, October 12, 1924.

An appointment had been made by me a week or two preciously with Mrs. Osborne Leonard, and she was under the impression that I would visit her in Hertfordshire accompanied by my wife, as I had always done hitherto. I had however, made this appointment with the object of taking with me Mr. Hannen Swaffer. We motored over together and until we arrived Mrs. Leonard did not know that Mr. Swaffer was coming with me. Her only previous meeting with Mr. Swaffer had been at one séance held at Dorincourt in February, 1924, under the mediumship of Valiantine, which is recorded in *Towards the Stars*, on that occasion she and Mr. Swaffer had chatted together for a few minutes, but beyond that had never spoken to one another.

Swaffer sat next to Mrs. Leonard, so that he could observe the expression of her face and her condition when she went into a trance, and I recorded the notes by the light of the little red lamp.

After Mrs. Leonard had gone into a trance, Feda spoke. The following report is necessarily abbreviated and in parts expurgated. The extracts quoted, however, are verbatim.

FEDA (greeting both of us): Good morning! Good morning! You know I spoke to you through the trumpet before, and I also spoke to Louise.[25] The Chief is here and also Warren and Annie.

Feda then went on to repeat the messages of Lord Northcliffe, given to her, but the majority of these messages were delivered in the first person and for fully twenty-five per cent of the time I heard Lord Northcliffe's voice as on a wire, about a foot away from the medium's head. A large amount of the conversation was recorded by me from the direct voice of the spirit of Lord Northcliffe, in the first person, before the message was repeated by Feda, through the mouth of the medium. This is quite a remarkable and extremely rare phase in the mediumship of Mrs. Leonard.

NORTHCLIFFE (to Mr. Swaffer): I am glad you have come. This is extraordinary, isn't it? I have so many things to say. You know, I have spoken to you recently, but then I could not say very much. Do you remember I touched you on the head—and rather awkwardly on the body or the arm?[26] I could have spoken longer but wasted the power. That was because I was suffering from suppressed excitement, but I shall understand conditions better later on. I felt myself more there than at the other sitting. I see Fatty is still existing—occasionally called Tubby. He is a self-important person who has a very soft spot in his heart for me. When on Earth I was rather impatient with Fatty. He was too lethargic.

(Here Lord Northcliffe mentioned the name Pearson, and afterwards the name Sim—or Simpson.)

Sim is a man who is still working at the office. Not quite in the office but in the building. He does supplementary work. Graham too. So many of them think of me and want to know whether I think of them. I do, because they don't feel the same in their work now as they used to do for me. Even if they did not like the things I did, they were fond of me.

---

[25] Louise Owen. This refers to the Dorincourt sitting on October 7.

[26] At a Dorincourt sitting, under the mediumship of my wife and, self, the spirit of Northcliffe spoke to Mr. Swaffer, who acknowledged he was touched by unseen hands.

(Here Northcliffe mentioned some intimate personal matters in reference to his life on Earth. Although the facts he gave were evidential, I do not consider that I am entitled to publish them. They were of an extremely delicate nature.)

(Then, in the independent voice, the spirit broke off and said to Mr. Swaffer:)

Hannen, is Bradley all right?

MR. SWAFFER: 'Yes.' Bradley is all right. You can say anything you like before him.

NORTHCLIFFE: I have been very much worried and annoyed at things people have said about me. Surely it is my business entirely. If I choose to be responsible I will see it through. I cannot do it quite in the way I should like. There is no one I could work through.

MR. SWAFFER: Can't Louise do it?

NORTHCLIFFE: I do not know whether I ought to draw her into it. I have got a new name for Louise: 2 LO. (Here more references of a private nature were volunteered.)

Do you remember my staying down there [27] and not being able to come up?

(Here Feda interrupted, saying that the spirit of Northcliffe was patting his hips.)

FEDA: This annoyed him very much. He hurt himself and couldn't come up to town. It was when he was at Broadstairs, and it was very awkward. This happened some time before he passed over; I think it was about two or three years before. He got away as soon as he could. It was not an accident, but the hip got especially bad.

NORTHCLIFFE There is a lady over here of whom I was speaking.

(An intimate reference identifying this lady was made here.)

She passed over rather suddenly. It was a great pity; at least one thought so at the time, it seemed like the cutting away of the ground. I was over here some time before she passed over. I felt she was coming but was not prepared for her then. I was anxious about her, but the uneasy feeling went off. She passed over about a year ago. She had not been at all well for some time. She passed over quickly and it all came as a shock. There is one of her children over here who passed over. She was very surprised to find it living over here.[28]

---

[27] The name of the place had been previously given by Northcliffe.

[28] The previous evidence given in these communications is quite clear. This child is not placed, but it may have been an embryo as I have been told

It is a curious feeling for me, now that I feel I cannot become too much involved with those on Earth. I adore children. (To Swaffer.) You and Louise knew more than anyone. Others did not grip the fundamental part of my personality.

The boy I was so fond of who passed over in the war—I had such great hopes for him. The boy passed over before me. There were so many things I thought I might do with him. I felt nearer to him than his own father. The boy was waiting for me when I passed over. People belong to each other through a soul relationship. In a way, there is a soul relationship between me and you, Swaffer, and there is between Louise and me.

MR. SWAFFER: Is there any message you would like given to your mother—Mrs. Harmsworth?

(The reply was given by Northcliffe with splendid delicacy, but I do not think I have the right to repeat it.)[29]

NORTHCLIFFE (breaking off from the subject under discussion): Bradley has great power (presumably meaning psychic power), and also his wife. He will do a great deal to convince the world that there is life beyond the physical, that the leap into the unknown—which is so terrifying—is only a step into the next room. This will take away the undermining fear which attacks people. Most people allow it to become the substance. Knowing this I want to lift that weight—that limitation from people.

HDB: When you came through and spoke at Dorincourt, you addressed Mr. Swaffer and Louise Owen, but you did not speak to me. Was that because there was no line of attraction between us?

I ask this question because I entirely disagreed with many of the views expressed by you on Earth, as doubtless you would have disagreed with many of mine. You appeared to me to be an extreme militarist, whilst I was, and am, an extreme pacifist.

NORTHCLIFFE: On Earth we should have both become irritated with each other, but these superfluous inhibitions don't count now. I have got to the essentials of things. I always had a gift for essentials.

---

on dozens of occasions by spirits that the embryo lives. The spirit of the child lives if it has existed in the womb for any period over nine days after conception. According to this there are innumerable spirits created on the Earth plane which pass away within a month or more of conception, without our being aware of their definite creation.

[29] Lord Northcliffe's mother died during the year following this sitting.

THE EVIDENCE OF LORD NORTHCLIFFE

MR. SWAFFER: Will you try and get through in your own voice at Bradley's again?

NORTHCLIFFE: Yes! I intend to come through again at Bradley's if he will allow me.

HDB: Am I to understand that you will endeavour to get through at Dorincourt, on occasions when Mr. Swaffer will not be present?[30]

NORTHCLIFFE: Yes! I would like to try.

HDB: If you do I shall be very pleased to welcome you. If I may I would like to ask you a question. What is your opinion of——?[31]

NORTHCLIFFE (in a very sharp and determined manner):——is hopeless. Give him up. Lose him. He has material power, but material power is nothing. Spiritual power will count for more at the present time than it has done for hundreds of years. Why, ——has not even got intellect!, He has remarkable mechanism, but very often that mechanism is only set going by other people's hands. Left to himself, what would he have done? Not much! He has only the remarkable gift for using other people's intellects, just as he would use their bodies, and even their souls, if he could get hold of them. He could not get you, Swaff.

Mr. SWAFFER: No! You know I always liked you, Chief.

NORTHCLIFFE: Don't say "like". Why don't you say what you mean? I love you, and you love me. Be hanged to like—love is the main-spring of life. Many loved me but there is love, and love. I loved them as grown-up children, stupid children, obstinate children. There was no one so surprised as myself when I came over to find that I was loved in the most unexpected quarters.

When I passed over here I was met by a boy quite young. Now he is grown up. On Earth I was very fond of him. He was rather thinnish and his hair was going grey. He used to look down a lot and held his chin down a good deal when he walked. When walking he did not pick his feet up; he shuffled. You remember how I used suddenly to surprise people by introducing little things which people thought I had not noticed.

Now that I am here my face is smoothed out. I felt so tired towards the end and my brain would not let me rest. It was working at ten times the rate it had ever worked before, but I found I could not keep it on a line, and I got ten thoughts all jumbled together. The result was confusion. I was using up the forces of my body. I was like a suppressed volcano.

---

[30] This he succeeded in doing later on as will be shown.
[31] The name of a famous person.

My mind could not work through that brain clot. I am sure that at the end I had got a clot—a small one—on the brain. It would never have dispersed, and, had I lived, I should have been miserable—in torture.

There was a friend of mine—a man I had known very well, who passed over about the same time—who was very closely connected with the building up of my affairs. We went over the old days together. The man I refer to I had not seen for some time before passing over. I used to admire him very much; he had marvelous ideas, but on Earth I thought of him as thinking up in the clouds. I may have hurt him by trying to counteract something in him. You know I used to break in suddenly on people, but it was usually apt.

Mr. SWAFFER: Yes, Chief; you could hurt!

NORTHCLIFFE: Yes, I did hurt, but it was a sort of cauterizing. I never meant to hurt stupidly. I only did it to wake them up—to stir them up.

MR. SWAFFER: Have you any advice for me?

NORTHCLIFFE: I am not speaking of psychic things—speaking of your personal affairs.

(Here Feda said that Northcliffe was putting his hands on Mr. Swaffer, and that he appeared to be lifting him out. She said: "He seems to be taking him to new conditions.")

I am not taking you off the Earth, although you would be much happier here. Swaff—you would expand here. People won't let you on Earth. You haven't been your real self yet—all yourself, not parts of yourself. I have got to help you to alter your Earthly conditions. You are coming into a happier, stronger and different condition in yourself, and outside, than you have ever been before. The work you are doing now is temporary. There is something much more important coming—not immediately. Have patience and you will do work in which you will be able to express yourself. You will leave certain people that you have had to do with. That will be a very good thing. Then you will be able to use your own power more in a new environment.

You will find a little trouble in your work almost immediately. There will be some opposition, but because of what I have said, don't exaggerate. It is not what has happened recently, but something is coming to a head. Don't give it the importance of a crisis. It is of secondary, and not primary importance. Put that in the background and go ahead again.

THE EVIDENCE OF LORD NORTHCLIFFE

(Breaking off.) ——[32] is not very pleased. That does not matter. His power is material. ——is afraid. The bully is always a coward.

MR. SWAFFER: How long do you think it will be before I shall be able to get ahead with something?

NORTHCLIFFE: I have got to pull so many strings. I have got to get a foundation.

MR. SWAFFER: Am I right in being patient just now, or is it cowardice?

NORTHCLIFFE: Cowardice is a virtue in this condition. It is better for you to be patient just now. There are things happening outside yourself all together. They will materialize later. Then you can strike. You are trying now to stay your hand.

MR. SWAFFER: Was I right in giving in yesterday?

NORTHCLIFFE: Yes! but it was not what you intended to do.

MR. SWAFFER (directly): You were just the same as.

NORTHCLIFFE: That's a nice thing! But I cannot say you are a heaper of coals. Yes—you were right, but it was not what I expected you to do. You were thinking of this matter the other day. I tried to tell you not to kick against it. I am on your side. Can you imagine my being inert with power, but apathetic? Was it my body that achieved the things I did? It was my mind that was the drawing force—drawn by my will. I have still got my mind. I am not helping you to be foolish—reckless. You must bide your time.

MR. SWAFFER: What is the best thing to do to get on with the job?

NORTHCLIFFE: I do not want you to do anything now—just go on as you are at present. You do not like it. Your dignity rebels against it. Another thing, do not anticipate. Go on each day, as it comes, Swaff; do not let it become an obsession. When you are not actually doing something about it, keep it off your mind. A little later on you will think you gave it too much importance. Bring tomorrow's searchlight to bear upon it. A lead maybe given to you very suddenly. Conserve your nervous force and energy for that. It will mean personal freedom. Then make use of it and enjoy it. I am backing you up here and I know you will come through—you have got help from this side; even without anything definite happening you will feel it supporting you spiritually and mentally. We shall not fail you. We will just keep at the back of you and help you internally and externally.[33]

---

[32] Name given of a famous person.
[33] Reference to Mr. Swaffer's political mentality; a General Election was imminent.

You have had it in you for years to work for us. Your approach was quite just. On Earth I was even a limitation to you. I kept trying to put you on to the planes you would not fit on to—kept giving you mental pushes. Now I recognize and see what you had in you then. I know you are going to work for me, to make yourself open to me to secure inspiration and impression. You have been too eager on the mental side. Now you are open to the spiritual. Bring the spiritual to function through the material. It is difficult, but bit by bit I shall help you to be strong. Strong, but not too positive. I can give you a good deal of stuff—stuff that has never been concocted by a twopenny-halfpenny literary mind before. Real stuff. Solid stuff. Original. Do not expect wonders just yet. Speaking of working—-

WARREN CLARKE (suddenly interrupting): Oiling the machinery.

NORTHCLIFFE: I expect that's it. You have got a difficult nervous system for me to work with, but I shall be able to help it to become absolutely under your control before long. You will develop your higher self—in thought or in action—and I can help you to everything. I wish I could talk to you without an intermediary, and then you would realize. I shall be able to give you confidence, poise—a foundation of spiritual strength. Bring spiritual into the physical. I will work through you mentally, not through automatic writing.

Most automatic writing is rot. It is the mind I can work through—the mind. I am practicing with you now, but at first only with little things.

To make yourself impressionable will you make your mind a blank for the moment? If you are in a hole I will give you an impression what to do. Don't do anything out of the ordinary at present. Walk warily, even though you despise yourself for a while. I shall speak to you again through the trumpet before long. At Bradley's, I take it—the necessary conditions are there.

WARREN CLARKE (joining in): You will be able to get more through next time. I thought the first time was quite wonderful.[34]

(To Swaffer I say, old chap, you must not mind the jazz band ...

(Here Mr.. Swaffer and I both laughed, thinking he was referring to the coming political election.)

MR. SWAFFER: You mean the political crowd?

WARREN CLARKE: No! ours is better than theirs. I mean at Dorincourt.

MR. SWAFFER: I thought you meant blue elephants and Manchester.

---

[34] Meaning the direct and individual voice.

THE EVIDENCE OF LORD NORTHCLIFFE

WARREN CLARKE: Ours is not political music. The jazz band which was played at Dorincourt may not be particularly good, but at least it was fairly decent! I know, Swaff, you did not care much for jazz music being played during the sittings, but you must remember that the psychic sign given by the playing of that band does help. It is not so trivial as one might imagine. It is extraordinary, and it does astound people, and with the luminous paint it is impossible for any human being to explain how it is done. It makes people think. Therefore, in its way, it is beautiful and uplifting.

(Feda interrupted and said that Annie was coming through, but that she could only stay for a minute, as she was in a great hurry.)

ANNIE: Herbert, I can only stay for a few minutes, but there are two things I wanted to tell you. With regard to your sittings, when you are holding them please try not to get so cross at home.

HDB: I am sorry, but I get so very nervy at times, especially so before the sittings, and sometimes I cannot help feeling irritable. Do you mean that this affects the power?

ANNIE: Yes! It does. And if you could try and get your mind a little more restful it would help us much more. The other thing I want to tell you is that I have just left Gert, and I am going straight back to her now. She has just arrived at Montana. She is all right up to the moment, but although there is no immediate danger she is in a very critical condition. She is very exhausted, but the journey had to be done. I was with her all the way, and I was trying to give her vitality, but her condition is so weak that it was almost impossible for me to impress her. At one point, just an hour or so ago, I thought she might not be able to survive the effects of the journey. A tiny point of extra strain might have been too much for her. I am going back to her now to watch over her. My love to you and Mabel.

NORTHCLIFFE; My best love to you, Swaff, and my best thoughts. All I can wish you that is good. Hang on!

The sitting ended.

With the exception of occasional interjections by Warren Clarke, and the one short poignant communication by Annie, it will be seen that Northcliffe held the conversation practically all the time.

I regard this sitting as extraordinarily evidential, especially as certain names were volunteered, some of which have to be omitted, and certain intimate and personal references were made which cannot be quoted.

The personality of Northcliffe was wonderfully dominating. The utterances of my sister towards the end were dramatic and evidential.

Neither Mrs. Leonard nor Mr. Swaffer knew anything of my sister Gertrude, or of her critical condition. At the time that Annie came through, at about twelve forty-five p.m., Gertrude had just completed the journey to Montana. This evidence was volunteered of her own accord by the spirit of Annie, and every reference to her condition—even to the one critical point when she was on the verge of collapse from the effects of the journey—was verified afterwards by Gertrude's husband, Mr. E. J. Fry, when he returned from Switzerland three days later. It would be difficult to conceive a more acute proof of survival than this communication. Not only was this communication valuable from the evidential point of view, but it can be taken as a proof of the care that the spirits can take of those they love by endeavouring, in times of crisis, to impress them, even to the extent of physical vitality.

I will now give the impression this sitting created upon Mr. Hannen Swaffer, which was published in *The People* of October 19.

"For nearly two hours Mrs. Leonard was in a trance. She sat in a room from which the light was partly excluded, a room in which many famous inquirers have sat with her. Mr. Bradley took a careful note which, in due course, will be added to the records of the Society for Psychical Research, a society whose tests Mrs. Leonard has passed.

"In my articles on this subject, I have taken a perfectly unbiased line, and merely written down what has happened without comment. But I must state that, in various ways, whoever was really speaking last Sunday gave considerable knowledge of matters that, presumably, only Lord Northcliffe would know about.

"There was a long reference to his mother, and to personal affairs known to very few. The voice spoke of people still in the Daily Mail firm, describing them. Now and then, name's' were mentioned. I find it difficult to describe this part of the conversation without possibly causing offence.

"My own personal worries were discussed, and advice was given me, similar to that which Lord Northcliffe used to give me during his lifetime. Now and then, a phrase characteristic of him was used.

"It all seemed so personal, so intimate, that when I was told 'I would like to sit in that chair with you for five minutes, Swaff, for then you would understand,' I felt as though a man whom I knew very well was really very near me. 'I am not dead, but alive,' said the voice, once. 'Can you imagine me inert? Was it my body that lived? It was my mind, driven by my will. My mind still lives.'

"I should need columns to describe the intimacy of this long talk.

"The leap into the unknown, which is so terrifying, is only a step into the next room,' the voice said to me last Sunday. 'It will take away the undermining fear which attacks people. Most people allow it to become the substance. Knowing this, I want to lift that weight, that limitation from people.'

"I find it hard to do anything but approach the whole subject with the deepest reverence. You scoff only when you first hear about it. As you go on you almost envy those who, in regard to spiritualism, delight in their conversion, declaring that it is the joyful explanation of everything for which they have been waiting for years."

6

THE MIRACLE OF THE DIRECT VOICE

Among other things, this chapter records a dramatic, poignant scene between Miss Frances Carson, the famous actress, and the spirit of her dead husband—he Editor of "The Tatler" asks a question about a dog and is given a correct answer—Mr. Donald Calthrop writes: "Thank you for my first real introduction to the world beyond"—Mr. P. G. Wodehouse fails to recognize a spirit voice—The author is advised to discontinue the sittings and is given the reasons thereof—Listening to a séance behind a closed door.

I

9:00pm Sunday, October 12, 1924.

ON the evening of this day I had invited to Dorincourt Mr. Edward Huskinson, the editor of *The Tatler*, Mr. P. G. Wodehouse, the famous novelist, Mr. Hannen Swaffer, Mr. Donald Calthrop, the well-known actor manager, and Miss Frances Carson, the celebrated young actress. Miss Carson is, I believe, Canadian born, but she made her name in America before coming to England, where during the last two years she has played many leading parts in the principal West End theatres. We all dined together, and the sitting took place afterwards, my wife and I completing the circle.

Again I must reiterate that the personal experiments I am engaged upon are made in order to obtain the direct individual voices of the spirits, speaking in their own tones, independently and from space, and giving personal and characteristic evidence of their survival after bodily death. It is the deepest probing into the secret problem of life that has ever been made, and its triumphant success marks an epoch, and represents the outstanding miracle of this or any other age in history.

In comparison with these discoveries, the marvels of wireless fade into pale significance, and assume no more importance than a child's material toy.

Scientists have said that if we could obtain even an unintelligible signal from the planet Mars, it would mean a step forward in knowledge.

Within the last two months at Dorincourt we have stepped past this unintelligible ambition, and arrived at the amazing condition of actual and audible communication with those who are living in other worlds.

The dark ages are past, and we can understand the Sphinx's smile, whose enigmatic meaning is: "You fools! There is experience, but never death."

Let me come down to cold experience. ... The luminous paint having proved so effective when used upon the amplifying trumpet, I had the drumsticks and sleigh bells also painted, in order that every movement would be visible. In the course of the séance, while the jazz band was played, the drumsticks could be clearly seen making the necessary movements, and the sleigh bells were repeatedly lifted, played, and then dropped far outside the circle of the sitters.

At about eleven o'clock Annie spoke in her direct voice which was clearly heard by all those present. She told me that Gertrude had survived the ordeal of the journey, that she was resting, and that she thought she was now in a slightly better condition and would pull through. This information was verified in detail by my brother-in-law on the following Wednesday when he returned from Switzerland.

I do not know whether I can convey the extraordinary effect of receiving two direct communications in one day on such an important personal matter as this.

Then the voice of a woman whom Mr. Huskinson had known spoke to him, and inquired why he had not brought his wife down. When he asked her if she remembered "Nigger," the voice replied, "Yes, he was a retriever dog." Another voice spoke to Mr. P. G. Wodehouse. This voice, however, was so faint that no recognition could be claimed.

THE MIRACLE OF THE DIRECT VOICE

Two spirit voices spoke at length to Mr. Donald Calthrop. One was that of his father, the actor, John Clayton, who had passed away in Mr. Calthrop's early youth and the other an aunt of his, for whom he had a great affection.

The spirit of his aunt it should be mentioned, spoke both in the independent voice, without the trumpet, close to Mr. Calthrop's face, and later at my request took up the trumpet and spoke through it—the voice then sounding considerably louder.

There followed one of the most dramatic scenes I have ever witnessed.

Miss Frances Carson is, I imagine, about twenty-eight years of age. No one in the room knew anything of her early history.

A man's voice called her by her Christian name.

"Frances, darling, it's Eric!" it cried, in an agitated manner.

Then for some four or five minutes a thrilling and emotional conversation followed, obviously between two people who had been all in all to each other.

They spoke of Devonshire, of the quiet lanes which she had walked through recently, of his speaking to her before he had passed away, of her success in London, which success she had always longed for when she was with him in America.

The voice, she told me later, was that of her husband, who had died suddenly from pneumonia on New Year's Eve, eight years ago. I have never listened to a more perfect, more beautiful love scene. One felt that it was too sacred for one to share in it.

Miss Carson knew nothing whatever of spiritualism and had never attended a séance. During the time her husband was speaking to her, she wept emotionally, and for some moments after her husband had gone she was deeply affected. She begged us to forgive her, explaining that she was not unhappy, for it was the happiest moment in her life. The revelation of an afterlife and of a possible communication with one whom one had loved, she said, was the most marvelous event in her life.

Three days after this Miss Carson sailed for America, and in a week or two I received a letter from her, written on board the *Olympic*:

"DEAR DENNIS BRADLEY,—I have been wanting to tell you so much, but I was afraid of the incoherency of my thoughts about the whole thing. You have given me so much, and I want you to know of my sincere appreciation of all you are doing. My personal experience quite stunned me. To hear a voice you had thought lost, and to be given tangible proof of the everlasting love—oh, it is too marvelous. I want to find out more and more, although I confess to feeling a wee bit scared. Yet, it has made me so happy. My sleep has been so deliciously peaceful, and when I wake I am certain that whilst sleeping I have been with him. It was never like this before. You see, I knew Eric when I was about sixteen, and we married. He was the definite influence of my life, and is even now, so long after his passing eight years ago.

"I felt that it seemed wrong to look back at one's greatest happiness, but I have always felt that no future could give me so much. It is really wonderful, and I am telling you all this to try and explain my personal joy and happiness on finding my lost treasure. What a wonderful evening. Do give other poor souls a chance on both sides. From the joy of their voices and the harmony that existed I am sure you are doing a great and constructive work."

Four out of the seven sitters on this evening had had no experience of psychic matters.

II

Although I usually enjoy perfect health, just prior to this sitting I had been feeling tired and overworked. On the following day I had a terrible headache, and so had my wife, and I was compelled to retire to bed early. I am inclined to think that the effect and strain of these experiments, and the fact, possibly, of sitting with various new sitters, were getting rather too much for me.

A day or so later I received the following letter from Mr. Calthrop:

"My DEAR MABEL AND DENNIS,—The wonder and beauty of last night is still so strongly with me that I really find it difficult to write to you, though I feel sure you will understand how much I want to say, to thank you for my first real introduction to the world beyond.

I am still rather stunned by it all, the Beauty was so great, and the Reality greater, I do not think I can ever doubt again. I pray not. Thank you so much."

Both Mr. Huskinson and Mr. Wodehouse told me on that night, and also on subsequent occasions, that they were deeply impressed by the extraordinary happiness they had witnessed.

Wednesday, October 15, 1924.
On the following Wednesday I held another sitting with my brother-in-law, Edward Fry, who had returned on that night front Switzerland.

THE MIRACLE OF THE DIRECT VOICE

There were six of us present, and it was purely a home circle. The usual phenomena took place, and it is unnecessary for me to give the details. I will only mention that Annie spoke for some time with us all, and told my brother-in-law that since he had left Switzerland his wife had been progressing favourably.

Three of the six people who were sitting had never sat before.

III

Saturday, October 18, 1924.
On this evening I held a sitting at which were present only my wife and her sister Ida, who had just arrived in England, having been abroad for several years, and myself. Ida had had no previous experience of séances.

Physical phenomena took place. The band was played, and the operatic music was brilliantly conducted. Sounds were heard moving across the room and Ida was touched on the shoulder by materialized hands and became frightened. I asked the spirits not to touch her again. The trumpet was lifted and her father, George Hunt, spoke with her for some two to three minutes. After this the spirit of Annie spoke to her.

IDA: Do you know where I am living now?

ANNIE: Of course I do, you are living in Chemnitz.

A little later I asked Annie how she thought we were progressing. To my astonishment she replied: "I am very sorry, Herbert, but I have got to tell you that you must discontinue these sittings."

I was exceedingly surprised and asked the reason.

"Because they are having a very injurious effect on your health," she replied. "Warren will come through presently and tell you how necessary this is."

A little later the spirit of Warren told me that it was absolutely imperative for me to stop for a while. I had a long conversation with him, in course of which he said: "I am very sorry, old chap, because I know how disappointed you will be, but we must consider your health first of all."

I asked him if this meant that I must stop altogether. He replied: "I cannot say at present, but if Valiantine should come to this country it will be all right for you to sit with him."

I asked him whether, in the event of Valiantine not being here, it would be permissible for me to sit in the case of a great emergency.

Warren replied: "Yes, but only in the case of great emergency."

As a matter of fact, I had been hideously overworked, for since the publication of *Towards the Stars*, I had been inundated with thousands of letters—most of them from total strangers—from all parts of the world asking for advice and help. I did not feel it human to ignore these requests, and that, with my literary and other work, had left me barely a moment to snatch a mental rest.

The development of mediumship and the series of dramatic experiences that had taken place had become fascinating and absorbing, almost to the exclusion of any other interest. It was a great disappointment to me to be told to stop for a while, but I understood the next morning how essential this was. I realized that it was impossible for me to go on working at this intensive pace without suffering from strain.

IV

Thursday, October 23, 1924.
I had invited to my house, as guests to dinner, Mr. Julian Shalders and two other people whose names I do not propose to print.

The invitations had been given about a fortnight before, and the guests had been looking forward to the experience of a séance. Unfortunately, on the previous Saturday I had been told that I must not sit again for a time. My wife suggested that she should sit with them, without me.

They adjourned to my study, placing the various instruments on the floor, with the luminous trumpet, etc., in the same disposition adopted during the sittings I had held before.

Directly I had left them I was overcome with curiosity as to what would come through. I got up and, unbeknown to them, stood outside the study door.

Four records were played on the gramophone, and after about twelve minutes some of the musical instruments were played. The sounds could he heard distinctly from outside the closed door. The effect upon me was rather peculiar, as although my house is kept quite warm with central heating, my legs, from the knees to the feet, became very cold, as if an icy draught were playing about me. This is the usual feeling I have at all sittings when psychic phenomena are taking place, but not nearly as intensely as on this occasion.

A little later someone called out that the trumpet was floating in the air, and that each of the sitters had been touched by it. I then heard a spirit voice calling "Edgar—Edgar." One of the sitters asked: "Is it you, Warren?" thinking it was the spirit of Warren Clarke.

The voice replied: "No, it's Reg speaking."

This spirit proved itself to be the brother of one of the nameless sitters. He had been killed in France. Afterwards this spirit also called on the second nameless sitter by the correct name. She had previously been a little nervous of being touched by the trumpet, and the spirit said to her: "Don't be frightened, I know you don't want me to touch you."

At the end of the conversation I heard the trumpet fall. It was again lifted and, I was told, hovered in front of Mr. Shalders. I heard a spirit calling "Father, Father."

Mr. Shalders answered: "Is it you, Owen?"[35]

Mr. Shalders was a little upset and did not endeavour to gain evidence; he volunteered certain statements to the spirit. One of these I heard him say was: "Your mother is quite well, Owen," at which the spirit laughed, and replied: "Well? Of course; I know she is!"

The drawing of the power and the forms of mediumship in connection with this sitting are explained fully in Chapter 9, which contains the record of a sitting with Mrs. Osborne Leonard.

V

The séance was remarkable because there are few instances on record of a sitting being heard from outside the circle. As a matter of fact, during the sittings held at Dorincourt both by myself and my wife, and also by Valiantine, voices have been heard at some considerable distance from the room, when the power was strong. On one occasion a very loud spirit voice was heard by people who were in the corridor on the next floor. On another occasion my wife listened outside the door for a while, and heard the conversations clearly and distinctly.

This ordered cessation in my experiments was apparently necessary. Momentarily I was irritated, although I realized its import. At first my mind rebelled against the unexpected ultimatum. The penetration had been so rapid, and the approach to the magnificent so imminent, that I felt resentful that such a puny consideration as my physical health should be accounted as of more importance than my research.

---

[35] This was the name of his son who had passed away a few years.

But the miracles of spirit communication have been irrefutably established. That is a concrete accomplishment.

And when the spirits gave me pause I did not realize their purpose. Yet their dual purpose must be apparent to all who read this book—they gave me pause in order that I should write.

7

FRAUD

Herein the author deals with false accusations against mediums—He tells the true story of Mr. De Wyckoff's charges against Valiantine and how he smashed them—He also tells of the strange communications between Mr. De Wyckoff and Mr. J Malcolm Bird of the "Scientific American," which account ends on a note of comedy—Captain Ben Hicks' exposure.

I

October, 1924.

BROUGHT suddenly face to face with inexplicable phenomena, the only explanation the unintelligent or the prejudiced can evolve is that phenomena which are inexplicable to him must of necessity be produced by fraud.

It is in a sense a purely comic state of mind: "I know everything possible, therefore what I do not know is impossible."

At one time or another, allegations of fraud have been made against most of the well-known mediums, often enough based on little or no evidence, and often due to the hysterical desire of the accuser to find a simple explanation, suitable to his simple mind, of phenomena which have disturbed and bewildered him. Again and again these accusations have been proved groundless, and it surely must be obvious that if the whole of the great study of spirit communication were based on fraud it would long ago have ceased to attract intelligent minds, and instead of obtaining fresh students daily cold and balanced searchers after the laws of a new knowledge—the band of so-called "spiritualists" would consist of a forceless group of mental unfits.

Whereas never before has its study attracted more attention, and never have its students included in their ranks men of greater eminence in the learned professions, men who accept as a proved fact the actuality of spirit communications, and are seeking to discover the laws which govern them.

But even yet, it is the general rule that when any accusation of fraud—no matter by whom or on what flimsy grounds—is made against a medium, it is everywhere accepted, and often on uncorroborated or prejudiced evidence, the whole of that medium's work is damned. Some base rumour, one insignificant incident maybe—indeed, has been—used to discredit the whole mass of accumulated and sifted evidence which stands to his record. These accusations, frequently inspired by personal prejudice, are usually hung on the thinnest of threads, and the slightest suspicion, founded on the most trifling incident, is too often accepted at once, without investigation or even criticism, and is used by skeptics and interested people to discredit the whole of the work accomplished.

One concrete case of this kind which came to my notice, and which I took the trouble to probe to the end, stands as typical of many, and for that reason, and because it is typical, I propose to deal with it at some length.

George Valiantine has on three occasions been accused of fraud; once by the Scientific American Committee in New York, whose findings were smashed by me after prolonged investigation; once by Mr. Joseph De Wyckoff, as recorded in *Towards the Stars*, and again by Mr. De Wyckoff in New York during the spring of 1924.

Before entering into details of these charges and their refutations let me give some idea of the medium. George Valiantine is a short, sturdy man, some fifty years of age, who earns his living by commerce in an American provincial town. He is slow of speech, but simple, direct and frank in all his conversation. His range of interests seems limited, as one would expect from his life and surroundings. His vocabulary is limited, and he would seem to have little knowledge of the value of words. His favourite description of anything that appeals to him is "Pretty good."

In short, the personal impression he conveys is precisely that a small tradesman or farmer in one of the unimportant English market towns would convey that of a thoroughly honest, hard-working, imperfectly educated individual, of necessarily limited views, and few opportunities to extend or polish them. Despite his lack of knowledge, he is innately refined, and possesses one of the most kindly and sensitive natures I have come in contact with.

It was not until he was forty-three, he told me, that he discovered his mediumistic powers. He developed them by gradual degrees, and at length achieved the direct voice, and also the phenomenon of materializations. The séances he held were unpaid, and his circle consisted merely of his personal friends and relations.

It was some four years ago that his extraordinary powers came to the knowledge of Mr. De Wyckoff, a wealthy American financier of Jewish extraction, who had for some time been interested in psychic matters. Mr. De Wyckoff entered into communication with Valiantine, and several times invited him to his country residence, Arlena Towers, for the purpose of holding séances, and for which he naturally and justly defrayed Valiantine's traveling and out-of-pocket expenses.

For some years Mr. De Wyckoff and Valiantine were in fairly close association in their experiments, and as I have recorded in *Towards the Stars*, Mr. De Wyckoff continued to display the utmost belief in the medium's powers. He was present at many of the séances held in London at Dorincourt in February, 1924, and he and Valiantine traveled back to America on the same boat.

II

It is peculiar to note that although the first two charges of fraud made against Valiantine emanated from two distinct sources, as an aftermath of the third charge the two individual accusers appear to have communicated and joined forces.

The publication of my strictures upon the findings of the Scientific American Committee had caused considerable comment in the American and British press. A leading article in *Light*—the weekly psychic journal—called for a reply by Mr. J. Malcolm Bird, the Managing Editor of the *Scientific American*, who was responsible for the reports of the Committee on Psychic Investigation. His letter was published in the issue of *Light* of September 20, 1924. It was a very guarded letter, in which, whilst acknowledging Valiantine's "remarkable showing in the field of subjective phenomena," he endeavoured to explain the attitude of his Committee by saying that they were only concerned with objective phenomena. His tone in defense was considerably chastened, but in the end paragraph of his letter he ventured to drop a veiled threat that he was in a position to publish another expose, the particulars of which he intimated that he had acquired.

Such a passage of misstatement, to say nothing of the innuendo contained in the last paragraph, demanded an answer. Evidently—by means at which I maybe permitted to guess—Mr. Bird had obtained information of a later séance in New York at which Mr. De Wyckoff had accused Valiantine of fraud, and on the data supplied him had made the rather silly threat to publish particulars.

Unfortunately, threats always affect me as a stimulant, and not as a depressant. So directly Mr. Bird indulged himself in what I cannot help regarding as the slightly contemptible "argument by threat," I determined to expose the whole incident and publish the full particulars.

In the issue of *Light*, dated September 27, 1924, there appeared the following letter from me."

"I have read Mr. Malcolm Bird's poor attempt to reply to my drastic criticism of the attitude of the Scientific American Committee in its investigation of the mediumship of George Valiantine in New York in July, 1923. My opinions of the Committee's methods are contained in my book, *Towards the Stars*; and they are based on the three-page report which appeared in the *Scientific American*.

"Mr. Bird refers to Valiantine as a 'message medium.' Valiantine is not a message medium—he is an independent voice medium; and the voices, when they manifest, are very often heard several yards away from where Valiantine is sitting.

"Valiantine did not appear before the Scientific American Committee to produce objective phenomena. He appeared before the Committee for three test sittings, having made neither promise nor guarantee of phenomena, in order that the members might observe any phenomena that might take place. Phenomena of various kinds did take place, and the Committee and even Mr. Bird, who had at that time made up his mind that spirit communication was a fraud, were nonplussed to find a reason for turning down Valiantine. He summoned up his wit, and evolved the childish argument that the chair upon which Valiantine sat, and to which an electrical apparatus had been secretly fixed, did not register the medium's full weight for fifteen seconds on one occasion, and at other odd times varying from one, three, six, nine and fourteen seconds. Despite this Mr. Bird is forced to admit that he held a long dialogue with one of the medium's spirit guides, whose voice came as he says from 'high in the air,' that conversation was carried on for ten times longer than the fifteen seconds during which it was alleged that full weight was said to be not recorded. How does he explain this? Does he suggest that Valiantine jumped in the air and opened the conversation for fifteen seconds, and then went back to the chair and continued it for two or three minutes? Wherein is the sense? According to Mr. Bird's report there was no point in Valiantine leaving the chair.

"Mr. Bird owns in his report that eight distinct spirit voices spoke to the assembly. In the séance room there were, I believe, between fifteen and seventeen sitters. Does Mr. Bird suggest that Valiantine, who is a heavy man and was wearing boots, was able to get up in the dark and dance like a Pavlova amongst the sitters without either being heard or discovered missing from the chair? If that is so, then Valiantine sat with fools. The chair theory does not account for the phenomena which Mr. Bird admits did occur.

"Mr. Bird in his July (1923) report in the *Scientific American* stated that if the weight resting on the chair was less than 12-pounds it would record the medium as being out of the chair. A month later—in August after the ectoplasmic theory had been advanced, he hedged by saying that a weight of nine pounds was sufficient to keep the lamp burning. Why did he not say so in his first report, instead of keeping what he regarded as important evidence until a month later?

"In my criticism I said that it is utterly impossible for anyone to sit perfectly still for half an hour without moving; and further, that when one is listening intently to catch a sound or to follow a voice, one leans forward involuntarily, and with one's hands on one's knees, almost the entire weight of the body is easily sustained, independent of the chair upon which one maybe sitting all this Mr. Bird ignores. To say the truth: we have far less proof that the lamp, which was in another room, was actually out, than we have that Valiantine was out of the chair. But whether he was in or out neither proves nor disproves anything, and the phenomena which were manifested still remain inexplicable to the slow mind of Mr. Malcolm Bird.

"Mr. Bird, referring to the theory of ectoplasm, says that I must have a precedent if I advance a theory. I would reply that there is never a precedent for a discovery; the faithful investigator is only concerned with the fact of the discovery. I censured the Scientific American Committee in its findings against Valiantine when it publicly rejected the genuineness of his mediumship. I gave it as my opinion that the decision was ridiculous. It cast an unjust stigma upon him not only in America, out in this country, where in several of our newspapers it was stated that the *Scientific American* had proved Valiantine to be a fraud. The gravity of the finding, based only upon a flimsy and an insignificant point, might have been sufficient utterly to discredit Valiantine, had he not succeeded in the spring of this year in establishing his powers beyond question before many of the most brilliant men and women in this country.

"What would have happened had I been careless enough to accept the loose finding of the Scientific American Committee? I should never have invited him to England, with the result that psychical research would have been deprived of a tremendous advance in knowledge, and a great mass of evidence of survival would never have been recorded. Valiantine had never set foot in England before February 1 of this year (1924), and he was taken by me from Waterloo to my country residence, Dorincourt, where I conducted experiments almost daily for five weeks. Over fifty people sat with him on various occasions: editors, novelists, dramatists, sculptors, artists, doctors, and scientists. Most of them were entirely unknown to Valiantine, and had not been introduced to him until after the séances had taken place in a darkened room. And yet at these sittings over one hundred different spirit voices manifested themselves, and carried on long pertinent conversations. Russian, German, Spanish, and even idiomatic Welsh were spoken in the independent voices of the spirits. Can Mr. Malcolm Bird offer any human explanation of these extraordinary phenomena? Can he offer any scientific explanation as to how it was possible for Mr. Caradoc Evans, the Welsh novelist, to converse with his father in Cardiganshire Welsh? Can he explain how it was possible for Mr. Harold Wimbury, the magazine editor, to converse on intimate subjects for over a quarter of an hour with the spirit of a journalist friend who had died about twenty years before?

"I maintain that the many evidences of survival and of supernormal phenomena under the mediumship of George Valiantine are more remarkable and of infinitely greater value than any yet recorded in the history of psychical research. Still the awful fact remains that this man was turned down by Mr. Bird's Committee, and the acceptance of his powers of mediumship might have been smashed absolutely by its unjust finding.

"In view of this Committee's dismissal of Valiantine and of the cold and contemptuous remarks of Mr. Bird in his report of July, 1923, it is amusing to observe Mr. Bird's complete change of attitude in his references, in last week's *Light*, to Valiantine. Late in the day as it is, I can now congratulate him on the paragraph in which he states that 'from numerous sources he has heard reports of Valiantine's showing in this field, indicating that there have been delivered through him independent messages in at least a dozen languages, each spoken by a native, and pertinent of the spirit alleged to be speaking.'

"What manner of investigator is Mr. J. Malcolm Bird, the managing editor of the very important *Scientific American*? What manner of reporter is this scientist? What manner of journalist is this journalist scientist? He concludes his letter to *Light* as follows:

"If a new edition of Mr. Bradley's volume should be called for I would suggest an additional chapter. This chapter would revolve about the séance where, in Mr. Bradley's presence, light was quite accidentally and in all good faith turned on a bit prematurely by one of the very props of spiritualism, who could not possibly be accused of bad faith in this slip. The trumpet was observed at somewhat less than its usual distance from the medium, and the medium's hand and arm were observed withdrawing from it. Examination of the trumpet developed the facts that it was quite warm at the point where a human hand would naturally and conveniently grasp it, and that the mouthpiece was damp.

"Will Mr. Bradley tell us about this sitting, or will he leave it to me to find a roundabout path into print for it via America? He need have no feelings of delicacy about telling us, because the name of the Unintentional engineer of this little expose already appears in full in Mr. Bradley's book in connection with other sittings of happier outcome—though Mr. Bradley had promised to use only its owner's initials.'

"I know of no such sitting. I made no promise to print only the initials of any person who sat with Valentine. Mr. Bird has introduced foreign matter into a sitting which took place at my house, and which is faithfully recorded in *Towards the Stars*. This was the séance during which the light was turned on by one of my servants in the garage outside, and came through the window above the top of the curtains. Valiantine was noted to be in great distress, breathing heavily and moaning, and the trumpet, which was seen in mid-air suspended supernormally in space, and some distance away from him, fell on the floor, where it remained until after Valentine had been taken to bed. Mr. Joseph De Wyckoff, who was present, realized with genuine alarm and grave concern that the turning on of material light was having the effect of hurling back the ectoplasm into Valentine's body, and was causing him great pain. He went to his assistance, and declared that the man was enveloped in a sort of whitish film. He called on a well-known London journalist, who was also present, to bear witness to his words. The journalist went over, and later described this film as being a 'slimy, frothy bladder, into which you could dig a finger, but through which you could not pierce.' It was half an hour before Valiantine was recovered sufficiently to be put in bed. Mr. De Wyckoff remained in the bedroom for about half an hour. I returned downstairs and gathered up the trumpets. In addition to Mr. De Wyckoff there were eight other persons present who can and will vouch for the accuracy of my statement.

"It will be noted that the light was not turned on by one of the 'props of spiritualism'; that the trumpet was not within an arm's length of the medium, and that the trumpet was not examined and found warm and moist.

"If Mr. Bird is willfully misleading the public, he is no scientist; if he has believed some garbled account, he is no investigator; if he has confused two sets of evidence, he is no journalist. His story is false. I fancy he built it up on a mixture of the Dorincourt séance, and a séance which took place in a New York hotel, and at which I was not present. Is that the roundabout, crooked way in which this scientist investigator-journalist gathers his evidence? Is spirit communication to be damned by such methods? I am now in possession of details of the New York séance, and of the part Mr. De Wyckoff and Valiantine and others took in it, and as this information is of the utmost importance, I propose to reveal the entire story in a coming issue of *Light*."

Mr. Bird, however, and his journalistic eccentricities seemed to me of small moment in comparison with the simple, the vital question as to the falsity or truth of Valiantine, and, after investigation, I published in *Light* on October 18, 1924, another letter in which I exposed the New York séance, on the results of which the third accusation of fraud has been made. Here is my letter:

"I had thought, maybe optimistically, that my incontestable evidence in *Towards the Stars*—much of it obtained in the presence of some of the most famous people in England—cleared the mind of any possible doubt as to the genuine mediumistic powers of George Valiantine. But I was mistaken. For a little over a month after my last sitting with Valentine—a sitting recorded in my book—a charge of trickery has been made against him in America. The charge has not been printed in America and has only been hinted at over here; it has been circulated by word of mouth in that country, and is doing much damage to the cause of Psychic Research.

"This is the third time Valentine has been accused of fraud. The first occasion was when he sat for the Scientific American Committee, whose unjust finding, the editor, Mr. J. Malcolm Bird, was compelled to contradict in his recent letter to *Light*, when he stated that he had received reports of evidential messages coming through Valiantine's mediumship in a dozen different languages.

"The second charge was made in America by Mr. Joseph De Wyckoff in November, 1923. Particulars of this appear in 'Chapter XI of *Towards the Stars*. I do not fancy Mr. De Wyckoff approves of this chapter, because it shows that he cannot be credited with the powers of a Sherlock Holmes. Anyway, Mr. De Wyckoff admitted his mistake to me at Claridge's Hotel, London, on December 5, 1923, and immediately cabled to Valiantine to that effect. This cable he confirmed by letter. Moreover, he made a personal apology again in my presence—to Valiantine on the latter's arrival in London in February, 1924.

"The third accusation is an alleged exposure of a sitting in New York reported to Mr. Bird by 'one of the props of spiritualism.' This is the séance at which the 'prop' is said to have seized Valiantine's trumpet and found it warm and moist. Mr. Bird says: 'Will Mr. Bradley tell us about this sitting, or will he leave it to me to find a roundabout path into print for it via America?'

" pass over the mentality of the scientific investigator who seeks roundabout paths. And, properly, I should ignore the scientific investigator who comes to a conclusion on an *ex parte* statement.'

"However, I am in a position to tell Mr. Bird the truth about this New York sitting, which he has mixed into such a sorry mess. And I will make the English public a present of the fact that Mr. Bird's reporter-prop is again Mr. Joseph De Wyckoff. As I have stated, the séance occurred about a month after Valiantine had left England, and before I tell the ugly, callous story of it, I will try and convey Mr. De Wyckoff's mentality immediately before it.

"Mr. De Wyckoff is a very shrewd and able financier. He has a dominating personality and has a great regard for material power.

In common with most financial magnates of his calibre, he is accustomed to his own way and is intolerant of suggestion, criticism and opposition.

"At the time, February, 1924, I was conducting a series of experiments with Valiantine at my house, Dorincourt, in Kingston Vale. There were several differences of opinion between Mr. De Wyckoff and myself. There was also dissension between Mr. De Wyckoff and his wife at the séances held on February 3 and 10, with the result that I refused to continue any further sittings with them unless they agreed to sit separately.

"On the Sunday prior to Mr. De Wyckoff's departure to America, I introduced to him the subject of a material project to Guiana in which he was interested, and in which the assistance of Valiantine was considered to be essential.

"Valiantine, a very simple man, and inexperienced in commercial undertakings, had consulted me in the matter. As his services in this project were regarded as indispensable, I inquired from Mr. De Wyckoff what recompense he was prepared to make to Valiantine for his time and his efforts. Mr. De Wyckoff disclosed to me his plans, which I regarded, entirely from Valiantine's point of view, as absolutely inadequate. The next day I informed Valiantine of these proposals, and strongly advised him not to agree to the undertaking unless Mr. De Wyckoff was prepared to sign an agreement, the rough draft of which I made out for Valiantine giving him equitable terms.

"Before leaving England Mr. De Wyckoff suggested that he should arrange for the publication of *Towards the Stars* in America. Although such matters are usually arranged through a literary agent, I agreed with the proposal, feeling that I would thus save time in negotiations.

"He cabled me from New York on April 8, saying that the Century Company was willing to undertake publication. The cable was definite, and I confirmed the matter with Mr. W. Ives Washburn, the London manager of the company, who by a later mail received excellent reports of my manuscript from the New York office.

"At this time Mr. De Wyckoff was arranging for the journey to Guiana with Valiantine, but acting on my advice, Valiantine then presented the draft of the agreement, which he asked Mr. De Wyckoff to sign before, setting out on the journey. The agreement was fair, just, and equitable, but Mr. De Wyckoff did not receive the proposal very graciously; he eventually signed it, and the signed rough draft is now in my possession.

"This represents the relations of the parties chiefly concerned, and the psychology of Mr. De Wyckoff and of Valiantine at the date upon which a séance was held at the St. Regis Hotel in New York on April 10 of this year.

"Mr. De Wyckoff had told Valiantine that he would like to hold a séance during that evening. So far he had one guest to sit with him and Valiantine. This guest was a Mr. Allan Miller, whom he induced to go and find two other men. Mr. Miller went into an adjacent restaurant and chanced upon two acquaintances whom he persuaded to attend the séance.

"Phenomena occurred, and spirit voices manifested. So much so indeed that one of the restaurant guests, after he had got into communication with a spirit purporting to be that of his brother, became so agitated and nervous that he had to ask permission to leave the room. Other manifestations occurred; and, as usual at the séances held through the mediumship of Valiantine, at the end Dr. Barnett, his spirit guide, closed the sitting with a short address.

"At the finish of Dr. Barnett's address the trumpet had fallen sideways between Valiantine's legs, with the small end against the edge of his chair. In a perfectly natural way Valiantine set the trumpet upright, as I, and many other sitters, have done dozens of times before at my own private sittings. As Valiantine was setting the trumpet upright, Mr. De Wyckoff struck a match, and scolded Valiantine for this action. Valiantine, upset and aggrieved, left the hotel.

"It is upon this incident that Mr. De Wyckoff bases his second accusation of fraud against Valiantine.

"Valiantine wrote to me the next morning, giving full particulars in a plain and straightforward manner. Mr. Allan Miller gave practically the same account to a Mrs. Rodems, whom I met later in London.

"By a strange coincidence, Captain Ben Hicks met one of the restaurant sitters, and he independently confirmed the version of the sitting given by Mr. Miller and Valiantine.

"Mr. De Wyckoff himself related the incident, exactly as I have described it, to my wife, when she was passing through New York from Los Angeles towards the end of April. Mrs. Bradley dismissed the story as trivial, and said that Mr. De Wyckoff appeared to be strangely obsessed in his endeavour to magnify its importance.

"Mr. De Wyckoff's attitude towards this matter requires careful analysis since he is responsible for the widely circulated and damaging rumours that he had succeeded in discovering Valiantine to be a fraud.

"Not the least curious and revealing point about his attitude would appear to be that communicated to me by Mrs. Rodems—who has no interest in psychic matters. She declared to me that Mr. Miller told her that, before the sitting, Mr. De Wyckoff asked him to attend an experiment, as he was 'going to try and catch a fellow out.'

"If that represents Mr. De Wyckoff's attitude towards Valiantine—with whom he had but recently purposed to enter into a commercial agreement—the curious procedure of picking up unknown guests in a hotel restaurant is explicable.

"It is significant that Mr. De Wyckoff, who left England on ostensibly friendly terms with me, did not write to me informing me of his 'alleged' discovery of fraud in Valiantine. Why did he not do so?

"I suggest that his attitude towards me and towards Valiantine definitely changed from the moment that Valiantine presented to him the draft of the equitable commercial contract which I had prepared for Valiantine in London.

Let us observe the sequel.

"On May 7 I received the following letter from Mr. W. Ives Washburn:

" . . I am compelled to be the bearer of unpleasant news in regard to your book, as I have just received the following cable from New York which reads as follows: "Inform Bradley cannot publish book; explanatory letter follows.—Century."

"It is too bad that this should have happened after the encouraging reports that you have had heretofore, but, of course, until the letter referred to arrives, I am not in a position to give you a satisfactory explanation of our action."

"In a letter from the Century people which reached me on May 21, the reason given was that it had been pretty clearly established that Valiantine is responsible for the spirit conversations which took place at his sessions, and De Wyckoff is of this opinion at the present time."

"I wish to make it perfectly clear that I do not blame the Century Company in any way for its decision. I consider that in view of the grave allegation made by Mr. De Wyckoff, it was absolutely justified in its action ...

"This, however, I am entitled to demand. Is there any conceivable justification for Mr. De Wyckoff's damaging allegation? He has branded Valiantine as a fraud and has stopped the publication of my book in America, and his action is calculated to cast a slur upon the great mass of evidence of survival collected through Valiantine's mediumship—evidence recorded by me in a work which entailed over a year's intensive and exhaustive study.

"Will Mr. De Wyckoff assert in public that Valiantine is a fraud and is responsible for producing and imitating the hundreds of various spirit voices that have manifested themselves during the recorded séances?

"Will he be willing to assert that Valiantine, simple and poorly educated man as he is, speaks cultured and fluent French, German, Spanish, Russian, and Italian, and Cardiganshire Welsh? And also that he has the ability to speak with the varied inflections of a man, woman, and child?

"Does Mr. De Wyckoff seriously presume to damn all this marvelous evidence because of one momentary, natural and logical action of Valiantine's—the lifting of a fallen trumpet from beside his chair?

"If Mr. De Wyckoff is an intelligent student of psychical research he must concede that the evidence obtained through Valiantine would be equally wonderful if no trumpet existed, and if Valiantine spoke with his own normal voice, as the usual clairvoyant mediums do.

"There is one other point to which I must refer, as it has a scientific importance. Mr. Bird, in his letter in, Light, says:

"Examination of the trumpet developed the facts that it was quite warm at the point where a human hand' would naturally and conveniently grasp it, and that the mouthpiece was damp."

"This is exactly what would happen with independent voice phenomena, and by this statement both Mr. DeWyckoff and Mr. Bird expose themselves as inexperienced investigators.

"During the last two months I and my wife have developed powerful forms of mediumship, and not only physical phenomena of an unusual and dramatic character have been produced in the presence of several witnesses, but with the use of a trumpet made so luminous that everyone in the room could see it, we have had on several occasions the independent voices of spirits, who gave their names and conversed with the sitters. During September I requested a well-known editor and a distinguished scientist to examine my trumpet before the sitting, and it was of course perfectly dry. When the sitting closed, I again asked them to examine it, and they found that the inside was moist, for the simple reason that it is necessary for a spirit to materialize the vocal organs and breath in order to produce its voice.

"I regard it as imperative to make public the details of the New York séance, and to make clear the flimsy basis upon which Mr. De Wyckoff's charge of fraud against Valiantine has been founded.

"If Mr. De Wyckoff has anything further to say let him say it in public. He is a frequent visitor to this country, and I am lecturing at the Steinway Hall on October 30 and to members of the Irish Literary Society on November 15. He can meet me. I am willing to meet him on any platform, in any court, or in the Press. If his opinions are reformed, and he does not desire to accept my challenge, it would be gracious of him, if he, is a sincere student of psychics, to tender George Valiantine his apology for the damage he may have done him."

But unfortunately for Mr. Bird and Mr. DeWyckof— strange associates!— the matter did not end here.

A day or two after this letter had appeared I received a call from Captain Ben Hicks, who had just returned from the Continent and had read my letter in *Light*.

He gave me further particulars in support of my views, and, in addition, wrote to *Light* as follows:

THE CARLTON HOTEL,
PALL MALL, S.W.

"I have read, with considerable interest, Mr. Dennis Bradley's letter on the séance held at the St. Regis hotel, in New York, on April 10 of this year.

"Mr. Bradley refers to the fact of my having met two of the sitters who were dining in the restaurant on that evening, and who were invited by Mr. Allan Miller to attend this séance.

These two gentlemen, whose names are Mr. Henry Anchester and Mr. Seamans, are very intimate friends of mine, and as I received from them a first-hand personal account of what transpired may I be permitted to give even more complete details than those given by Mr. Bradley?

"They told me that on the evening of April 10 they were dining in a small restaurant opposite the St. Regis Hotel, having practically finished their dinner. Mr. Joseph De Wyckoff and Mr. Allan Miller were also dining at the restaurant. Mr. Miller, leaving Mr. De Wyckoff, addressed my friends, saying: 'I have a very funny proposition to make. My friend, Mr. De Wyckoff, is going to hold a spiritualistic séance in my rooms at the St. Regis Hotel; would you care to attend?' They answered: 'We have never been to one of these things before, but we should certainly like to go.' Mr. Miller told them that he had never been to a séance either, and added that he felt a trifle nervous of these things.

"The gentlemen were then introduced to Mr. De Wyckoff, and they all adjourned to Mr. Miller's apartments in the St. Regis Hotel. Manifestations took place, and were so astounding and so convincing that one of the gentlemen, Mr. Anchester, was compelled to leave the séance before it was ended, and, as a matter of fact, fainted in the hallway of the hotel. He was joined a little later on by Mr. Seamans, who also left before the séance was over, because he felt somewhat scared. Both these gentlemen told me that this séance was the most marvelous thing they had ever witnessed.

"Mr. Bradley now informs me that Mr. De Wyckoff alleges that he has discovered George Valiantine to be a fraud. This allegation is made upon no positive foundation, but only upon a ridiculous incident which occurred after my friends had left the room. I understand that Mr. De Wyckoff suddenly struck a match whilst Valiantine was setting upright the trumpet that had fallen by the side of his chair. This is no proof whatever of fraud, but Mr. De Wyckoff's action in striking a match whilst Valiantine might have been in a trance condition was a highly dangerous one, and as Mr. De Wyckoff well knows, might prove dangerous to the health, or possibly the life, of the medium. It is astounding to me that Mr. De Wyckoff should have, deliberately assumed this responsibility.

"Now, knowing Mr. De Wyckoff as well as I do, and having a great regard for his intelligence and knowledge of the world, I fail to reconcile his statements. He has, to my knowledge, been in close contact with George Valiantine for four years, and he has personally described to me on many occasions the marvelous, indisputable evidential facts he has received through Valiantine's mediumship. It is therefore inexplicable to me that he should now attack him, as surely during this long period he should have had plenty of opportunities to form a definite judgment as to whether Valiantine was genuine or not.

"If Valiantine could successfully trick Mr. De Wyckoff for four long years he must be possessed of the most remarkable mentality ever known.

"There is one point which I deeply regret to have to make. It appears to me that there is some ulterior ... motive which has caused Mr. De Wyckoff to attack George Valiantine's integrity and honesty, and if this is the case, so far as Mr. De Wyckoff's study of this subject is concerned, one can only regard it as psychical suicide.

"If I maybe permitted to say so, I feel that I may claim to have a very considerable knowledge of psychical research in its various forms. I have had the privilege of sitting at séances with George Valiantine on occasions when both Mr. De Wyckoff and Mr. Bradley were present, and during my sittings I received extraordinary personal evidence. I am compelled, therefore, to disregard Mr. De Wyckoff's accusation entirely, and to subscribe my judgment that Valiantine is not only genuine, but that he is a medium whose powers are remarkably highly developed."

This letter was set up in type, and a proof of it was sent for corrections, if any, to Captain Hicks at the Carlton Hotel, London, on October 18.

Strangely enough, just at this time Mr. De Wyckoff arrived in this country from America, and by chance met Captain Hicks. They two had a very long discussion. Captain Hicks showed him the proof of the article; Mr. De Wyckoff tried to persuade Captain Hicks to withhold the letter, saying that he would make a public explanation.

This was never done, although the columns of *Light* were open to him to make an adequate explanation or to offer a public apology.

I publish the whole particulars of this matter because it is of paramount importance to prove that this is not the first time that loose allegations have been made, great and powerful mediums been discredited and crushed, and the whole science of psychical research thwarted.

This chapter ends upon a note of comedy for, strange to relate, within a short time of this controversy Mr. Malcolm Bird switched completely over in his views, and has since been lecturing in America on the truth of psychic phenomena. He is now secretary of the New York Society for Psychical Research. He has affirmed his belief in the supernormal, and I offer him my congratulations upon his conversion.

8

WASTE OF TIME

A few characteristic thoughts on fools and charlatans—The medium who bandaged her eyes and delivered "unutterable, meaningless drivel"—The investigator is indignant with vulgar trickery designed to impress the weakly credulous.

~

October, 1924

IT would be foolish to deny that fraud exists in every calling in life. There are many fraudulent mediums, but the majority of these adopt the easy form of what is termed the "clairvoyant mediumship."

Human nature is still gullible—in spite of the self-valuations of certain of the opponents of spiritualism and only the fool makes his own will, or keeps his treasury notes beneath his pillow because an occasional solicitor is struck off the rolls, or an odd bank manager absconds. So only the fool condemns a great study on isolated instances of charlatanism and deceit on the part of a few rogues who profess to be adept in it.

In the course of my investigations I have come across more than one medium who has appealed to the worst side of my suspicious nature, and it maybe of interest to the general reader to give a typical example of a sitting which, to say the least of it, aroused my suspicions and evoked my contempt.

In the middle of October, 1924, I received a letter from one of the most arduous experimenters of psychical research, in which he said that he had heard of a clairvoyant medium residing in London, but had had no opportunity of testing her powers. He asked me if I would care to call on her and conduct an experiment, as he himself was too busy at the moment.

The fame of this medium seemed to have spread in some way until it had reached circles genuinely interested in the exploration of this new world, and I therefore thought it advisable to visit her, and to glean what further knowledge she could enable me to obtain.

So an appointment was made, and accompanied by another man I visited her. I had a preliminary chat with her and found her to be one of the ordinary professional clairvoyant mediums—the lowest form of whom occasionally clash with the police over the official view of what constitutes fortune-telling, and who, as a rule, charge a nominal fee of a guinea for each sitting.

Before commencing operations, this medium proceeded to bandage her eyes, telling me as she did so that she was about to go into a trance condition, in which she would be controlled by a certain foreign character.

A minute or so passed, and then she spoke in certainly broken English, but the voice and accent were entirely her own.

She did not appear to me to be in any trance whatever. For twenty minutes I listened to the most unutterable, meaningless drivel, the medium suggesting name after name, which conveyed nothing whatever to me, and I observed that the names were all of the most usual type, such as John, Peter, Paul, Bill, Ted, Arthur, and so forth. Then, failing to strike a masculine chord, she essayed the feminine, and plied me with the ordinary female names, none of which I recognized.

After enduring half an hour or so of this procedure, a name—quite a usual name—was mentioned which might conceivably have applied to the man who was with me, but no further evidence of identity was given, and it would have been stupid credulity on his part for him to have accepted the name as evidential, as, when asked as to the cause of death, most of the diseases from which humans die were mentioned.

Bored, and more than a little disgusted, I suggested that the sitting should be closed. In her own voice, but speaking as the control, the medium agreed. She asked that we should wait until the trance was at an end. I ventured to hope that it would end very speedily, which, incidentally, it did.

The only thing in favour of this medium which I can conscientiously admit is that she refused to accept the fee for the appalling performance.

I wish to make it clear that I was in no way antagonistic to this medium. I went to her with the genuine desire to benefit by whatever powers she possessed, but what I am compelled to call the obvious "faking"—to be crudely expressive—got on my nerves after a time.

I can only say that if this woman has any mediumistic powers they were in abeyance at the time of my visit, and, in their place, I was the reluctant witness of what I personally am convinced was vulgar trickery designed to impress the weakly credulous. At the close of the sitting she seemed to be unduly nervous lest she had been discovered.

One maybe pardoned a certain indignation with such cases for it is so-called "mediums" of this type and class who disgrace and bring ridicule upon this great science, and inexperienced people maybe induced to visit them and discard the entirety of truth because of one insignificant lie.

But, as I have said, it would be as absurd to permit such an experience to affect one's views on the study itself, as it would be to allow a defaulting bank cashier in a small provincial town to render one nervous as to the credit of the Bank of England.

9

THE SEARCH FOR REASONS

The spirit of Warren Clarke explains why the author was advised to discontinue the Dorincourt sittings, and counsels him about a proposal made by the Research Officer of the Society for Psychical Research—He is also warned of certain financial irregularities—A question about the powers of mediumship and the answer—A forecast of the great psychical upheaval—"Telepathy: the banal refuge for uneasy souls."

I

Tuesday, November 18, 1924

IN view of the advice I had received I determined to give up the direct voice sittings for a time, but I was naturally curious as to the reasons which had brought about that advice.

It is not that I believed or believe that séances have an injurious effect on one's physical health. A certain amount of power would appear to be taken from one, which one automatically regains after the necessary rest, but, as I have explained, I was at this time overworked in many other directions entirely unconnected with my psychic studies, and I was no doubt feeling the strain of a surfeit of activities.

With a view to finding out in detail, if possible, the reasons for the stopping of my personal direct-voice séances, I arranged a sitting for my wife and myself with Mrs. Leonard at her cottage in Hertfordshire as the only channel through which I was likely to obtain a full explanation.

With the exception of a few omissions of conversations relating to purely personal matters, the following is a verbatim record of what took place.

II

FEDA (after the usual greeting): We wanted you to come; both Warren and Annie are here.

WARREN: There are many things we wish to talk about with you. To start with, don't worry about the stopping of the sittings at Dorincourt. You will not lose the power; it is not evaporating—you will find that it will be very much stronger later on. The character will be slightly altered, but you will gain by the rest which you are taking. We were compelled to stop the sittings for several reasons. The stoppage was made not entirely on account of your health. There was another element coming in, and we could see the plans at the back of certain people's minds.

You were on the point of agreeing to give a series of sittings to the Society for Psychical Research.[36]

You would have been disconcerted and worried had you agreed to this. It is possible that a lot of complications would have been set up, and there were certain plans to be tried on you. We feel that they would have been inclined to impose ridiculous conditions, which would have possibly made it necessary for the guides to withhold phenomena. Others there might have been inclined to endeavour to kill the phenomena. You must leave these experiments, under such conditions, until the power has become sufficiently strong to resist all complications and difficulties. Later on, you will be able to suit other people's conditions.

---

[36] On Saturday morning, October 18, I had received a five-page letter from Mr. E. J. Dingwall, Research Officer of the Society for Psychical Research, urging my wife and me to give a series of experimental sittings in their séance room. I had practically decided to agree to this. On the same Saturday night at a sitting held at Dorincourt both Annie and Warren told me that it was essential that we should have no more sittings from that date and until they gave us permission to resume.

THE SEARCH FOR REASONS

HDB: But had we agreed to sit with the S.P.R., I should have imposed the conditions.

WARREN: They would not have taken them.

HDB: You think, then, that we should have achieved poor results?

WARREN: I do, and these results would have reacted on the controversy with De Wyckoff and Valiantine. You have had quite enough worry and work already in disproving those implications.[37] In addition to this there were several other reasons which made it necessary for you to suspend the sittings. The conditions at the S.P.R. and the general atmosphere of everything would have made it bad, even for mediums whose power was fully developed. All reasons combined made it essential for us to stop for a while.

MRS. BRADLEY: You said the sittings were having an injurious effect on Herbert's health.

WARREN: Yes! Because, as a matter of fact, he was suffering from overwork, and he was trying to do too much. He could not have gone on under those conditions. You see, when Herbert is engaged in study he gets into a certain state of congestion and nerves. When sitting with the S.P.R. it is very likely that he might have lost his temper, and there would have been a good shindy all round, and with these people it can do a great deal of harm—especially after the Joe[38] episode. Later on it may become easier for Herbert when he is in a fit condition to tackle people. He has too much to do to attempt this just yet.

MRS. BRADLEY: Have you been seeing Dennis[39] lately

WARREN: Oh, yes—I am keeping my eyes on him; attending to him and pummelling it out of him. Of course he wants to stuff in mentally everything he can. He has ambition.

(Here followed a spontaneous and volunteered reference to a certain man—giving his name—who handled much of my finance. It was a derogatory reference, and coming from Warren was a complete surprise. It was a warning of the utmost importance. In February of 1925, nearly three months later, I discovered that this man had been robbing me for years of thousands of pounds.)

WARREN (continuing): In the meantime, Herbert, take things easily for a while, and gain a little more equilibrium.

---

[37] This refers to the allegations made by Mr. De Wyckoff against Valiantine in America. See Chapter 7.

[38] Mr. Joseph De Wyckoff. See Chapter 7.

[39] Dennis Anthony Bradley.

Going back to your condition, just lately you were getting into the same condition in which you were in at the time you were writing your last book—all nerves.

HDB: I should like to ask you, Warren, a question about the powers of mediumship. We are not sure whether the power by which we get the voices comes from Mabel or comes from me.

WARREN: You, Herbert, are the supplier of the power and Mabel is the conductor. Herbert could change over to conductor, but we prefer him as the supplier. The power is their drawn through Mabel, and the method we use is to get the power as far away as possible. We try so as not to get the voices near her.

HDB: Do you think that I could get the voices alone, Warren?

WARREN: Yes! You could do so, but it is much better as a combination between you and Mabel.

MRS. BRADLEY: Could I get the voices alone, Warren?

WARREN: Yes, you could, because you store up the power, and under ordinary conditions you could draw upon this power when the reservoir is close to you. Herbert is the reservoir and you, Mabel, charge your aura with power from him.

HDB: After the time you told me that I was not to sit again for a while, one further experiment was conducted by Mabel, under her mediumship, without my being present in the circle, or in the room. On this occasion I was standing outside the closed door, and I listened to the conversation being carried on with the various spirit voices. How was the power working on that occasion?

WARREN: It was working intermittently. The power was not flowing in a regular way. You, Mabel, felt a constant pull upon you like a stretching.[40] You had got some power, but not nearly so strong as under ordinary conditions. There is another point I want to deal with in regard to your sittings. I must tell you that the luminous paint which you use neutralizes the power considerably.

HDB: Do you suggest that we should not use it?

WARREN: It makes it more difficult for us. Don't use so much of it. It would be better to try it with a certain number of little spots on the end of the trumpet only.

HDB: You know, Warren, that the effect of this luminous paint was very impressive on all those who sat with us.

---

[40] My wife said afterwards that she felt as if something was being pulled from her.

THE SEARCH FOR REASONS

WARREN: Yes, but you were overdoing it with the paint. I will explain just for ourselves. Whenever we use power, if any light is close to the direction in which we are using it, the power becomes weakened; it breaks it up. When only part of the trumpet is painted it give us a chance of getting away from it as far as possible. During your sittings we were using the trumpet front inside the end.

MRS. BRADLEY: When we resume these sittings, how many sitters would you advise us to limit the number to?

WARREN: Not more than two or three.

HDB: Shall we include Hannen Swaffer?

WARREN: Yes, I think he will be all right for one, but you should never include in the circle more than one person who has never sat before.

HDB: You know, Warren, that Dennis is going to make his first experiment to see if he can obtain the voices at Cambridge next Saturday, in company with two or three other men.[41] Do you think you can help him?

WARREN: I cannot say at present how much power he has got, but both I and Annie will do our best to help him. Mediumship is an undeveloped force. It is right to tell people—everybody—to make experiments and endeavour to develop. The powers of mediumship are not limited to just a few extraordinary people. It is a power that is in everybody, and it can be shaken loose in anybody; it is a power which can be cultivated.

HDB: Have you seen Northcliffe lately?

WARREN: I told Northcliffe that you were not sitting at present. He has been to Dorincourt once or twice, but Northcliffe has not much patience; he is anxious for you to start again.

HDB: When do you think it would be advisable for us to resume?

WARREN: I should think you might start again early in the New Year.

HDB: Do you think we might resume before January 20. At any rate, as far as I am concerned, I should like to start well before then, because Hannen Swaffer is lecturing at the Queen's Hall on that date.

WARREN: I shall be able to impress Mabel when I feel it will be all right. She is a conductor to sensitive vibration, but, unless anything unforeseen happens, I think the New Year would be quite the right time.

ANNIE (joining in): I am glad to see you are so much better, Herbert. Neither you nor Mabel could have stood the strain as you were going on. I do want you to make it a rule until further notice to be very careful whom you have as sitters with you.

---

[41] The experiment was made at Cambridge and was not successful.

HDB: How often would you advise us to sit?

WARREN: Only once a week for a start. You see these sittings are still in the experimental stage and with sympathetic sitters it is quite all right, but any new sitter is apt to disturb the conditions. Especially when voices are trying to say something evidential.

HDB: With regard to the Society for Psychical Research, if Valiantine agrees to sit for them, would it be all right for Mabel and me to accompany him?

WARREN: Yes, but you are not to sit alone with Mabel for them. Don't be led into promising this. You must build up the power with Valiantine. First of all try your experiments with the three of you.

HDB: They tell me with regard to the voice mediumship, Warren, that as a rule particular guides are appointed for this form.

WARREN: Annie and I are both your guides, but John King is the one particular guide who is helping in the voice manifestations.

FEDA (interposing): I know John King; he often helps with the voices. He was a pirate, but he is most respectable now. He has been on the other side for 200 years. He is a great soul. He has an enormous voice. It is a mixture of Dr. Barnett and Kokum. There is a kind of freemasonry amongst the guides. John King was with a man called Husk. You can read about him. He used to do all the materializations. When he comes through to you, you must not be surprised at the loudness of his voice.

MRS. BRADLEY: Have you seen Bob? And do you know whether he has seen Winifred at Brighton?

WARREN: Bob has been down with them and has had some interesting experiments. He was very delighted with that lady. He likes her; she is a good soul. Bob says: "Tell them she is on the right lines. Give Alice my love-best love—and say that I tried to send a message to her through that lady."[42]

There has been rather a gathering of the guides round them to see if they can develop them later on. Bob says that the psychic power with women is more mental —auric.

Bob was worried because Alice felt cold. He says Alice has got more power than Winifred. Will you tell her? She feels Bob when he is near her—in a curious way, as if he enveloped her. At these times she feels as if her face were not quite her own.

She feels as if part of it had drifted away. That is when Bob is in her aura. Twenty years ago great power could have been developed in her.

---

[42] These references regarding the experiments, etc., were found to be correct.

HDB: Have you been with Pat[43] lately?

WARREN: Yes! And so has Annie.

HDB: Of course, Pat never met Annie in life here.

ANNIE: But he knows me more now than if he had met me. Pat will be able to draw inspiration. A little later he will have a guide who will draw through him.

MRS. BRADLEY: Will he sing?

ANNIE: Yes, he understands rhythm. He will be good at music and painting, although drawing is not his natural gift.

HDB: What about Dennis?

ANNIE: Warren and I are often with him and he is sometimes impressed by us, but we cannot impress him so easily as we can impress Pat. You see, this knowledge came to him later on when other ideas had become fixed in Dennis's mind first. Dennis now finds it rather trying to fit this idea on to his other impressions.

With regard to his psychic experiments, I shall stop Dennis unless he feels that they are for his good. You must tell Dennis to reason for himself, to prove that the right inspiration shall be given to him. At present he is not sure, and it is not right for him to sit unless he feels that it is quite right.

He must make up his mind firmly first and then go ahead. He has a fine temperament, but sometimes that temperament makes things difficult for himself. He is clever, but it would not be good for his mind to be torn in two just now. He is very impressionable, but sometimes he puts up a big resistance against impressions. He must try to find himself.

Herbert is, of course, quite sure of himself, and the sittings with Valiantine helped him enormously. It was a splendid combination.

HDB: That is why I regard mediumship as the greatest thing the world has ever known.

WARREN: Yes, but there is often a very great difficulty in supplying the necessary power.

HDB: I think that despite the difficulties the work that Mabel and I did alone in our recent sittings at Dorincourt did achieve extraordinarily good results. What we found was that everyone who came there was not only amazed, but was absolutely convinced of survival. They seemed to marvel at it all the more because there was no professional medium present.

ANNIE: Yes! You managed to get some splendid results.

---

[43] My younger son.

HDB: At any rate it made them all talk in the West End—not that the West End counts for very much in the scheme.

WARREN: Yes, and it made "Old A" sit up and rub his eyes. We have already impressed a great number of people, and even if you finished now you would have done a great work.

HDB: Were you at the Irish Literary Society on Saturday last, Warren?[44]

WARREN: Yes, and I thought they were astoundingly ignorant, but there was one man there who was just pulverized; the big man sitting just near you. He appeared to be saying to himself throughout: "Good gracious me!" He was a perpetual note of exclamation.

HDB: I am afraid that after the lecture, when the debate started, I was rather irritable in the way I answered some of the questions.

WARREN: Yes, I think you might have made the replies a little more flowery; you were a little abrupt, but many of the questions they put were particularly stupid. Surely some of them could read something of the subject. I could see you getting more and more purple. There was one particularly stupid little man—another mosquito; he could never have thought. Had he been at Dorincourt for ten years of experiments he would never know anything. He has a mentality like a lump of damp cotton wool. The big man was not so bad, but altogether they were rather a queer set of people. Yet, despite all that, the effect upon them afterwards was very great.

HDB: At any rate, I do not want to lecture again for a while—I want to take a rest.

WARREN: You can't have one; you will be resurrected very soon, and it is quite different to holding séances. It is hard work, but it is straight hard work.

HDB: Were you at the Steinway Hall?[45]

WARREN: Yes, we were all there. It went splendidly The parson, Drayton Thomas, said it was splendid.

HDB: You know, Warren, I never use psychics for any material purpose, but at the same time, I do want to ask you one question.

Do you remember on Thursday last, at about one fifteen p.m., under peculiar conditions I did ask you to impress Sirett?

WARREN: Yes, I know quite well. I put it in your head to ask me.

---

[44] I lectured to the members of the Irish Literary Society on Saturday, November 15.

[45] I lectured at the Steinway Hall on October 30.

THE SEARCH FOR REASONS

HDB: As a matter of fact, in some peculiar way, I just felt that I would like this sign.

WARREN: Yes, and we were able to give it to you. It was just a symbol of power—to show you can link up with us. Even when things are going wrong. We can do this sometimes in an extraordinary way.

HDB: You know, Warren, that every day I always say "Good morning" to you and Annie. Do you hear me?

ANNIE: Yes, of course I hear you. I hear you when you are walking along.[46]

MRS. BRADLEY: Do you know that Dennis has had an offer to go into a publishing business?

WARREN: Yes! But I am not taking that seriously. In any case I am not very keen on it for him.

HDB: I have heard from several sources, Warren, and it was indicated to me during the sittings in February last by Dr. Barnett, that there is to be a great physical upheaval during the next few years. Will you tell me whether you know anything of this?

WARREN: Yes. You see the world, at the present moment, is spiritually at sixes and sevens. Doyle has been told of this upheaval and he has got most of it right, but he is very much inclined to exaggerate. It will come in a great shaking up of the Universe.

MRS. BRADLEY: Only as a spiritual shaking up?

WARREN: No, both mentally and physically as well. A great psychical upheaval must react upon the physical. Herbert feels himself that people must be shaken out of this awful apathy. Look at those Irish Literary Society people; look at the years they have had for study. They are all educated, and have had many advantages in life, and yet they appear to know nothing of any real value. It seems useless to wait for their minds to grow gradually. It would take too long.

These great psychical manifestations may come with peculiar forms of upheaval. It will be psychical and super-physical. There will be storms—great storms, great winds, Earthquakes and tidal waves.

HDB: Could you give us the time during which we are to expect these manifestations?

WARREN: It might be next year or within the next two years.

MRS. BRADLEY: In what part of the world?

---

[46] This is correct since I usually pass my greeting whilst walking alone along the country road away from my house.

WARREN: Especially in Europe. But Europe will not be wiped out. Neither will England. The upheaval will be more noticeable and more striking than anything before. The actual death-toll will not be much greater than that of the big epidemic of influenza which occurred a few years back. That was, in a way, an upheaval, but the people only regarded it as, more or less, a glorified cold in the head. With the coming upheaval there will be Earthquakes in England, and the great majority of people will be terrified—it will make their hair stand on end. This physical and psychical upheaval will be a spiritual sign, and many manifestations will be made from our side. Then the world will know that there must be spirits. These great psychic signs come in times of calamity; after wars and during them. Although war is most unspiritual, even then many of the poor soldiers at the front had manifestations.

You, Herbert, will have power to be able to hand comfort out to the people to enable them to bear up during this time of panic.

HDB: What do you mean, Warren? With the leaders?

WARREN: Yes! Doyle will be able to lead if only he keeps his health. Doyle will lead on the spiritual side. You and Mabel will be able to show that communication with the spirits is possible. You will be able to take away from them much of the fear of death. Various spirits will speak through you, and during the time of this upheaval the Saints will be speaking to many people, but they will only come to those who are ready for them.

(A slight pause.)

WARREN: The Master came back to those who followed him on Earth.

HDB: During this time will physical protection be given to those who are of service?

WARREN: Yes. You have nothing to fear. We shall help the four of you; you and Mabel and Dennis and Pat. We shall protect those who are helping us, and the protection will be physical, mental and spiritual. You, Herbert, will have to live as long as you can. We have a lot of work for you to do.

(Here Warren spoke to Mrs. Bradley with regard to the condition of her health. It is impossible for me to give these details, but it was a most important and remarkable analysis of her condition, and treatment was discussed. My sister Annie came through, and went thoroughly into the details with her, and gave her advice on the matter. Certain affairs were discussed, and correct information volunteered, of which even I had no knowledge.)

THE SEARCH FOR REASONS

HDB.: Can you tell me how Gertrude is going on?

ANNIE: She is a little better.

HDB: Do you think she will pull through?

ANNIE: I cannot say, but she is certainly better than she was.

MRS. BRADLEY: Can you tell me what effect the pneumothorax treatment is having?

(Here Warren joined in the conversation with my sister. They explained Gertrude's condition thoroughly, dealt with two individual forms of ailment, and explained the difficulties of treatment which would help one but hurt the other, and explained also how necessary it was to be careful in the usage of this treatment.

They said that one of the two forms of ailments was disappearing, which was a good thing as it was drawing So much upon her system.[47]

WARREN (at the close of the discussion): I never thought a few years ago, Mabel, that I should be here talking about internal organs.

I want to say that I feel very much better about Dorothy, also the "old man" has bucked up considerably.

HDB: That was probably on account of Ida talking with them. Were you there?

WARREN: Yes, but not exactly as an accomplice, even although we are clever, but we did succeed in impressing Ida what to say to them.

HDB: Do you think Ida is likely to develop powers of mediumship?

WARREN: I cannot quite say. In new mediums it takes very much longer. You know, she is very much impressed with the experiments at Dorincourt.

MRS. BRADLEY: Yes, but she seemed to be very nervous.

HDB: When we resume our sittings would you advise us to continue the experiments with the jazz band? I am not, as you know, at all keen on physical phenomena, but I have found it does astound people.

WARREN: I should go on the same as you started, but don't put so much of that paint on them. I take great care of my hands now.

(Here Warren broke off and said that Tanner[48] was getting on very well. He also added that we might expect some signs from De Wyckoff[49] shortly, and that De Wyckoff was in a chastened frame of mind.)

---

[47] The diagnosis volunteered was absolutely correct, and less than a week after this sitting I received a note from Gertrude in Switzerland saving that the doctors had decided to stop the treatment.

[48] The spirit referred to in my last book.

[49] Subsequently De Wyckoff made two endeavours to resume friendship with Valiantine, but Valiantine ignored him.

WARREN: My love to you both, and to Dennis and Pat.
Here the sitting closed.

III

At this sitting, with hardly a moment's pause, communications and conversations with Warren Clarke and Annie continued for just over two hours. This is a fair example of the amazing powers invariably manifested under the mediumship of Mrs. Leonard.

It will easily be understood that it was of the utmost importance for me to ascertain not only the precise reason for the abandonment of the direct voice sittings at Dorincourt, but also to find out, if possible, when it would be advisable for me to resume them.

After the stoppage on October 18 I fully realized how essential it was to take a rest on account of overwork, but it came as a surprise to me when I was told by Warren that a further reason for the stoppage was because I was on the point of agreeing to sit for the Society for Psychical Research.

I have always implicitly followed the advice given by the spirits, and I have never been misled. Therefore when this communication came through to me, I decided at once that I would not sit with my wife for the Society for Psychical Research until the power had been more fully developed, and until I was advised that I may do so.

The manner in which Warren dealt with the powers of mediumship is interesting, and from these communications I am convinced that in the near future the powers of mediumship will be scientifically explained in such a manner that everyone can understand the methods of producing the phenomena.

It was also interesting to learn of the dual form of mediumship of my wife and myself—with my function as the supplier, and she as the conductor. It was instructive to know that by some means a reservoir of power has been created in me which can be drawn upon.

Warren's remarks on the luminous paint which had been used on the trumpet, and on the various instruments, are of considerable practical value. They explain, to a very great extent, why a complete darkness does assist the spirits in materializing their voices and speaking to us.

The theory I had formed that practically everybody possesses the latent power of mediumship—some in a very undeveloped state and others more completely developed—was confirmed. It is as Warren

THE SEARCH FOR REASONS

Clarke says, a great and undeveloped force, the use of which a few of us are on the fringe of discovering.

For the past seventy years many of the great scientists of the world have taken a medium, studied him, his methods, his powers, the phenomena produced, and so on, but none of these scientists has experimented on himself for development. Everyone should experiment. Without experiment we can learn nothing. Mediumistic powers, as Warren says, are not limited to a few extraordinary people; tens of thousands of people may possess them, but they are uncultivated, and without cultivation it is impossible for them to develop.

Communication with the spirits in their actual voices may, within this century, become as simple as the telephone or the wireless. In fact, it seems to me that it is a new and phenomenal form of wireless communication.

There can be no question that a new and inexperienced sitter does have some peculiar effect upon the communications, and sometimes a disturbing influence upon the power of communication.

That explains why, in so many cases which have been recorded in the past, when a medium is taken before a body of investigators, under test conditions, to produce the phenomena which have been proved and established with other experienced sitters, the results under new conditions are often entirely negative, or extremely poor.

The manner in which Warren criticized the audience at the Irish Literary Society proved that he was there. The two or three characters he referred to were very palpably recognized by me. He was not particularly complimentary in his criticism, but he was right. In the debate which followed my lecture there were one or two brilliant speeches, but the others were deplorably stupid, and showed not the faintest glimmer of comprehension or intelligence.

The Sirett incident was amazing. It proved the knowledge of Warren Clarke of something which had happened in a peculiarly dramatic way. Of this incident I can say no more.

For the reason that from various psychic sources in America, in England, in France, and in Germany entirely apart, and having no connection with each other—communications have been coming through during the last year of a great upheaval in the near future, I asked one question. It is dangerous to prophesy, neither can spirits foretell the future with any degree of certainty, but because this possibility has become an almost worldwide rumor, I asked my question. Whether the upheaval, which Warren referred to in guarded terms, happens or does not happen, will not affect the incontrovertible evidence of direct communication with the spirits.

The diagnosis of Gertrude's condition—at the time I am writing she is still in Switzerland—was correct in every detail, and displayed an absolute and intimate knowledge beyond and outside that of ours. The probable effects of a certain form of treatment which was being given to her at the time of this sitting was described, and the effect it was actually producing upon her. The doctors, discovering these effects, stopped this treatment a few weeks later. This is unique evidence of superhuman knowledge.

If we are foolish enough to assume that even a minimum part of the communications (the majority of which imparted information beyond my knowledge) made at this sitting were due to human telepathy—a primitive theory presumed to account for spirit communication which is still stupidly clung to by many scientists, and by a proportion of the members of the Society for Psychical Research—then all I can say is that the results of this form of telepathy applied only to the minimum part of the communications were astoundingly brilliant, and shine amazingly in comparison with the trifling experiments conducted by Professor Gilbert Murray and Lord Balfour in thought reading, the results of which were published in December, 1924, and which can only be considered as deplorably infantile.

Throughout the last two years I have been in constant communication with the spirit of Annie, and with the spirit of Warren Clarke. Under certain conditions it is far easier for me to talk with both of them at length than it is for me to talk with any human being. Even psychic researchers and spiritualists may wonder how it is that these communications are so extraordinarily complete. The reason is that not only am I in tune with both of them, but that our respective minds are in tune. It is only fitting that I should receive the information I do from them. The reason for failure maybe that many who attend séances are not, and perhaps cannot be, in tune to the same extent with the spirits who endeavour to speak to or communicate with them. They are not accustomed to the communicating spirit or spirits, or to accept them to the same extent as I do. Therefore the harmony being less in tune, and the mental vibration more flimsy in character, the information they receive is weak in substance.

This, after all, is a condition of affairs to which one is accustomed in the present life. Sympathy—or understanding, or affinity, call it what you wish—makes us infinitely more in tune with some of our fellows than with others, and with them we often seem to share in common a certain understanding of conditions and ideas without words. It is not telepathy; it might be more readily described as a common outlook, based on a common sympathy.

Telepathy, of course, is the banal refuge for the uneasy souls who, for some inexplicable reason, shrink from the bare idea of survival and the possibility of a communication with those who have passed away out of this life. As a rule, however, they carefully refrain from any definition of telepathy. One gathers that "telepathy" is a convenient shibboleth which dispose at once of the unknown, and therefore uncomfortable.

No telepathic theory can dispose of the phenomenon of the direct voice. No telepathic theory can dispose of the phenomenon of the trance mediumship of Mrs. Leonard.

No modern scientist is likely to achieve any progress in psychical research until he discards the negative theories of telepathy and the subconscious mind, as applied to direct spirit communication. Both these theories have been utterly refuted by the evidence which has been accumulated during recent years.

10

A VOICE MEDIUM SÉANCE

A Scottish correspondent draws the author's attention to the Sisters Moore—Arthur Brandise on Mr. DeWyckoff's estate—Unquestionable evidence obtained—The secret of obtaining mediumistic power.

I

November 20, 1924

From a correspondent in Scotland I had heard that two Scottish mediums, the Misses Moore, were visiting London. He also told me that he considered them to be the best of the few voice mediums in North Britain.

The arrangements for their sittings were made by Miss Estelle Stead, and through her I fixed an appointment for my wife and myself. At the last moment, however, my wife was unable to accompany me, and I took with me another lady whom I called "Miss M.B." The sitting was held at 5 Smith Square, Westminster. I am known personally to Miss Stead, but I introduced the lady to her under the pseudonym.

There were no other sitters present but Miss M.B. and myself.

The Misses Moore hold their sittings in complete darkness, in the manner of George Valiantine.

We formed a circle of four, the trumpet being placed in the centre, well away from any of us. Music was played on a musical-box. After a few minutes one of the mediums' spirit guides came through and spoke for a short time. He was followed by another spirit guide, named Angus, who also addressed us. Then came a spirit who spoke to the lady who accompanied me, calling her by her Christian name. The spirit announced itself to be Diana, a cousin of the lady's, who had died some few years back. The conversation, which was evidential, continued for two to three minutes, the voice being fairly clear and distinct. Complete recognition was established. Another spirit addressed my friend by her correct name. This time it was a masculine voice, which announced itself to be Cyril ——[50] Although Cyril while on Earth was not in any way intimately associated with the lady, recognition took place, and identity was established.

A spirit, speaking in a materialized voice, addressed me as Mr. Bradley.

HDB: Who are you?

THE SPIRIT: My name is Arthur. I spoke to you in America.

HDB: Were you living on Earth when you last spoke to me?

THE SPIRIT: I spoke to you at a sitting there. Don't you remember I was talking about the Estate?

HDB: Are you Arthur Brandise?[51]

THE SPIRIT: Yes. I do not think the estate is much good to Joe.[52] He is very lonely there. Someone ought to tell him to get rid of it.

After Arthur Brandise had gone the spirit of my friend's grandmother came through to her and spoke to her for some considerable time on personal matters.

The sitting was short but successful, especially as there was no possibility of the mediums knowing the lady who accompanied me. This was the first séance my friend had ever attended. She was somewhat astonished at the results.

The Misses Moore are unquestionably reliable mediums.

---

[50] Full name given.

[51] I had hardly remembered this incident until he mentioned the Estate as I had not placed very much significance upon the incident. It is, however, recorded in Chapter II of *Towards the Stars*. I gave a lead here by giving the full name.

[52] Mr. Joseph De Wyckoff.

A VOICE MEDIUM SÉANCE

II

The study of mediumship and methods, especially direct voice mediumship, is of considerable interest to me, and is also of considerable scientific value to the world.

I therefore asked the Misses Moore, who are round about the age of thirty, to let me have particulars of their career, and to tell me how they discovered their power.

Until nine years ago, in 1917, neither had any interest in spiritualism. During the latter part of that year they were introduced to a family of spiritualists, with whom they attended some meetings and séances. Their interest became aroused, and a little later they began a series of sittings for automatic writing, but with results which could not be described as particularly good. At one of these sittings the advice came through to them to sit regularly in the dark with a trumpet, in order to develop the direct voice mediumship. The communicators declared that this power could be developed, and the statement was subsequently confirmed by some trance medium speaking from a public platform. They decided to sit to endeavour to obtain the direct voice, and formed a family circle with their friends. They sat for some few months with this circle, but no results were obtained.

Experimental sittings were then abandoned on account of illness. Sometime later, they formed a new circle at a friend's house. They sat regularly every week for several months before anything happened. Then faint tapping's were heard on the trumpet. They regarded this as distinctly encouraging, and encouragement was certainly required by them, as the experience of sitting for so long without anything taking place was beginning to tax their patience.

This faint sign, trivial as it may appear, brought about new conditions in their circle. Would-be sitters expressed a wish to join, and immediately it would appear the condition brought by the new sitters retarded their development.

They were introduced to a lady clairvoyant and lecturer in Scotland. She joined them in their sittings, and it was during a series of these sittings that they first heard a spirit speak to them in the direct voice. They said that it was difficult for them to describe the feeling of wonderment and joy they felt when they heard this voice.

From that time the development was quick, and for months afterwards they sat, usually twice a week, and, eventually, as many as ten distinct spirit personalities came through and spoke.

The results varied according to conditions brought by those who sat with them. They observed that with one single sitter who appeared to be skeptical or unsympathetic the séance was adversely affected, and the phenomena often poor.

Since developing the powers of mediumship they have held sittings which have been entirely blank of result, and on other occasions the phenomena have been very poor. They say that on the blank occasions they feel there is no power whatever in the room, and that the whole atmosphere seems deadened.

The more I study the development of the well-known mediums the more I can see that the development of my wife and myself in direct voice mediumship has been unparalleled in its rapidity.

It appears to me that the few good mediums in the world have developed because of their extraordinary patience. I very much doubt whether, had I personally been compelled to sit for several months without anything whatever happening, I should have conjured sufficient patience to continue.

11

A TRANCE MEDIUM

Mrs. Scales, a clairvoyant and clairaudient medium—The question of control—An extraordinary transformation—Annie comes through, whereon occurred one of the most impressive and memorable experiences of the author's life.

I

November 27, 1924.

I was invited by Mrs. Gaston Sargeant to attend an experimental sitting at her house in Chelsea, with the medium, Mrs. Scales, whom I had never met before.

Mrs. Scales is a clairvoyant and clairaudient trance medium, and during the whole of her sitting is under control. Hers is a similar form of mediumship to that of Mrs. Osborne Leonard, inasmuch as throughout the sitting she is in a trance condition. The difference is that whilst Mrs. Leonard is controlled throughout by the spirit of Feda, Mrs. Scales is often controlled by more than one spirit.

Mrs. Gaston Sargeant used the utmost care that my name should not be disclosed before the séance, even to the servants in the house.

The sitting took place at about eight forty-five p.m., and was held in the drawing room in full electric light, so that I could take notes throughout. I was also permitted to smoke.

The three of us sat together: Mrs. Sargeant, Mrs. Scales, and myself. Mrs. Scales, holding her hands over her eyes, gradually went into a trance.

There followed three minutes before the first movement was made. The hands were removed from her face and her eyes were twitching rather violently.

She was then controlled by a spirit called Chloe, speaking in quite a different voice to that of the medium and in broken English. Chloe, I was told, was the spirit of an Indian girl.

As first her utterances were very chaotic, and I could not make very much out of them.

CHLOE: There is a big Indian standing behind massy and he want to come through my medium, but me say "No, not yet."

(To Mrs. Sargeant) The Chief[53] is standing behind you.

(Again addressing me) K. is standing behind you now; big flame just over the top of your hair. I see there are three different bloods in you.

HDB: I know of only Irish and English.

CHLOE: It comes from a long way back, from your ancestors. You may find out later on.[54]

There is a spirit here called John, and he is showing a small coin like a 6d.

I do not understand how it is you have got so much power; you have the power for materialization. Later on you will be able to get materialization. If, when you are in bed you were to ask four or five times they will be able to build up.

(Breaking off from argument) I see an American flag; it curls up into the big letter A. (Here the medium held my right hand.) It builds up into a lady, and there is also a gentleman piccanniny (meaning boy, I presume). He calls you "Uncle Herbert."[55] He is of close blood to the lady.

---

[53] Mrs. Sargeant tells me that this refers to her husband, whom the control always refers to as the "Chief".

[54] Since the first edition of this book was published, I have discovered that my great-great-grandfather was Alexander Saphne, who escaped through the barriers in the French Revolution.

[55] She got this name with difficulty.

(Breaking off again the Control spelled out the letters: TANNER. At this I could not help laughing, because although the whole of the communications had seemed jumbled and practically valueless, suddenly a certain meaning dawned on me so I said: I think I know what you mean now.)

He tells me that it was a joke that John was playing on you.

He says that I am to tell you that the two brothers are here, and he wanted you to know that he was here.

(Note the peculiar way in which the evidence of this name came through. First, John holding a 6d, the colloquial term for which is a "tanner," and later, the medium, spelling out the name TANNER. I knew a Mr. John Tanner, who passed away a few years back, and also his brother, who passed away a year or so ago. The two brothers were much together.)

John says that he could enlarge on this, but Annie is here and wants to come through.[56] Kokum[57] is here too, and John and he are going for a walk together.

(A slight pause)

(To Mrs. Sargeant) Annie says: "It is perfectly sweet of you to bring my brother here."

Mrs. SARGEANT: I was only too delighted to do so.

CHLOE: Annie says she has brought Georgie[58] with her. She says: "Have you got the trumpet in your room now?[59] Ask Mabs to bring it."[60]

(Here Chloe said twice: "Door in the court, door in the court." I presumed later that she meant "Dorincourt")

Annie says she is going to see Pat. She says a long way back she (Annie) was called Nancy.[61] She sends a message that you are to expect some news concerning an old gentleman—closely connected. He may take a journey soon. (Here Chloe spelled out "Galway."[62])

---

[56] Name given out clearly and without hesitation.

[57] Kokum is one of George Valiantine's guides.

[58] Georgie was Annie's son, who passed away several years ago.

[59] The trumpet which I use for the direct voice séances at Dorincourt had been sent to Cambridge.

[60] "Mabs" is an abbreviation which Annie very often used when addressing my wife Mabel.

[61] 2 Perfectly true, and exceptionally evidential.

[62] 3 This is the part of Ireland in which my father was born.

A spirit has just been, here who passed over with a nasty cough. He was in the circle for a little while, but he did not want to wait in case his condition might choke the medium.⁶³

(To Mrs. Sargeant) The Chief says that he would like to help the pretty lady—Annie—come through and take control. (Meaning to take control of the medium in place of Chloe.)

Here the question of the change of control was considered for two or three minutes, with Chloe speaking and interpreting for the spirit of Mrs. Sargeant's husband. There followed quite an extraordinary discussion. She said that Annie was timid of making the endeavour as she has never manifested in this way before. She was nervous of occupying the medium's body, and did not know whether she would be able to control and use the organism. Eventually she was persuaded to make the attempt. The medium fell back in her chair and we waited for some two minutes.

Mrs. Scales is a very fat, short woman. Her ordinary accent is, to put it politely, commonplace. Her face is one which might be termed pleasantly plain and homely.

Gradually the whole of the expression of the medium's face changed completely. It was a transformation.

Whilst the outline remained, the eyes and the expression became beautiful. This was not hallucination. My faculties are as keen or keener now than they have ever been, and it must be remembered that this amazing change was seen not only by me but by Mrs. Sargeant in a full strong light.

At first it was only with very great difficulty that the first few words were articulated. It was as if they were produced with considerable effort. Within a little while, however, the power strengthened considerably, and the spirit of my sister was able to assume complete control.

It was my sister. It was her spirit, using the organism of another physical body, and speaking to me in her own voice. I do not care if the inexperienced skeptic may feel inclined to laugh at this, but those who have studied spiritual phenomena will know and understand. I have

---

⁶³ 4 If one assumes that the spirit of Warren was referred to, and assumes also that there was the question of his taking control, this might have caused a slight choking effect, as it had been observed that when a spirit takes control of the medium for the first time, the conditions under which he passed over are conveyed. Warren Clarke died of heart trouble.

had communications in almost every form from her now for nearly two years. I have spoken to her in the independent voice in the presence of celebrated witnesses on hundreds of occasions. I know her personality, and I know her spirit.

Annie's voice possessed its old beauty; the quality was the same, and every syllable of every word was perfectly enunciated, in the manner which was so characteristic of my sister when she was on Earth. No actress living could have simulated this wonderful individuality. It was two souls talking together on a plane of understanding. She discussed with me all the delicate intimacies of her life here.

She had always been the one soul, the one woman allied to me by blood, for whom beyond all sexual ties, I had the greatest and purest love it is possible to conceive. I think that I alone knew and understood her soul. In the finer regions of the mind when on Earth she was always beyond me, just as she was infinitely beyond all those with whom she came in contact. With that big mind of hers she helped me enormously, in the most gentle and subtle manner, to develop any latent possibilities in my character and, as I know now, she has helped me to an even greater extent since she passed over to a higher sphere.

During this wonderful scene, whilst she was using the organism of another person, she gave me the most intimate and exceptional evidence of survival. Name after name and fact after fact were discussed: my wife, Pat, Dennis; everything.

There was a great tragedy in her life—just barely indicated, but veiled in *Towards the Stars*. This tragedy—the details of which have never been published, and are not known to more than two or three living people—was discussed by her.

She spoke to me of my son Anthony at Cambridge, who, incidentally, knew her when he was a very young boy, and has spoken to her in the direct voice several times since she has passed over. She sent messages to him. Throughout there were so many communications and gestures that it would be utterly impossible for any writer to attempt to put them on paper. I can do no more than say that this was one of the most marvelous experiences of my life.

Imagine, if you can, the complexity of my emotions. For here, before my eyes, was the spirit of my sister occupying and controlling the mechanism of another person's body. That it was my sister was proved by the abundance of the evidence she gave. Yet, though the accents were hers, and the expression of the face transformed before my eyes was the physical body of another.

It was a peculiarly difficult situation for me to conduct. Existing and apparent were the splendid spirit, but also the disturbing physical form through which it was expressing its love.

Within me raged the conflict of spiritual attraction and physical aversion. There are some scenes in life you cannot describe. This was one of them. They have to be lived through and experienced to be understood.

After this Chloe came through and asked me if I would bring Mrs. Sargeant back into the room. I have omitted to mention that shortly after the opening of this scene Mrs. Sargeant, of her own accord, suggested that it would leave us freer to discuss certain questions if she left the room.

I called Mrs. Sargeant, and she came into the room. Shortly after this the medium was controlled by the spirit of Mrs. Sargeant's husband.

Again the whole condition of the medium changed. It was the voice of a man speaking in cultured masculine tones. It is not essential for me to refer to the conversation which took place between Mrs. Sargeant and her husband. After speaking to her for a while, he spoke to me, and told me that he had been present during the conversation with my sister, and that they on their side regarded Annie as one of the divine spirits. It was good for me to hear him say this. She certainly was one on this sphere, and I feel that she is also one on the sphere in which she is now existing.

II

On the following morning I telephoned to Mrs. Sargeant to ask her a question, which I had forgotten to put to her. I asked her to describe the voice which she heard when my sister took control. This I did to check any possible doubt as to the tones being produced by my imagination. Mrs. Sargeant said, in describing the voice of my sister, that the delivery was slow, and the enunciation exceptionally sweet and clear. This was characteristic of Annie's speaking voice when she was on Earth.

12

THE NECESSITY FOR CRITICISM

*Some remarks on the mediumship of Mr. Evan Powell—
Miss Madeline Cohen's mother—Lord Northcliffe talks to
Lord Beaverbrook—Mr. Bonar Law's faint whisper and Lord
Northcliffe's reply—The late Mr. Harold Ashton's talk about Mr.
A. G. Hales, the war correspondent.*

I

December 8, 1924.

PRIOR to the sitting, which I am about to record, I had three previous experiences under the mediumship of Mr. Evan Powell. One occurred in July, 1923, and is recorded in *Towards the Stars*. This sitting was not a very successful one, as no voices whatever were heard, and the phenomena—which were entirely physical—consisted only of the movement of various objects.

The second time I attended, at the invitation of Sir Arthur Conan Doyle, in Westminster, when there were several other people present. Several voices came through, although for only a very short time and spoke very little. These sentences were spoken whilst a musical-box was played. None of my personal friends came through, but one spirit, speaking to me in two or three phrases, announced itself to be Arthur

Brandise, saying that he had spoken to me in America at Arlena Towers. This fact could not then have been known by the medium.

In addition to this, a spirit, purporting to be that of William Stead, spoke to me in reference to my literary work. Other spirit voices addressed various members of the assembly, and I do not know if any evidential information was given. There appeared to me to be far too much volunteering of information by the sitters, which merely called for acquiescence by the spirits.

I feel, however, that I can assert that there can be no question that Mr. Powell is a genuine medium, and he is also one of the most honest and straightforward men I have ever met. I am of the opinion that his powers of mediumship may get stronger.

On the third occasion I attended a sitting with Mr. Powell at the British College of Psychical Science. It was not particularly good. There occurred various physical phenomena, and one or two voices came through and spoke, but nothing of an evidential character was obtained.

II

The fourth Evan Powell sitting was held at Dorincourt on December 8. There were present, in addition to Mr. Powell and myself, Mrs. Bradley, Anthony Bradley, Mr. and Mrs. Hannen Swaffer, Miss Madeleine Cohen, Miss Louise Owen, and Lord Beaverbrook.

Lord Beaverbrook arrived just prior to the sitting, as it was only arranged at the last minute that he should come down. Mr. Swaffer and I are sure that Mr. Powell was not aware of Lord Beaverbrook's identity.

The medium insisted on being tied to his chair with ropes. He was tightly bound hand and foot. The ropes were passed underneath the chair and tied in such a manner that it was utterly impossible for him to move. This was done by Mr. Swaffer and by Anthony in the presence of us all. The knots of the ropes were sealed with wax. In addition to this the right thumb was tied with cotton, and the thread taken across to the left thumb, and tied so that any movement would break the thread.

As far as I am concerned, it does not interest me whether Mr. Powell is bound or not, as in this study I rely only upon mental evidence for proof, and not upon physical phenomena.

In talking to Mr. Powell before the sitting, he told me that he had heard that my wife and I had obtained the direct voices. I suggested to him that, in addition to his own trumpet, which is a long, black,

THE NECESSITY FOR CRITICISM

leathery instrument (quite light in weight) we should also place in the centre of the room my own aluminium trumpet.

My illuminated trumpet was, therefore, placed in the centre of the room, and Mr. Powell's leather trumpet was placed outside the circle on a writing-table.

The gramophone was played, and within a minute or so Mr. Powell went into a trance, and was controlled by his spirit guide, Black Hawk.

It must be understood that when Black Hawk speaks it is through the medium's lips and vocal organs, and that Black Hawk's voice, although he speaks in broken English, is very similar to that of Mr. Powell. Therefore, a critical observer is quite justified in being entirely unimpressed by his remarks, as they could easily and consciously emanate from the medium. The generalities given forth by Black Hawk have no actual value.

It is only the direct voice spoken through the trumpet or independently at some distance away from the medium that is phenomenal.

The first independent voice that spoke addressed Miss Madeleine Cohen, calling her "Maddy" (the name by which she is known to her friends). This voice, which claimed to be that of Miss Cohen's mother, could hardly get a sentence or two through, and evidently could not sustain the power.

A little later on a spirit, announcing itself as Northcliffe, came through and addressed Mr. Swaffer as "Poet,"[64] and Miss Louise Owen as Lulu.

He said to Mr. Swaffer: "I did get the name through. I am so pleased."

Lord Northcliffe added he was glad that this particular séance had been arranged.

The voice was either speaking independently, or was using the black trumpet, which, of course, could not be seen. The spirit did not stay very long, and only got through a few short phrases, none of which could be regarded by a skeptic as of an evidential nature.

Suddenly Black Hawk, through the mouth of the medium, called out: "He is talking to you, Lord Beave!"

MR. SWAFFER: He is talking to you, Lord Beaverbrook.

NORTHCLIFFE: My God, Beaverbrook, if you only knew how difficult it was.[65]

---

[64] 1 The term by which Lord Northcliffe addressed Mr. Swaffer when on Earth.

[65] 1 Perhaps this remark was meant to imply how difficult it was to materialize his voice to speak.

A little later on the voice said, "Law is here."

Here Black Hawk, speaking through the medium, said that there was standing behind Lord Beaverbrook a tall, dark man, very reserved, but very eager with a little cough. He also said that he had lost two sons, the loss of which had hastened his death.

Black Hawk added that this spirit was too full of emotion to speak yet. He said that he was trying to touch Lord Beaverbrook, and asked him whether he felt it. A little later Lord Beaverbrook was touched, and admitted that he felt the touch.

A spirit voice saying it was that of Bonar Law spoke in a faint whisper.

BONAR LAW: Keep on as you are going; I will try to get through and help you. Don't commit yourself just yet.

LORD BEAVERBROOK: What shall I do about——?

No answer was given to this question. Northcliffe came through again, and during the conversation Lord Beaverbrook asked him whether he could obtain an answer to the question put through Bonar Law.

LORD BEAVERBROOK: Will you ask him what I shall do about——?

There was a pause for a full minute.

NORTHCLIFFE: In favour. Law says you should give your consent; it is the only thing to do.

Black Hawk said that he would bring a spirit light. A spirit light appeared, like a round flame, about three inches in diameter. It floated up and down, and round the circle.

Warren spoke, as he usually does, to several of us, using my illuminated trumpet, He talked for some little time with my wife, with me, with my son, with Mr. Swaffer, with Lord Beaverbrook, and one or two others.

As he was using the illuminated trumpet I asked him whether he would take the trumpet to the ceiling, which, as I have before stated, is some twelve feet from the ground, and right out of the reach of anyone. The trumpet was taken up to the ceiling, which was touched several times.

During the time that Warren was using my trumpet it was taken all round the circle, and even outside the circle, the effect of which is impressively phenomenal.

The spirit of Annie spoke a few words to several of those present.

A spirit, saying it was that of Harold Ashton, spoke to Mr. Swaffer.

HAROLD ASHTON: I have got rid of the hydrochloric.[66]

---

[66] Harold Ashton who was well known to Mr. Swaffer, had taken hydrochloric before he died in 1917.

Black Hawk joined in the conversation, and referring to the spirit that had just spoken, said "his innards had gone."

Harold Ashton made some remarks about "Smiler."

MR. SWAFFER: You mean "Smiler" Hales?

LORD BEAVERBROOK: Who is "Smiler" Hales?

HDB: A. G. Hales.

MR. SWAFFER: The war correspondent.

Later on came through a spirit purporting to be that of Keir Hardie, and spoke to Lord Beaverbrook and then to Mr. Swaffer.

This spirit made a reference to Bruce Glazier, and a short discussion on democracy ensued.

The spirit of Bonar Law came through a second time, and speaking in a faint voice, addressed Lord Beaverbrook, calling him "Beaverbrook" and saying: "It is Law speaking."

LORD BEAVERBROOK: Why do you announce yourself as Law, and address me as Beaverbrook?

BONAR LAW: You will know my reason for this later.

BLACK Hawk (to Lord Beaverbrook): Law says will you get a sitting with Mrs. Osborne Leonard, and see that the appointment will be made anonymously?

Annie again spoke to us, and also Feda, who only stayed for a short time.

Then —

NORTHCLIFFE: Law is full of emotion; that is why he finds it so difficult to speak.

During the conversation Northcliffe also said to Lord Beaverbrook: "This is a new revelation; it is the great reality."

Black Hawk, having said that the power was waning, the sitting was closed.

Then lights were turned on, and Mr. Powell was still in a trance; his head was bent down, and he was tightly roped, and the thread across the two thumbs unbroken.

III

On analysing the results of this sitting, taking a critical and impartial view, I should feel inclined to say that from an evidential standpoint the results might be regarded as comparatively negative, and this is the view that I expressed to Lord Beaverbrook in our conversation afterwards.

It must be clearly understood that when I say this sitting was comparatively negative, I say so only from the point of view I should adopt if it had been my first séance. My impression in such a case would be that I should feel it was necessary for me to obtain far more striking proofs before I could accept the fact of survival after death.

All the voices, with the exception of that of the spirit purporting to be that of Bonar Law, were quite distinct and clear. The conversations, however, were very short, and by no means fluent, and each spirit seemed to have considerable difficulty in sustaining the power to speak for more than a minute or two.

The voices certainly did come from all parts of the room, and in speaking to the various sitters, moved across to different positions. Each voice expressed a different accent and individuality. During the sitting both trumpets were used at various times.

13

A MIXTURE OF EMOTIONS

The recorder is irritated—An appointment with Mr. F. F. Craddock—The late Alfred Russell Wallace recants his theories in his book "Man's Place in the Universe"—The author's mentality on sitting with fresh mediums.

I

December 5, 1924.

A DIRECT voice medium of whom I had heard from various sources is Mr. F. F. Craddock, and I decided to obtain an appointment with him. An appointment was made for me by introduction, and the sitting took place at the medium's cottage in the country, some thirty miles front London. I may mention that I am cognizant of all Craddock's history

The sitting was held in the afternoon, and there were present the medium, my wife, and myself. We sat in a small room, quite dark—with the exception of a tiny red light in a corner of the ceiling of the room, which was so faint that it might not have been there since one was unable to distinguish the figures of anyone present. The three of us sat close together, side by side, in a line, facing a very large, fixed trumpet.

A musical box—a particularly large and heavy one, switched on by the medium himself—was played practically throughout, even when the various voices were speaking. Personally, I find the playing of music whilst the voices are speaking is disturbing and irritating. The spirit voice speaking in absolute silence is infinitely more impressive, and it is in this way that the voices come through at all the Valiantine séances, and also at those held under the mediumship of my wife and myself. The voices very often come through at our home sittings whilst the gramophone is being played, but we stop the music immediately, so that they maybe more audible.

Through the large, fixed trumpet there came the voice of one of Craddock's guides, called Joey,[67] with whom we talked for a while. There also spoke through the trumpet another guide of Craddock's, called Dr. Ord—or the name sounded something like that to me. He spoke of the planets, and gave a short description of the type of beings inhabiting Mars, who, he said, were far more highly developed than we on this Earth.

Another of Craddock's guides, named "Sister Amy," said she was a Canadian nun, who passed away about a century ago.

Joey made one or two references to *Towards the Stars*.

A spirit saying it was that of Alfred Russell Wallace spoke to me, referring to a book of his which he said was called *Man's Place in the Universe*.[68] He said that his book is all wrong, that he wished he had not written it, and that if it were possible he would like to recall all copies and burn them!

One of the guides told me that a new and big revelation would be made to me some time in February next.[69] My attitude is Asquithian and non-committal. I shall merely wait and see.

A spirit announced itself as John Bradley. He said that he too had been a writer. I have no knowledge whatever of John Bradley.

A voice, speaking in French, announced herself as "Cerise."

There came through the trumpet two or three people, addressing me as Herbert, and my wife as Mrs. Bradley. Although I spoke to and encouraged each of these voices, I could not succeed in getting their names through. Neither could I get anything whatever to suggest any evidence of their personalities.

---

[67] I was given to understand later that this spirit purported to be that of Joseph Grimaldi, the famous clown.

[68] I have not read this book, nor do I know if this is the correct title.

[69] Some suggestion of this was also made at a sitting with Mrs. Scales.

A MIXTURE OF EMOTIONS

Frankly, not one of these spirits was recognizable, and the conversation with those purporting to be friends was very short—only two or three banal phrases, whilst I was endeavouring to ask questions. Then the voices disappeared.

The voices of the guides were quite clear, and not only through the trumpet, but independently just behind our heads, and sometimes just in front of our faces.

It was an interesting sitting, but it offered no evidence of the survival of personality.

I always make a point, at any fresh sitting, of leaving my mind open and of regarding the sitting and the phenomena exactly as I should regard then if it were my first experience. There are many great difficulties in this study, and it is quite impossible for any medium to guarantee or produce results to order.

It is very essential in the study that one remains critical on the value of evidence. Each new experience should be weighed and tested by itself.

II

Since Craddock knew my name, and who I was, if he were fraudulent it would have been an obvious course for him to have produced a reiteration of some of the information which he could easily have obtained from *Towards the Stars*. In fact, that would have been the first source for him to turn to for information. Though I could claim no recognition whatever of any of the spirit voices, and though no personal evidence of any description was acquired at this sitting, it would not be fair to assume that the phenomena produced by him were not genuine.

Analysing my feelings at this sitting, the whole effect produced seemed to me to be a curious mixture of emotions. Throughout, I could not help feeling the suggestion of supernormal impersonation.

On the whole, I am inclined to think that Craddock has considerable powers, but I should imagine that these powers vary.

His guides certainly appear to have distinct individualities. At the same time, careful and encouraging as I was in speaking with them, they appeared to me to be very evasive in their replies to questions verging on any evidential point. I am inclined to think his mediumship is more upon the physical than the mental plane. I asked certain questions very guardedly, and it was quite apparent that the communicants had no knowledge of any of the personal spirits who had communicated with me before. They seemed to me to be on an entirely different sphere.

14

THE MEDIUMSHIP OF MUNNINGS

A discourse on Cabinet Ministers, barristers, actors, painters, poets, and newspaper proprietors as a preface to the record of a sitting with Mr. F. T. Munnings, a direct voice medium—Dan Leno sings, George R. Sims offers a Limerick—His favourite dog comes through to Mr. J. M. Dick, the sporting journalist—Animals in the spirit spheres—Dr. Ellis Powell as Mr. Munnings' guide—The psychic chord—Lord Northcliffe speaks with Mr. Swaffer and Mr. Dick.

I

December 18, 1924.

FEW of the professed skeptics have gone to more trouble and spent more time in attempting to analyse the mediumistic fraud than I have done.

A medium—like a Cabinet Minister, a barrister, an actor, a painter, a poet, or a newspaper proprietor, may in his private life be all that is undesirable, and yet may possess undoubted psychic powers. When one looks at a great picture one does not ask if the artist's marital record is blameless, or if his credit is unimpeachable in his butcher's eyes; and the indiscretions of a poet, a Cabinet Minister, or a newspaper magnate have little interest save to future collectors of garbage in the shape of intimate reminiscences, and should have no bearing on the assessment of their accomplished work. So the fact of a medium possessing an equivocal past—while it may, and does form good ground for a close scrutiny of his work—by no means disproves his possession of the mysterious psychic powers, of the laws of which we are at present in almost complete ignorance.

Were Mr. Lloyd George suddenly to discover an amazing mediumistic gift, it would be fatuous for the Tory searcher after truth to allow Mr. George's material past to damn his psychic future; should a new Lenin or a new Crippen appear as mediums, their pasts would not affect my desire to investigate their claims and to observe their accomplishments. I should use my faculties, and if genuine and indisputable phenomena were produced by them, I should accept it, just as I should accept it from the most noble character that ever breathed.

The phenomena and the personal character of the medium must be dissociated by the conscientious observer, just as the artist forgets that Turner drank and died in a squalid boozing den in Chelsea, that Shelley's marital affairs were complicated, and that Kit Marlowe would not have decorated an Archbishop's drawing room.

II

Mr. F. T. Munnings is a "direct voice" medium, and was used by a journalist, a Mr. Sydney A. Moseley, for the purposes of a "stunt" exposure of spiritualism in *John Bull*.

According to Mr. Moseley, Munnings had been accused of certain conduct on matters entirely apart from and unconnected with psychics. Yet Mr. Moseley used this record illogically. Obviously, he felt that, so far as moral character was concerned, here was an ideal "stunt" instrument. Knowing every detail of this gross usage, and although I am international in thought, I thank God I was born a pure-bred Irishman.

I had been told by a large number of psychical students that Munnings—whatever his character, and they know it far better than the bright Mr. Moseley—is a very powerful medium, and that remarkable results had been attained at his sittings. I therefore determined to investigate the matter for myself and arranged a sitting at Dorincourt.

THE MEDIUMSHIP OF MUNNINGS

There were present, in addition to Mr. Munnings and my wife and myself, Anthony Bradley, Mr. and Mrs. F. A. H. Eyles, Mr. Hannen Swaffer, and Mr. John M. Dick, the well-known sporting journalist.

Mr. Dick had never attended a séance before. He was not introduced, and the utmost care was taken that his name was not mentioned in the presence of the medium, who arrived at my house five minutes before the sitting took place.

Munnings has a shortish trumpet, which is often used for the production of the voices, although some of the voices come through independently, and do not feel the necessity of amplifying the sound and using the trumpet. Mr. Munnings' trumpet was slightly and very faintly luminous on the *inside*. As a matter of fact, one could hardly see a glimmer of it. Before the sitting, I asked Munnings whether he would have any objection to my luminous trumpet being used as well. It may here be mentioned that it is necessary to ask a medium whether he objects to the conditions, because a change of conditions will very often affect the phenomena. Munnings agreed that both the trumpets should be used.

The sitting opened, and after about ten minutes one of the medium's purported spirit guides, Emanuel, spoke. Emanuel speaks in a very distinct voice, and the accent is certainly entirely different to that of Munnings.

After Emanuel had spoken there came another of his guides announcing himself as Angus Stern. Angus said that he acted as a messenger to the other spirits.

He spoke in a very strong Scottish accent.

Emanuel then said the spirit of an elderly lady was inquiring after Alec Huntley (my chauffeur).

A voice spoke to Mrs. Eyles and mentioned something about "father." Mr. Eyles seemed to claim some recognition of this character, and he gave the name of "Newson." It will be observed that the spirit did not volunteer the name. A short conversation took place.

The voice spoke through Munnings' trumpet, and not through mine.

After this there came through another of the medium's guides—Dr. Ellis Powell—who spoke to us for some little time.

A spirit voice saying it was Dan Leno spoke to us in a general sort of humorous way. I can only record that if it were not the spirit of Dan Leno, it was the most marvelous imitation I have ever heard. I knew Leno's work on the stage very well, and I occasionally met him in private life.

Mrs. Bradley asked Leno if he would sing to us. The voice then sang a verse each of three songs: "The Midnight March," "The Recruiting

Sergeant," and "If you won't marry me I will marry you." Each of these three verses was sung in the remarkable and characteristic manner of Dan Leno.

At the end of these songs Leno talked for a short time and said that Herbert Campbell wished to send his regards to old friends. He added that he would like Stanley Lupino to come to a séance, because he would like to talk with him, and he also remarked that once he had nearly frightened the life out of Stanley.

Leno said that he would not come back to this earth if he were offered all the money in Drury Lane—an ambiguous remark, perhaps, since Mr. Basil Dean's financially unsuccessful production of "A Midsummer Night's Dream" was then being performed.

After this a spirit saying it was that of George R. Sims came through and talked with Mr. Eyles for some little time about a book which Mr. Eyles had assisted in compiling.

Here I must remark that none of these voices spoke through my luminous trumpet; they either spoke independently or through Munnings' trumpet. The only use that was made of my trumpet was in wafting it about different parts of the room.

A voice announcing itself as "Grandfather Bradley" addressed my son as Dennis, my wife as Mabel, and myself as Herbert—the point of this being that this is the personal way in which my son and I are known to the family, whereas outside he is known as Anthony and I am known as Dennis. This spirit voice said: "You know, when I speak of Dennis, I mean your son. We know you as Herbert." It was impossible for me to claim any recognition because I never knew this grandfather, who died nearly forty years before I was born. I endeavored to get some evidential information as to the part of Ireland in which he was born, but directly I framed my first question the spirit disappeared.

Emanuel said that the spirit who had just spoken was a very advanced spirit who had come down from a very high plane. He added: "I can tell you he is on a very much higher plane than I am."[70] Then in the center of the circle a dog barked. It was a loud and very distinct bark. Wough—Wough— Wough—Wough! There was then a pause for about six or seven seconds, and then again: Wough— Wough—Wough—Wough! Then followed a sort of moaning as if the animal wanted to come to someone. Mr. Dick appeared to be very amazed. A voice then spoke, and announced that it was Bloomfield, of Yeovil, the keeper of the dogs

---

[70] This is in no way evidential but is flattering to patriarchal conceit.

in the spirit spheres. Bloomfield said that the dog had belonged to one of those present. Mr. Dick asked: "Is it Bogey?"

It was a pity that Mr. Dick volunteered the name, but this was remedied afterwards.

Bloomfield replied: "Yes, it is Bogey." I then asked the voice whether he could tell us the breed of the dog. This was a direct question calling for an evidential reply.

Bloomfield: It is a very large dog—a Great Dane.

The dog continued to bark for a little while in the same manner: four deep barks each time. After the first few barks of this dog there came back an answering bark of my Alsatian wolfhound in an out-house some distance away from the room in which the séance was being held. Each time the bark of the Great Dane was heard in the séance room, the replying bark came from my Alsatian wolfhound. Mr. Dick told us that he was astounded by this phenomenon and declared that he should recognize his dog's bark anywhere. The dog had been a great friend of his and of his wife's, and they had had a very deep affection for it. This dog would always bark in four distinct barks at a time, and this was one of its chief characteristics.

Shortly afterwards there came through a spirit purporting to be that of Harry Hawker (the airman). This spirit stated that he lived quite close to Kingston—at Hook. He said that before he passed away, he had been warned by a spirit voice that when he was in the middle of the Atlantic, he would get a cold douche. The voice said to him: "You are all right this time, Harry, but be careful the next time." (This reference was taken to refer to the time when Hawker was given up as lost, but eventually turned up safely after some days.) The voice continued saying: "I was reckless again, and so here I am. I found the physical parting with my wife very painful at first, but I am perfectly happy now; I should like the opportunity of speaking to her."

Emanuel said that he had heard that I and my wife had obtained the direct voices at Dorincourt; and that if he could be of any service to us, he would be only too pleased to endeavor to help us when we resumed the sittings.

The guide, Dr. Ellis Powell, said that if he could help us in any way he would also be glad to do so.

EMANUEL: With regard to your mediumship, it is at present of a sort of dual character between you.' During the sitting Munnings said that he saw the psychic chord very clearly passed right across the circle from him to me, joining up from the solar plexus.

A spirit announcing itself as that of Husk, the famous medium, came through and spoke to Mr. Eyles and to me for a while. He said that his mediumship on Earth had been of assistance to him when he passed over to other spheres.

During the early part of the evening, when Emanuel was speaking, Mr. Swaffer in a very guarded way said to him: "There is one special friend of mine, whom I should like you to bring through if possible."

EMANUEL: Yes, I will do try best. Is it George Charles William?
SWAFFER: No!
EMANUEL: Is it Charles William?
SWAFFER: Yes, I think we might place that.
EMANUEL: Is it Alfred Charles William?
HANNEN SWAFFER: Yes![71]
EMANUEL: Would he not be sixty on July 15?
SWAFFER: I don't know—he might be.
J M Dick: Yes, that is right. That is the Chief's birthday. I know because my birthday is within a few days of his.

It was only afterwards that a voice purporting to be that of Northcliffe spoke with us. The voice could not, in, any circumstance, be recognized as belonging to Northcliffe. It appeared to me and to Mr. Swaffer that it bore a great similarity to that of Emanuel. The voice spoke to us for some time, greeting Mr. Swaffer, greeting Mr. Dick, and greeting me. The greeting to Mr. Dick certainly had a significance as the voice went straight over to him saying, "Hullo, John," and later in speaking with him referred to him two or three times as Dick.

When the voice had gone, Mr. Swaffer said that he could not say that he recognized the voice as Lord Northcliffe's. Immediately upon this the voice of Emanuel came through and said, "I must tell you that Viscount Northcliffe had great difficulty in materializing his voice, and I had to help him very considerably. I had, at times, to lend him the use of my vocal organs, therefore the voice may have sounded very much like mine."

III

This séance was peculiarly mixed. There was an absolute scarcity of actual evidence and of personal identity. It maybe noted that neither Annie nor Warren Clarke made any attempt to come through. Whenever

---

[71] These are the three Christian names of Lord Northcliffe.

they speak they give evidence of their identity immediately. I could not claim any recognition of the purported spirit of my grandfather, and Mr. Swaffer does not claim that he could recognize the voice of Lord Northcliffe, or that any evidence whatever was offered proving it was Northcliffe.

The recognition of J. M. Dick, both in Christian and surname, must be placed on the credit side.

The incident of the barking dog was remarkable, and evidential information certainly came through when the "spirit voice" said that it was a Great Dane.

I must mention that on one previous occasion at which I sat with Munnings, another dog came through and barked. Apparently, the entity of Bloomfield has in some way attached himself to Munnings' sittings, and he does occasionally bring through the spirits of dogs who once belonged to sitters. There is no need for the skeptic to laugh at the idea of a dog which has died coming through. Why should not the spirits of dogs exist in after life? I am a lover of dogs, and I have a greater affection for some of my—— than for the majority of the people I have met in life. In addition to this Warren has told me that there is an Animal Kingdom, and that animals do continue their existence. In my opinion, F. T. Munnings is a very powerful voice medium. The voices came through from all parts of the room, right away from the direction in which the medium was sitting. Some of the voices were quite independent, and the trumpet, when it was used by other voices, could be discerned moving around of its own accord. The presence of my luminous trumpet assisted the impressiveness of the séance, as not only was it lifted to the ceiling and to all parts of the room, but it acted on occasions as a reflector of the movements of the other trumpet, which one could see pass by it. When my trumpet was being wafted round the room and carried to the ceiling, Munnings was the most astonished man in the room. He exclaimed that he had never seen anything like it before.[72]

Whether the power for the moving of our trumpet was taken from myself or my wife I cannot say, but it is unlikely that any power would be taken from either of us for the voices on this occasion.

After the sitting, Mr. Swaffer and I were extremely critical in discussing the matter with regard to the scarcity of evidence we had acquired.

---

[72] In a later edition HDB updated his summary of this sitting: see appendix A.

Mr. Dick, however, said it was the most remarkable evening of his life. He added: "That was my dog and I know it!" There is this to he said: whether we managed to acquire any evidence or not, there is no living person who can produce fraudulently the remarkable phenomena which took place for over two hours. I would defy any one man, or any three of the greatest mimics or actors living, after careful rehearsal, to hold a fake séance and produce one quarter of the results. Such an attempt would be an utter fiasco. The personal character of the medium does not matter to me one iota. It is for the investigation of any form of phenomena that I am engaged in this study.

Munnings' services should certainly be utilized by scientific researchers. A day or so afterwards Mr. J. M. Dick wrote to me, and the following is an extract from his letter: "I am still in a state of amazement at the revelations made at your place the other night. The barking of my dog left me no room for doubt, and yet the revelation was so astounding that my mind as yet seems unable to grasp its full significance."

IV

Munnings is now a man of about fifty. He tells me that he did not discover or develop his powers of "voice" mediumship until when he was over forty, some nine years ago. It was quite by chance that he attended a direct voice séance, where a voice told him he had mediumistic powers, and he at once decided to form a private circle, to see if his powers could be developed. He commenced his experiences with a few friends at table sittings. Remarkable messages were received by taps. One of the messages gave him the measurements of a trumpet, which he was instructed to have made. Although he sat with his friends regularly once a week for nine months, and received many messages by taps, it was not until the end of this long period that a voice came through. Munnings said it was weird and strange, but unmistakably a voice. From that time onwards, the voices have gradually improved and become clearer and clearer.

15

THE PHILOSOPHY OF JOHANNES

HDB renews his acquaintance with the spirit of Johannes, the philosopher whose observations appear in "Towards the Stars" —Automatic writing—Johannes discourses on the future of spirit communication, the Northcliffe evidence, Oscar Wilde, the symbols of the Trinity, ethics and morals, energy and sloth, and attacks some of the critics of his philosophy as written in the book mentioned above.

I

December 22, 1924.

MRS. TRAVERS SMITH, one of the best known of the automatic writing mediums, is the daughter of the late Edward Dowden, Professor of English Literature, the author of a standard *Life of Shelley*, a psychical research student, and a Shakespearean scholar. She has had few psychical experiences beyond automatic writing or Ouija board writing.

As I have stated, in these sittings for automatic writing I never make the attempt to gain evidential information, my questions being, as a rule, of the philosophical order. The one evidential point, however, which maybe regarded as a confirmation that the communications of Johannes, who is in control of Mrs. Travers Smith, come directly through his spirit, is the fact that on several occasions during the sittings held with Valiantine in February, 1924, at Dorincourt, Johannes came through and spoke to me in his own voice, referring at length to the various philosophical discourses we had had together through the mediumship of Mrs. Travers Smith. It must be understood that Mrs. Travers Smith was not present at these Valiantine sittings, nor had any of the witnesses who listened to our conversations any knowledge of Johannes or of his discourses, since they were not then published.

II

The experiment of this date was arranged to enable Mr. Swaffer to observe the phenomenal rapidity with which the answers could be given to any philosophical question which might be put to Johannes.

The last time I sat with Mrs. Travers Smith was on January 7 of this year, which completed a series of sittings recorded in *Towards the Stars*. The same procedure was used between her and me as on previous occasions. Mrs. Travers Smith sat with the Ouija board, and I sat opposite her, with writing-pad and pencil, to record the replies as they came through her.

The sitting took place after dinner in the drawing room at Dorincourt, with full lights on.

In addition to Mrs. Travers Smith and myself, there were present, as observers, Mr. Swaffer, my wife and my son Anthony. The questions which were put to Johannes were entirely spontaneous, coming either from myself or from the other sitters. The replies came with such rapidity that it was only with difficulty that I could keep pace in recording them.

HDB: It is some considerable time since I last spoke to you, Johannes. This sitting has been arranged just in order to enable Mr. Hannen Swaffer to observe this particular form of communication.

JOHANNES: I know quite well why I am called here; I must say at once that I feel the task is going to be a difficult one for me tonight.

HDB: Why, where does the difficulty lie?

JOHANNES: I am not permitted to explain exactly, but there are other forces here so strong that part of my forces maybe kept back. I have been told by my child[73] that I must keep this influence from

---

[73] Johannes means Mrs. Travers Smith.

her, and I shall do it. You must excuse me if I cannot give you what you ask me.

(It maybe taken by this that Johannes meant that he did not wish to reply to any questions which might be put, by Mr. Swaffer regarding the spirit of Lord Northcliffe. Mrs. Travers Smith had previously said that for private reasons she did not wish to be involved in the Northcliffe controversy.)

MRS. TRAVERS SMITH: Can you tell us anything about the circle here tonight, Johannes?

HANNEN SWAFFER (interposing): On a previous occasion, Johannes, I have heard you speak in your own voice.

JOHANNES: That is quite true. I was able to do so in this house, and I found the conditions excellent. Regarding tonight, you add considerably to the strength of the circle; you have a curious mentality—it seems to me that you have a certain physical strength which helps the more powerful influence of the psychical force.

HDB: On a previous occasion have you heard Mr. Swaffer talking?[74]

JOHANNES: Yes!

HDB: Have you heard any of the criticisms which have been passed on the published record of your philosophy?[75]

JOHANNES: Yes! I have sometimes been anxious to have the opportunity of giving messages through in contradiction to some of my enemies who are anxious to expound their own theories. I should like to give those messages through tonight if you will allow me.

HDB: Are you referring to reincarnation?

JOHANNES: Yes!

HDB: I know, Johannes, that you do not believe in the reincarnation of the spirit in the physical body on this Earth plane. Am I to understand, by the use of the term "enemies," you mean those one or two literary critics on Earth who have attacked the statements which you have made; because these statements do not agree with the formation of their theories?

JOHANNES: I have frequently spoken to many on this subject. I am so anxious not to be misunderstood. I have not said that the soul would not be reincarnated. The whole of life is a continual evidence of the same spark flowing from the greater life behind, without any change

---

[74] Mr. Swaffer was present at a Valiantine sitting when Johannes spoke to me in the direct voice.

[75] Many of the literary critics of *Towards the Stars* referred to Johannes, and *The Occult Review* had several leading articles on Johannes's views of reincarnation.

of spirit. There will be a change of soul, but no change of spirit. The fundamental spark or spirit is ever the same. Thus the spirit reincarnates, but not in the physical body, only in the innermost soul, and we pass on to an existence which enfolds greater life.

HDB: Can you tell us anything of the occasions on which you spoke to me in your audible voice? And also how that form was accomplished?

JOHANNES: I remember having spoken to you then through a method which was new to me. As far as I am concerned, I found a part of the physical body which was adaptable for me to use, and through this I made an impress around the medium, and impressed, not through the breath, but through an actual physical throat. It became as if I had passed into a condition almost in accordance with yours. My words came through with a curious rhythm. This condition was one to which I was unused, and at times I was entirely ignorant as to whether I had succeeded in making the correct impression.

HDB: I was able to hear you quite distinctly; you made quite good impressions, and gave me confirmatory evidence.

JOHANNES: Now I find it easy to speak to you through my child. Even under other conditions it could not be attained without help. I find a harmony here tonight.

HDB: You know that throughout I have been in agreement with your philosophy.

JOHANNES: That you have been gradually filtering. There is so much to study before the time that all is pieced together and the full philosophy of the universe will be discovered. It is all founded on the teachings which can be read in the New Testament.

HDB.: What do you think will prove the most convincing form of spirit communication during the next year?

JOHANNES: I am interested in answering that question. Over here at present there is a feeling that something must be given to the world—a wider significance than the evidence which has been dropped in slowly for some time past. We have taken counsel as to what must be exhibited to convince. We believe that a certain number of cases must be put before you, giving tangible evidence—evidence actually to be handled and seen.

You may look forward to a number of cases, such as the Glastonbury one.[76] At times it maybe actually there before men's eyes, so that no one

---

[76] This refers to the Glastonbury script obtained through Mrs. Travers Smith and recorded in the books of Mr. Bligh-Bond.

can possibly dispute that we have sole inspiration from this side. These are the first steps, and a great deal will be done by some individuals. The cases which are being made public are increasing in number as we find persons who will consent to act over here. The net result will be that the subject will become an article of the educational faith of the people in every country in time. Education is what we are striving for at the present.

HANNEN SWAFFER (to Mrs. Travers Smith): Would you mind my asking a question regarding a lecture which I am to give at the Queen's Hall next month?

TRAVERS SMITH: Certainly, if you wish.

HANNEN SWAFFER: Can you tell me, Johannes, if it is within your knowledge, what is the value of the Northcliffe evidence to be brought forward at the Queen's Hall meeting?

JOHANNES: My opinion is founded on what we have spoken of only on my side. I feel as if this is going to be the centre of a series of rays which will extend from it as its inmost part. It is all-important that the evidence given to the world shall be of public interest. For that reason we have been discussing who should be called upon to continue what is already begun. The case in which my child was concerned was entirely a matter of chance. She acted for a while as the interpreter of one who was tied closely to the Earth.

HDB: Do you mean Oscar Wilde?

JOHANNES: Yes! In this instance the desire was there to speak, and the chance was offered to him. Wilde was given an opportunity, and allotted the task of making his literary gifts felt again as a piece of evidence. Now, this new evidence is of another character. It is chosen because the man in question has the requisite personality. Personality means force—the force which is necessary at this time. The news must now be pressed into the minds of the common herd. So many remain in willing ignorance of the life beyond; life which does not differ altogether from the life they are living on Earth.

This is what we are aiming at. We want a forcible personality. A character that is entirely indisputable in the evidence he affords so that no one can deny the proof of his continued existence.

(Here Johannes paused for a few minutes at my request, on account of my hand being tired with writing. I took a short rest in another room.)

HDB (returning): There is one question I would like to put to you, Johannes. Have you met or seen the God of the Universe? And, if you have, or if you have not, can you tell us your conception of Him?

JOHANNES: That, I think, I have answered before. I have not met the God of the Universe. You call him "God"—we call him "Life." The Life which is behind all of us who have not passed into the state which is pure spirit, but which is beyond the soul.

Life is threefold: Son, Father, Spirit. Of the ultimate state we cannot understand more clearly than you. We know that all life has sprung from this. It is an intelligence beyond all human comprehension. Commanding all so that nothing can be wasted—even imperfect creatures who are sent into the world and used, and then used again until, as perfect beings, they become threefold, as I have said. Behind all is the symbol of the Trinity, which explains creation. On your Earth plane there is the trinity of the father, mother and child, as in the later state of civilization there is the Son, Father, and the Spirit, which is over all, and permeates the world, after the body, which is the child, has vanished, and has been sacrificed.

HANNEN SWAFFER: If all worldly religions are merged into some form of Unitarianism, why is it that all spirits who speak at spiritualistic circles use terms which refer to Christ?

HDB: Please try and give a short and concise answer, Johannes, and endeavour not to dictate quite so fast.

JOHANNES: I shall try to give it easily. You are right as to our giving you the symbols which are peculiar to you. We give you your religion as we give you familiar clothes, but, in addition, there is another point that you have passed over. Your mind has been trained in one particular channel, that continues in the afterlife, because this development of the soul finds its familiar ideas and surroundings more congenial to its growth than if it were plunged into a fresh sea of ideas. The same religions and beliefs continue, and even the Christ was not a myth, but a living soul sent into the world as a purpose, which he fulfilled.

ANTHONY BRADLEY: What is the standard of ethics on your side? Does it coincide with our English morals?

JOHANNES: Not by any means, my dear man. Such a question seems to me to be very elementary. If you give me time, I shall take your code of morals, bit by bit, and explain. The rents are very wide. When you come over here you will find the values of your virtues changed in almost every instance. It is part of the change in the general condition here. Mental sight is considerably widened, and the far-reaching consequences of certain judgments are made plainer. You must understand that so-called virtues, especially points of honour, are not quite so immaculate as you imagine.

ANTHONY BRADLEY: Will you tell us the value of energy, as opposed to apathy and sloth?

JOHANNES: That is a most important point. Energy is life. If you misuse energy, you misuse life. Sloth is the most evil of all vices. Nothing is so degenerating as any failure to use the strength within. It is almost better to be energetically evil in life than to lie prostrate under the force that dominates you in any way.

I can assure you that the most severe punishment you attain is to be confined in a place where you are unable to use the most dominating force that is yours.

ANTHONY BRADLEY: Can you tell me whether I have any strength for mediumship?

JOHANNES: I will tell you. I find in you a sensitiveness, but no practise so far for the motor side. The psychic side is there. You have the sensitiveness of mind to obtain clear impressions and to convey them to your consciousness.

III

Mrs. Travers Smith contends that a certain contribution is made by me to the power during my sittings with her. My contention is that if that is the case, it is psychic and not consciously mental, for during these sittings I am so occupied in recording the replies to the various questions that I have no conception of their value or intelligence until I read my notes afterwards at leisure.

My mentality and thoughts have no influence whatever on the replies. It might be argued that, subconsciously, my mind might influence a reply to my own question, and that the philosophy expounded by Johannes at times appears to coincide with the philosophy I had hitherto arrived at. In the philosophical section of *Towards the Stars*, which contained the "Conversations with Johannes," the record of a long series of my sittings with Mrs. Travers Smith, it was suggested—with a certain logical amount of justification—by Mr. J. A. Spender, in a special article in the *Westminster Gazette*, that the communications of Johannes were coloured by my mentality. But there were recorded many replies to questions which were not mine, and questions and answers on subjects of which I had no knowledge.

No programme of questions was arranged for this particular sitting. I had one or two to ask for my personal knowledge, but, as a test, I asked

Mr. Swaffer and my son Anthony to keep on putting any question that occurred to them on the spur of the moment. The phenomenal point is that they were answered with such rapidity that my arm ached in recording Johannes's replies, and several times I was compelled to ask him to stop.

In all, the conversation and the replies amount to 2,323 words. Allowing for the one or two short pauses for rest, the time occupied was half an hour.

16

A DISCUSSION ON "VOICE" POWER

The Second Munnings Sitting[77]

Mr. Munnings' trumpet interests the investigator—Nevertheless the happenings of this sitting are recorded faithfully: how the spirit of George Herbert Lee Mallory came through, what the guide Emanuel said to Anthony, how Dr. Herbert Fullerton Ransome examined Mrs. Bradley and H.D.B. and the results of that examination.

I

December 31, 1924.

This sitting took place at Dorincourt. I was anxious to make further study of the mediumship of F. T. Munnings, and in addition I wished to see if it were possible to obtain any information regarding my own mediumship.

There were present, in addition to Munnings, Mrs. Bradley and myself, Anthony Bradley, Miss Queenie Baylis, and Alec Huntley—my chauffeur.

---

[77] See Appendix A for the third sitting and HDB's exposure of Munnings.

I had asked Huntley to sit in this circle, as a reference had been made to him at the previous sitting with Munnings. Huntley had become interested in spiritualism but had never sat at a séance.

In addition to Munnings' trumpet, which I have already described, my trumpet was also used.

A Battistini record was played on the gramophone, and after a second operatic record was put on my luminous trumpet was lifted and carried to the ceiling, which was hit several times.

After this a jazz record was put on, and syncopated time was tapped inside the trumpet in perfect time.

Emanuel—Munnings' guide—spoke to us. Munnings asked Emanuel whether it would be possible for him, at future sittings, to dispense with the trumpet altogether, and whether the spirit voices could manifest without its use. Emanuel replied that in all probability it would be possible for them to do so, but that it would be just as well to have the trumpet there in case the power was not sufficient for the spirits to materialize their voices sufficiently without using it. The trumpet aided them in amplifying the sound.

I asked Emanuel whether he could give us any information with regard to the personal mediumship of my wife and myself. Emanuel replied that he knew we were going to resume our private sittings quite shortly.

The guide, Angus Stern, came through and greeted us.

Emanuel said that there was a spirit there—not personally known to us—who wished to have the opportunity of practising in speaking and in materializing his voice. The spirit then came through, announcing itself as George Herbert Lee Mallory. He said he had spoken on one or two previous occasions, and he was hoping later that he would have the opportunity of speaking to his wife.

Mallory: I got to the top.[78] Irvine did not get so far. When I passed over, I felt the separation from my people. [*Here he mentioned Godalming.*]

It would be the joy of my life if I could get through to my wife, and to my own people. I want to report on things—family matters. Our bodies are still under the snow. I hope later to have the opportunity of coming through and recording my experiences. My passing over was painless, and I saw visions just before the end. People on this sphere have been very kind to me, but at first I was a little Earthbound. God bless you!

---

[78] Meaning Mount Everest.

A DISCUSSION ON "VOICE" POWER

Emanuel said that several of the spirits were scrambling for the trumpet in their endeavour to speak. He added: Emanuel: I may tell you that some of them are not above telling little fibs, but we guides see that anything that comes through to your plane is authentic.

H.D.B.: Will you tell me, Emanuel, why it is that you are willing to devote so much of your time in acting as a guide at these séances. Is this of any value to you with regard to your own personal progression?

Emanuel: Progression comes through the schooling given by other people. Guides are not tied to the apron strings of the medium. Munnings has been more trouble to us than most mediums.[79]

The guides acquire their position voluntarily, and it means progression for the spirits to take up work of their own will.

Answering a question put by Anthony, Emanuel said: "Any good deeds one performs will always over-balance the little mistakes of life. One day I will tell you all about my life on Earth."

H.D.B.: Were you a Cambridge man?

Emanuel: Yes, I was at Cambridge.

Anthony: What college were you at?

Emanuel: Clare. Where are you?

Anthony: I am at Trinity.

Emanuel: In my time they used to say, "Oxford for muscle and Cambridge for brains."

Anthony: Yes, but the saying may have been reversed now.

Emanuel (laughing): Surely not now that you are there!

The conversation between Anthony and Emanuel continued for some little time. Later, Emanuel inquired of me whether there was a man named Shepherd Scott connected with the house. I replied that there had been a man of that name. He had been my head gardener a year or so back.

During the time that Emanuel was talking, the luminous trumpet was moving about with peculiar sweeps. The sweeping movements were made in precisely the same manner as the movements made on occasions when the spirit voices have been talking to us at Dorincourt during our private sittings.

On account of this I asked Emanuel to give me the reason for the quick sweeping movement of the trumpet at intervals.

Emanuel: It is necessary to move the trumpet in this way to scoop up the power. I am an expert in picking up the ectoplasmic power to

---

[79] A peculiarly amusing remark.

use for the materialization of my voice. During a sitting, this power is hanging about the circle in different parts. I collect sufficient to enable me to speak; that is the reason why the trumpet is wafted from point to point.

You and Mrs. Bradley are giving power the whole of the time. I know you have both been shut off from holding your private voice séances, but, at the same time, we do collect from you a certain amount. This power circulates from left to right.

Emanuel asked if we would play a little music, as he wished to bring the spirit of a Dr. Ransome to examine Mrs. Bradley and myself with regard to our mediumship. A little later, the spirit voice of Dr. Ransome spoke to us. This voice was an extraordinarily individual one, and entirely different from any other voice which had spoken at any of our sittings. It spoke in quick but kindly accents. The voice reminded me very much of that of my friend, Dr. George Cathcart, the famous throat specialist.

Dr. Ransome asked us to be sure and get his name correct—Herbert Fullerton Ransome.

Dr. Ransome: It has occasionally been said that two people in one family—both being mediumistic—should not sit together. That is absolute nonsense. In this case it is right for you both to sit together whilst holdings your private sittings. In this form of mediumship there is a perfect understanding between you, Mr. Bradley, and your wife. I would advise, when sitting for the voice, that one does not sit without the other. If one is ill, it would be better not to sit at all. If you will give me a little time I should like to examine your throats. (To Mrs. Bradley) Just open your mouth, please.

On examination he said that Mrs. Bradley was perfectly fit. Right close to her mouth, about six inches away, there was emitted from the luminous trumpet a very strong blowing sound. A little later he examined me.

Dr. Ransome (to H.D.B.): The power of the mediumship is a joint production of both. In this respect there is almost an affinity between you. I would advise you, when you resume your sittings, not to sit more than once a week, and I think you might start in about two weeks' time. You need not worry about the power of mediumship—it is still there, and it is likely to become very strongly developed. In the future you will obtain something much more advanced in phenomena than anything you have obtained before.

You, Mr. Bradley, are quite healthy, but occasionally you have slight congestion of the liver.

A DISCUSSION ON "VOICE" POWER

You usually feel very drowsy after lunch, don't you?[80] It would be as well for you to drink a glass of warm water each morning and night.

You have no need to worry, I see longevity established there.

H.D.B.: Can you tell me whether my heart is quite all right?

(During the time 1 was conversing with Dr. Ransome the luminous trumpet was put very close to me, within perhaps less than a foot of my face.)

Dr. Ransome: Your heart is quite sound, but since you have stopped your sittings you have had some slight attacks of palpitation, but you need not worry about this. It is just caused by a little wind round the heart—I will remove this for you.[81]

H.D.B.: I have a very important reason, Dr. Ransome, for desiring to hold the first of my private sittings on Thursday of next week. Would this be advisable?

Dr. Ransome: Oh, yes. I think that will be quite all right, and in any case, I will make a point of being present on that day to observe if there is any undue strain.

Mr. Bradley: Would you be kind enough to examine my son, as he suffers from headaches periodically?

(The illuminated trumpet then went over to Anthony, and whilst the examination was being made Dr. Ransome carried on a light, characteristic, and humorous conversation with him.)

Dr. Ransome: You get your headaches right across the top of the forehead, don't you? It feels as if there is a big weight being pressed there, doesn't it?

Anthony: Yes, that is right.

Dr. Ransome: That is what makes you frown [laughingly). If we do not cure them you will have lines there before they should be, and it will make you look quite old {laughing). The cause of your headaches is that you make too much blood. There is an excess there. I do not mean

---

[80] For some time I have invariably felt drowsy and enervated after luncheon, although I only take quite a lightish meal. Strangely enough, I never feel tired after dinner, and often remain up working or pleasure seeking until two to three in the morning.

[81] The symptoms diagnosed by Dr. Ransome in regard to my heart were correct. 1 had not mentioned the fact of the attacks of palpitation to anyone, as I detest parading any indisposition before other people, but this had happened during the last two months or so on several occasions, and during the attack I felt completely breathless. Later on these attacks ceased and I have not experienced them since.

to say there is any clot of blood, but a certain blood pressure is there. This is affected by a certain formation of your spine.

After Dr. Ransome had gone, a spirit voice spoke, announcing itself to be Henry Withall. and addressed me. He stated that he had been connected with *Light*. He wished to tell me how interested he was in my mediumship, and he added that it was going to develop into a very extraordinary power.

A spirit endeavoured to speak to Huntley, but the voice was very indistinct, and no identity could be established.

Early in the evening I had asked Emanuel whether it would be possible for him to bring through the spirit of Cecil Husk, who was one of the famous mediums of the nineteenth century. Towards the close of this sitting Husk came through, announcing himself by name, and speaking to me.

The voice was entirely unlike that of any spirit who had spoken that evening.

H.D.B.: I have been told, Mr. Husk, by a friend of mine, Mr. Hannen Swaffer, who had a sitting quite outside this circle, that you desired to speak to me.

Cecil Husk: That is quite right. I sent a message that I wished to speak to you with regard to your mediumship. I am most interested in the mediumship of you and your wife. I wish to help you in every way that I can in your personal sittings, and I shall attach myself and act as one of your guides, in order that I may impress and advise you how to act, and in order to take care of you. Your mediumship will develop to a very powerful degree, and you will receive great help from this side. Later on, phenomena of a very exceptional character, and of a different nature to any that has previously taken place, are likely to occur.

H.D.B.: I hope that when we sit again neither my wife nor I will have to be put under trance conditions.

Cecil Husk: No! I shall see that this does not happen. It will not be necessary. You will develop in a natural way and will remain quite normal throughout. It is infinitely better to avoid a trance condition. If you remember, I suffered so much during my Earth life through going into a trance state during the séances held under my mediumship. I lost my sight through it.[82] I do not want anyone to suffer as I did. You will have the best guides that it is possible to obtain. On this side there is John King, who was my guide when I was on Earth. He will help you,

---

[82] Cecil Husk went blind.

A DISCUSSION ON "VOICE" POWER

and he is really the most powerful of all voice guides on this side; when he manifests and speaks you will find that his is the loudest and most powerful voice over here.

Mrs. Bradley: Is his voice louder than Kokum's?[83]

Cecil Husk: Yes! I think you will find it at times even louder than Kokum's.

The conversation on points of mediumship continued for some time, and among other things I asked whether the taking of alcohol in any way affected mediumship.

Cecil Husk: No, it does not matter at all in moderation. Go on precisely as you have been doing and take whatever you feel you require. Only, on the days you are sitting, do not smoke excessively, as sometimes this affects the vocal organs, from which we have to use part of the ectoplasmic forces.

Husk struck me as being an extremely sympathetic character.

After this a voice spoke through the trumpet in a very agitated, husky, and indistinct whisper. It addressed itself to Mrs. Bradley. The voice was so quick and excited that we could not decipher what it wanted to say. It called Mrs. Bradley "Mabel," but we could only understand that he had passed away just recently in Sydney—Australia—in an accident, and that he knew both my wife and me, and had been present at our wedding. The voice got so agitated that at the end it used a sort of shouting, incoherent whisper.

On several occasions two spirit voices were heard speaking at the same time; sometimes Emanuel would be speaking at the same time as another spirit, and on one occasion to another spirit, and these two voices were heard talking to each other in the centre of the room.

At the end of the sitting Emanuel came through and asked us if, before closing, we would sing something, and he would join in. We sang, and Emanuel's baritone voice was heard loud, musical and distinct, high up in the room. My wife and I took 'particular notice that the medium was singing at the same time.

---

[83] Here Mrs. Bradley refers to Kokum, one of the spirit guides of Valiantine, who possesses the loudest voice I have ever heard. It can be heard two hundred yards away.

II

My analysis of this sitting is that nothing occurred which could be recorded as being of a personal evidential nature. At the same time it was a most interesting sitting. I have given only a brief outline of the conversations which took place, as the sitting lasted for two and three-quarter hours.

The characters and the voices of Cecil Husk and Dr. Ransome were remarkably impressive in their individualities.

It seems to me that with Munnings one does not appear to be able to get any personal evidence. Why this is so I cannot say, except that perhaps his mediumistic powers and ectoplasmic forces are of such a character that the personal spirit friends find it difficult to manifest.

17

A NEGATIVE EXPERIMENT

The private sittings are resumed, and inasmuch as the séance recorded below proved negative, the author offers his observations on his illuminated trumpet, psychic power, musical instruments, as means to confound materialists.

I

January 8, 1925.

DURING the sitting with Mrs. Osborne Leonard on November 18, 1924, in the communications I received from the spirit of Warren Clarke I was told that we might resume our private sittings for "voice" conversations early in the New Year.

As Mr. Swaffer had agreed to lecture at the Queen's Hall on January 20, I invited him to be present on this occasion in case it were possible to get into communication with the spirit of Lord Northcliffe.

Three months had now passed since I had been requested by both Annie and Warren to cease holding these sittings. It was therefore peculiarly interesting to me to resume my experiments.

My mind was entirely open, and I told Mr. Swaffer that it was impossible for me to say whether anything would happen or not, as I fully realized that spirit communication in the direct voice could not be obtained to order. At the same time, I certainly felt that it was probable that we should receive some communication in the direct voice.

I followed the instructions given to me by the spirits implicitly, and there were only five sitters present Mr. Hannen Swaffer, Miss Madeleine Cohen, Mrs. Bradley, Anthony, and myself.

In accordance with the instructions given, I had the illuminated stripes running from the end of the trumpet altered to several spots of about half an inch in circumference and about one inch apart. The luminous band at the widest end of the trumpet was left as before. The lights were turned off, and various records were played upon the gramophone. For thirty-five minutes nothing whatever happened; after this, the illuminated trumpet was lifted a little way in the air for a short time, and was then replaced in the centre of the room. About ten minutes later, the trumpet was lifted, moved all round the circle, and then put back.

After we had been sitting for about an hour the trumpet was taken up, moved all round the circle, and each of us was touched, but we could get no voices at all—not even the faintest of whispers.

I then asked aloud the question: "If the power is weak will you please try and tap once on the trumpet." A very faint tap was made in the affirmative.

Feeling that the power was not very strong, and that it was unlikely we should obtain any personal phenomena, I asked aloud: "Do you consider it advisable for us to close this sitting? If so, will you please tap once?" A tap was given and after this the sitting was closed.

II

Throughout this sitting the atmosphere in the room appeared to me to be somewhat dead, and after the first twenty minutes or so I did not feel that any results would be obtained.

These notes are written immediately after the sitting, and I wish to record that I do not feel at all disturbed because at this first resumption of our private sittings no results of value were obtained.

I am in no way affected by this apparent failure; on the contrary I am quite confident that the mediumistic powers of my wife and myself are intact, and will gradually develop to a considerably higher degree than hitherto.

In this study of mediumism there is so much to be learned, and it will become part of the study of the future to ascertain exactly why it

A NEGATIVE EXPERIMENT

is that on certain occasions nothing happens, just as it is equally part of the study to learn why and how things do happen.

No musical instruments were placed within the circle. This form of phenomenon does not interest me, except for the reason that it has been found useful for confounding materialists.

18

A SUCCESSFUL RESUMPTION

Mr. John De Forest has a dramatic experience: Theodora giving him a message to "Napper"—The spirit of T. W. H. Crosland tries to speak and fails—The author is satisfied.

∼

I

January 12, 1925.

AFTER the failure of my first experiment on my resumption of personal mediumship, I had no intention of holding a further séance until a full week had elapsed. On this day, however, a friend of Anthony's, Mr. John De Forest, a younger son of Baron De Forest, was dining with us. Mr. De Forest had no knowledge of spiritualism, but having heard of certain of my experiences, introduced the subject and discussed it with avidity. After dinner he was extremely desirous that we should make an experiment. I was not at all anxious to go, but eventually, as my son was also keen, and as he was returning to Cambridge the next day, I agreed.

The circle therefore consisted of my wife and myself, Anthony, and Mr. John De Forest.

Anthony asked me if I would mind the jazz instruments being placed in the middle of the circle. I told him that he could do exactly as he pleased. The luminous trumpet was, as usual, also placed in the centre of the room. Lights were turned off and the gramophone turned on. Within five or six minutes after the second record had been played, the luminous trumpet was taken up, moved quickly all round the circle and taken up towards the ceiling. On a jazz record being played, the drum and cymbals were played in syncopated time. When Galli-Curci and Battistini records were played, the trumpet was lifted and the songs were conducted. I asked the question: "Was that Palastrina conducting?" and a very loud tap on the trumpet came in the affirmative.

After about twenty minutes the trumpet was lifted and a feminine voice spoke to Mr. De Forest in a somewhat excited manner.

MR. DE FOREST (apparently recognizing the voice) Are you Theodora speaking to me?

THE VOICE: Yes.

THE VOICE: Will you tell "Napper" about this?

As I had no knowledge as to the identity of "Theodora," or as to whom the name "Napper" referred, I said to Mr. De Forest: "Do you know who 'Napper' is?"

MR. DEFOREST: Yes, it is the name by which we call Dean Paul.

HDB: Did you notice that the "spirit" volunteered this name?

Immediately I made this remark the luminous trumpet switched away from Mr. De Forest and came straight over close to me, saying: "Yes, I did."

The trumpet then went back again to Mr. De Forest, and a further conversation was carried on between them.

Mr. De Forest informed me afterwards that Theodora was a young lady friend of his who had died a fortnight previously of typhoid fever. He was greatly impressed by the phenomenon, saying: "It is simply marvelous."

Annie spoke to Anthony, to my wife, and also to me. I asked her if it were quite all right for us to resume our sittings, and she replied that it was.

The power did not appear to be very strong, and the conversations could be maintained for only a very little time.

After a short interval, another spirit came through in an extremely agitated manner, speaking in a very hoarse whisper which it was most difficult to interpret. All we could get from him was "Crosland"—the name was repeated twice. I tried to encourage the voice, and to get some information, but it was quite impossible, and the luminous trumpet fell clattering to the ground.

I lifted it and then asked: "Was the last voice that spoke T. W. H. Crosland?" and a loud tap on the trumpet came in the affirmative. We sat for another ten minutes, but nothing occurred, whereon the sitting, which had lasted for about one hour, was closed.

II

Neither the power nor the strength of the voices seemed to be nearly as strong as on occasions of the last experiments in October. At the same time, I was quite satisfied with the results of this second experiment after the resumption, and the point of evidence given through by the volunteering of the name "Napper" was of distinct value.

19

AN IMPORTANT MATERIAL WARNING

The spirit of Gaston reminds Mrs. Gaston Sargeant of a social duty to her friends the Lowthers—Warren Clarke talks about his daughters—HDB's sledge-hammer tone of voice in print—Annie warns the author of financial deficiencies.

I

January 15, 1925.

THIS was my second sitting with Mrs. M. Scales. It was conducted in full daylight at three p.m., and took place at Mrs. Gaston Sargeant's flat in Chelsea. On this occasion I was accompanied by my wife, so there were present, in addition to the medium, my wife, myself, and Mrs. Sargeant. Mrs. Sargeant left the room after the first few minutes.

The medium went into a trance, and there was a pause of some three or four minutes before she spoke.

Mrs. Scales as I have mentioned in a previous chapter, is controlled by various spirits, and the communications are made through her mouth.

The first control which came through was that of Gaston Sargeant—the name of Mrs. Sargeant's husband—speaking in the first person.

A short, intimate conversation took place between Mrs. Sargeant and Gaston.

GASTON (to HDB): You have been suffering a little from nerves lately. I will endeavour to see that a battery is put upon you.

HDB: I do not really mind nerves. As a matter of fact, I usually work on them, but the study of this subject does rather take it out of one.

GASTON: Yes, once the study is taken up it lives with the individual. To the good lady (the medium placed her hand on Mrs. Bradley) I would say: Not too many sittings. It is not good for her to give out too much of herself.

(Turning to Mrs. Sargeant) The Lowthers go away to Africa tomorrow morning. You have not written to them. You should get on the phone to them at once.

Mrs. Sargeant informed me that she had forgotten to write to her friends, the Lowthers, and she then left the room and got on the telephone to them.

A little later Chloe, Mrs. Scales' control, spoke through the medium.

CHLOE: "The Massa"[84] says that you want electricity.

Chloe then went on to say that there was present the spirit of a man, of whom she gave a faint description. She said he was calling for Mabs. He wanted to remind my wife of a recent anniversary of his passing over.. She then mentioned 3 and 1 and December 3 and 1.[85]

Chloe then mentioned "W."

CHLOE (to Mrs. Bradley): Now he is whispering. He says: "I am privileged to walk into your bedroom without his (*HDB's*) permission." Now he is going like this—Here the medium held her chin high in the air and moved her head to and fro. She then stroked her chin in a peculiar manner. These two gestures were striking characteristics of Warren Clarke.

CHLOE: Annie is coming along with Georgie.

Chloe said that the man was saying something about the "voices," and that these had something to do with some big writings. He was showing two books.

The messages from Warren Clarke were given through by Chloe, who prefaced each reply by "He says." Therefore, to make the account clearer, I have assumed in the following communication that it was Warren who gave these messages, and I have recorded the replies under his name.

---

[84] The Massa" and "The Chief" are the terms by which Chloe refers to the late Mr. Gaston Sargeant.

[85] This—December 31—was the date upon which Warren Clarke died.

AN IMPORTANT MATERIAL WARNING

HDB: Can you suggest me a title for the new book?

WARREN: This time it should be "Beyond" instead of "Towards." (Here he mentioned a name.)

MRS BRADLEY: How do you think she is getting on?

WARREN: She is not going on; to my mind she is going off. It makes me feel like going to church and saying: "Lighten our darkness, we beseech thee, oh Lord." (Suddenly the name "Betty"[86] was volunteered.)

HDB: Have you any advice to give about Betty?

WARREN: I would not presume to know better than you on this matter, but Betty's chest should be kept warm. I did not like the cough I had on Earth myself. It was a damned nuisance.

HDB: Well, you've got rid of that now.

WARREN: Yes, but we cannot patent the elixir. (The name "Phyllis"[87] then came through.) Of course she matters, but not so much as Betty.

(To HDB): You must not be coerced to deviate from the sledge-hammer tone of voice in print. You must give it to them straight from the left.

HDB: Am I getting too mild?

WARREN: Don't pander to certain types.

HDB: Some say I am too outspoken.

WARREN: On your plane they are very much asleep. We do not mind that so much if when they wake up they will be sensible.

(The conversation went on for a little time in a humorous manner.)

I wanted to cheer you up. What damnable atmospheric conditions you have been nursing. It is not exactly like Italy.[88]

HDB: Will the voices develop?

WARREN: Rather!

HDB: Warren, would you be able to control the medium and speak direct through her?

WARREN: Perhaps I will next time, but I do not wish to try it today.

HDB: How do you think things will progress next February when Valiantine comes over?

WARREN: I shall be staging big things then.

HDB: Have you found out anything about my guides?

WARREN: When you are holding your voice sittings they will be all walking round the room. They are there to create power.

---

[86] This is the name of Mr. Warren Clarke's younger daughter.

[87] The name of Mr. Warren Clarke's second daughter.

[88] Warren was with me in Italy in 1922.

When Valiantine comes, I would advise you to use the musical instruments. I think you will be able to startle everybody with the results.[89]

After this communication Chloe, through the medium, said that there were a lady and a young boy there, and, if we would wait a little time, the lady would control the medium and speak to us. After a pause of three minutes a phenomenon took place similar to that described in Chapter 11. The medium's face was gradually transfigured, and the voice which addressed us through the medium was precisely identical with the voice of Annie. The articulation at first appeared to be difficult, but the tones later were exactly the same as those used by my sister when on Earth.

A delicate conversation was carried on between Annie, my wife, and myself, which continued for some twenty minutes. Matters were discussed which were of a private and personal nature. Annie volunteered several names, and gave evidence of her surviving personality. Among other things she referred to certain financial affairs of mine, and displayed an absolute knowledge of them. It was here that I got my second warning on a matter of exceptional material importance. To my unutterable surprise I discovered serious embezzlements of my money in February of 1925—a month after this sitting and three months after the first warning.

The conversation which took place was precisely as if she were in the body on Earth, not only in everything that she said, but in every inflection of the voice to the peculiar soft manner in which she laughed. It was a slight, little, trilling laugh, during which the medium turned her head slightly on one side—a peculiar characteristic of Annie's when on Earth. My wife, who had not previously experienced this extraordinary form of phenomenon, was deeply impressed, and said that she regarded it as remarkable.

II

I have no hesitation in saying, after my two experiences with Mrs. Scales, that she is, in her own particular form of mediumship, exceptional.

---

[89] They were used on two occasions during Valiantine's visit. The results are recorded in later chapters.

AN IMPORTANT MATERIAL WARNING

It is quite conceivable that her powers may vary at times, but the personal evidence which I received from Annie was incontestable. Names were mentioned, and certain information was volunteered which my wife and I alone knew, and to each of us certain true things which the other did not know. Apart from its intimacy, it would be of no purpose for me to publish the details, because throughout *Towards the Stars* and throughout this book her identity is established beyond question.

During our conversation I asked Annie why it was that neither she nor Warren came through to speak to us at sittings with Munnings, and she replied that it was on account of some of the conditions through which they did not care to penetrate.

20

A WONDERFUL EVIDENTIAL SITTING

Lord Northcliffe gives certain evidence of the survival of his spirit—This chapter is the record of a most amazing sitting; the author regrets the expurgations relating to matters of a private nature—an attempt at materialization—Northcliffe's twenty-one statements, many of which are confirmed by Miss Louise Owen in the neat chapter.

I

11 a.m. Sunday, January 18, 1925.

This was the Sunday prior to Tuesday, January 20, the date on which Mr. Hannen Swaffer had undertaken to lecture at the Queen's Hall on Spiritualism, under the title of: "Is Lord Northcliffe Dead?"

For three months Mr. Swaffer had pursued his investigations, with many of which I was associated. The meeting was to take place under the chairmanship of Sir Edward Marshall Hall, and, in addition to Mr. Swaffer, the speakers were to be Sir Arthur Conan Doyle, the Rev. Vale Owen, Miss Louise Owen (no relation to the Rev. Vale Owen), and myself.

There had been a tremendous demand for seats, and although the Queen's Hall holds 2500 people, every seat had been booked a fortnight before the lecture was to take place.

Just prior to this, Mrs. Osborne Leonard had been ordered to take a rest, and was recuperating at Whitstable. At my request and because of the importance of this meeting, she traveled to town, and a sitting, under her mediumship, was held at Dorincourt on this Sunday morning.

There were present only Mrs. Osborne Leonard, Mr. Hannen Swaffer, and myself.

Mrs. Leonard was about four minutes going off into a trance. During the last minute an undistinguishable whispering was continuing through her lips until she became coherent. Then Feda took control.

The first few communications through Feda came in the second person, but after a short time the communications changed to the first person from the communicant.

The following is a record, with the exception of a certain number of necessary expurgations which relate principally to matters of a private and personal nature.

FEDA: Good morning: I am so glad to be here. The Chief has come, and he says that he is glad to be able to speak without so many intruders.[90] He says he sends his thanks to you, Swaff, and to you (HDB). The Chief is patting you on the back, Swaff.

NORTHCLIFFE: Keep up your spirits, Swaff, we shall pull you through. Will you please keep a little quiet before the meeting. Don't go off into what is called "the deep" beforehand. If you will leave yourself quiet, I shall be able to control you and help you at the meeting. I have been through to you many times since I last spoke to you through Feda. You have been thinking of me too much lately. You have been concentrating on me, both consciously and subconsciously, and this concentration has often kept me mentally in the background. At several of the sittings you have shown too much anxiety for me to come through.[91]

I have a strong feeling that I shall be able to come through to you mentally more easily later on, especially when this meeting is over.

---

[90] This maybe taken as referring to other séances at which Northcliffe has communicated when several others have been present.

[91] I have been told on several occasions that when a sitter concentrates too much on one spirit it makes it more difficult for this particular spirit to volunteer their statements. This is a point for sitters to learn.

This is a time of nervous strain for you, and even for me. We have a nervous system over here just as you have. This is not open to the same conditions as you, but we feel the same anxiety to succeed in our ambitions as you do.

I did try to show myself to you, Swaff.[92] With more practice I think I can show myself more easily to you, but I have not yet done so.

(Here a few personal references of no moment were made.)

Lately you have been feeling a little depressed, I have been trying to lift that depression. Have felt better?

SWAFFER: Yes.

NORTHCLIFFE: You know the one I called "Mac". Will you give Mac's love to Louise? He is very pleased with what she tried to do recently. Tell her not to worry because one part of the plan had to fall through, There was something she could not carry out about the child. She did more than I had ever expected she would. Mac has been very worried about one of his children, but not so much at the moment. I would like to help poor old Mac occasionally. Materially things are not so right as they should have been.[93]

Especially this morning I am trying to give you things you do not know. I tried to walk on one foot and could not. I started to go out, and had to come back. It was an actual pain, and I got in a temper about it. I think you will find that Louise had reason to remember this because I tore up something—a paper. On this occasion it was rather an important paper. Afterwards I wanted to find out certain details, and put the pieces together again. Louise has usually an excellent memory, but at times it is rather erratic. She supplied me with the details and enabled me to patch up this matter. You might say to her that the delay in finding the paper caused a rift in the lute. My lute must have had a great number of strings to it. A few of them survived. "Lute" is a kind of clue to it. I think this will be found to be essential. I am trying to give you evidence, and that is why I am boring you with these details.[94]

WARREN CLARKE (interposing): That was what I was always hammering at.

(Feda said that the Chief did not like being interrupted and just looked at Warren.)

---

[92] This refers to an attempt at materialization at a sitting which Swaffer attended, but the attempt was not successful.

[93] See question No 1 put to Miss Owen in Chapter 21.

[94] See questions No 2, 3, 4, and 5 put to Miss Owen in Chapter 21.

FEDA: He has got a look sometimes. ... His eyes are not wide; he just looks quietly.

NORTHCLIFFE: Who called it a three-volume look? Ask Louise.

SWAFFER: Yes, Chief, you had a novel way of looking at people.

NORTHCLIFFE: Yes, not exactly what you would call a £10 look, but a three-volume look.[95]

Will you tell Louise I have been helping her on several occasions? I think she knows. I stroked her hair. I am helping her with material plans, to carry them through to a successful issue. I know that things have been difficult for her in the past, but she will be better now. She had a hard struggle at one time. Now she, you, and I are working to make the common lot easier.[96]

Will you ask Louise about my disappearing? I used to tell her tales of how I disappeared and eluded people in a very funny way. I mean that I had a very novel way of eluding people. She remembers. She and I often chuckled over it.[97]

FEDA: Sometimes he laughs without laughing. He makes a funny noise and pats his head.

NORTHCLIFFE: Many people look at evidence from a different point of view.

I saw Louise sewing ribbons on a garment. She was putting the ribbon on the wrong edge. She will laugh when you tell her of this.

She was rather cross with the ribbon straps.[98]

I am bringing along a band of spirits on Tuesday, because I think there will be an element there which will try—not to break up the meeting—but to disturb it in some way. We shall use our power to keep them quiet and suppress them. There is so much willful misunderstanding and we are not going to have it. Don't worry, Swaff, if there is an antagonistic feeling. We shall try and keep the conditions clear, right, and harmonious.

We want to create and keep the right atmosphere. (Feda said that Northcliffe was putting a book in front of Swaffer.)

We shall do a lot for the book after the meeting. I have a good deal of material to impress you with.

(Here Feda said: "Now he has two books," and asked: "Are there two books?")

---

[95] See questions Nos. 6 and 7 put to Miss Owen in Chapter 21.
[96] See question No. 8 put to Miss Owen in Chapter 21.
[97] See question No. 9 put to Miss Owen in Chapter 21.
[98] See question No. 10 put to Miss Owen in Chapter 21.

A WONDERFUL EVIDENTIAL SITTING

One is for Swaff.

HDB: Whom do you think should publish it?

NORTHCLIFFE: Independent people. (Feda said Northcliffe was coming over to me.)

HDB: What does he mean? Is it anything to do with my publisher?

NORTHCLIFFE: Yes, that is my reason for mentioning it. You had a letter from him a little while ago[99] You will get another letter later on; wait for it.

(To Swaffer) I want a strong publisher. Someone who will have faith in it and the courage to stand by it.

(Warren again interposed and a short argument took place between Warren and Northcliffe on publishing, in which Feda joined in. Northcliffe appeared to be a little impatient at the interruption.)

WARREN: Just one word, please—this is my room, and I have the right to speak when I wish. . This is where I work.

NORTHCLIFFE (to Swaffer): You know that you will have to give other lectures.

SWAFFER: I think we could have filled the Albert Hall for this meeting.

NORTHCLIFFE: Yes, I have already told you that the Albert Hall could have been taken. Later on it will.

SWAFFER: Do you think we could fill it?

NORTHCLIFFE: Oh, yes, I think so if the conditions were right, and if there were no fog.

WARREN (again interposing): I will clear the fog if there is any.

(Feda said Northcliffe was not at all impressed by this remark of Warren's.)

NORTHCLIFFE (to Warren): I do not think powers could be used to affect such conditions.

WARREN: Oh, yes, they could, I know more of such powers than you do.

NORTHCLIFFE (changing the subject): We are all in this subject up to the neck. It is the biggest thing, Swaffer, that you have yet touched. When we get our own papers we should be able to give it to them properly.

---

[99] I cannot place this. I had received two letters from two firms of publishers making me offers for my next book (i.e., this one) and also a letter from my own publisher—Mr. Werner Laurie—asking me when my next work would be completed.

You have got to be independent.

HDB: It is all very well to talk about papers, but what about the financial side?

NORTHCLIFFE: That will come; it will be arranged.

WARREN (again interposing—to HDB):Mable is always quaking in her shoes about your psychic studies. She thinks that this may affect your material interests, but don't worry, Herbert, we shall look after that.[100]

NORTHCLIFFE: It is necessary to look after the material interests as well. You must not neglect them, Swaff. You must attend to your own work or I cannot help you as I wish.

SWAFFER (suddenly): Can you tell me, Chief, where Louise is now?

NORTHCLIFFE: How do I know whilst I am here… Wait a minute. (A pause of about thirty seconds.) She is not far away, and I am getting her thoughts very strongly.

FEDA (interposing): Is she going between two places this morning?

NORTHCLIFFE: At this moment—will you please take the exact time[101]—Louise appears to be sitting still in the midst of movement. Perhaps it is a temporary stop. She appears to be close to a window or glass.[102]

She has forgotten something.[103]

She was wanting to wire—to send a telegram to someone.[104]

She has altered the plans of her journey. This journey was not just as she thought of arranging it at first.[105]

I am a little puzzled how to get this through.

Has she heard recently of an accident?[106] You see, I have to get her thoughts like a wireless. I have to tune my mind into the condition of the necessary apparatus. It is difficult for me to act as transmitter and receiver at the same time. I am seeing a place—in the wave sense, if you understand—a place which is rocky or stony. There are very high cliffs on the one side and lower cliffs on the other. I see a gulf—enormous depth—and on the right side an even deeper gulf. There is a huge boulder.

---

[100] They unquestionably were looking after my material interests as will be shown in Chapter 26.
[101] The time was 11.42 a.m.
[102] See question No. 11 put to Miss Owen in Chapter 21.
[103] See question No. 12 put to Miss Owen in Chapter 21.
[104] See question No. 13 put to Miss Owen in Chapter 21.
[105] See question No. 14 put to Miss Owen in Chapter 21.
[106] See question No. 15 put to Miss Owen in Chapter 21.

A WONDERFUL EVIDENTIAL SITTING

(Here the independent voice of Northcliffe came through, speaking the last sentence clearly and distinctly. The voice was about a foot from Mrs. Leonard's head.)

This boulder seems to be balanced in rather a precarious position. I keep on getting through the thought of an accident. The thoughts of you people on the Earth plane are passed on to us by our thinking of them. We reconstruct their thoughts.

The accident I get through Louise's mind might be in the immediate present or in the past. We have as much to learn about this thought transference as you. You have not yet given us the opportunities to develop this. We and you should both co-operate.

If this accident is in the past it is very, very recent.[107]

FEDA: He (the Chief) has got a habit of repeating words. He is saying: "I am sure of it; I am sure of it."

NORTHCLIFFE: Have I mentioned that before I passed over—I had a peculiar pain on one side of my face? I think the effect of it was visible. It was on the right side—like a contraction. One or two people knew of this.[108]

Here the telephone bell in my study rang continually in an annoying manner for a minute or two. I had no intention of answering it. Then the communications went on whilst the bell was ringing.)

NORTHCLIFFE: The telephone used to annoy me considerably. Do you remember, Swaff, the silent one I had?

SWAFFER: No, I don't remember.

NORTHCLIFFE: There were three telephones. Two of them were fairly close, and another one just outside. I often used to blame Louise when she went to answer it for not shutting the door.[109]

Another thing I want to mention, which you might know about. Some little yellow flowers—primroses. Will you ask Louise about them, and ask her about the double supply which someone sent to me? I appreciated them more than she knew at the time.[110]

Will you ask her also whether she remembers the fuss I made when I had the place upholstered?[111]

(The telephone, not having ceased, I moved across the room and took the receiver off.)

---

[107] See question No. 16 put to Miss Owen in Chapter 21.
[108] See question No. 17 put to Miss Owen in Chapter 21.
[109] See question No. 18 put to Miss Owen in Chapter 21.
[110] See question No. 19 put to Miss Owen in Chapter 21.
[111] See question No. 20 put to Miss Owen in Chapter 21.

NORTHCLIFFE (referring to me): I felt him pass me like a breeze.

WARREN CLARKE (interposing): Yes, Herbert is much more like a breeze than a draught.

FEDA: The Chief is taking something in his hand—a long thing—he is writing with it. Something with a sort of tube at the end of it.

NORTHCLIFFE (to Swaffer): Do you remember that, Swaff?[112]

SWAFFER: Um——

NORTHCLIFFE: It's no good saying "Um." Say you know, or you don't know. You have seen it—you have got to find out, all these little things are important. You should remember.

FEDA: The Chief is saying something about his brother dropping something. This is only for your own edification. He is dropping some enterprise. The last thing you would have thought he would have parted with.

NORTHCLIFFE: You will be surprised about this, Swaff—astonished. He is already moving about it secretly.

Bradley, don't let Swaff forget about this.

HDB: You know, Northcliffe, that I am engaged in writing a new book on this subject? And in it I shall have to deal with this conversation with you.

NORTHCLIFFE: Yes, quite right. That will not affect the other book. You will find that one book will dovetail with the other.

(To Swaffer) Were you disappointed at a sitting just recently?

FEDA: The Chief says: "Do you remember a lady at one sitting coming through to you? She was very anxious to come through."

SWAFFER: Give her my love, Chief.

NORTHCLIFFE: You are to hold on to——. You remember I teased you about it once—at a sitting.[113]——comes into our plans in a sense—don't be too impatient. You know you are very irritable.

SWAFFER: I can't help being irritable on the telephone.

WARREN (to Northcliffe): You would have been more irritated. If a woman had telephoned you, and you had not answered it, she would have wriggled through the other end.

(Feda said that Northcliffe did not like the interruption, and said that he took no more notice of Warren than of a fly.)

NORTHCLIFFE: Never mind what Warren says. ——will be useful. I had one in my life. It just reminds me of my particular one. I don't mean Louise; Warren was thinking that I was.

---

[112] See question No. 21 put to Miss Owen in Chapter 21.

[113] Apparently referring to a sitting which Mr. Swaffer attended.

A WONDERFUL EVIDENTIAL SITTING

FEDA: Warren has no right to think.

NORTHCLIFFE: (to Swaffer) I can't get into your extraordinary mind, Poet.

SWAFFER: You said that reminded you of someone in your life. Do you mean——?

NORTHCLIFFE: Yes. Do you remember her lace cap? On Earth she certainly did worry me.

SWAFFER: Yes, I suppose I should have chased you if I had been a woman.

NORTHCLIFFE: I am thankful for small mercies. I think you would have been particularly obnoxious as a woman. I suppose there was something that reminded you of——.

SWAFFER: Yes!

NORTHCLIFFE: She has done some writings lately. She has some felonious intention of publishing them. I do not think they are very good. Do you remember the place with the large pool—a long made pond with a rim round. Louise will know.

(Here followed a lengthy discussion on journalism, during which time Northcliffe volunteered the statement that Swaffer would shortly be writing for the *Sunday Express*.[114] Immediately after this conversation, Feda said that Northcliffe had stepped back.)

WARREN: Herbert, will you give Mabel my love, and also Mabel's mother?

HDB: Yes, I will. Can you tell me, Warren, how you think the home "direct voice" séances are developing?

WARREN: They are going on quite well.

HDB: We are holding a séance tonight. Will you help Northcliffe to come through in order that he may speak to us in his own materialized voice?

WARREN: Yes, Annie and I will do our best to help.

FEDA: I shall come through and speak, too. (To HDB) I hear you say "Good morning" to me. You say it when you are walking along the road; when you have got outside the gate. I always hear you.

(This was a spontaneously volunteered statement by Feda, and a true one. When I am walking along the Portsmouth Road each morning, after I am, outside the gate of Dorincourt, I say "Good morning" to my sister and Warren Clarke, and to Feda, as I would do if I met them in the flesh. I have never mentioned this fact to anyone, but I have had

---

[114] His proved afterwards to be a correct prognostication.

the corroboration of this volunteered by Warren and by Annie, and now I have had the volunteered corroboration from Feda.

SWAFFER: Did you hear me drinking—our health last night, Warren?[115]

WARREN: Yes, I did.

SWAFFER: I drank your health in coffee. You did not give me a tap in reply.

WARREN (humorously): We do not tap for coffee.

HDB: I would like to ask Northcliffe one question. Did you come through when we had a sitting with Munnings?

NORTHCLIFFE: Yes, I did.

HDB: Warren, I want to ask you a specific question. I know that with direct voice mediumship there are always experienced guides appointed on your side. Can you give me the name of them?

WARREN: Yes, one of the guides is John King.

Have you met Husk and Dr. Ransome?

WARREN: Yes, I have met Husk.

HDB: Have you met Emanuel?

WARREN: I do not know Emanuel very well.

Here the power was getting very weak, and, with the usual greetings, the sitting ended at twelve thirty-five p.m.

The examination of Louise Owen on the twenty-one volunteered statements by the spirit of Lord Northcliffe—all of which were completely outside the knowledge of Mr. Swaffer, Mrs. Osborne Leonard or myself—will be found in the next chapter.

---

[115] Often when I am alone I drink a toast to Warren. I speak my toast aloud, and an answering tap frequently comes in reply. This is not imagination, for the taps come from any part of the room on request.

21

ESTABLISHMENT BY EXAMINATION

An astounding evidential interview, in the course of which Miss Louise Owen is examined as to Lord Northcliffe's twenty-one statements.

~

8.30 pm Sunday, January 18, 1925.

DURING the remarkable sitting which took place at Dorincourt in the morning, the conversation never ceased for over an hour and a half, and the individual surviving personalities of Lord Northcliffe and Warren Clarke were apparent in every characteristic, mannerism and expression. To me the force, determination, and impatience of Northcliffe were apparent throughout, and the light humour and knowledge of Warren Clarke were equally significant of his personality.

I took notes throughout, and, afterwards, in analysing the context, I found that Northcliffe had volunteered twenty-one specific statements on matters which were completely beyond the knowledge of Mrs. Osborne Leonard, of Mr. Hannen Swaffer, or of myself.

It was palpable to me that Northcliffe, in volunteering these statements, had a purpose of import in view. He was making an effort not only to establish his own identity, but to give us information on matters to which no theory of human telepathy could apply.

THE WISDOM OF THE GODS

The majority of the statements were made in reference to Miss Louise Owen, and I can vouch that none of the three sitters know where Miss Owen was on the morning in question, or what she was doing.

Working with Mr. Swaffer during the afternoon on the verbatim notes of the script, I framed twenty-one questions to be put to Miss Owen in such a way that they could not convey to her mind a correct and intelligent reply, unless they were matters within her knowledge.

Mr. Swaffer suggested to me that if we found she was in town, he and I should lunch with her on the nest day—Monday—and put these questions to her.

At about six-thirty we rang up her flat in Buckingham Gate to ascertain if she was in London. At the moment we rang up we found that she had just arrived in town. We then asked her if she could motor straight out, and after a slight demur she agreed to do so.

She arrived just after dinner had been served and was ushered into the dining-room. The conversation during dinner was general, and no clue was given nor was any mention whatever made as to what had transpired in the morning.

After dinner Mr. Swaffer and I asked Miss Owen to remain with us in the dining-room, and the questions were put to her in the following order. I explained to her that I had a reason for putting a series of questions to her in what must appear to be a somewhat abrupt manner. The replies made by Miss Owen are recorded as follows:

QUESTION No. 1: Have you done anything recently about Mac's children?

LOUISE OWEN: Yes. I took one boy with me to Switzerland for a month and brought him back to Paris with me. He has had a little lung trouble, and I thought a holiday in Switzerland would do him good. I am going back there in a fortnight's time. If possible, and his mother would agree, I would like him to spend six months in the mountains. His holiday did him a lot of good—he did not look the same on his return. I wanted him to stay longer, but he would not stay alone.

This is a confirmatory and evidential reply to the eight-word sentence question put to Miss Owen. She mentioned Mac's full Christian name. Mac passed over some time back, and she has been making an effort to help one of his children.

QUESTION No. 2: Do you know of any trouble Northcliffe had on Earth with his feet?

LOUISE OWEN: No, I cannot quite remember anything in particular. He may have had corns.

ESTABLISHMENT BY EXAMINATION

Evidently Northcliffe thought she might remember a certain trouble he had had at one time.

QUESTION No. 3: Do you remember any trouble over Northcliffe tearing up some papers angrily?

LOUISE OWEN: I cannot say anything in particular. He was often angry, and he often tore up papers, but it does not convey any particular incident to my mind.

QUESTION No. 4: Did you ever refresh his memory on any of the details concerning the tearing up of any papers.

LOUISE OWEN: Yes, I did do this. There was a certain instance of the tearing up of letters in reference to——. I could not place any particularly important incident, but these occurrences often happened. I remember another incident over a letter with "K.J."[116]

QUESTION No. 5: Can you connect any incidents with a "rift in the lute?"[117]

LOUISE OWEN: No, that conveys nothing to me. I remember quarrelling with Northcliffe over the papers mentioned. —— wrote to Northcliffe abusing me, and I have the letter in my possession now, but it is too private to publish, as —— passed over in 1923.

QUESTION No. 6: Northcliffe had a peculiar way of looking at people. He states to us that this particular look was not referred to as a "ten-pound look." Have you ever heard it referred to by a similar phrase?

LOUISE OWEN: No, I cannot remember that.

QUESTION No. 7: Was this look ever referred to as a "three-volume look?"

LOUISE OWEN: It may have been, but I cannot say that I remember that particular expression.

QUESTION No. 8: Have you thought at any time recently that Northcliffe has touched you?

LOUISE OWEN: Yes, several times.

HDB: Have you ever thought that he has touched you on the hair?

LOUISE OWEN: No, I cannot say that, but I have often felt that he has touched me.

QUESTION No. 9: Do you remember Northcliffe ever mentioning anything about disappearing?

LOUISE OWEN, (quickly): Why yes, of course. He would often do this. Sometimes he misled people. When on the Riviera he would

---

[116] Kennedy Jones
[117] Northcliffe humorously emphasized "lute" and not "loot".

sometimes endeavour to pretend to be someone else. On occasions he would wire me: "Where am I?" Afterwards we used to laugh about this.

When one refers to the verbatim communication front Northcliffe with regard to his disappearing, it will be seen that he said he used to tell her tales of how he disappeared and eluded people in a very funny way.

Miss Owen volunteered the statement that she and he used to laugh over it, and on the verbatim notes it will be seen that the communicating spirit of Northcliffe says: "She remembers how she and I chuckled over it."

QUESTION No. 10: Have you been doing any sewing lately:

LOUISE OWEN: Yes, quite lately, I do quite a lot of my own needlework.

HDB: Can you remember quite recently any particular garment you were sewing?

LOUISE OWEN: Yes, in Switzerland I was doing some needlework on my court dress—the one I wore when one of my adopted daughters was presented last year.

HDB: Were there any ribbons on the garment?

LOUISE OWEN (quickly and spontaneously): Yes There were. I sewed the ribbons on the wrong way. I put the ribbon binding on the wrong side of the edge of the lace where the train was cut off the Court dress, and had to unpick it all.

HDB: Were there any ribbon straps?

LOUISE OWEN: Yes! I got rather cross with the ribbon straps. I got them too tight.

QUESTION No. 11: Where were you at eleven forty-two a.m. this morning (Sunday, January 18)?

LOUISE OWEN: I think about that time I was going into the restaurant car. I traveled from Paris on the ten o'clock train to Calais.

HDB: Was the train moving or at a standstill?

LOUISE OWEN: I am not quite sure; I think it stopped somewhere about that time near Abbeville. I remember mentioning to Barbara, who was with me, things about Abbeville and the war.

QUESTION No. 12: Did you forget anything?

LOUISE OWEN: Yes! I forgot to bring with me a bottle of scent which I required.

QUESTION No. 13. Were you intending to send a telegram?

LOUISE OWEN: I had intended to send a telegram, but then I thought that I would not send a telegram to Mary—my adopted daughter—whom I had left in Paris with a French family, as I feared, not knowing them very well, it might disturb them on a Sunday.

ESTABLISHMENT BY EXAMINATION

QUESTION No. 14: Did you alter your proposed plans for this journey?

LOUISE OWEN: Yes, I did alter my plans. I had intended to catch the twelve o'clock train from Paris, but found it was impossible to reserve a cabin, so I was obliged to travel by the ten o'clock train instead, knowing the boat would not be so crowded.

QUESTION No. 15: About this time—eleven forty-two a.m.—did you hear of, or were you thinking of some accident?

LOUISE OWEN: Yes, I was thinking of an accident. You see, we were going through a fog, and I thought of some of the French railway accidents, and also of the possibility of an accident in crossing the Channel. I said to Barbara, who was with me: "How dreadful if there were an accident—I hate fog."

QUESTION No. 16: Was your mind at that time on any particular form of accident? If so, did you in any way visualize the way or the place in which such an accident might occur?

LOUISE OWEN (after a few seconds pause): Wait a minute—that's rather funny. I had the Continental *Daily Mail* with me, and I was looking at a picture published on the back page of the *Daily Mail* of a skier aged three years. This photograph I had sent to them from Switzerland.

HDB: Can you describe the scene of the picture?

LOUISE OWEN: The picture was taken in the Alps. I have got a copy, and I will send it on to you. It showed a great ravine. We had been discussing several times the accident mentioned, and then looking at the child's picture. I thought of the father—a well-known guide for the Jungfrau—and I thought what a terrible thing for the child if the father ever lost his life, and I pictured the Jungfrau facing Wengen, where we had been for a month. In front is a huge ravine.

QUESTION No. 17: Do you remember any peculiar pain Northcliffe had in his face?

LOUISE OWEN: Not any peculiar pain, but he sometimes had trouble with his teeth.

(Here Miss Owen involuntarily put her hand up to the right side of her face.[118])

QUESTION No. 18: Do you know anything about a silent telephone of Northcliffe's?

---

[118] When Northcliffe's communication came through with regard to this pain, he referred to the right side of his face. This point, though confirmatory, has no essential value.

LOUISE OWEN (quickly): Yes, of course! He had a silent telephone; one which made no noise. A telephone one could whisper into. He used to call it his "silent telephone". He used to say: "Don't shout, I'm using my silent telephone."

HDB: How many telephones had he?

LOUISE OWEN: He had his own private telephone and the ordinary Exchange, also a private one direct to his office.

HDB: Was there any telephone outside his room which you used?

LOUISE OWEN: Yes!

HDB: Did you occasionally use this whilst he was there without shutting the door? And did this create a disturbance?

LOUISE OWEN: Yes, he often blamed me for not shutting the door. He said my chatting annoyed him.

QUESTION No. 19: Do you remember anything in connection with Northcliffe with regard to primroses?

LOUISE OWEN: Yes, I was only thinking of that yesterday. N.N.[119] used to send them to him.

HDB: Do you remember anything about a double supply.

LOUISE OWEN: I remember a box of primroses being given to him and I remember them being passed onto someone else. We laughed about it at the time.

QUESTION No. 20: Do you know anything of any communication with Northcliffe regarding upholstery?

LOUISE OWEN: No, not in particular, but so many things were at times upholstered. I could not place any particular incident in connection with this.

QUESTION No. 21: Do you remember a long thing like a sort of tube—not a pen—he used to write with?

LOUISE OWEN: No, I do not say I do. I only remember that he used exceptionally long pencils.

Of these twenty-one communications made, all of which were entirely outside our knowledge, eleven of the replies were absolute confirmations of exceptional evidential value, six replies were made which might be taken as correct, but which had no evidential value, and the remaining four were on incidents which had escaped her memory.

---

[119] Miss Owen volunteered the name.

22

THE MIRACLE OF THE "VOICES"

Wherein Lord Northcliffe again speaks—Warren: "I am not experienced enough to be the Chief Guide"—Confirmatory evidence of a Munnings' sitting—" Northcliffe is pleased with Queens Hall arrangements".

I

About 9.30 pm Sunday, January 18, 1925.

This sitting took place in my study immediately after Mr. Swaffer and I had examined Miss Owen on the communications from Northcliffe.

This was the third experiment for the direct voice, since our resumption in January, under the mediumship of my wife and myself. There were present, in addition to my wife and myself, Mr. Hannen Swaffer, Miss Louise Owen, Mrs. Osborne Leonard, Mrs. Hunt and Miss Madeleine Cohen.

My luminous trumpet was placed in the centre of the room and the lights were turned off. After the third gramophone record had been played, the trumpet was lifted up for a short time and then dropped. After another record had been played the trumpet was again lifted and a spirit voice, not at all distinct, addressed Mr. Swaffer.

The first few sentences we could not catch, but then the voice got through, somewhat impatiently: "It's Northcliffe; it's Northcliffe!" The spirit then spoke to Mr. Swaffer, to Miss Owen, and to me. He referred to the Queen's Hall meeting. Amongst other things he told us that the meeting would do much to help to spread Spiritualism all over the world.

Feda came through and spoke much more clearly and distinctly than Northcliffe. She used my trumpet which was wafted about from place to place as she addressed each of the various sitters. On several occasions she gave that merry, characteristic laugh, which we all of us know so well.

It was interesting to hear her chat with Mrs. Leonard, for although Feda is her control, Mrs. Leonard, when in trance, is completely unconscious of what transpires during the sittings held under her mediumship. Mrs. Leonard says that it is one of her greatest joys to be able to sit and talk to Feda in the direct voice, as she did on this evening.

Feda referred to the communications made during the morning to Mr. Swaffer and to me. Then she flitted around the circle, and spoke to my wife, and to Miss Owen. Feda is a spirit unique and unmistakable in character. She is now one of the famous personages of the psychic world, having been the means of bringing through an irrefutable mass of evidence of survival. Feda's voice always enlivens a circle, and one feels a regret when she has to go.

Warren came through. He said that he thought the voice development was progressing very well. He talked freely but said that the conditions were a trifle difficult on this evening for prolonged conversations.

HDB: Can you tell me, Warren, who is the guide for the voices here? I know that both you and Annie help, but I would like to ask you if you are the chief guide?

WARREN: I am not experienced enough to be the chief guide.

HDB: Can you tell me who is the chief guide?

WARREN: Husk!

HDB: Is John King connected with Husk?

WARREN: Yes![120]

A little later on Northcliffe came through again and spoke to us with reference to the Queen's Hall meeting. Feda spoke with us again for the second time. So also did Warren.

---

[120] This is rather an important point, because it is confirmatory evidence of the Munnings' sitting, at which Husk said that he would be present, and that he would look after the voice phenomena, and also of the Leonard sitting in which John King was referred to.

THE MIRACLE OF THE "VOICES"

WARREN: Northcliffe is very pleased with the arrangements which have been made for Tuesday. He says that it is his meeting. But we shall all be there with you. During the sitting, when operatic records were played on the gramophone, the luminous trumpet was lifted on one occasion and used as a baton, and the whole of the operatic selection was conducted with the magnificent gestures of a musical genius.

II

The sitting was very successful, but it is necessary to record that the voices were still not quite as powerful and distinct as they were at our private sittings during October last. Yet the evening was brilliant and miraculous. The sitting was late and all of us were tired; I certainly had experienced a strenuous and amazing day, the record of which has involved three chapters to retail.

23

A BARREN JOURNEY

Concerning a pilgrimage to a simple-minded medium in the North of England—The author returns after a disappointing visit.

January, 1925.

Sometime in November, 1924, I received a letter from a correspondent in the extreme North of England. He said he had read an account of a lecture of mine at the Steinway Hall, in which I said that the "direct" or "independent" voice was the most rare and intensely dramatic form of mediumship.

My correspondent, who, apparently, had not read my book, shall be nameless, because I do not wish to hurt him by my observations. He wrote me a long letter in which he said that, in his own home, this form of phenomenon had taken place for the last thirty years. He invited me to visit him, and stated that no one outside his own circle had been asked before to witness this phenomenon, but that if I could make the journey, he could promise me that I should be able to talk with the spirit of those who had passed on, just as though I were speaking to any living person, and that no instruments, such as a trumpet, etc., were used at his sittings.

As I was, desirous of probing every conceivable channel of knowledge, I wrote to him—presuming this to be one of the rare cares of the independent voice—saying:

> "I shall be indebted if you will be kind enough to tell me whether you actually get the spirit voices, and if so would you mind telling me what is the volume of sound? By this I mean, are the tones of the same power as our ordinary speaking voices?"

He wrote in reply saying that my query amused him a little, and that the volume of sound was sufficient to satisfy anyone, and could be heard in the next room, with the door shut. Also, that the voices come in the most natural way, in full daylight in the middle of the day or in the middle of the night, or in the middle of a field, and that if anyone who had passed away wished to speak to me personally, I should have no difficulty in recognizing the voice.

Among other things, this letter went on to say that, after a sitting there, I should realize how badly misled I had been.

I wrote back saying that the phenomenon of obtaining the voices at any time, in the fields, etc., appeared to me to be quite exceptional, and that I should like him to explain what he meant by saying that I should realize how badly I had been misled hitherto.

In reply I received a very long, dogmatic letter. It made all sorts of extraordinary assertions as to the various phenomena which had taken place in his own home. It was evident that my correspondent had not studied the subject or the works of any of the great writers on psychical research, and I wrote him to that effect. At the same time, I determined that should an opportunity occur I should visit him, as it would be interesting to study the development of these private home circles, and especially so in the case of a medium who—as I imagined—had obtained the independent voices.

Despite my strain of overwork I made the long journey North towards the end of January to investigate the claims of this medium. I arrived at the house about two o'clock in the afternoon. My correspondent was living in a small, but scrupulously clean little villa. The medium, I had been informed previously, was his wife. I found them both to be simple and kindly people—the hard—working Northern type.

The three of us sat in the full daylight. My host smoked a pipe, and I a cigarette. As they had said that the voices manifested themselves at any time I was quite interested, and alert to observe this phenomenon.

A BARREN JOURNEY

I was both surprised and amused to find that, instead of a form of independent voice mediumship, it was a case of primitive trance mediumship. His wife went into a trance—a genuine trance—and the control, some Zululand guide—a girl—for one hour and a quarter proceeded to give me indifferent interpretations of Bible passages in a more uneducated mentality than one finds in the average Mission Hall.

No evidence of any description was given as to any personal character, with the exception of a few jumbles connected with well-known personalities, whose names had been recently published in the newspapers.

It was a futile journey of six hundred miles for nothing of value.

These people were sincere and truthful, but here was a case of absolutely undeveloped mediumship, and they, in their simplicity, had imagined it to be more marvelous than anything which had occurred in the history of psychical research.

24

THE THIRD EXPERIMENT WITH MUNNINGS

The author pauses to make a few observations on Horatio Bottomley —The supernormal movements of H.D.B.'s trumpet— Spirit lights in the room.

I

January, 1925.

Despite the fact that the spirits had warned me of over-work and had advised me to refrain from holding too many séances under personal mediumship, I felt that this should not preclude me from pursuing my psychical experiments with other mediums.

Mr. Hannen Swaffer, one of the few fearless editors and critical journalists, had said to me, "You can't use Munnings." But Munnings as a psychological study interests me much more than does, for instance, Horatio Bottomley, for Munnings has the advantage of possessing psychical faculties, beside which his trifling social delinquencies are relatively insignificant. So why on earth should anyone say, "You can't use Munnings?"

I know Munnings' history, and I shall not satisfy prurient curiosity by repeating his little lapses from virtue. They were not of a very serious character, and had no bearing whatever upon psychics. In this

THE WISDOM OF THE GODS

England of ours the lives of many notorious men endure their ups and downs, and the patriotic Bottomley, who, during the great war made soul-stirring recruiting speeches at the Empire Theatre, and received a personal fee of one hundred pounds a night for doing so, is now, where I hope he will remain, in gaol. Bottomley was at times amusing, but Munnings is more so, and that is why I asked him to Dorincourt for a third time.

Munnings, who arrived after dinner, was not introduced to my guests in ease any evidence should be later volunteered—which it wasn't.

II

It was in the latter part of January that this third experimental sitting was held under the mediumship of Mr. F. T. Munnings. There were present, in addition to my wife and myself, Dr. V. J. Woolley, Honorary Research Officer of the Society for Psychical Research, Mr. P. G. Wodehouse, Miss Leonora Wodehouse, and the Baroness Kakucs.

Mr. Munnings informed me before the sitting that he was feeling unwell, and had been suffering from a bad cold.

Of the sitters the Baroness Kakucs and Miss Leonora 'Wodehouse had had no previous experience of séances.

I explained to Dr. Woolley beforehand I had found at previous experiments with Munnings that it was seldom one received any actual evidence of personal identification of the communicating voices.

Dr. Woolley also understood that this was not a case of test research work, but that it was to be regarded merely as an experiment to observe any supernormal phenomena which might occur. Dr. Woolley was sitting next to Munnings.

I placed my own illuminated trumpet in the center of the circle, and, on this occasion, Munnings, having observed the striking effect of the movement of my illuminated trumpet at the two previous sittings, had painted his trumpet with two vivid, luminous stripes in a similar manner. The effect of this was very good, as both trumpets could be clearly seen. The two trumpets were placed about a foot apart.

Three or four records were played on the gramophone before anything transpired.

Munnings said that he felt the conditions were peculiar, and appeared to be surprised that we had to wait so long before any phenomena took place. He said that he did not know what was wrong,

THE THIRD EXPERIMENT WITH MUNNINGS

and that he had never had to wait so long before. I knew why,[121] and I was very amused.

It appeared to me, and to the other sitters—towards the end of the fourth record—that one of the trumpets was moving towards the other one. Dr. Woolley said that he did not think it had moved. During the time that the fifth record was playing my illuminated trumpet was suddenly lifted into the air, and moved all round the circle—touching each of the sitters. It was then taken higher into the air, and I asked whether it could be taken to the ceiling. It was taken to the ceiling, which it rapped several times.

Whilst my trumpet was lifted to the ceiling I engaged Munnings in conversation, so that there could be no doubt in the mind of anyone that either he or I or anyone else was moving. I do not know whether Dr. Woolley happened to observe this fact.

The movements of my trumpet were supernormal.

A little later the voice of Emanuel came through, using Munnings' illuminated trumpet.

Emanuel said that the power was rather weak, and that the spirit communicants would have to draw a certain amount of power from me and from Mrs. Bradley. I replied to Emanuel, saying that I did not wish him to draw very much power from me, as I had been advised to be careful of the strain of mediumship.

Emanuel said that they would be careful as to how much power they took from us.

The few voices which came through during the evening were weak and disconnected, and they seemed unable to hold the power for more than one minute or so at the time.

A spirit purporting to be that of Dan Leno sang the verse of a song, but the voice was not very good, and certainly could not be established with the same certainty as on the previous sitting with Munnings, when this communicant manifested.

A spirit voice came through announcing itself to be that of Lord Grenfell, whose funeral had taken place on that day. Lord Grenfell, I learned later, was interested in spiritualism, but the voice did not volunteer any information which could be regarded as evidential.

Husk talked to my wife and me on our mediumship. Husk seemed to be disturbed; his voice was not very distinct, and although I asked certain questions which might have been of considerable value, I obtained no evidential replies.

---

[121] The adverse vibrations of one of the sitters.

During the evening certain spirit lights appeared in various parts of the room.

It is significant to note that neither Annie nor Warren have ever attempted to speak at a Munnings' séance.

III

The sitting was devoid of any evidential proof of the personality of the communicating spirits. That supernormal phenomena occurred is, however, indisputable.

The voices which came from space appeared to be laboring under some difficulty in carrying on a conversation.

25

DRAMATIC MATERIAL DISCOVERY

A thrilling experience—A sitting on the results of which many thousands of pounds depended—Spirits locate incriminating ledgers—"The fact remains, that without any outside medium, I and my wife have conversed for hours and hours with the spirits of my sister Annie and of Warren Clarke, and these spirits have talked in their own individual voices, clearly and distinctly from space"—On the threshold of the Temple of knowledge.

I

Sunday. January 25, 1925.

For a very important purpose, I held a private sitting at Dorincourt on this night for the direct voice. There were present only my wife, her mother and myself.

My illuminated trumpet was placed in the centre of the room, and operatic music was played upon the gramophone. The first selection played was a Curci record. There appeared to be a peculiar acuteness in the atmosphere, and the voice of Galli-Curci, singing "Dov'è L'indiana Bruna," sounded to me finer than I had heard it. I thought that this was possibly due to my imagination, but to my surprise my wife made the remark that she had never heard her voice so pure, or so clear.

Then as Galli-Curci was singing Verdi's "Tutte le al Tempio," the illuminated trumpet was lifted, used as a baton, and the song was conducted. The time was actually controlled. The luminous baton vibrated with the music; the spirit of the great composition was vividly brought to life. It was thrilling and supernatural, for the material instrument of the gramophone was made subservient to a higher intelligence.

Warren Clarke came through.

His voice was not loud, but it was quick, decisive, and alert. I had some important personal questions of considerable significance to me which I wished to put to him.

The answers he gave were direct, and of great and immediate value.

During the past two months references had been made by Warren and by Annie to certain matters affecting my material—or financial interests. The first indications which came as a warning are recorded in Chapter 9 and in Chapter 19 in Book One of this work.

It is seldom that material interests are discussed by the spirits, and although I did not entirely realize it at the time, this matter was one of tremendous importance to me. It was only later that I found out how gravely my interests were affected. I discovered that it was a case of treachery and injustice, and it is, apparently, only in such cases that the spirits will intervene upon material issues.

I was advised exactly what to do, and I acted upon the advice given.

Within a fortnight of this sitting, I made astounding discoveries. The investigation I undertook involved study of accounts for a period of several years, and the accounts amounted to, in all, over a million of money.

Fortunately, I am an expert accountant, and although the necessary work entailed an almost super human effort, it was between Friday night and early Saturday; morning, on February 1, at two a.m., after a concentrated study, that I found and proved the defalcations. Prior to this, I had been told by the spirits exactly which set of accountancy books to examine first. All these books were the most unexpected, an ostensibly insignificant set at which I should probably never have looked but for their advice.

Subsequent to this I had to prove these to three firms of chartered accountants, and throughout the examination I was enabled by supernormal means to find my evidence in several unexpected quarters.

The embezzlements had continued persistently for years, and had been most cunningly covered. It was a terrible case, and, but for the advice given me by the spirits, these embezzlements would have probably continued indefinitely, and would have entailed me in the loss of many more thousands of pounds.

This dramatic incident serves to show that the spirits can and do help those with whom they communicate, and that, in addition to their spiritual advice, they can and do protect us from material injustice.

After my conversation with Warren, Annie came through and confirmed the information which Warren had expressed, and then she told me the correct time at which I should act upon my new purpose. She also discussed the condition of my sister Gertrude, who was, still very ill. Before going she told me that Husk was there and wished to speak to me.

Husk came through after a while, and talked with me and with my wife. During the conversation, he said that he felt it right to advise us not to sit again until Valiantine was here, as he felt it was too much for us at present. He knew that there was a tremendous amount of intricate work that it was now imperative for me to do. He said later that we would be impressed as to when it would be advisable for us to resume our private sittings.

II

The communications I received were remarkable, but again it came as a surprise to be told to stop holding these sittings. On reflection, however, I realized that I had an excessive amount of work to get through, and to continue to hold private voice séances as well would be too severe a mental strain. I expressed the hope, however, that my own and my wife's mediumistic powers would develop considerably during the series of sittings which were to take place in the spring of this year, under Valiantine's mediumship.

This private voice sitting was of inestimable value to use.

III

We are living in an age of miracles, miracles beyond any that have ever taken place. It is difficult for the human mind to conceive that the barrier of death has been broken down.

My wife and I can sit together, and talk at length and with fluency upon all matters of moment with the spirits of those who are closely attached to us, and who have passed on from this Earth plane.

Were I to advance this statement without corroboration from outside witnesses, I should not expect the world to believe me. It is a matter almost beyond comprehension, but the established fact remains, that, without any outside medium, I and my wife have conversed for hours and hours with the spirits of my sister Annie and of Warren Clarke, who have talked in their own individual voices, clearly and distinctly from space.

Many famous people have heard us and them, and have also spoken in my house to their own spirit friends.

It is not so much the marvel of the universe, it is the truth of the universe.

Today, those of us on this Earth plane are but infants but tomorrow we maybe taking our first few step towards divine knowledge and wisdom.

From all that I have seen and learnt, I am convinced of two things: that there is no mysterious fetish in mediumship, and that the power, the force—call it what you will—is inherent in each of us.

Each man, woman and child has this mysterious attribute, an attribute in the vast majority of cases entirely latent, in a few cases acknowledged, in fewer still both acknowledged and cultivated.

The world stands at the threshold of a vast new Temple of Knowledge, virgin, unexplored, the majesty and beauty of which excel all other shrines raised by human hands.

BOOK TWO
VALIANTINE AND THE VOICES

1

*George Valiantine comes to England and is met by HDB—
Follows a remarkable sitting, at which old friends from
"Towards the Stars" come back—I know there is no death.*

∼

I

Friday, February 13, 1925.

GEORGE VALIANTINE arrived in England from the USA on February 12.

The Berengaria was late on account of the fog, and it was past midnight when I met him at Waterloo and motored him to Dorincourt.

It was in response to innumerable requests from prominent students of psychical research that I had invited him to make his second visit to this country.

It was pleasant to meet this simple, honest man again. I find that when I am in his company Valiantine has a soothing effect upon the nerves, whereas, prior to his visit, I had endured the strain of a tense period of intricate work.

The day following Valiantine's arrival was spent quietly at Dorincourt—my wife being ill in bed. In the evening the two of us held a sitting together.

We at opposite each other some six feet apart; on the floor between us two trumpets, one his and one mine.

Eleven distinct and individual spirit personalities spoke with us. Only two used a trumpet. The power was so strong that nine of the spirits spoke independently of the megaphones, their voices being clear and recognizable and in mid-air.

Annie discussed with me in her independent voice several important and intimate questions.

Warren Clarke discarded the trumpet and spoke at considerable length in the independent voice. He also dealt with certain intimate subjects, and gave me most valuable advice on the financial investigations I was engaged upon with three firms of chartered accountants.

Feda came through and spoke is her usual joyous manner, welcoming us both and interspersing her speech with her merry little laugh.

It was a great joy to speak to Valiantine's guides,[122] each are characteristic and outstanding personality, both in the manner of phrasing sentences and in their intonations: Dr. Barnett spoke to us in his wise and determined manner: Bert Everest in his light humour; Pat O'Brien in his rich Irish brogue; Kokum and Hawk Chief[123] in their tremendous resounding voices; some of them sometimes speaking together and sometimes to each other. All the spirits sympathetically referred to my wife. Whilst the two Indian guides were talking, I asked them to speak as loud as they could, so that possibly my wife might hear then. Although Mrs. Bradley was in bed on an upper floor (not over the room where we were sitting), some thirty or forty yards away and with all the doors closed, she told me afterwards that she had heard the speakers distinctly.

This was not to be wondered at, as when they raised their tone their voices could be heard quite a hundred yards away.

The spirit of little Honey spoke, so also did that of little Bobby Worrall.[124]

The conversations were carried on fluently and practically continuously for so long that eventually I asked Dr. Barnett whether we should close the séance. Immediately I asked this question, Bert Everest said that they did not wish to close then because Johannes wished to speak to me.

Johannes then spoke to me without using the trumpet. His voice was slow and his tones cultured, in the measured accents of a brilliant intellect. It was a tremendous pleasure for me to talk with him.

---

[122] Valiantine has an exceptional number of spirit guides: Dr. Barnett, Bert Everett, Kokum, 'Pat O'Brien, Honey, Hawk Chief, and Bobby Worrall.

[123] All these "spirit" personalities are described in *Towards the Stars*.

[124] All of these characters appear in *Towards the Stars*.

He said that he had attached himself to me as one of my guides, and that in my literary work he would always endeavour to help me. I told Johannes that, for a while, I should not have the leisure for creative literature, and all that I could do was to record the psychic happenings.

The conversations were carried on with eleven individual spirits, each speaking easily, fluently, liquidly, tenderly, intimately, and brilliantly. Each sentence spoken was pregnant with meaning and knowledge. Each of the speakers I knew so much more truly than the majority of the men and women I meet on Earth. Each lives on a plane infinitely beyond that upon which I exist. Not one expressed a thought but what is noble. None exuded an atmosphere but that of tranquility and love. Each breathed the rarest breath of life—the life beyond our comprehension.

I know that there is no death, but there are degrees of life, and it is the spirits who are completely alive and we who are comatose.

This vivid evening was a splendid augury of the future, when this new and magnificent truth maybe incontestably proved to all this strife-stricken world.

2

The author is infuriated—The negative effect of a materialistic sitter—A case of sleepy sickness is discussed and Dr. Barnet gives a prescription.

I

Sunday, February 15.

When reading these records of the phenomena which took place during the long series of Valiantine sittings the reader will appreciate that only a bare and abbreviated account, containing points of psychological interest or evidential information can be given. If some of the later chapters appear cold and brief, it is not because of a lack of material, but because of a surfeit of it and of the necessity for compression. Otherwise, this book would run to thousands of pages.

On February 15 I invited to Dorincourt Mr. Hannen Swaffer, Miss Madeleine Cohen, Miss Winifred Graham, Mrs. Robert Graham, and a gentleman who shall be nameless. George Valiantine and I completed the circle.

Just prior to the opening of the sitting, the nameless gentleman said to me: "Bradley, I do not want my name to appear in any book, because there are two members of my family who are leaving me a considerable sum of money in their wills. They detest spiritualism, and if they read that I was sitting at séances they would cut one out."

This remark incensed me. Since I was first engaged in this study of the greatest subject in the world and have made considerable sacrifices in order that the knowledge might be established, it was galling to come in contact with such a mentality. I knew from the moment we started that the sitting would be smashed.

We waited for a quarter of an hour, and I then said, "I wish to tell you that I consider it futile to proceed with this sitting."

Evidently my feelings had permeated the room, for the gentleman in question offered to leave. He left.

I told the others that I was willing to continue for a short time, but I feared, on account of this disturbance, that communications would be either extremely difficult or impossible.

After five or six minutes the voice of Dr. Barnett spoke, but the power was not very strong.

There was a very momentous question which had arisen during the day, and one which I desired to put to Dr. Barnett. I will explain the importance of this question. A local doctor was attending my wife for her illness, and during the morning he told me he was also attending a case of a rare disease. A patient of his—the son of a Mr. R. H. Saunders—was stricken with sleepy sickness. I answered that we were holding séances at Dorincourt under the mediumship of George Valiantine, and that on occasions most remarkable advice had been vouchsafed by the spirits. I added that one of the spirits, Dr. Barnett, possessed a knowledge of medicine. My wife's doctor suggested that, at the first opportunity, I should ask Dr. Barnett for advice on this case.

I asked Dr. Barnett whether it would be possible for him to give us advice or to obtain advice on their side as to the treatment of a case of sleepy sickness.

Dr. Barnett said that he could give advice.

I asked him whether it would be necessary for me to bring the doctor there so that he could take down the treatment.

DR. BARNETT: No—I will give it to you now. Please write it down.

I wrote down the treatment.

DR. BARNETT: Tell your doctor to give the patient every two days—an injection of Antimony and Oil of Chaulmoogra. Tell your doctor also to manipulate the arms and shoulders of the patient from the hips, whilst he is in a relaxed position.

I had to ask him to spell "Chaulmoogra" since it was a word none of us knew.

Immediately after the sitting had closed I telephoned to my doctor and gave him the treatment suggested.

It must be remembered that I knew nothing about antimony and none of us had ever heard the words "oil of Chaulmoogra"; my doctor was astounded at the prescription. He told me that he would phone to a West End specialist with regard to the quantities, etc. and added that to the best or his knowledge Oil of Chaulmoogra was used occasionally in cases of leprosy.

3

A daylight sitting at which the spirits talk with Pat, the eight-year-old son of the author—Mr. Greville Collins attends a sitting and appears to be upset and is taken out of the room—Miss Madeline Cohen's mother addresses her daughter—Evidential information—The spirit of Arthur Playfair talks with Mr. Swaffer: Miss Phyllis Monkman mentioned—The late William Archer's regrets.

I

Monday, February 16, 1925.

An extraordinary event took place, and I will relate the incident as it was told to me by my son Pat, aged eight years. He was sitting with Valiantine in my study in the morning, and the room was flooded with strong sunlight. Pat, who knows quite a considerable amount about spiritualism, asked Valiantine to let him talk to the spirits. Valiantine laughed and said they might try. Then Valiantine held the trumpet up at arm length, at right-angles from himself, and in a minute or so Pat heard a voice speaking to him. For six to seven minutes Pat carried on a conversation with Annie; then with Warren Clarke, who talked of Phyllis and Betty, two playmates of Pat; and later on Kokum talked to him, and then Bert Everett. Pat told me all the things they said. This is a very remarkable phenomenon, as it is rare that the spirits can manifest their voices in broad daylight.

II

Wednesday, February 18, 1925.
This sitting was held in my study at Dorincourt at about eight forty-five p.m.

In addition to Valiantine and myself, there were Miss Louise Owen, Miss Kate Goodson, Miss Madeleine Cohen, Mr. Greville Collins (the theatrical manager), and Mr. Swaffer.

The two trumpets were used—my own trumpet, and Valiantine's, which has an illuminated star inside.

Miss Goodson and Mr. Greville Collins were not introduced to the medium.

To me it appeared that the sitters were in a somewhat excited and restless condition.

Two or three records were played on the gramophone before any phenomena occurred, and then several of the sitters were touched, both with the trumpet and with, presumably, materialized hands.

One of the illuminated trumpets came over to me and rested for quite a time on my knee.

Mr. Greville Collins was touched on two or three occasions, and appeared nervous.

The voice of Bert Everett was heard high up in the room, giving a loud laugh. Dr. Barnett said: "Souls, don't be afraid." At this Mr. Greville Collins appeared to be quite upset, and said to me that he could not stand it any longer, and that he must get out of the room. I took him out; gave him a strong whisky and soda, and left him comfortably by the fire in the drawing room.

On my return Dr. Barnett almost immediately spoke again. He said that there was too much excitement among the sitters, and that this made the conditions difficult for the spirits to speak.

Miss Madeleine Cohen's mother addressed her. They spoke to each other for some little time on personal and family matters. The voice of Mrs. Cohen was indistinct at first, but gained power later. Some points regarding a sale were discussed, and mention was made of some of the family, certain members of which were at Monte Carlo. Mrs. Cohen volunteered the information to Miss Cohen that Hilda (Miss Cohen's sister had recently been shocked by a certain incident.[125]

---

[125] Quite true, and of an evidential nature.

VALIANTINE AND THE VOICES

A voice spoke to Mr. Swaffer, and announced himself to be Arthur Playfair. Arthur Playfair spoke for quite a little time to Mr. Swaffer, and also to me, although I did not know Mr. Playfair when he was on Earth. He addressed Mr. Swaffer as "Swaff," and also made several references to Phyllis Monkman, whom he first referred to as Phyl and later, on request, volunteered her full Christian and surname.

It must be noted here that Valiantine, who is a stranger in this country, knew nothing about Arthur Playfair, who died some few years back, nor was he likely to have any knowledge that Playfair was a friend of Phyllis Monkman's.

Playfair thanked me for what he called "the great work I was doing," and also thanked Valiantine for giving him the power to be able to speak to us.

William Archer came through. He was indistinct at first, but the voice improved considerably as it went on speaking. He talked for some time with me. He said that his boy was with him on the other side, and that he (Archer) was so sorry now that he had kept this truth back whilst he was on Earth. He added that he had known how true it was for some long time, and that he was deeply regretting that he had not made his knowledge public.

Mr. Archer also spoke with Mr. Swaffer regarding the book which Mr. Swaffer was then writing.

Later a spirit voice called "Kate-Kate." Miss Goodson immediately replied, and the voice said at once that it was her father. Miss Goodson and the spirit talked for some long time about family matters, Miss Goodson crying during most of the conversation.

The spirit referred to her sister Annie and her baby, who, he said was a sweet child, and was growing up in the spirit world.[126] He added that the three of them were there together, and were as happy as could be. He asked if Miss Goodson could bring her mother so that she could talk to him. "Please give her my love and kiss her."

This is a mere indication of the communications made by this spirit.

Dr. Barnett said that we should close the sitting. I got up to turn on the light, and whilst I was standing up the voice of Annie spoke to me within about a foot from my face and without using the trumpet. Her tones were heard distinctly by everyone present. She just said: "Herbert, there are a lot of spirits here tonight; I am sorry we have to close, but it is necessary this evening!"

---

[126] Apparently, the baby referred to had died.

III

This séance was fairly successful, but I did not feel that the conditions were very good. There was an entire lack of passivity, and much movement and restlessness on the part of all those present.

4

A helpful passivity that made a successful sitting—Little Bobby Worrall and Pat—A spirit whistles a military tune—The Martians: their mentality and their bodies—Mrs. Helen White's testimony— "Perfectly natural."

Thursday, February 19, 1925.

This sitting was remarkably successful. There were four sitters: Mrs. Helen White, Captain C. J. Astley Maberley, Valiantine, and myself.

I knew at once that the conditions were extremely good. There was a very helpful passivity in atmosphere.

Dr. Barnett greeted us, and there came through falsetto Valiantine's spirit guides, Bert Everett. in his falsetto voice; Kokum in his loud tones, and Pat O'Brien. They all spoke to each of us.

Little Bobby Worrall came through in his childish accents and told me how he had talked to Pat in the daylight of the previous afternoon.[127]

Mrs. White's mother spoke to her daughter on personal matters, and also spoke to Captain Maberley. A voice whistling a military tune then

---

[127] On the previous afternoon, in the full daylight, Pat had again sat with Valiantine, and had spoken to Annie, and also to Bobby Worrall. On that occasion Bobby said that he had read through some of Pat's books with him, giving the names of those books.

came close to Captain Maberley. Captain Maberley asked the whistler for another military tune known to him, and this was given. A voice apparently that of the whistler spoke to Captain Maberley and together they conversed for some time. This voice also spoke to Mrs. White.

Another spirit voice manifested itself to Mrs. White, announcing itself as Canon. Mrs. White and Captain Maberley recognized this personality, and they discussed certain matters.

Annie talked for a short time with me on private matters.

Towards the end of the evening, Dr. Barnett came through, and gave a long, brilliant discourse on Mars, and the condition of the inhabitants of Mars. They were far more intellectual beings than those on the Earth plane, and far more developed both in science and in spirituality. Their physical bodies are smaller than ours, and they possess many senses that we have not.

Before long they will be able to communicate with us; they are trying to do so now. They will get through to us before we will get through to them. The Martians have established communications with spirits to a higher degree than we have; in fact communication with the spirit spheres from Mars has become a very simple matter.

Bert Everett gave a spiritual address.

After the sitting Mrs. White said that she considered that the experience was absolutely marvelous, and that until now she had never felt absolutely convinced of survival. She was overjoyed at being able to get into direct communication with her mother and the most remarkable thing to her was that it had all seemed so perfectly natural.

5

The author enjoys a stimulating relaxation from psychics—Mrs. Bradley sits alone with Valiantine—Only a universal spiritual movement can prevent war: Dr. Barnett's solemn warning—An ideal mediumistic combination.

I

Friday, February 20, 1925.

THIS was the date of the first night of the production of the "Grand Duchess" at the Globe Theatre, with Miss Margaret Bannerman in the lead. I had made an engagement to attend this performance. Although the English adaptation of this French work did not prove a commercial success, Miss Bannerman gave a brilliant performance of a most difficult part. Afterwards, at the invitation of Mr. Anthony Prinsep, my friend Charles Sykes and I joined the company to sup and dance. A stimulating relaxation from psychics.

This evening my wife, who was convalescent after her illness, sat with Mr. Valiantine alone in my study at Dorincourt. The trumpets (Valentine's and mine) were placed in the centre of the room. Conditions were perfect; and it was not necessary to play the gramophone.

Within a few minutes the first voice manifested and spoke to Mrs. Bradley—the voice announcing itself to be that of Georgie,[128] calling

---

[128] Full Christian and surnames being given.

her "Auntie Mabel." This voice was that of Annie's son, who had passed away some few years ago at the age of seventeen. He said that he wanted to talk to Uncle Herbert[129] on certain matters and also that he had tried to get through to Dennis at Cambridge, but that he had found it too difficult, as there was not sufficient power there.

Later, Annie spoke independently and without using the trumpet, referring to the sitting at which she had taken control and spoken through Mrs. Scales.

Warren sent his love to his children, Phyllis and Betty. He spoke of their illness, and volunteered a statement with regard to the health of my wife's sister Ida, who was then in Germany.

While he was speaking of the illness of his children, he told how the illness had been contracted.

In talking to Dr. Barnett, my wife referred to the upheaval which had been forecasted, and asked if, among other forms, there were likely to be Earthquakes. Dr. Barnett said that there would be certain Earthquakes, and added that there had been one or two slight tremors just recently on the Earth plane.

DR. BARNETT: There is a very grave danger of another great war during the next two years, and only a universal spiritual movement can prevent it. If this war takes place it will be a catastrophic war in the air; Germany and Japan are preparing in secret. Japan is now engaged actively in getting huge fleets of aeroplanes ready.

MRS. BRADLEY: Are there any means by which it can be prevented?

DR. BARNETT: It can be prevented only by the people on the Earth plane spreading the truth of spiritualism. This is the only way.

Bert Everett came through and spoke to Mrs. Bradley for some time. Kokum also. Dr. Barnett closed the sitting.

Mrs. Bradley says that the conversations were easy and fluent, the voices coming through without the slightest difficulty. It maybe noted that the same thing happened during on the previous occasion when I sat alone with Valiantine.

During the last series of experiments which were conducted in February of last year, we found that on the occasions when the three of us sat together my wife, Valiantine, and myself—the conditions were perfect. The communications came through with wonderful ease and fluency; evidently this combination makes an ideal one for the voice vibration.

---

[129] H.D.B.

6

HDB deplores the number of ladies at this sitting: the atmosphere of a tea-party—The late Mr. Scott speaks to his widow—Spirits speak in German—The spirit of Major Dighton-Probyn on the prevention of wars—A remarkable letter.

I

Saturday, February 21, 1925.

THERE were present, Valiantine, Mrs. Dighton-Probyn, Mrs. Kinloch, Mrs. Scott-Nelson, Mrs. Benvenisti (who translated *Towards the Stars* into German), her secretary, Miss Engster, Lieutenant-Colonel Miles Tristram, his daughter, Miss Tristram, and myself.

It was a conglomerate assembly, and there were far too many ladies present. I had invited one or two people to be present and, inadvertently, my wife had invited others. Of the sitters, five of the ladies had never sat at a voice séance.

The sitting took place at Dorincourt, and, although all the ladies were very charming, I felt the atmosphere was that of a tea-party, rather than that of a séance. I was exceedingly irritated by the continual chatter, and in consequence I should regard the conditions as the reverse to ideal.

The majority seemed restlessly excited, sectional in their thought and sectional in their anticipation. But, despite these poor conditions, fourteen different and individual spirit voices manifested.

Dr. Barnett spoke on several occasions and so did Bert Everett, Kokum, Pat O'Brien, and Honey. Feda spoke to me and to another sitter, and Warren Clarke had a short conversation with me. All the guides and Warren Clarke spoke in their independent voice without using the trumpet.

One of the illuminated trumpets was lifted and a spirit voice spoke to Mrs. Scott-Nelson, announcing himself by name as Jack Scott.[130] A long and personal conversation ensued between them. Many matters too delicate to be published were referred to.

Mrs. Scott-Nelson was emotional throughout the conversation, and she expressed herself to me afterwards as being enormously impressed.

Spirit voices of two of Mrs. Kinloch's relatives spoke with her for some long time, and as she asked each of these spirits to bring other of her relatives through I began to get nervous that the séance might continue throughout the entire weekend!

Two different spirits carne through and spoke to Miss Engster and also to Mrs. Benvenisti; both of these spirits spoke in German. They were very indistinct and it was difficult to translate their communications.

One announced itself to be the mother of Miss Engster and the other to be her father.

A spirit voice of a relative of Colonel Tristram spoke with him and with Miss Tristram, and I heard the voice address Colonel Tristram as "Miles." Miss Tristram evidently recognized the communicant, and the voice made references to a trip Miss Tristram proposed making to Canada.

The spirit of Mrs. Dighton-Probyn's husband, Major Dighton-Probyn, of the Royal Garrison Artillery, who died at the age of fifty-one, spoke to her for some time. His voice was fairly distinct and recognition was claimed by Mrs. Dighton-Probyn. He talked with her on personal matters, and he also came over to me and spoke to me on the imperative necessity of mankind preventing future wars. He complimented me on some of my literary work.

Dr. Barnett closed the sitting.

---

[130] This is the name of Mrs. Scott-Nelson's first husband. It was unknown to me.

II

Owing to the number of people present and the animated discussion which followed, I forgot to question Mrs. Benvenisti's secretary with regard to the communication she received.

I remembered afterwards that I had not asked her whether her mother and father were alive or dead. This is an important point, since none of us, with the exception of Mrs. Benvenisti, had any knowledge of her. Neither did we know her name.

I wrote to Mrs. Benvenisti the next morning, reminding her that Dr. Barnett had deliberately said that the voices which had addressed her secretary were the voices of her father and mother, and asking her if she would be good enough to inform me on this point.

Mrs. Benvenisti wrote to me that her secretary's name was Miss Engster, adding: "I wish to state that Miss Engster is only twenty-four years old, and has, unfortunately, lost both parents during the last few years. I can vouch for the fact that no one present knew anything about her. When she was addressed by the two voices, she answered them in the Swiss-German dialect of her home. The voices were very indistinct, and it was difficult to understand what they said beyond a few short sentences. During the sitting Miss Engster was touched on the forehead, and she asked in the Swiss-German dialect incomprehensible to any of the others present—that her head might be touched again, upon which she was touched twice on the forehead."

7

The spirit of Bert Everett sings a duet with a gramophone record of Galli-Curci's: the comedy makes Dr. Barnett laugh—Miss Winifred Graham's father speaks to his daughter—More about the prescription for sleepy sickness—Life in the spirit spheres.

Sunday, February 22, 1925.

On this evening, in addition to Valiantine, there were present my wife, Mrs. Graham, Miss Winifred Graham, and myself. The conditions were very good and the voices manifested without any difficulty. Ten spirits spoke.

Dr. Barnett spoke to us several times on various subjects, and so also did Bert Everett. Both Hawk Chief and Kokum spoke in their usual loud tones, and Pat O'Brien came through twice and talked jovially with each of us in his Irish brogue. Bobby Worrall spoke of Pat. He also said that he was with Valiantine, Pat, and myself in the morning when we walked along by Beverley Brook.

On this occasion we used my illuminated trumpet and one of Valiantine's trumpets, which I had painted with a thick band of luminous paint and with two rather large stars on each side.

I asked Pat O'Brien if the strong luminosity made any difference to the power of the personal spirits in lifting the trumpets, and he said that he did not think so. He added: "We will lift them now." And immediately he took up Valiantine's trumpet, which was wafted rapidly round the room, and taken up towards the ceiling.

BOBBY WORRALL: I will see if I can lift both trumpets.

Whereupon both the trumpets were moved across each other and whirled round.

During the time a Galli-Curci record was being played on the gramophone, Bert Everett joined in. His voice, very high up in the room, was shrill, and although one could not say that it was wonderfully musical the shrillness of his notes was certainly phenomenal, so much so indeed that it made everyone laugh. He did this on one or two occasions, and during the time that he was singing there came through the deep resounding laugh of Dr. Barnett from the middle of the circle.

Georgie, Annie's son, announced himself by his full Christian and surname. This was the first time he has spoken to me, although he had, on a previous occasion, spoken to my wife. During his life on Earth he and I were great friends and it was a pleasure to me to be able to speak with him again. He told me that he had tried to get through several times, but had found it very difficult to materialize his voice. He was very anxious to speak to Dennis. Dennis and he were very fond of each other, and had been much together during their early youth. Annie spoke to me, my wife, Mr. Valiantine, and to Mrs. Graham. Warren spoke to us all in his usual cheerful manner.

There then came through the spirit of Mrs. Graham's husband, Bob. His voice was at first a little indistinct, but it improved as he went on. He spoke for some little time to his daughter, Miss Winifred Graham, who heard all that he said. Unfortunately, Mrs. Graham is a trifle deaf, and could not manage to catch all the sentences, but during the time he was addressing his wife and his daughter, he called them by their Christian names, Mrs. Graham "Alice" and Miss Graham "Winnie."

Bert Everett spoke to Mrs. Graham, and referring to this spirit said: "Now he is on this side he has shaved his beard."[131]

Towards the end we discussed with Dr. Barnett the treatment for sleepy sickness. He said that the injection of antimony should be made every two days, and that the one dram of Chaulmoogra Oil should be taken in a capsule, and not administered with milk. He again emphasized that the patient's arms should be manipulated from the shoulder to the hips while the patient was in a relaxed position, and also the necessity of keeping the bowels well flushed.

At the close Bert Everett gave an impressive address on the conditions of life in the spirit spheres. He said that he was living with the spirit of

---

[131] Mr. Graham wore a beard while on Earth.

his mother in a beautiful little house; that each of the various rooms of this house had one predominating colour, and that the walls were decorated with flowers, which blended with the colour scheme.

Answering a question, Bert Everett said that they walked on solid ground, and that there were various beautiful temples of learning. He also added that there were rivers, and seas, and crystal gliders, upon which they could travel at great rapidity on the ether waves.

8

Mrs. M. I. Ellis has a private sitting with Valiantine—Two spirits speaking at the same time—Mrs. Ellis's account of talking with her daughter and Sir Ernest Shackleton.

I

Monday afternoon, February 23, 1925.

IN response to a particular request made to me by Mrs. M. I. Ellis for a private sitting with Valiantine, he visited her in her flat. They were the only two present. Valiantine had never met her before.

Dr. Barnett, Bert Everett and Kokum came through and spoke with Mrs. Ellis, and also Feda.

Of the personal spirits, three addressed her, identifying themselves and giving names, and a personal conversation was conducted.

In addition to these, another spirit stated that it was a guide of Mrs. Ellis's.

The illuminous trumpet was used by the personal spirits and moved in the air. At one time two of the spirit voices were speaking at the same time; one independently and the other using the trumpet.

II

Here follows Mrs. Ellis's account of her experience:

"We sat in my rooms at three forty-five p.m. The first *spirit voice* was that of a spirit friend, known when he manifests in public as 'G.S.' As a record with which we had started the séance progressed, a hand touched my head with firm, warm fingers. The metal trumpet was used by this spirit with difficulty.

"Second—Without any wait or interval my little girl Sybil manifested with difficulty: she said she could not give the violets as I had requested her to do to the medium, because he was a stranger. 'Give them afterwards,' she said, 'please.' The medium then remarked that he felt a cold breeze.

"Third—At once a man's voice, still very husky, said he was Sir Ernest Shackleton, and recalled to my remembrance some time back, when he brought snow into my séance room, which actually melted on our hands. He laughed, recalling my astonishment at the time.

"Fourth—Mr. Valiantine's guides, especially Dr. Barnett, spoke very graciously and with greater clearness than my own personal friends had been able to do.

"Fifth—Feda came and spoke very sweetly, and recalled her other visits to my little séance room.

"Sixth—Sybil again spoke, or rather murmured, that a stranger was present. (seventh) Sybil, and G.S. and another spirit [eighth] speak together, using two trumpets.

"Ninth—A spirit who claimed to be a guide of mine, and who spelt his name for me, Alla Pasha, I remarked, 'Surely a Turk or an Egyptian.' He replied that he was from India, and a Hindu, and that he was here to help me to get the direct voice, which I should get in less than a year.

"G.S., who had not left the room, again touched me, and, on my chaffing him about his gurgling voice on the trumpet, he said: 'Oh, this trumpet! I can touch you through it; I can put my hand through it easier than I can put my voice through it!' The same spirit then requested me to put on the same record with which we had started the séance, and as, Dr. Barnett, the medium's control, had said that he was retiring, with the medium's permission I turned on the red light. G.S. then removed my papier maché trumpet from the corner of my séance room into the cabinet, and kept time on it to the music of the record which was being played. The spirit friends came quickly, but had only power to whisper, and all the time had to keep very close to me. The manifestations were very rapid, but the time was too limited. We only sat three-quarters of an hour, and the feeling of haste was very intense. No help by singing or music was given to encourage the voices."

9

The holding of two sittings on one day weakens the power—
The question of strain and the difficulty of manifestation.

~

I

Monday evening, February 23, 1925.

ON the evening of the day upon which Valiantine had held a private sitting with Mrs. Ellis, I had invited two guests to Dorincourt for a séance. It was unfortunate that two appointments should have been made for Valiantine on one day, but owing to certain circumstances this was unavoidable. I consider it very inadvisable for a voice medium to hold two sittings in one day as I feel this is too great a strain, but it was impossible for me to put my guests off.

This second sitting at Dorincourt took place at about eight forty-five p.m.

In addition to Mr. Valiantine and my wife, there were present Priscilla, Countess Annesley, Major Colley, and myself.

Lady Annesley, whom I have known for many years, had often told me how interested she was in psychic studies, but this was the first occasion upon which she had experienced a séance.

Mr. Valiantine's illuminated trumpet and also mine were placed in the centre of the circle.

The conditions did not appear to me to be very good, and the power was certainly not strong. It was half an hour before any manifestation whatever occurred.

Then the deep voice of Dr. Barnett came through from the centre of the room, giving a short sentence of greeting. Bert Everett spoke from high up in the room, and Kokum spoke to us in a very loud tone. Pat O'Brien addressed me, and then my wife and Lady Annesley.

I asked Pat O'Brien, who came through, if he felt the power to be weak, and if he thought that any personal spirits would be able to lift the trumpet. Immediately both the illuminated trumpets were lifted and whirled in the air.

After a while, Valiantine's trumpet was taken over towards Lady Annesley. It touched her on the knee and on the head, and with great difficulty a voice came through. It was terribly indistinct, almost indecipherable. However, the voice managed to get out the word "Ethel."

For a long time this voice persisted, but, although we got a certain number of phrases, it was impossible to obtain any definite identification or information from this spirit. Lady Annesley, however, said that she knew an "Ethel" quite well who had passed away.

My illuminated trumpet was lifted and a voice spoke to Major Colley. This voice was also extremely indistinct, and we could only get through that it was "Arthur" (the second name could not be deciphered). The voice persisted, and tried very hard for six to seven minutes, but we could not understand what was said.

II

The evening was a very poor one, the poorest since Valiantine arrived in this country. I am inclined to think that the afternoon sitting had used a considerable amount of power, and that this rendered the manifestations extremely difficult.

10

A wait of three-quarters of an hour—A voice addresses the Countess Oeitiongham—A conversation in Chinese dialect—"Information that maybe of the utmost value"—Lord Northcliffe suggests a title for Mr. Swaffer's book.

I

Wednesday, February 25, 1925.

THIS sitting was held at Dorincourt at eight-thirty p.m. Present: Valiantine, Mrs. Bradley, Mr. Hannen Swaffer, Mrs. Kennedy, Mrs. Reynolds (Mr. John Galsworthy's sister), the Countess Tyong Oeitiongham, Dr. V. J. Woolley, and myself.

Of the sitters, Mrs. Reynolds and the Countess Oeitiongham had never sat at a voice séance.

The two luminous trumpets (Valiantine's and mine) were placed in the centre of the room.

The conditions appeared to be difficult, as it was some three-quarters of an hour before any movement was observed or any voice heard, although during this time all of the sitters notified that they had been touched.

The first manifestation occurred when the voice of Dr. Barnett came from the middle of the circle, saying "Have patience, friends."

A little later, Bert Everett came through from high up in the room. His voice appeared to me to be much weaker than usual.

Whilst a gramophone record was being played, the loud voice of Kokum also spoke. A little later the Irish accent of Pat O'Brien was heard, and he spoke a few sentences to me.

During this time my illuminated trumpet was lifted on two occasions in the air.

When we had sat at least one hour, one of the trumpets was lifted close to the face of the Countess Oeitiongham, and a voice addressed her in a foreign language.

The Countess answered in Chinese, but the voice was so indistinct that she could not decipher what was said.

The power appeared to be weak, and the trumpet was dropped.

After an interval, during which the gramophone was playing, the trumpet was lifted to the Countess, and the voice addressed her in the same tones, and again she answered in Chinese. Whilst the voice was endeavouring to speak we encouraged it to persevere, saying that we knew how difficult it was to materialize the vocal organs.

Four times the same effort was made by the voice, until it became strong enough and distinct enough for the Countess to understand what was said.

The conversation then went on for a short time between them in Chinese.

Immediately after the spirit had gone I asked the Countess, "Did you get any information of value?" She replied, "What he said maybe of the utmost value." Another sitter then asked: "Could you tell us what was said?" The Countess replied: "I should prefer not to say."

There was, of course, no curiosity on our part in wishing to know the nature of the communication, which was possibly of a very personal character. It was sufficiently phenomenal for us that Chinese had been spoken by an unknown spirit, which had been understood by the Countess.

DR. BARNETT (to the sitters): That was the lady's father who was speaking, and he sent a communication through her to her mother.

It was confirmed later by the Countess that her father was dead, and that her mother was living.

There was no one in the circle who could speak Chinese, and, in discussing the matter afterwards, the Countess stated that there were at least twenty different dialects in Chinese, each of which might have been used. She added that the voice spoke to her with two dialects mixed, in a way in which no European—even if he were able to speak Chinese—could do. One of the dialects was one in which her father used to speak with her when she was a child, and the other was one which they spoke together after she had grown up. This is obviously a point of the utmost evidential importance.

Feda addressed Mrs. Reynolds. Her voice was somewhat faint, but she spoke independently without using the trumpet.

Feda told Mrs. Reynolds that a spirit was there who wished to communicate with her, but could not obtain sufficient power. "It is very difficult for them tonight."

Whilst Feda remained, she spoke to Mr. Swaffer and to one or two of the other sitters.

Towards the close a voice came through in the independent voice- without using the trumpet saying "Swaff, Swaff, it's the Chief!"[132]

This voice, although not powerful, was very distinct, and everything that was said was heard by everyone in the room. Northcliffe and Mr. Swaffer discussed the book which Mr. Swaffer had just completed, and Mr. Swaffer, amongst other things, asked: "Have you got a title for me, Chief?"

LORD NORTHCLIFFE: Call it "Northcliffe's Return."[133]

Directly the spirit had gone, Mr. Swaffer asserted with great firmness: "That was Lord Northcliffe's own voice! I know it."

After the sitting Mr. Swaffer said that Lord Northcliffe's voice was better than he had ever heard it before.

Dr. Barnett closed the sitting.

II

The conditions did not appear to me to be at all good.

Of this sitting, it must be recorded that it was a very remarkable thing to succeed in getting a conversation carried on with a voice in Chinese. It must also be recorded that Lord Northcliffe's voice was clear and distinct.

I am not sure whether Valiantine was slightly nervy because of the presence of Dr. Woolley, but it must be noted that the power throughout was by no means strong, and that the majority of the communications were short, and lacked fluency.

---

[132] Lord Northcliffe.

[133] Mr. Swaffer used the title for his book *Northcliffe's Return*, which was published on July 3 1925

11

HDB's hundred-guinea challenge to Captain Maskelyne—The conditions—Throwing up the sponge—Why Captain Maskelyne withdrew—An illuminating confession of ignorance tickles the author's ironic sense—"Conjurors and illusionists are dull."

February 26, 1925.

AT this time there had been considerable publicity in the Press with regard to Valiantine's visit to this country, and press men, interviewers, photographers, etc., were clamouring each day to see him.

Some days previously Captain Clive Maskelyne, hearing that Margery (a well-known amateur medium and the wife of Dr. L. R. G. Crandon, of Boston, U.S.A.) was likely to visit this country, had issued a challenge that he could produce any of the psychic phenomena she was said to have produced in America.

Whilst the *Daily Sketch* was interviewing Valiantine and myself, I mentioned that I would issue a hundred guinea challenge to Captain Maskelyne that he could not produce phenomena similar to those which we were obtaining through Valiantine. Much fuss was made in the newspapers over this, and Captain Maskelyne accepted the challenge, declaring: "I am convinced that I can do all that Valiantine can do."

This was a peculiarly foolish and rash statement on the part of Captain Maskelyne. I stipulated that Captain Maskelyne must accept, and work under, the same conditions as Valiantine; that is, that he must sit in a room, six guests to enter the room, without their being introduced to Captain Maskelyne. The lights must then be turned off immediately, and Captain Maskelyne must produce voices that would speak to the various sitters, and the voices must establish the identities of the speakers.

Captain Maskelyne had accepted the challenge without the faintest knowledge of this vast subject.

When he was told of what was taking place, and what he would have to do, he threw up the sponge, and admitted that he could not do it. He stated that he could produce any physical phenomena, but was told that in this advanced study of psychics we no longer considered physical phenomena to be of any value.

Captain Maskelyne called to see me, and told me that he would not attempt such a performance. Therefore, he withdrew from his acceptance of my challenge.

In my talk with him, which was quite friendly, Captain Maskelyne told me that he had never attended a séance in his life, and that he knew nothing of mental phenomena, and had no knowledge of modern psychic literature. An illuminating confession of ignorance which tickled my ironic sense.

It was a little disappointing, however, that my challenge so avidly accepted should be so quickly dropped. I was looking forward to a performance. It promised a rest from the appeal of the stars, and the new diversion of a pseudo-understudy. When one has realized the divine comedy of the Universe it is an amusing relaxation to observe the ludicrous gyrations of material farce.

Captain Maskelyne maybe an efficient conjuror and illusionist—most of them are ineffably dull and all such forms of entertainment leave me bored and unamused but he fell into the same error into which so many conjurors have fallen before, by imagining that physical tricks have anything whatever to do with the authentic and established fact of direct spirit communication. No human being on Earth can produce by artificial means the voices of the spirits of another sphere, who give vocal and mental evidence of their individual identities. We advanced students are not interested in comic and primitive material illusions, we are only concerned with the great mental and spiritual realities.

It is symptomatic that in the infancy of this great study of the psychic forces, which embrace scientific and philosophic problems of the utmost importance to our civilization, that the heels of the leaders are followed by the clowns, who turn grimacing to the herd and by their comic contortions endeavour to inspire a ribald laughter.

12

Pat O'Brien speaks with Sir Oliver Lodge—"Pat" Raymond Lodge speaks to his father—Admiral Henderson and a strange reference to Joseph Honner—Sir Oliver discusses ether with a spirit—Dr. Barnett's sleepy sickness prescription is tried—Footnote: The victim of sleepy sickness is cured—The author unburdens his mind on the S.P.R.—Comments on "Raymond"—HDB states his spirit philosophy.

I

Friday, February 27, 1925.

This sitting was held in my study at Dorincourt at about eight forty-five p.m. In accordance with the usual procedure, none of the sitters were introduced to the medium, Valiantine.

Mr. Valiantine sat in my study, and those who were present walked straight in when the lights were turned off within a few seconds.

There were present Sir Oliver Lodge, Admiral Wilfred Henderson, Mr. Lionel Corbett, Mrs. Bovill, my wife, and myself.

It maybe presumed that Valiantine would know Sir Oliver Lodge, since his portrait has appeared in so many papers, but he was not introduced, neither did Valiantine know any of the names of the other sitters.

Although my study is well warmed by central heating, during a séance the atmosphere often changes and the room becomes quite cold.

I therefore advised the sitters to take in wraps with them, and Sir Oliver Lodge took in and wore a fur coat.

The two luminous trumpets were placed in the centre of the room. The conditions appeared to be very good.

During the time the first four records were played on the gramophone, many of the sitters were touched on the knee, hands or head, by what maybe presumed to be materialized hands.

The first voice to be heard was that of Dr. Barnett, speaking in deep clear tones, close to the floor, in the centre of the circle. He gave us a greeting.

A little later the loud tones of Kokum were heard speaking, whilst a gramophone record was being played.

During the evening, from high up in the room, there came the shrill voice of Bert Everett, who also spoke with us on two or three occasions later. Hawk Chief, on request, gave a penetrating whoop. Pat O'Brien, in his rich Irish brogue, carried on a conversation with Sir Oliver Lodge.

Bobby Worrall talked with us and with two or three of the sitters, and referred to watching Pat playing with a toy railway during the day in the nursery.[134]

Feda came through, and spoke with several of the sitters, including Sir Oliver Lodge, and gave her peculiar little laugh.

All these spirits spoke independently, without using the trumpet, and their voices appeared from different parts of the room.

Of the personal spirits, quite early in the evening, we heard an independent voice close to Sir Oliver Lodge, calling: "Father!" Almost immediately following this, the luminous trumpet was lifted, and taken very close to Sir Oliver, who was touched on the head and on the body.

The voice then said: "It's Pat, father!" And then added, as if announcing himself to us all: "Pat Raymond Lodge." Sir Oliver Lodge told us that Raymond was often addressed by the family as "Pat." A conversation ensued between Sir Oliver and Raymond on family matters, which lasted for some little time. Names were volunteered by the spirit. Three times during the evening Raymond came through to Sir Oliver Lodge.

An independent voice came through, addressing me, giving full Christian and surnames. This was George, my sister's young son.

He talked with me and with my wife, and said that he was going to make the endeavour to speak to my son Dennis at Cambridge on the following evening.

---

[134] This I found later to be correct.

A little later the luminous trumpet was lifted and taken in the direction of Admiral Henderson. It hovered close to him and a voice, which at first was very indistinct, spoke to him. All that we could catch was "Honner." Admiral Henderson, who is slightly deaf and has to use an ear instrument, did not appear to place the name. The voice then went on to say, "Knew you forty years ago." The name "Honner" was repeated and a little later some of the sitters distinctly heard the voice volunteer "Joseph Honner." Admiral Henderson then said that he recognized this name and added that he had served with a Joe Honner some forty years ago, saying also, I think, that he had not heard of him for over thirty years. The voice was weak and only one or two sentences were exchanged, but Admiral Henderson appeared to be somewhat surprised at the name volunteered by the voice.

This incident is interesting because I was seated next to the Admiral and, weak as the voice was, I distinctly heard the words "Joseph Honner." So also did Mr. Lionel Corbett and Admiral Henderson, who both corroborate me in this. Sir Oliver Lodge, however, said, after the sitting, that he thought the full name "Joseph Honner" was suggested by the Admiral. The point is important because the voice certainly said something about "Forty years ago" and certainly said "Joseph Honner," and the Admiral had to search his mind before he could recognize the name. The voice said "Joseph," and the Admiral referred to him as "Joe," the abbreviation by which he would be likely to remember a young shipmate.

Now although the full and somewhat uncommon name volunteered may only have been given as an evidential reference for identification, it was assumed that this was the spirit of Joseph Honner endeavouring to speak. Three months later, however, we learnt that the Joseph Honner referred to was alive.

The exact record of this incident is verified by Admiral Henderson, who adds: "I asked the voice one or two questions about the then Mediterranean Station and, curiously enough, I got quite reasonable and intelligent answers. The incident is full of interest. The facts are too genuine to be ignored. I am quite sure that the fact of Joseph Honner's existence had never entered my mind for at least thirty odd years."

After this incident a voice came through, announcing itself as George Hunt, my wife's father (full Christian and surnames being given), and talked with me and with my wife. He said that he was anxious to have the opportunity of speaking to his wife.

Two individual spirits came through and spoke to Mrs. Bovill, and also to Mr. Lionel Corbett. These spirits gave full Christian and surnames, and a short personal conversation ensued between them.

Suddenly, in the middle of the sitting, one of the luminous trumpets was lifted, and it was whirled round the circle at a lightning speed. It was then taken up to the ceiling—high up in the air—and the ceiling was rapped.

Towards the end of the sitting, Dr. Barnett spoke to us again, and there then ensued between Dr. Barnett and Sir Oliver Lodge a long discussion upon the ether. Sir Oliver Lodge asked questions of Dr. Barnett with regard to the make up of the human body. The manner in which Dr. Barnett replied to each of Sir Oliver's questions was fluent and intelligent. The discourse went on for over a quarter of an hour. The methods by which spirit communication in the actual voice could be obtained was discussed between them. Sir Oliver asked whether, on their side, this was a question of the fourth dimension, and Dr. Barnett, giving, as he did several times throughout, his characteristic and stentorian laugh, replied saying that there were several dimensions beyond ours.

Dr. Barnett dealt with the various forms of life of humans, animals, trees, plants, and so on, and stated that life survives in every form and that it is impossible to destroy life.

In answer to a question from Mr. Lionel Corbett with regard to psychic upheavals, Dr. Barnett again gave a very grave warning about the secret preparations of Japan and Germany for war in the air. On several occasions Dr. Barnett has referred to this, and although any forecast is problematic, yet he insists on the point that the next war will be comparatively soon and that it will be the most terrible that human civilization has had to endure.

Dr. Barnett added that he was very annoyed that the doctor had delayed so long in administering the treatment he had given for sleepy sickness. With regard to this point, I had telephoned the father of the patient on the morning of this night, and he had said that it was only on the previous night that the doctor had administered the treatment which had been given through by Dr. Barnett twelve days ago.[135]

I referred to the coming sittings we had arranged to give in Tavistock Square to the Society for Psychical Research, and said that I hoped we

---

[135] Four administrations in all were given, and whether it was due to this or not, the patient has now completely recovered.

would get good results, although I was not certain that the conditions there would be entirely satisfactory.

Dr. Barnett laughed and said: "We will do our best, but you should ask yourselves whether your intellects are not superior to theirs." This, of course, is quite true. As a matter of fact, I, personally, have learnt so much during the last two years of study, with my own mediumship, and with the enormous number of sittings I have had—not only with Valiantine, but with other mediums—that my experience in those two years amounts to more than the whole of the Society for Psychical Research put together for the forty odd years of their existence. And it must also be borne in mind that present at this sitting was Sir Oliver Lodge, past President of the Society and the greatest scientist in Great Britain.

Dr. Barnett, at the close of the sitting, speaking to my wife, said: "I wish to speak to you about your pet animal. (Meaning my Alsatian wolfhound!) You must give it Vermifuge. The dog has worms; that is why he scratches himself. You must give him a tablespoonful after meals."

II

All those who were present were impressed by the phenomena that had occurred.

I had a chat afterwards with Sir Oliver Lodge, who expresses his conviction of spirit communication far more freely and convincingly in conversation than he does in his public writings. He referred to the communications he had received during recent years from the spirit of F. W. H. Myers. Since the publication of his excellent book *Raymond*, he has not, I believe, published any further work on psychical research; his genius has been devoted to the solution of material scientific problems.

In the compilation of *Raymond* Sir Oliver based his evidence of survival chiefly on the communications received through clairvoyant mediums—that is communications made through these mediums' mouths and lips. To appreciate the great advance that has been made recently it maybe noticed that there is no record whatever in *Raymond* of evidence obtained by the direct and independent voice speaking from space, which is the rarest and most dramatic form of phenomenon yet discovered.

At the time that *Raymond* was published Sir Oliver had, apparently, no personal experience whatever of this form, and, although since that date he has heard the "independent voices," I gathered from him that his knowledge of "voice" phenomena is extremely limited. This is not to be wondered at since "voice mediums" are so rare that only a handful are known to the world. In fact, only a year ago Sir Oliver told me that he did not think the chief research officers of the Society for Psychical Research had ever heard the independent voice.

It is necessary to emphasize these facts because a week or so subsequent to the Dorincourt sitting at which Sir Oliver was present, in a letter to me he raised one or two points which demanded an immediate and thorough analysis. He said, "that the thing that impressed him most was the sailing round of the illuminated trumpet at a considerable speed high up." Now, although I agree that this may have appeared amazing to those who have witnessed such physical phenomena for the first time, I have become so accustomed to various manifestations of this description that I have ceased to regard their significance.

The most important point raised by Sir Oliver was his suggestion regarding the control of the medium. Here I was compelled to join issue with him. In his letter referring to the "voice" communications he said:

> "To make them really evidential some control of the medium would have been essential. I have no reason to doubt his (Valiantine's) genuineness, but a scientific report must lay stress on the guarding of all loopholes for normal production of phenomena."

Now, on the evening that Sir Oliver was at Dorincourt, from his conversation during the séance and afterwards, he certainly appeared entirely convinced of the fact that supernormal voices were speaking from space. A personal affirmation, however, is different from a scientific confirmation, and when one comes in contact with a discovery of infinitely greater importance than the discovery of wireless, it is only right on an initial experience that every aspect should be carefully reviewed.

It was imperative, therefore, for me to prove to Sir Oliver that the physical control of a medium, though essential for scientific establishment of physical phenomena, could have no bearing whatever upon the scientific establishment of the psychical or mental phenomena of "spirit voices" volunteering evidence of their surviving identities. This I did in the following reply:

"With regard to the phenomenon of voice mediumship, I feel that I understand more of this than any scientist in the world, because during the last nine months both my wife and myself have developed as voice mediums and, beyond the few odd accounts which you have read, astounding evidence of surviving personalities has been established in the presence of witnesses of repute.

"I do not believe in controlling a medium. If anybody suggested that I should be controlled I should feel insulted, and I refused to do this with Valiantine, although he brought over from America a net with a lock acid key, which he asked me to use. I think such methods are stupid when one is collecting mental proofs.

"How can you account for Chinese, Russian, German, Italian, and practically every language being spoken in the independent voice of a spirit? Could any form of control account for this?

You must forgive me, Sir Oliver, if I analyse your letter.

We have, apparently, entirely different minds with regard to the value of the various phenomena. You say that the thing which impressed you most was the sailing of the luminous trumpet through the room at considerable speed high up. That, I may mention, is the incident which impressed me least of all. I have had in my own house, under my personal mediumship and also with Valiantine, physical phenomena beyond anything of which I have read. I have had a whole band playing, and I have had the most brilliant solos played, without any material music, by the spirits, but I count physical phenomena as of comparatively little value. They would never convince me of survival.

"In your letter you say, 'with regard to voice communications,' to make them really evidential, some control of the medium would have been essential, and that in a scientific report one must lay stress on the guarding of all loopholes for the normal production of phenomena.

Since you have, as I understand, secured one of Mrs. Osborne Leonard's sittings each week for several years (records of which are never published to the world), do you control her and do you disregard any evidence that comes through her mouth? If you do not, how can you disregard any evidence that comes through an independent voice from space?

At a considerable sacrifice of time I have hardly ceased for one day in my psychical studies for the last two years. During that period I have attended some hundreds of séances, and I have gained a great advance in knowledge. I assert unhesitatingly that the idea of controlling a voice medium represents a primitive conception of this form of phenomenon, and maybe likely to smash the instrument or affect the sensitive vibrations, and annihilate progress.

I have studied the life of every medium with whom I have come in touch, and I have observed how the powers of many have been destroyed, and how the power of an infinitesimal few has been developed.

"Please do not think that I am writing in an unfriendly tone. I have the utmost respect for you as a great scientist, but on the study of sensitive mentalities and on the value of any psychological points of evidence which maybe volunteered, I yield to no authority upon this plane beyond myself.

"The Society for Psychical Research fail because of their attitude and their lack of experience and knowledge. They think only in terms of suspicion and doubt, and can evolve nothing more original in thought beyond the tying up or the caging of a medium.

"When the volume of the long series of experiments upon which I am engaged is published it will be found that there has been accumulated a vast mass of volunteered evidence obtained directly from the spirit voices. This evidence is irrefutable, and has been given to people of keen intellect whose words the world will take, and who are, one after the other, coming out into the open and pronouncing their new conviction."

Since the date upon which I wrote this letter to Sir Oliver Lodge a further tremendous advance in psychical research has been established. At Dorincourt the spirits have conversed in audible voices in full daylight in the presence of several witnesses.

It was essential for me to point out to Sir Oliver, when he raised the point of control, the analogy between the communications and evidence he received through Mrs. Leonard and other clairvoyant mediums, upon which he based his conviction of survival, and the communications and evidences which are now being received in the more amazing form of the direct and independent voices of the spirits. If, as a scientist, he felt that the establishment of survival could not be claimed scientifically on the evidence of "independent voices" without the medium being controlled, it would be paradoxical to claim survival scientifically on communications coming through the mouth of any clairvoyant medium, with whom the suggestion of such form of control has never been advanced, and would, of course, be considered absurd.

If control were the establishing crux then *Raymond* is valueless and all Sir Oliver's psychical studies have been wasted time.

But *Raymond* is not valueless; it is the carefully compiled work of one of our greatest thinkers, who will thoroughly understand the opportunity for the exposition of these arguments which he had afforded me.

To control a voice medium is not only foolish, but detrimental. It is what the spirits say that counts. Either they prove to you by evidence their identity, or they do not. If they do, you are convinced of survival; if they do not you remain in doubt. Whether the medium is or is not controlled matters not one iota.

The medium is merely the passive instrument, and in this rare form is ultra-sensitive. To control or disturb in any way is likely to cross the vibrations. I am not theorizing, I am speaking with authority, for as a voice medium myself I know more upon this subject than any living scientist.

Control? The Spirit of God, in His wisdom, gives us all free will to progress or stagnate. Control is anathema to the artist. Can one control love? It is easy to control the physical manifestation of love, but can one control its mental exercise? That would be devastating.

Wireless is not an invention, and spirit communication is not an invention. They are both new and great discoveries. A few years ago we should have ridiculed the idea of listening to voices speaking through space from America, now we do not ridicule the fact that we can listen to voices speaking to us from another world.

We are living in an age of miracles. Miracles infinitely beyond those recorded two thousand years ago. Our faith is no longer based on flimsy legend, it is based on adamant fact.

We are on the eve of new and momentous discoveries.

13

A sitting in an unsuitable room at 27 Trinity Street, Cambridge—'Impossible to go on,' says Dr. Barnett—HDB's address to the Heretics.

∼

I

Saturday, February 28, 1925.

Having been invited to lecture to the Heretics Society at Cambridge on Sunday, March 1, I motored down over the weekend, and held a sitting in my son's rooms at 27 Trinity Street on the evening.

There were present: Valiantine, Dr. Broad, Mr. I. A. Richards, Mr. Jack Baines, Mr. W. Laurence, Miss Margaret Gardiner, Mrs. Bradley, Anthony Bradley, and myself.

The room in which the sitting was held was rather large, and unsuitable for a séance. The curtains were not heavy, and the light from outside penetrated through in places. Of the sitters, there were four who had not had any previous experience.

The conditions appeared difficult, and the sitting was comparatively poor. Only three voices were heard. Dr. Barnett, speaking from the centre of the room, gave a short phrase. Bert Everett spoke and also Kokum.

An independent voice was heard quite close to Miss Gardiner, calling: "Margaret, Margaret!" but we could get nothing further than this.

At one period, the luminous trumpet was lifted and floated round the room, touching the various sitters; it then collapsed on the floor.

The voice of Dr. Barnett came through, and said that it was impossible to go on. The sitting, which had lasted less than an hour, was then closed.

II

On the following evening I addressed the Heretics Society on "The Recent Advance in Psychical Research." The Liberal Club, in which the lecture was delivered, was filled to capacity.

The President of the Heretics, Mr. P. Sargent Florence, was in the chair.

Mr. Hannen Swaffer also addressed the members of the Society.

It was a particularly keen and intelligent audience, and the questions which were asked afterwards were many and varied, the majority being of a studious character.

After the meeting we adjourned to some rooms in college, and to my amusement a number of the undergraduates who had been present at the meeting flocked in, and asked me whether it would be possible for a séance to be held then and there.

14

*"Women," states the author, "are better sitters than men" —
A father meets his daughter in the spirit—Miss Ida Cohen talks
with her dead aunt—Seventeen voices speak.*

~

Monday, March 2, 1925.

THE sitting took place in my study at Dorincourt.
   Present: George Valiantine, Mrs. Bradley, Miss Ida Cohen, Mr. L. Gainsmore, Mrs. Hunt, Mrs. W. Johnstone, Mrs. H. Whittet, and Mlle. Bechard. None of the new sitters was introduced to Valiantine, nor did he know their names.

I was not at the sitting, as I was speaking at the Lyceum Club on this evening.

Of the sitters, with the exception of my wife, Mrs. Hunt and Mrs. Whittet, none of those present had ever experienced a séance.

The conditions appeared to be fairly good, and a long period of observation leads me to assert that the majority of women are infinitely better sitters than men. The following account is written from the record taken by Mrs. Bradley.

Of the guides, five manifested and spoke during the evening. Dr. Barnett and Bert Everett on several occasions, also Kokum, Hawk Chief, and Pat O'Brien.

Feda spoke to two or three of the sitters.

With regard to physical manifestations, during the evening one of the luminous trumpets was lifted and whirled round the circle at lightning speed, and was then taken outside the circle, high up in the air.

A trumpet was taken in the direction of Mrs. Johnstone and a voice called: "Kitty, this is father!" Father and daughter talked together for some time on personal matters.

A little later, after other voices had spoken to various sitters, another voice spoke also to Mrs. Johnstone, announcing itself to be "Elsie," and calling Mrs. Johnstone by her Christian name. A conversation was carried on between Mrs. Johnstone and this spirit. Mrs. Johnstone asked the question: "Were you happy in India?" to which the voice replied: "No," in a decided manner.

Identity was established by Mrs. Johnstone of both the voices which spoke to her.

Through, the trumpet a voice addressed Mr. Leo D. Gainsmore, giving the name of "Lou." A voice also addressed Miss Cohen, calling her "Ida," and a conversation ensued.

Another voice addressed Miss Ida Cohen, announcing itself to be "Louisa." This voice continued to talk with Miss Cohen and with Mr. Gainsmore on personal matters. Miss Cohen informed the sitters afterwards that she had been speaking with her Aunt Louisa.

Through the trumpet a voice addressed Mrs. Hunt, announcing itself by the full name of "George Hunt." Another voice, addressing Mrs. Hunt, announced itself as "Carrie."[136] The voice continued to speak with my wife and with Mlle. Bechard.

Warren spoke to my wife, with Mrs. Hunt, and with Mlle. Bechard, regarding his children, Phyllis and Betty.

When the voice of Carrie was speaking Mlle. Bechard said: "Do you know what Phyllis did this morning?"

CARRIE: She fell!

Mlle. Bechard stated afterwards that, during the morning, Phyllis had fallen in a faint.

Two individual spirits came through to Mrs. Whittet. One announced itself with: "It's your Gordon, mother." Whereupon they talked together on personal matters. The second voice spoke through the trumpet, saying "It's Girlie." This was the voice of another of Mrs. Whittet's children, who had passed over.

A voice addressed Mlle. Bechard, to which she replied in English. The voice then replied to her in French, and they then conversed for a while.

---

[136] Mrs. Hunt's sister.

THE WISDOM OF THE GODS

The voices were fairly continual throughout the evening.

It will be observed that during the evening seventeen voices—masculine and feminine—spoke, and of these, seventeen most, of them gave their names and identified their personalities to the sitters.

15

A poor sitting—An untranslatable message—A persistent voice—Bert Everett tries to help but fails.

Tuesday, March 3, 1925.

This was a poor evening. There were present: George Valiantine, my wife, the Hon. Richard Bethell and Mrs. Bethell, Mr. N. P. Whaddia and his friend Mr. Dharwar, Mr. Hannen Swaffer, and myself. With the exception of my wife and myself, none of the sitters had ever been to a voice séance before.

After about a quarter of an hour the voice of Dr. Barnett gave us a greeting Bert Everett spoke a sentence or two and also Kokum. Very considerable effort was made in getting through a spirit speaking in the independent voice, and then using the luminous trumpet to Mr. Whaddia. This spirit was speaking in a foreign language. The voice was very indistinct, and Mr. Whaddia and Mr. Dharwar in answering spoke in some Indian dialect. Although the voice replied, and persisted for some little time in endeavouring to make some communication, Mr. Whaddia said it was impossible to understand what was said. The voice, of course, was heard by us all and was moderately loud, but no one could translate the message. The persistence of this voice apparently used up a considerable amount of the power. The luminous trumpet moved from Mr. Whaddia to Mr. Dharwar, and the continuous effort which was being made proved a little tiresome to the other sitters. After this incident Bert Everett said: "Mr. Maddia (it sounded like that, and not Whaddia) it was your father speaking to you." Then Dr. Barnett said the conditions were not good and closed the sitting.

16

A spirit tries to speak to Mr. Austin Harrison—the spirit of William Archer makes an explanation—The plot of "The Green Goddess"—Feda rebuffs the anonymous Mrs. X.—Mrs. X.'s confession—The author's letter to Mr. Harrison—Photographs of Ectoplasm.

I

Wednesday, March 4, 1925.

This sitting was held at Dorincourt at about eight forty-five p.m. in the presence of Valiantine, my wife, Mr. Hannen Swaffer, Mrs. Kennedy, Mr. Austin Harrison and Mrs. X. (a lady whose name I prefer not to mention), and myself. Mr. Harrison had had no previous experience, and Mrs. K. has sat only once previously at a direct voice séance.

The conditions appeared to me to be quite good, and I felt that the sitters would form a good circle.

Again, however, the séance was what I should term a more or less negative one.

Dr. Barnett came through after ten minutes, and gave us a greeting, afterwards speaking with us several times at odd intervals.

Bert Everett also spoke on two occasions, Kokum once or twice, and Pat O'Brien spoke to me and to several of the sitters. Feda spoke on two or three occasions.

Of the personal spirits, Lord Northcliffe addressed us independently, and spoke with Mr. Swaffer and with Mr. Harrison, but the power was not sufficient for him to keep the conversation going for long.

A voice speaking independently, and just passing Mr. Harrison's head, called twice, "Harrison-Harrison." The luminous trumpet was then lifted in an endeavour to address Mr. Harrison, calling him "Austin." Again the power seemed to be weak, and no recognition could be established or claimed, and the trumpet fell to the ground.

Another voice, speaking independently, said in clear tones that it was William Archer. Mr. Archer spoke to Mr. Harrison and to me. In conversation with this spirit, I referred to the statement made in the Literary Guide in regard to a paragraph which had appeared in the Press, in which I had stated that William Archer had sat with me at Dorincourt whilst he was on Earth when he spoke to his son and referred to his work. When this was referred to in the Literary Guide in their current issue, it was stated:

"Not long before his death Mr. Archer assured us that he was not in any sense a believer in spiritualism." to which I replied:

"This statement was refuted by William Archer in his long letter to John Middleton Murry, published in *The Adelphi* this month in which he said:

"'I am absolutely convinced, from repeated experience and observation, of the genuineness of a very great number of the phenomena, and of the crass stupidity of the men of science and others who simply denounce and refuse to study them.'"

William Archer, in replying to me this evening, told me that he did believe in spirit communication whilst he was on Earth.

MR. HANNEN SWAFFER: Where did you get the plot of "The Green Goddess?"

WILLIAM ARCHER: From my son.

The trumpet, then traveling in the direction of Mr. Harrison, said: "Harrison, this is the one great Truth."

The trumpet moved towards Mrs. Kennedy and addressed her, the voice saying: "It's Paulie, mother." A personal conversation continued between them, and afterwards Mrs. Kennedy said that she knew it was her son Paul, and the announcement of his name as "Paulie" by which he was known, was very evidential to her.

Shortly after this the trumpet was lifted and an independent voice spoke in the direction of Mrs. X. The voice was indistinct, and it was impossible to get any proper communication through. Two attempts were made, and each time the trumpet fell to the ground.

The independent voice of Feda came through again, and speaking to Mrs. X. said: "You must not try to touch the trumpet!"

Mrs. X. seemed a little agitated and replied: "All right, I am very sorry; I won't do it again."

DR. BARNETT: There has been a disturbance going on, here tonight, and we shall have to close.

Mrs. X., who is a very charming lady, was extremely upset, and openly told us that during the sitting she had been stretching her arms out on occasions when the trumpet had been in the air in the endeavour to get behind it and see if it was being held by anybody, and once or twice she had touched it. She found that no human hand was holding it, but when she had touched it, it had fallen to the ground.

This action of the arms waving behind the trumpet was, probably, affecting the ectoplasmic forces.

Mrs. X. told me afterwards that she was frightfully sorry she had done this, because a previous sitting had convinced her of survival. When she had described the phenomenon of the luminous trumpet moving in the air to a very close relation of hers, he had asked her whether, on the next occasion, she would get her hand behind the trumpet in order to ascertain that no one was holding it. She added that she only did this in order that she might be able to say that she was certain the movements were supernormal.

She told me that what she had done that night had given her wonderfully convincing proof, but had realized afterwards that by her action she had destroyed the power for mental communication, which is, of course, the one thing of real value.

II

From the evidential point of view, of course, the evening must be regarded as poor, and the length of the conversations was quite short. At the same time, the rather unfortunate incident had a certain value and added to my knowledge. I can see that one has to face, in the future, with skeptics or inexperienced sitters, the possibility of many of them stretching their arms out in the dark, thus destroying the sensitive forces and preventing voice communications from coming through.

After the sitting, the discussion which took place was more or less confined to the incident which had disturbed the phenomena.

As a result of this there was a somewhat amusing aftermath.

Austin Harrison is an intimate friend of mine of long standing. He was for many years the editor of *The English Review*, and is also the author of several brilliant books.

During the six months or so prior to this sitting I had seen very little of him, and had no opportunity of discussing the subject of psychics with him.

I mention this because some little time after this sitting an article written by him appeared in the *Sunday Pictorial* in which he recorded his one experience in a rather humorous manner, and raised the question as to why people should not put their hand behind the luminous trumpet if they wished, and why it was that spirits could not speak in the daylight. I therefore wrote him the following letter:

"Your article comes to me as a refreshing breeze of humour. It is as if a Georgian coachman walked into the works of the Rolls-Royce Company for the first time, and, looking at a stationary engine, thought he understood it.

"The article is full of amusing psychological contradictions and affirmations.

"You say that the spirits abominate light, but since you were at Dorincourt we have obtained the voices in the full daylight, and all these records will be published in my book.

"What have you to say to this?

"In your description of the one séance you attended you give your impressions of certain (to me, quite ordinary) psychical phenomenon, and say to yourself 'but this is miraculous.' Of course it was. But then, after the séance, because I, with tremendous experience, say there was nothing 'evidential' you say that you protest that you 'had experienced a lot.'

"You itemize the facts."

"You say: 'First, inanimate bodies have moved freely in the air, apparently of their own volition. Secondly, I had been mysteriously touched on the leg and on the head. Thirdly, a cool blast had rippled my brow. Lastly, I had heard beyond a doubt various voices, and had spoken with two dead people, both known in life to me. If this is not "evidential" what is evidence? Only one factor was missing—light. An important factor.'

"I can show you that we have overcome even light.

"Now, the strange part to me, Harrison, is this. You, on your first experience, accept as 'miraculous' and 'evidential' an accumulation of minor incidents which I, in my advanced knowledge, record as nonevidential. For, on the incidents which you observed and heard, I should never claim the establishment of survival.

"You say: 'I feel annoyed at people who regard a floating trumpet as "non-evidential." To me such a phenomenon is fantastically evidential. But of what? That is the question.'

"I must reply to you, Harrison, that the 'floating trumpet' is merely evidential of the supernormal movements of a physical object. In itself, this alone could never convince me of survival. The trumpet is used only as an amplifier of sound, in order to enable the materialized spirit voice to be more distinctly heard, and it is only when these voices volunteer information which enables us, beyond doubt, to recognize their living personalities, that we can accept the survival of their spirit.

You also say, with reference to physical manifestations, that the learned (one of whom I presume you mean me to be) assure us they are purely preliminary. These physical manifestations are preliminary, and have been proved and tested by scientists in many countries. I have proved and tested them and got far beyond them, and unless through these first preliminary steps I had succeeded in arriving at an advancement in mental knowledge, I should long since have ceased to pursue my studies.

"The physical does not appeal to me, because it is a blind alley, and the progress of psychical research must depend, in future, entirely upon the knowledge that can be gained through mental phenomena.

"Had you experienced all that I have during the last two years I am quite sure you would be inclined to regard as comparatively poor that which you regarded at Dorincourt as 'miraculous.'

"I thought you knew, but perhaps I omitted to tell you, that during a long series of experiments my wife and I, without any professional medium being present, have obtained voices and evidential communications in just the same manner as happened with Valiantine. This has been the result of my studying how mediumship can be developed.

"This has proved the fact of the supernormal faculties of man and also the fact of the survival of the spirit, and of the actuality that audible conversations with spirits can be carried on by us on this plane. If I merely stated this I should not expect to be believed, but I have proved it before witnesses of repute."

The few queries made by Mr. Austin Harrison in his article were of the character invariably raised by those who, for the first time, witness psychical phenomena. Mr. Harrison regarded ectoplasm and the ectoplasmic forces as mere assumption. Ectoplasm is not an assumption; it is an established scientific fact, and the complete accessible particulars of the nature of ectoplasm are to be found in the books of Baron von Schrenck Notzing, Madame Bisson, Dr. Geley, and Dr. Crawford.

Baron von Schrenck Notzing, the leading psychical researcher in Germany, held séances with the celebrated French medium, Eva C., for four years, and with a subdued red light two hundred and twenty-five photographs of ectoplasm were taken under the strictest conditions.

The scientific works of the writers I have mentioned form the textbooks from which the inquirer may begin his studies. They form the basis of psychical knowledge, but the proved fact of the existence of ectoplasm and the proved fact of the supernormal movement of objects is not a sufficient basis for the acceptance of the survival of man's spirit after bodily death. It is only from an accumulation of irrefutable evidence of surviving personality volunteered by the discarnate spirits themselves that it is possible to establish this claim. That is why what Austin Harrison regarded as miraculous and evidential I was compelled to regard as non-evidential, even though it was phenomenal.

17

When publicity becomes aggravating: Valiantine's fame and the ridiculous position of the Society for Psychical Research—The S.P.R. séance room: mediaeval in conception and inquisitorial in design—The author is incensed—How the first S.P.R. test sitting was smashed—The moribund S.P.R..

I

Friday, March 6, 1925.

THE Society for Psychical Research, of which I am a member, had approached me, before Valiantine arrived in England, with regard to obtaining a series of experimental sittings with him in their séance room.

Since the date of Valiantine's arrival in England, enormous interest had been developed in the British press on the various phenomena which had been produced at the sittings which had been held. Many of the newspapers gave columns of description of the various happenings which had taken place at Dorincourt, and I was snowed under with applications from persons—famous and otherwise—requesting the privilege of a sitting with Valiantine.

When it was reported that he was about to give a sitting to the Society for Psychical Research, undue prominence was given to this event, and its import was absurdly exaggerated.

The Society for Psychical Research was referred to by one newspaper as the most important body of its kind in the world. This is quite ridiculous, since the great bulk of recent research work has been conducted, not by the Society, but by individual students.

Before proceeding with a record of this sitting I am going to analyse the status of the sitters representing the S.P.R., and in justice to the many brilliant intellects who are studying this subject, I must analyse their intelligences by comparison.

The first sitting I was able to arrange for them took place at about eight-thirty, at 31 Tavistock Square. London.

II

There were present Dr. V. J. Woolley, Mr. E. J. Dingwall (both research officers of the S.P.R.), three lady members of the Society, whose names I do not know, Mr. Hannen Swaffer, Mrs. Bradley, Valiantine, and myself.

The séance room of the S.P.R. is recently built, and equipped for the purpose. The room has been seldom used, and the atmosphere is aggressively new.

In a corner stands a huge cage, big enough to incarcerate a full-grown man. It is a sinister-looking contraption, mediaeval in conception and inquisitorial in design.

The room, I was informed, had been used only once before during the last few months; that was for a series of experiments with a physical medium—not a voice medium.

These experiments consisted of articles being placed in the cage, while the investigators sat outside holding the hands of the medium for considerable lengths of time in order to observe whether the articles moved or not. Sometimes the articles did move, and sometimes they did not. I cannot help feeling that the hands of the sitters must have become unpleasantly clammy during the long waits for this soul-stirring event, and I am perfectly certain that had I been one of the sitters, my mind would have become clammier even than their hands.

This phenomenon may have proved peculiarly interesting from a scientific point of view to the novitiate, but such a phenomenon would now leave me utterly bored. It was a very primitive form of mediumship—a form many of us have long since passed. If an article happened to lift itself two inches into the air, this would not prove survival to anyone. So far as physical phenomena are concerned, on many occasions at Dorincourt we have had some of the most marvelous physical, as well as mental, phenomena the world has ever known.

The circle of nine at the S.P.R. sitting was rather large. The two luminous trumpets were placed in the centre of the room, and underneath Mr. Dingwall's chair was a small, luminous spot. Another luminous spot was on the wall, facing Mr. Dingwall. I do not understand the purpose of the two spots, unless the Committee thought that the medium might walk round and round the circle trying to overtake the trumpet in order to speak through it.

I had explained to the research officers that any form of physical phenomena did not interest me in the slightest, and that only mental communications, to my mind, possessed any real value whatever.

Of the sitters, Dr. Woolley, I think, has had only four experiences of the direct voice séances, all of which I provided him with at Dorincourt.

The extent of Mr. Dingwall's experiments I do not know, beyond the fact that he attended one direct voice séance—a poor one—at Dorincourt, under Valiantine's mediumship, in February, 1924, and that he had investigated Margery, the USA amateur physical medium.

Mr. Dingwall informed me that he was much more interested in physical phenomena than in mental phenomena, and that he did not regard himself as a good sitter for mental communication.

These two gentlemen are charming and intelligent men with whom I get on excellently.

With regard to the three lady members of the Committee of the S.P.R., and who were invited to this sitting, I believe that none of them had had any previous experience whatever of a direct voice sitting.

The results of the sitting were practically negative. The temperature of the room was fairly warm, but the pervading mentality was to me excessively cold.

Mr. Dingwall manipulated the gramophone. There was a selection of only jazz records. I have no fault to find with jazz music, but as an evening's entertainment it is inclined to become boresome. Operatic selections are a relief.

One of the ladies objected to music being played. She said that she thought it would be better if we recited prayers or that we maintained a complete and holy silence.

This incensed me. Although I approach this study in the sincerest spirit, I know that in addition to the philosophical issues, these communications depend upon a scientific regard for the vibrations when the voices are endeavouring to manifest under difficult conditions.

After waiting three-quarters of an hour, during which time I was unutterably bored, eventually we heard the voice of Bert Everett saying: "Good evening, souls." The voice came, as it usually does, in a shrill, falsetto tone, high up in the room. We waited on for half an hour longer, and then the anonymous lady made another inexperienced remark, which I pounced upon in fury, and this smashed the evening.

Immediately after this the voice of Dr. Barnett said "Goodnight, friends."

The whole thing was ludicrous.

It was a complete waste of time. Here was a gathering of what is assumed to be the one great society for psychical research in Great Britain. What did we find? We found it represented by elderly ladies, who know practically nothing of the modern development of the subject.

I told Dr. Woolley that I should refuse to sit again. Firstly, because the company would bore me; secondly, because I felt that the members of the Society did not understand the proper conditions for this direct and sensitive form of phenomena; and thirdly, because I know that I should get so irritable that it would have a deterrent effect on any manifestations which might occur.

I have studied and know what conditions mean. I know the sensitiveness of mediumship, the sensitiveness of atmosphere, and the mentality of sitters. I know Valiantine's powers, and I know how my own and my wife's voice mediumship developed.

My personal feelings on my first experience with the members of the Society for Psychical Research were that of amazement at their lack of knowledge of the rudiments of phenomena, and astonishment during my conversation with them at the naive manner in which they exposed their ignorance.

III

On the following day, Una, Lady Troubridge, who is a member of the S.P.R., telephoned me to say that she had been asked by Dr. Woolley if she and Miss Radcliffe Hall, who was for some considerable period on the Council, would sit in the Society's séance room with Valiantine. Lady Troubridge told me that she did not wish to sit there because she thought the conditions were not good.

"Can I come down to Dorincourt," she asked, "and sit with you? I will only sit with them at the S.P.R. if there is no other opportunity, but I know it is almost impossible to obtain good results with the conditions that exist there."

The next day Lady Troubridge wrote to me this letter:

"Following our talk on the telephone, I write to remind you that Miss Radcliffe Hall and I will hold ourselves ready at any date or time to sit with Valiantine at your house if you are so kind as to arrange a sitting. I have written to Dr. Woolley to say that in view of the inclusion of novice sitters in their circle, we do not care to take part, as we only consented to doing so in the belief that the circle would be limited to S.P.R. investigators of experience, yourself and Mrs. Bradley, and anyone you should recommend as experienced in the conduct and attitude needful if any results are to be obtained.

"I cannot feel that they will get anything at all from which to form a judgment if they include people who have no experience of any kind of phenomena."

Lady Troubridge, whom I know personally, has a knowledge of psychics, although her study has been mostly confined to clairvoyant trance mediumship. Apparently she felt that the conditions at Dorincourt were conducive to results of value, and that the conditions and the organization by inexperienced people at the S.P.R. headquarters were not conducive.

The great wave of knowledge of psychics has apparently swept past the Society for Psychical Research. At the moment it is evidently in a moribund condition.

18

The author emphasizes the importance of harmony—Voices speak within thirty seconds—Some remarks on bad plays and stupid people—Further advice on financial affairs—Dr. Barnett's discourse on the planet Mars—Bert Everett on the ethereal body.

Saturday, March 7, 1925.

ON this evening, as a relief from the boring tensity of the conditions and the odd mentality of the Society for Psychical Research, we decided to hold a private sitting at Dorincourt. Only three of us sat: my wife, Valiantine, and myself.

Students should observe the immense importance of complete harmony when they wish to obtain communications in the direct voice through from the higher spheres.

I am not giving theories; I am giving knowledge. I know conditions. These pseudo-researchers do not.

The three of us walked into my study. We required no music for vibrations; we knew that we could get into direct communication at once.

The luminous trumpets were placed on the floor, but they were never used. Within thirty-five seconds, in the independent voice, the spirits began to speak to us, and they never ceased for longer than a minute, when a pause was made to enable another voice to come through.

Seven spirits spoke to us with great fluency and at great length. It was as if ten people, instead of three, were sitting in a room talking. Each of the seven unseen personalities was vivid, attractive, and distinctive. More so indeed than any seven people we might invite to our house could ever be, for the handicap of the physical body so often engenders the irritating cultivation of posturings, posings, mannerisms, and affectations.

Bert Everett said how easy it was for him to talk with us under harmonious conditions, and how pleasant it was to be able to talk with just the three of us.

Kokum, the Indian guide, talked with us in his great voice for a long time.

We questioned Dr. Barnett about the conditions of the previous evening, asking him how it was that they had been unable to materialize their voices and speak with us, as they were speaking this night. He said that there the sitters created an atmosphere which formed an impenetrable barrier, that we might sit there only once or twice more, and unless they could penetrate the conditions and obtain good results it would be wise to give up such attempts, as it was dissipating valuable time. He said: "Mr. Bradley, you must try and control your nerves." I am quite aware of the wisdom of his advice, but, nevertheless, being human, I cannot control my nerves with certain irritating types, and I shall refuse to sit with them in future. When I see a bad play—and the majority of plays are inartistically bad—I feel a nausea, and when I sit with stupid people, on the research of a great study, I feel a ten times worse nausea.

My wife asked how the man with the sleepy sickness was getting on, and again Dr. Barnett said that he was very annoyed they did not follow out the instructions given quickly enough.

Pat O'Brien came through and spoke at great length. His pleasant Irish humour was a magnificent sedative.

Georgie, speaking independently, talked with my wife and myself, expressing a wish that he might speak with his grandfather and grandmother, my aged father[137] and mother who are still alive.

Annie talked with the three of us in her splendidly distinct tones, and said how glad she was to be able to speak to us freely and lovingly, without the restrictions imposed by other sitters, and by the necessity, which it was important for them on their side to regard, of bringing other spirits through to talk with their friends.

---

[137] He died four months later.

She told me again how she was helping me in my literary work, and also in certain very essential material issues which I had to contend with. In our talk she said many things which cheered me up in a way it is impossible for me to describe.

Warren talked with my wife and me for a long time. He said that the material matters would be straightened out for me quite soon, and that they were helping me. He discussed in detail many important private matters.

Both my sister and Warren discussed the dramatic developments that had taken place since the Osborne Leonard sitting some three months previously when Warren came through, and giving me the full Christian and surname of a certain person, told me that I should have to be careful and that I should have to watch certain matters. Annie had also warned me, saving there were material issues that were imperative for me to regard, giving me another and direct line of observation.

On these important financial matters I was told precisely what to do, and the moment at which to act.

On the date of this sitting, March 7, I was still continuing my investigations which had already resulted in the disclosure of the embezzlement of tens of thousands of pounds. This subtle and malevolent treachery, emanating from an unexpected quarter, had been persistent, and might never have been discovered but for the communications I received from my two great spirit friends. This incident is a remarkable example of how the spirit forces can counteract a material evil.

After Warren had gone, Dr. Barnett came through again, and in his philosophical wisdom said that whilst we were on this material plane it was necessary for us to take care of the material issues. He said: "Your sister and Warren warned you what was taking place. Not only did they speak to you, but they impressed your mind as to exactly how to act."

Later on he said that they, on their side, were building up tremendous proofs of the actuality of spirit communication for us to give out to the world.

In answer to a question put to him as to the physical stature of the Martians, Dr. Barnett said that they are shorter than we are, the average height being about four feet three inches, but they are perfectly proportioned.

He said that they had often tried to speak to us by wireless, but had been unable to make us understand. He said that life on Mars is much more beautiful and more spiritual than upon this Earth plane, and that the majority of the inhabitants, when they leave the physical body, go straight to the seventh plane instead of to the lower planes, to which most of us go when we have left this Earth. He said that the communication between those in the physical body on Mars and those who had passed away in spirit into the other spheres, has long been a generally established fact, and that it is normally accepted by the Martians.

I asked Dr. Barnett whether the spirits of those who had passed away from the Earth plane mixed with the spirits which had passed away from Mars and from the innumerable other planets? Dr. Barnett said that surrounding this Earth and the various other planets were the spirits of those planets, and that the spiritual communications which came through were to those on the planet on which they had lived, but that he, and the majority of spirits who had lived on Earth, could communicate with the spirits of those which had lived on Mars and on other planets. He said that, just as they communicate in their spheres with the spirits of those who have inhabited the physical body in other planets, so in the future might we communicate with those living their physical existence on other planets. This fascinating possibility opens out immense fields.

During the evening we all chatted with Bert Everett at great length. I asked Bert to explain to me his condition when speaking to us on this plane in his own voice. I told him that I understood that the ethereal body of the spirit was more or less the same in form and in senses as the physical body we inhabit here. I asked him to tell me whether, when he was speaking to us, here in this room, he left his ethereal body in the sphere in which he lived. I explained to him that what I wanted to know was, as they had so often told us that they possessed an ethereal body which is more or less the same as ours—whether, when they came through to talk to us, they brought into the séance room a complete ethereal body, or whether they only materialized their voices and left that ethereal body in the plane on which they existed.

To make it more clear, I explained to Everett that he had once told me that he lived on the same plane with his mother, in a beautiful abode which he had described to us. I asked him: "Do you leave your ethereal body in that particular home with your mother, and can she see it there, while you are here talking to us here is your materialized voice?"

He said: "The ethereal body is there, although I could bring it if I wished. I can travel here as quickly as thought, but it is not necessary for me to bring my ethereal body; I can bring my spirit and materialize my voice to speak to you. In addition to this we can, under proper conditions, materialize our hands, and touch you with them."

During a chat with Dr. Barnett he suddenly said to us: "Your dog wants to come into the room." A moment or so later we heard my Alsatian wolfhound scratching outside the door. I went out and took him away in case he should disturb.

Warren came again and talked with us intimately and characteristically, and while he was speaking I could see his spirit form moving about the room to each of us as he spoke.

Bert Everett again came and said: "Mrs. Bradley, I want to tell you that you may sit again, alone with Mr. Bradley, for the voices and then we will come through and speak to you."

Dr. Barnett joined in and said that he would also endeavour to speak with us when we sat.

Suddenly, in the middle of a long discussion, Dr. Barnett said to me humorously: "Your butler is listening outside the door." Upon my questioning my butler on the subject afterwards he frankly and openly said that he was outside the door on this evening and that on several occasions during the last few weeks he had listened and heard the various voices speaking to various people and that those voices were entirely unlike any of those people whom he had ushered into the house.

This sitting was absolutely marvelous. It is utterly impossible for me to convey any graphic impression of the conversations which took place. I realize that I cannot do justice to the extraordinary conversational brilliance of Dr. Barnett or indeed to the other spirits who communicate with us under perfect conditions.

Let the scientists and the Society for Psychical Research make some endeavour, as absolute infants, to learn what harmonious conditions mean—then perhaps they may gain something of value to themselves.

19

People who make good and bad sitters—A password with a spirit—Mrs. Dawson Scott is spoken to by her grandfather—A dead friend addresses Mr. Dennis Neilson-Terry—The late Harry Pelissier comes through to Miss Fay Compton—Pelissier plays tricks with the gramophone—Laughter the best vibration for voice phenomena—The spirit of Billie Carleton—The impressions of Miss Fay Compton and Mr. Dennis Neilson-Terry.

I

Sunday, March 8, 1925.

IN obtaining the direct voice, the study of conditions, both atmospheric and mental, is of paramount importance.

I have found that, of all the classes and types, the finest sitters are the great artists of the theatrical world.

I have also found that, with the exception of Sir Oliver Lodge, who is a perfect sitter and brilliant talker, the average scientist has a cold and destructive influence, and in these sensitive psychic studies the majority appear to exhibit infantile intellect.

On this occasion there were present: Miss Fay Compton, the famous actress whose art is beyond and independent of her entrancing beauty; Mr. Dennis Neilson-Terry, an actor of considerable artistic ability; Mrs. Dawson Scott, the well-known novelist; my wife, Valiantine, and myself. Neither Mrs. Dawson Scott nor Miss Fay Compton had previously experienced a direct voice séance.

With the stress of the work, and the tiresome necessity of accumulating evidence at Dorincourt under the test conditions of not introducing any of the sitters to Valiantine, I had decided that at least my Sundays should be free and pleasurable days. Therefore, these three new sitters came to my house about six o'clock and were introduced by their correct names to the medium. We chatted and dined, and sat at about 8.15 p.m.

Although the names were given to him, I feel sure that Valiantine knew nothing whatever about them, beyond the fact that they were all extremely interesting and attractive people, and that they gave him considerably more pleasure than many of the sitters whom he had been compelled to meet on previous occasions.

During the evening fourteen different and distinct personalities spoke with us.

Of the guides, there were Dr. Barnett, Bert Everett, Pat O'Brien, Kokum, and Bobby Worrall.

For twenty minutes at the close of the sitting Dr. Barnett discussed with us every conceivable question that we could put to him.

The guides came through with ease, and spoke on several occasions.

On the previous evening I had arranged with Bert Everett to give me, early in the evening, a password which was to signify if he considered the conditions would be good for manifestations. The password arranged with us was "exquisite."

Early on this evening I asked Everett the question "how are things tonight, Bert?" The password was at once given to me, so I knew that we should get very good results; and my mind was set completely at rest.

Bobby Worrall, who impressed all the sitters, spoke at some length to each of us, and was charming. Whilst he was talking with me, I asked him whether he had been with Pat on that day, and he said that he had seen him walking with me during the morning, and had seen the horses being chased about the fields.[138] He also said that he had seen Pat playing with his railway, and that he had kept the trains on the lines. This referred to a peculiar incident, because during the day Pat had fixed his rails from a window-seat to a chair, then on to another chair and back to the window-seat; the train having traveled all round, strangely enough, kept to the higgledy-piggledy rails without falling off—a unique performance which created much astonishment.

Bobby Worrall said that he had been able to keep the trains on the lines. This may sound a stupid little incident, but it is extraordinary, because, on these flimsy rails with the jolts and the joints, both Pat

---

[138] Three horses in a field opposite my house had gone wild.

and my wife were astounded that the train had gone round without falling off.

Feda came through and talked gently in her independent voice with several of us.

Of the personal spirits there came through a voice, addressing Mrs. Dawson Scott. Mrs. Dawson Scott had written a short, private note to me, saying that she had a very particular reason for seeking an opportunity of a sitting with Valiantine, but she did not tell me what that reason was.

When Feda was through she said to Mrs. Dawson Scott: "Mr. Dawson is here." Later a voice, using the luminous trumpet, spoke to Mrs. Dawson Scott, saying "It's Grandfather Dawson speaking." Together they spoke for a little while. Grandfather Dawson told Mrs. Dawson Scott that he was helping her, and impressing her in her literary work. Mrs. Dawson Scott, who is a very charming woman, with a slight affliction of highbrowishness—a libel which has, on occasions, been cast upon me, so, evasively, I therefore cast it upon her—rather resented this, and told him that she did not want him to help her in her work. She added that she wanted to create her own work. This remark had not the slightest effect upon the spirit, who said that he would continue to help her.

I can quite understand the exhibition of Mrs. Dawson Scott's ego. It is almost justifiable; which is a compliment one can apply to very few people. I had considerable difficulty in shedding my own ego with regard to the help one gets from the higher intelligences. Now, I am only too willing to accept any impression I may get from another intelligence on any sphere, so long as it is on a higher plane than my own.

A little later another voice came through, using the luminous trumpet and speaking somewhat indistinctly to Mrs. Dawson Scott. I told her to ask: "Is it a relative?" She put this question, and the voice replied: "Yes, I am as near as ever I can be to you." This was clearly heard by everybody. While the voice was speaking Mrs. Dawson Scott could not quite hear what was said, but Mr. Dennis Neilson-Terry, who was on her left, heard very distinctly. The luminous trumpet moved to Mr. Terry as he joined in the interpretation of what was said, saying: "I am her husband." Going back to Mrs. Dawson Scott the voice said: "You are my wife."

With reference to the communications to Mrs. Dawson Scott from her husband and her grandfather, it is interesting to mention that she had not told me before she came that she had that week received messages from some source unknown to me, saying that if she could come to

Dennis Bradley's she would receive communications from both these identical characters, and that she would then hear their voices, and know the truth. This is precisely what happened. It should be noted, from the evidential point of view, that her grandfather volunteered the correct name of "Dawson."

During the evening there came through a voice speaking to Mr. Dennis Neilson-Terry, calling him "Dennis." Recognition was established between them, and it appears he was a cousin of Mr. Terry's, named Frederick Morris, who had died during the war. Although the spirit answered to the name of Frederick, Mr. Terry addressed him as "Bay." Mr. Terry said that during the morning he had spoken over the telephone to Mr. Morris's brother, to which the voice replied: "Yes, I know." The voice also volunteered "I have been with you and your kiddies." As far as strict psychical research is concerned, there was nothing very evidential in this conversation except that Valiantine did not know whether young Mr. Dennis Neilson-Terry had any kiddies or not.

A voice then came through, which addressed Miss Fay Compton. The luminous trumpet was lifted, and hovered around her, touching her several times. The voice then said that it was her father. Miss Compton talked with him for a little time, and the voice concluded the conversation by saying: "Harry is here—he wants to speak to you."

A little later the luminous trumpet was again lifted, a voice saying, "Fay, it's Harry." Together Miss Compton and the voice talked on quite joyously for some little time. Recognition was almost immediately established. The voice was that of Harry Pelissier, Miss Compton's first husband, the most brilliant burlesque actor of this century, who passed away some few years ago. Three or four times during the evening the spirit of Pelissier came through and talked with her.

The most remarkable thing to me was the vivid personality of this spirit. Pelissier made us all roar with laughter in the séance room, just as he had done with his genius on the stage when he was on this Earth plane. Several times his voice gave a splendid laugh of humour; not only did he laugh, but he played many amusing tricks with the gramophone. While I was working the gramophone and while the records were being played, with the lid closed down, he manipulated the needle in such a way that the records did not cease, but were made to give strange sounds throughout, owing to the movement of the needle. This is somewhat difficult to describe, but all I can say is that we rocked with laughter. On one occasion when I went to put on another record and had placed the sounding-box down to commence it, the sounding-box was lifted

VALIANTINE AND THE VOICES

up, carried right away from the record, and placed in my hand. Pelissier is a fine spirit to get through because he inspired us to laugh, and laughter is the finest vibration for voice phenomena. Laughter creates the greatest harmony, because when certain physical manifestations or a point of humour is given by the spirit, the whole of the sitters laugh in one accord. That is harmony!

While we were all laughing Bert Everett came through high up in the ceiling, laughing with us, and then volunteered the statement: "That was the lady's husband doing that." That I regard as evidence, because, although we had all dined together, I can vouch that Valiantine was not told anything about Miss Fay Compton.

Somehow the spirits seemed to be attracted to Miss Compton. During the evening she asked Dr. Barnett whether it would be possible to bring through the spirit of Billie Carleton. Later on a voice came through and said to Miss Compton: "It's Billie." The voice was not very strong, and could only speak with difficulty. They talked together for a very short while, but one could not record anything that was said as being of evidential value. I was rather sorry for this, because on the day of her tragic death, which occurred on the day after she had attended the great Victory Ball held at the Albert Hall in 1918, I was lunching with a particularly intimate friend of hers, who left me in good spirits to go and see her, and, on arriving, found her dead.

This is probably the first time that the spirit of Billie Carleton has spoken, and the voice was therefore rather weak, and could not hold out for long, so I had no opportunity of asking a few questions which might have been of considerable evidential importance. Billie Carleton might have volunteered a name which I knew, but perhaps she will do so at a later date.[139]

Annie spoke to me for a short time, and also to my wife. She referred to the slightly disturbing worries I had recently been through. Warren talked with me, and with my wife, and we introduced him to the other sitters, to whom he spoke a few words. I shall collect no further evidence from either my sister or Warren. It would be a surfeit if I did. I talk with them only on the plane of cultured understanding.

In reference to these two spirits, Mr. Dennis Neilson-Terry afterwards said that he was enormously impressed with the extraordinary

---

[139] The opportunity did occur later and is recorded later in this book. I obtained the evidence I desired. The above notes were dictated exactly as they appear before this happened.

personalities of the two voices of Annie and Warren. To him, he said, they stood out as two remarkable individualities. I have said so much of both these two great spiritual characters, who speak in their own voices to me, that I can say no more. It is only a confirmation to me when others, who have heard then for the first time, are impressed in the same way that I have been impressed for the last two years.

It was a fluent evening throughout. At the close Dr. Barnett asked whether we wished to put any questions to him, and for twenty minutes or so a rain of questions was poured in upon him. A number of questions were put to him by Mr. Neilson-Terry and by Miss Fay Compton; and also by Mrs. Dawson Scott.

In answer to certain questions, he said that with regard to the brilliance in art, in literature and in acting, the inspiration comes by impression from a higher sphere than ours.

When Miss Compton's father was speaking to her, he told her that he helped her, and that he impressed her in her work.

Dr. Barnett, in confirmation of this point, said that artistic genius was invariably impressed by the intelligences of the spirit spheres.

MR. TERRY: Is Christ the Son of God

DR. BARNETT: Christ was the son of man; of a material father and mother.

I have asked this question before, and I have received the same answer each time.

This brilliant man, who has confounded the greatest living scientists, had no hesitation in pronouncing his knowledge. He said that Christ was a very great Spirit, and that He existed in the Seventh Plane of the Seventh Sphere. Christ was one of the greatest spirits that had lived in the physical body on the Earth plane, and His influence would be of even greater value to this Earth in the near future than ever before, because the spirituality and the great philosophy of Christ could save our civilization from material destruction.

Dr. Barnett spoke with the utmost veneration for the spirit of Christ, whom he regarded as approaching the divine and incomprehensible intelligence of the great God of the Universe. The Seventh Plane of the Seventh Sphere is only an approach to the colossal intuitiveness and wisdom of the great God, who is the Ruling Intelligence, not only of this insignificant Earth planet, but the unknown multitudinous planets of the vast and unknown Universe in space.

It was a brilliant evening.

There was complete harmony, and the communications were of absorbing interest. Harmony is the one essential condition we have to cultivate and learn.

II

As a matter of valuable interest, I give Mr. Neilson-Terry's independent account of his impressions and experiences at this sitting.

"I have found it excessively difficult to record any impression of the séance that was held last Sunday night, without entering very deeply into a description of that séance, and, on thinking it over, I have decided that, so far as I am concerned, the only way to record my impressions faithfully is to give a thorough and unbiassed description of what occurred, and leave whosoever reads to form his own conclusion as to my impressions.

"In the first place, I want to place on record that I was at Mr. Dennis Bradley's house, Dorincourt, Kingston Vale, on Sunday, March 8, as his guest. Mr. Bradley is a friend of mine, and I should indeed be impertinent if I inquired into his moral integrity. Mr. Bradley has brought over from America Mr. Valiantine, a very well-known American medium, and it was for the purpose of attending what is known as a direct voice séance that I was invited to Mr. Bradley's house.

"I arrived at six o'clock, and we had a delightfully informal chat, and later an equally delightful informal dinner, and the actual séance took place in a medium sized sitting room, and lasted from eight-thirty till eleven-thirty. I met Dennis Bradley's wife for the first time that evening, and a Mrs. Dawson Scott, and also Miss Fay Compton, whom I have known for many years. We discussed spiritualism, the theatre, books, people—in fact, we had a general conversation.

"After dinner, which finished about eight-twenty, I went into the small sitting room with Mr. Bradley and Mr. Valiantine, and the ladies went into the drawing room whilst we were preparing certain cylinders or trumpets which were used during the sitting. I should like to state here that Mr. Valiantine is a thick-set, somewhat stout, American citizen, with a very definite American accent, and there is nothing about him which any ordinary person, or even an artistic person, could describe as supernatural—in other words, I have seen 'Mr. Valiantine walking about the streets during the thirty years that I have lived. The actual preparation that was entailed, in so far as the cylinders were concerned, was this: they were placed in an alabaster lamp, that was lighted, in order to make their ends and their sides, which were painted with some form of phosphorescent paint, glow in the dark. (The object of this will be seen later.) I should here like to state that I am over six feet tall, and that if I stood on an ordinary chair with either of these two cylinders in my hand, stretching them upwards to the full length of my arms, I should have been unable to touch the ceiling. There was a gramophone in the room, on which, during the sitting, records of John McCormack, Clara Butt, Galli-Curci, and jazz music were played, but when any voice spoke the gramophone was stopped by Mr. Bradley. The room, which was curtained so that no light came in, was warmed by some radiator, and had one door, but it was closed throughout the sitting. Mr. Valiantine never went into a trance throughout the proceedings, and spoke quite a deal during them, but never to the best of my recollection when any of the spirit voices are speaking. He has a quaint manner of saying 'pretty good,' and laughing rather heartily at any proceeding that appears to amuse him.

"Dennis Bradley was nearest the door; on his right was Mr. Valiantine; on Mr. Valiantine's right, Mrs. Bradley; on her right, myself; on my right, Mrs. Dawson Scott; on Mrs. Dawson Scott's right, Miss Fay Compton; on Miss Fay Compton's right, Mr. Dennis Bradley. The gramophone was between Mr. Bradley and Mr. Valiantine. In the centre of this circle were placed the two trumpets or cylinders; the lights were turned out, and we commenced the sitting. Clara Butt sang on a record, and, when she had finished, the Lord's Prayer was said perfectly reverently and simply. Apart from this, and the singing once of Onward Christian Soldiers, there was no religious ceremony whatsoever; indeed, the proceedings were pretty light-hearted, and remarkably natural so far as we were concerned.

"Now to what actually happened. The first unusual occurrence was that I was touched very distinctly. This I mentioned, was told to thank for it, and did so. I then said that I was accustomed to the general procedure at a séance, and, indeed, did not desire any further instruction. The ends and sides of the trumpets were glowing in the dark, and I shortly saw one of them move towards me slowly without any visible means of support. Later on some sound was made, which appeared to come from the ground. Dennis Bradley said: 'That is the voice of Dr. Barnett saying good evening.' Almost immediately afterwards a voice with a distinct Irish brogue, which appeared to come from nowhere in particular, made some statement. Mr. Bradley introduced this as the voice of, I believe, Pat O'Brien. Then a strange booming voice introduced by Mr. Bradley as that of Kokum. Then a small, almost childish, feminine voice introduced by Mr. Bradley as the voice of Feda, the spirit control of Mrs. Osborne Leonard. Then, very high up in the room, came a very shrill, almost parrot-like voice, and here I must say a voice that was to me almost uncannily curious in its clarity and pitch. This was introduced by Mr. Bradley as the voice of Bert Everett, who, I understand, is a dead brother-in-law of Mr. Valiantine. Mr. Bradley asked Bert Everett how the conditions were that evening, and the voice replied: 'Exquisite.' I cannot say I like Mr. Everett's voice; it was not musical and is most unnatural, but it is very, very clear.

"Of these voices, Dr. Barnett and Bert Everett spoke again, Everett on and off throughout the sitting and Dr. Barnett for a considerable period at the end of the sitting. The rest never appeared again. Again, I would emphasize that Everett always spoke from high up in the room. Dr. Barnett seemed to be on the floor, in fact, it seemed that if one took one of the trumpets up from the ground one would find Dr. Barnett sitting quietly underneath it. Dr. Barnett's voice was very deep, and he answered questions whenever spoken to, quickly and clearly, and he had a curious laugh. Without prejudice, I don't think he had a very great opinion of our, or shall I say my, intelligence, as, at the end of each reply he made to any of my questions, he laughed, but not heartily.

"In the midst of this sitting one of the trumpets moved in the air, circling round, and floating above our heads, and, at one point going as high as the ceiling, and fluttering against the ceiling like a moth. (I heard the tapping of it on the ceiling.) The trumpet circled round, and finally seemed to rest in space in front of Miss Fay Compton. Again I wish to emphasize that one could see this trumpet quite plainly, as it was painted with luminous paint. Through the trumpet some voice attempted to whisper, or speak, to Miss Compton, and finally her father, Mr. Edward Compton, spoke, and later said that 'Harry was there.'

"Harry turned out to be Harry Pelissier, and Miss Compton kept up a considerable conversation with this spirit in ordinary, everyday tones. At one point, Miss Compton was unable to catch precisely what was said through this cylinder or trumpet, and, as I clearly heard what was said, I told her, and immediately the trumpet flew round to me, and a voice through it said: 'Thank you, sir!' and then the trumpet flew back again. At one point, the spirit sent a kiss through the cylinder, and finally the cylinder floated back again on to the floor.

"Miss Compton then herself expressed a desire that this same spirit should go and talk to me, and also that if it were possible that the spirit of Billie Carleton should speak to her. Both things occurred as desired, at different moments. I had a slight chat with the spirit of Harry Pelissier concerning the time when he was at the St. Mildred's Hotel, Westgate-on-Sea, and Billie Carleton had a very casual conversation with Fay Compton, and incidentally sent about eight kisses through the cylinder, of a very different calibre to the one that Harry Pelissier had sent.

Shortly after this, whilst Mr. Bradley was putting on a new record, and, certainly during a portion of the sitting, the gramophone, which was fully wound up, played different times, paused, and altogether acted in a strange manner. It was suggested to Bert Everett, who again arrived on the scene, that it was Harry Pelissier playing practical jokes; to this Everett readily agreed, exclaiming: 'That was the lady's husband. He is very humorous.'

"I might as well say that each time any spirit spoke through the trumpet (with the exception of Dr. Barnett, who appeared to be talking from under the trumpet) the cylinder elevated itself into space with the large end slightly above the level of one's mouth, when sitting in a chair, at about an angle of one hundred and thirty-five degrees.

"To Mrs. Dawson Scott, through one of the trumpets, there came two spirits, one representing himself to be 'Grandfather Dawson' and the other her husband. I am not very clear as to what they said, I did not hear very well, and I don't think that Mrs. Dawson Scott was very helpful, if indeed help was needed. To myself there came a spirit voice, which, after considerable trouble and much coaxing on my part, announced itself to be 'Freddy.' I accepted it as such, and addressed it as 'Bay,' which was the nickname of a cousin of mine called Frederick Morris, who was killed during the war. He spoke to me as interested in my children, and I told him how sorry I was he had been killed. He said: 'Oh, don't you worry, I am alive all right,' and I believe, but I am not dead sure, that he sent his love to someone called 'Louise' or 'Louisa'; to the best of my knowledge I know no one of that name. I would also like to say that no one in the room knew I had a cousin called 'Freddy' who had been killed in the war. That makes six spirit voices that spoke through the elevated trumpet. None of them to me had any particular strength of personality, with the exception of Harry Pelissier, and I am, personally, not capable of judging whether he phrased as he did when he was alive. A little boy called Bobby spoke during this sitting. He spoke with a slightly American accent, saying:, 'Yes, sir,' and 'No, ma'am.' I had quite a little conversation with him as to whether he liked boys or girls best, and I told him I had two little girls of my own. He expressed a desire to see them, and when I acquiesced he suggested that he should come along with me that evening after the sitting. I told him I was afraid he would find them asleep, and he said: 'Oh, don't you worry, I shan't disturb them.' He then said he would try and come and see me next morning, and tap somewhere near my bed. I told him not to come too early, and he said: Oh, d'you stay in bed all day?

I said: 'Fairly late sometimes,' and that is all I know about Bobby. He certainly was a charming child, and I was sorry to miss him next morning.

"I do not want anybody who is reading this to imagine that there was an accumulative arrangement or effect as if working up for the grand climax, or dramatic denouement. The order in which I have described these occurrences is in all probability faulty, and I have purposely left to the last what was to me a most striking phenomenon. I sensed a seventh presence in the room—something much more tangible than anything that I have heretofore described—and finally a well-modulated, middle-aged voice spoke to Mr. Bradley, and again to Mrs. Bradley. It was the voice of Warren Clarke, so Mr. Bradley said. He spoke of his great desire to see and speak to certain people. He was most insistent that they should be brought there, and as he spoke to Bradley and Mrs. Bradley one could almost feel his voice move from one side of the room to the other, and with very great speed. He was talking to Mrs. Bradley, when he was introduced to Miss Compton, and he said: 'I am very glad to see you here, Miss Fay Compton.' It almost seemed as if you could feel the turn of his head as he went from Mrs. Bradley to Miss Compton. The same strength of personality, the same clear speaking, the same well-modulated voice, but this time in feminine tones, occurred when Mr. Bradley's sister also spoke, as she did during the sitting. In the same way I could sense her personality; I could almost feel her movements. These two spirits, Warren Clarke and Mr. Bradley's sister, were more definite in human personality than any of the others. The fact that they came and spoke in tones that were perfectly ordinary and straightforward, as yours and mine, made the situation that had arisen a very strange one. I can find no normal explanation for this matter, though I have turned it over in my mind many times. If Mr. or Mrs. Bradley had told me that such a thing could occur I might have been incredulous, but I heard both spirits and sensed both spirits, and I place on record that I do believe that I heard the spirits of those two people speaking in that room last night.

"At the very end Dr. Barnett spoke for some considerable time. He asked us whether any of us wanted to ask any questions. Many were asked and replied to, but I do not intend to go into these now. I will just state one that I asked and his answer. The question I asked was this: "Was Jesus Christ the Son of God?" He answered, "The Son of man, of a material father and mother, the same as you or I." I cannot help if the question was rank blasphemy on my part: it was asked seriously with the desire to know from someone who, if he were dead, according to my religion should be in a position to know. I merely place on record his answer. Shortly afterwards the sitting closed, and the lights were turned up. It had lasted for three hours. Everything, so far as I could see, was as it had been before we turned the lights down.

"I would like to add that when the little boy Bobby was speaking he was asked to lift one of the trumpets; this he did. He was then asked to lift both; this he also did, so that both trumpets were floating in the air. I examined the trumpets afterwards and they were covered with moisture. Mr. Valiantine seemed in no way tired, nor were his vocal chords in any way strained, nor was there any form of perspiration on his brow. He was as cool and collected as he was when I first met him before dinner. I found him a very charming man, and I thanked him for a very amazing experience. I cannot explain this experience. I can only record it at the request of my friend, Mr. Bradley, by whose courtesy I was introduced to Mr. Valiantine."

III

Two days later I received an enthusiastic letter from Mrs. Dawson Scott, in which she said, among other things:

"I write to thank you for conclusive evidence as far as I am concerned. You have given me what I needed!"

Also this from Miss Fay Compton:

"I write to thank you for the wonderful experience you gave me on Sunday night. I am so grateful. If I might come again and bring my husband (Leon Quartermaine), who is tremendously interested, I can't tell you how pleased I would be."

20

Another sitting at the headquarters of the S.P.R.—A fatuous evening—The author, who is not present, attacks the conditions prevailing at the S.P.R.—Unintelligent handicapping.

Monday, March 9, 1925.

THIS was the evening arranged for the second sitting with the Society for Psychical Research in Tavistock Square.

On the previous Friday I had refused to sit there again. This sitting, therefore, took place without my being present.

In addition to George Valiantine, there were present my wife, Dr. V. J. Woolley, Mr. E. J. Dingwall, Mr. Hannen Swaffer, and two of the ladies who were present at the previous sitting, who still remain anonymous to me. The third anonymous lady, who had been present at the previous sitting, and who had aroused my ire by her foolish attitude and complete inexperience, was not present.

The two ladies who sat on this occasion had had no experience of a direct voice séance.

The sitting lasted for an hour and a half or so, and nothing whatever happened. No voices of any description were able to manifest or penetrate the atmosphere. It appears to me that one of the first things that the Society for Psychical Research will have to study is the conditions under which phenomena can take place. Atmosphere, vibrations, situation, and mentality are of paramount importance in order to obtain results.

In its present stage of development the voice phenomenon rests upon the most delicate thread. Under varying conditions the voices which are heard may, either be extraordinarily clear, moderately distinct, or extremely poor in articulation, whilst on some occasions the voices cannot manifest at all.

The medium is merely a passive instrument, who himself can speak with the voices, or speak simultaneously with them.

I am a member of the Society for Psychical Research, and it was I who was the first means of introducing them to this rare form of phenomena.

No voice sitting, to my knowledge, has ever been held at the Society for Psychical Research until the one recorded by me in Chapter 17, on March 6, 1925.

During the present series of experiments with Valiantine, every sitting that has been held has been what maybe termed a test sitting. We test at Dorincourt, as rigidly as at the S.P.R. offices, or elsewhere. The test is the amount of evidence which is volunteered by the voice as to identity and as to surviving personality.

I am able now, after my prolonged experience, to tell almost immediately when the atmosphere and vibrations are good, and when they are impossible.

Both Dr. Woolley and Mr. E. J. Dingwall are ostensibly anxious to do all in their power to assist this research work. This being so I shall certainly offer them further opportunities for the observation of the voice phenomenon.

With my personal knowledge, as one of the most advanced scientific investigators of this form. of phenomenon, I shall, however, insist that every experiment is made under conditions likely to obtain the best results.

This study is mental, and not physical.

I have had dozens of applications from members of the Society for Psychical Research who wished to attend the experiments taking place at Dorincourt.

In one of the chief London papers about this time it was stated that a prominent member of the Society had said:

"In the special séance room we have a wire cage, and it was proposed that Valiantine should ultimately, be placed in this during the séances, to ensure that the phenomena would be produced under real test conditions."

That wire cage stood in the séance room on the first evening I attended. To me it was an offensive-looking object. I did not know if it was the intention of the Society to use it—and Dr. Woolley assures me that it was not—but if such a thing were suggested, I should refuse to allow it to be used, because I should feel it to be insulting to my intelligence as an investigator.

Does this prominent member of the Society imagine that this is a conjuring entertainment?

Communications in the independent voices giving evidence of their identities have now been made in every European and in many Eastern languages. That is marvelous mental evidence, and it is mental evidence alone that we are striving to obtain.

This is research work of such importance that it will ultimately influence the opinion of the whole world. There must be no unintelligent handicapping of this great study.

21

*The spirit of Dr. Barnett tells what is wrong with the S.P.R.—
Northcliffe speaks to Mr. Gonnoske Komai, the famous Japanese
poet—The Hon. Mrs. Fitzroy Stanhope receives evidence—A
conversation in Japanese—Countess Ahlefeldt-Laurvig talks
with a spirit in Danish and Russian.*

I

Tuesday, March 10, 1925.

VALIANTINE was anxious to find out from his chief control, Dr. Barnett, exactly what was wrong with the conditions at Tavistock Square, and, although we had arranged for guests to come down on this evening, he asked my wife if she would sit with him alone for a few minutes after dinner. They sat in my study. No music was played, and the voice of Dr. Barnett came through within three minutes.

Mr. Hannen Swaffer, who was present on this evening, remained with me in the drawing room, and from this room we heard them speaking. We then went and listened outside the study door. The three voices were talking with one another—Valiantine, my wife, and the loud voice of Dr. Barnett.

This was the first occasion on which Mr. Swaffer had heard a spirit voice from outside the door, and he was deeply impressed. We heard every word.

VALIANTINE AND THE VOICES

The following is a brief account of the conversation which took place:

MRS. BRADLEY: You know why we are here, doctor, don't you?

DR. BARNETT: Yes, I heard you discuss the matter.

MRS. BRADLEY: Well, can you tell us what was wrong last night, and why you were not able to get through?

DR. BARNETT: No, I will not talk about that subject at all; I would rather not.

VALIANTINE: Won't you tell us why it was so difficult, doctor?

MRS. BRADLEY: George[140] is so worried about it.

DR. BARNETT: The spirits are insulted by the attitude towards us. This is a subject which must be approached with reverence, and not with tricks and contraptions.

MRS. BRADLEY: Yes, doctor, I understand, but I am sure Dr. Woolley and Mr. Dingwall are only too anxious to get the right conditions, and to do anything that you think would be best.

DR. BARNETT: They cannot do anything until their minds are different.

MRS. BRADLEY: Would it be better if we sat there in the little room we first go into to have coffee?

DR. BARNETT: No, the whole atmosphere is bad.

MRS. BRADLEY: Well, doctor, if we get Dr. Woolley here, in this room, will you tell him yourself just what is wrong, and what is the best thing for him to do?

DR. BARNETT: Yes, I will do so.

After the negative sitting at the S.P.R. on Monday, March 9, Dr. Woolley had called on me the next day and requested me to ask Dr. Barnett at the next meeting we held what was wrong with the conditions. It must be observed that this request by Dr. Woolley to ask a spirit voice for instructions is peculiarly significant. Dr. Woolley has heard Dr. Barnett speak now on four occasions; therefore he knows the intelligence of this spirit.

---

[140] Valiantine.

II

Ten minutes after Valiantine had spoken to Dr. Barnett my guests for the evening, arrived. Valiantine was not introduced to them; he did not even see their faces until we walked into my study, and the lights were turned off within two or three seconds.

Our guests on this occasion were the Countess Ahlefeldt-Laurvig, the cultured wife of the Danish Minister; the Honourable Mrs. Fitzroy Stanhope, and Gonnoske Komai, the famous Japanese poet. None of these sitters had had any previous experience of the direct voice; neither could they be described as what are usually termed spiritualists.

In addition, there were present Mr. Hannen Swaffer, my wife and myself, and Valiantine.

The conditions were excellent, and there appeared to be complete harmony amongst the sitters. It was quite a brilliant evening. In all eleven distinct spirit voices spoke with us.

Of the guides, Dr. Barnett and Bert Everett spoke with us on several occasions.

I received the password from Bert Everett that the atmosphere was "exquisite."

Pat O'Brien spoke to several of the sitters, and Kokum and Hawk Chief on two occasions spoke in their tremendous voices. Bobby Worrall stayed for some little time, speaking with most of us, and carrying on quite a delightful little conversation with Gonnoske Komai.

The luminous trumpets were lifted, and whirled all round the room at lightning speed, and were also raised to the ceiling by Hawk Chief. Both trumpets were lifted simultaneously by Bobby Worrall.

Warren spoke easily and fluently in the independent voice with my wife and with me.

Lord Northcliffe came through, speaking with Mr. Swaffer on two occasions. He also talked with Mr. Komai, whom he knew personally, for Northcliffe, when he was on Earth, had a great respect for Komai's literary gifts.

To the Hon. Mrs. Fitzroy Stanhope a voice came through, using one of the trumpets; the voice volunteered the name of Evelyn and established its identity, and talked with her for some little time.

A voice spoke to Mr. Gonnoske Komai in Japanese. This voice was at first indistinct, and, although the personal identification of this spirit was not established, Mr. Komai said that the voice volunteered certain names and places, and also said that he had committed "Harikari."

Although Mr. Komai could not definitely place the identity of this spirit, he said that he had an idea who it was.

None of the rest of us, of course, knew Japanese, but, during the conversation, the Countess Laurvig said that she distinctly heard certain Japanese words spoken by the spirit.

A voice addressed the Countess Laurvig, and she replied to it in Danish. The voice, in replying to her, said: "Speak to me in Russian," and announced that he was her brother Oscar. Together they talked for a little time in the Russian language.

I regard this evening as a very remarkable one. What finer test could there be than to have three sitters ushered into the room, entirely unknown to the medium, and, during the evening, to obtain voice communications in Danish, Russian, and Japanese?

The foolish folk who talk of caging a great medium like a monkey should endeavour to realize that this evening was one of the severest tests possible to conceive.

III

Two days after the sitting recorded in this chapter I received a letter from the Hon. Mrs. Fitzroy Stanhope, saying:

"It was so absolutely convincing, and it was such a joy to get my message."

Mr. Gonnoske Komai, in thanking me for what he described as a "unique and wonderful opportunity of witnessing the voice experiment," wrote, among other things:

"I shall never forget it! I greatly regret that I could not recognize the gentleman who tried so hard to communicate with me in my native tongue. But I suppose I must not be 'over anxious' to do so, according to the Doctor's advice given us that evening.

"I also wanted to ask Dr. Barnett many questions— international— but I was very shy at the time, it being my first night I ever encountered such a wonderful experiment."

The Countess Ahlefeldt-Laurvig also wrote:

"Thank you for your great kindness in allowing me to be present at that wonderful sitting last night. I cannot tell you how much I appreciated it, and how very grateful I am to you for giving me this extraordinary and unforgettable experience, especially as I know the whole of Great Britain asks you for admittance to your séances."

On the following morning after this sitting I received a letter from Captain C. J. Astley Maberley, recording an incident which I regard as of considerable importance, and enclosing me a copy of the letter which he had written to the Society for Psychical Research. This letter is of such interest that I think it is worth quoting:

"I wish to inform your Society that at a sitting held at Mr. H. Dennis Bradley's house on February 19 last (under the mediumship of Valiantine), amongst the many voices which manifested was that of 'Bert Everett,' one of Valiantine's guides. This spirit assumes a voice, not his material one, for reasons which he has explained, and this voice is of quite a distinct character. On March 7 I attended a sitting at Hockley House, on the invitation of my host, the Rev. L. Corbett. Mr. Corbett had also heard Everett speak at Mr. Bradley's house, though not upon the same occasion as myself.

This Hockley sitting was held under the mediumship of Evan Powell.

"Amongst many others, a spirit voice came through, giving his name as 'Bert Everett,' but immediately he spoke, and before giving his name, both Mr. Corbett and myself recognized the voice as that of 'Bert Everett, the tones being the same, though not so loud as those heard at Mr. Bradley's house.

"Presently I asked him to speak to us in his own voice—which he did. The spirit voice is assumed for purposes of vibration. Mr. Evan Powell has never met or sat with Valiantine, and has had no opportunity whatever of hearing Everett's voice. This I regard as an important point, as it is a cross establishment of the same spirit voice."

This is a very remarkable piece of evidence, as it records the recognition of the absolute tones of the voice of the spirit of Bert Everett by these two gentlemen who had both heard him speak on separate occasions at Dorincourt, and who then heard the same voice speak in Hockley.

22

Mr. Hannen Swaffer's account of a successful sitting—Kokum sings his favourite song—Charles Garvice's message to his wife—Northcliffe finds a secretary for Miss Louise Owen—Dr. Barnett's new word: "hypostatic."

I

Wednesday, March 11, 1925.

I WAS not in the room on the occasion of this sitting, as I was resting in the drawing room which adjoins my study. Throughout the evening from where I was sitting I could distinctly hear several of the various spirit voices in conversation with the sitters. I give Mr. Hannen Swaffer's account of what took place.

This sitting was even more remarkable than that on the previous evening. Bradley was not present, but sat in the room adjoining.

The circle consisted of Mrs Alice Graham, the mother of Winifred Graham, the authoress; Alfred Morris of Tankerton, Whitstable; Louise Owen, Madeleine Cohen, Mrs. Bradley, Valiantine, and myself. Perfect harmony was immediately established, the consequence being that, almost immediately after the Lord's Prayer was recited, Dr. Barnett's voice said: "Good evening, souls." Then, soon after the voice of Bert, the second guide, greeted us from high up in the room, and when asked what the conditions were like said, "Exquisite." And they seemed to be.

Then, in turn, Pat O'Brien arrived and said a few sentences, speaking to most of the sitters and making himself known to new ones. Hawk Chief said a word or two, and Kokum shouted out so loud that you could have heard him in the road. After pressure, he sang his favourite song, "La Paloma," which comes from some Italian opera. He produced, while singing this, a terrific volume of sound.

Feda, who came along early on, spoke to me first, saying: "Good evening, Swaff."

Her voice was a miracle of clearness, twice as loud as I have ever heard it before. She engaged in conversation with most of the sitters, one after the other, joked with Mr. Morris, whom she called "Alf,"[141] and, after a most pleasant conversation, said: "Mrs. Graham, your husband is here."

Mrs. Graham had been present at two other Valiantine sittings in the hope of speaking to her dear one. The first sitting was more or less a failure—her husband did not arrive. The second time he spoke; but she could not clearly distinguish all he said. Mrs. Graham is a little deaf, so it was fortunate that I was sitting next to her.

Mr. Graham's voice, however, was clearer than such voices usually are. The attitude of the luminous trumpet during his visit was what I should call affectionate. It nestled on Mrs. Graham's head and stroked her arms.

"Tell Winnie I have been helping her with her book," he said. "I am always in the house. Give her my love."

There were several sentences like this, all expressed in an anxiety of affection.

"I will give her a title for her new book," he said.

Mrs. Graham then said: "I do wish Garvice would speak."

Charles Garvice, the novelist, was a very dear friend. Immediately after Mrs. Graham spoke, the trumpet came towards her again. It would seem as though she possessed some intuitive sense that Garvice was there; for it was Garvice who addressed her.

"Give my love to my wife," he said, and then spoke about his daughter, who is alive, and his daughter Olive, who died four months ago.

"She is with me," he said.

A little later the luminous trumpet went to Mr. Morris, and said something I could not hear.

---

[141] Feda has, I believe, often before spoken to Mr. Morris through the mediumship of Mrs. Osborne Leonard.

"Is that you, Alstrom?" said Morris.

"Yes," came the answer in a very clear voice, which from then continued to be remarkably clear.

Charles Alstrom, who was a maker of office furniture, doing business in the same building in Great Eastern Street where Mr. Morris's business is, passed over only a few months ago, and when Mr. Morris spoke to his father the other day, he was told what great progress Alstrom was making on the other side; it was obvious from the clearness of his speaking that this was true.

Mr. Alstrom sent his love to his son, and, in talking with Mr. Morris, expressed his pleasure that he was now negotiating for a lease of the premises which Alstrom formally occupied.

The meeting to a stranger would seem very sensational, so greatly in understanding did Alstrom and Morris seem to be. This sort of spirit visit only happens, I notice, when the sitting is a very harmonious one and no doubts are cast.

Then the Alstrom spirit told Mr. Morris that he was always with Mr. Morris's father, and that they were great friends in the other world.

Immediately afterwards, Mr. Morris's father came through and confirmed all this.

Had Mr. Morris been a new sitter, the evening, to him, would have been a great revelation. As it was, this was by far the finest sitting he had ever had, for, although he had been inquiring into spiritualism for years, the best experience of his life up to that time was when he sat with me at an Evan Powell sitting arranged by Conan Doyle.

Then Feda came back and said: "The Chief's here."

According to Feda, who told Mrs. Bradley so at another sitting, the spirit world now calls Lord Northcliffe "the Chief." It seems to have heard it called that so often recently at sittings that it has got used to it.

After a little pause the Northcliffe voice spoke independently about six feet up in the room. It was louder than I have ever heard it before.

I forget what Lord Northcliffe said to me—he spoke to me first—it was a few words; but, immediately afterwards, he went across to Miss Owen, called her "Louise" and told her "to go on with the secretary."

This was a piece of evidence, for the other day Louise Owen got a message from Northcliffe in automatic writing, saying that he had found for her a spirit secretary. She had not told anyone this; yet the Northcliffe at our sitting had known all about it.

A little later, Northcliffe said to her: "Thank you for the flowers. I know you brought them for me," and he gave a loud chuckle, exactly as

Lord Northcliffe used to do in Earth life. This was a characteristically Northcliffean thing, for the truth is that Miss Owen brought down some flowers for Mrs. Bradley, and Northcliffe, who, always in life, would fasten on to himself something; intended for someone else, was obviously joking by pretending that the flowers were for him. In life he was very fond of flowers. They were found in all his rooms.

Northcliffe, following his usual custom, only addressed the people he knew of the sitters. The only third person addressed was Madeline Cohen, to whom Northcliffe said: "Madeline, I am glad to see you here."

Those were all the personal messages of the evening, which was remarkable for the rapid interplay of conversation and the way in which the spirit guides dodged in and out of the gathering, each one a definite characteristic personality with a voice his own, a manner his own, an accent his own. It was also a better sitting than usual, in the sense that Valiantine, immediately after a spirit has spoken, involuntarily remarked something, every now and then, a second or so after a spirit voice. In some cases the spirit voices were probably eight feet away from him, yet his remarks always came, as usual, from his seat, immediately afterwards.

The sitting was also remarkable for the fact that, when we asked Kokum to lift the trumpets, as we had done once before, he seized them in a second and whirled them like Indian clubs, high up near the ceiling. They looked as though some giant were standing in the room, except that no giant could have whirled them with such a carelessness and yet with such a sureness of direction. Once, too, Feda was asked to lift the trumpets, and she gave a sort of childish imitation of this, directly she was asked to, in such a way that no medium could have risked doing it.

I regard these things, pantomime though they may seem, as highly evidential.

At the end, Dr. Barnett said the power was going, and, as usual, we had a little talk with him. Speaking to me he said: "Mr. Swaffer, your name is inscribed on the history of the spirit world because of the great work you are doing."

I said that I had received great help in my work from the other side, and having been complimented like this, I ventured to ask Dr. Barnett if he would go out of his way and help our sittings at the S.P.R..

"I know it is silly," I said, "but it is a silly world, and we can only deal with the world as we find it. I quite appreciate your point of view, and in many ways I agree with you, but I do feel that, as Valiantine has started these S.P.R. sittings, he should go on with them, and you should make them successful."

Dr. Barnett, who, hitherto, has expressed great contempt for the whole thing, seemed more inclined to help.

"Shall we get Dr. Woolley down here on Friday?" I said.

"I will speak to him and discuss the whole matter," he said.

Then he said something about "I am sorry for those souls who do not realize there is a life hereafter. These people are not hypostatic."

"What is that word, Doctor?" I said. "I never heard it until last week when you used it."

"It means not in harmony," he said. "H-y-p-o-s-t-a-t-i-c!"

Dr. Barnett then urged on us the need for trying to stop wars, this being, of course, a frequent warning at séances. "Otherwise," he said, "a long series of catastrophes and wars must follow. It was for us to do the best we could."

The lesson of this sitting is all-important for people who wish to communicate with their friends who have passed over. If you approach this subject of spiritualism in loving and sincere sympathy, you get results. If you start cross-examining spirit friends, as though they were burglars or pickpockets, they naturally resent it. Besides, sittings of this kind leave you in a much finer spiritual condition than the silly sittings with skeptics present which I have sometimes attended. You come away exalted, feeling better.

I should like to place on record here, that after the sitting, Mrs. Bradley told the sitters what she had told me before, that on the Friday, twelve days before, Sir Oliver Lodge told them of an experience he had had with his family on Christmas night at dinner.

Lodge has twelve children, who sat around him at the table.

"Now, let's play a game," he said. "You will pretend that I am dead, and you cross-examine me as to whether I am your father or not. Ask me all the questions that you think would prove it."

For an hour they asked him about things in his past life and theirs, and he couldn't remember one of the things they could remember. So, at the end, he said "That proves it's not me. I'm not your father!"

II

Immediately after this sitting I received a letter from Mrs. Alice Graham, in which she said:

"A wonderful night and such marvelous spirit manifestations."

Mr. Alfred Morris wrote:

"The sitting with that great medium, Valiantine, was not only remarkable; it was very, very evidential."

23

The riddle of Dr. Woolley's quest—Una, Lady Troubridge and Miss Radclyffe Hall at Dorincourt—Lady Troubridge receives evidence—Miss Radclyffe Hall's father speaks to his daughter— Mental proofs again established.

I

Friday, March 13, 1925.

THE last séance held in Tavistock Square, in the séance room of the Society for Psychical Research, having proved negative, Dr. Woolley had asked me to inquire from Dr. Barnett what was wrong when he called upon me during the week. I informed him what Dr. Barnett had said.

Dr. Woolley was only too anxious to do everything possible to obtain incontrovertible and volunteered proofs which would be of great value to the work of psychical research.

Whether, however, Dr. Woolley is more interested in the study of supernormal faculties in man, or whether he is desirous of proving the survival of man's personality in the spirit after bodily death, I do not yet know. Personally, I am only interested in the proofs of survival, for the great fact of survival is, to my mind, the one thing which civilization needs beyond all else.

It is my desire to give the Society irrefutable evidence, which can be placed upon their records.

Together we arrived at the decision that the atmosphere and the vibrations at Dorincourt having been proved to give the best results, two of the chief investigators of the Society, Una, Lady Troubridge, and Miss Radcliffe Hall, should come down there for what might be termed a stringent test séance, the results of which, and the evidence obtained, if any, to be placed on the records of the Society.

Miss Radcliffe Hall had sat upon the Council of the Society for Psychical Research for several years, and she and Lady Troubridge had provided during the last eight years some good evidence of survival obtained through the mediumship of Mrs. Osborne Leonard. Both Lady Troubridge and Miss Radcliffe Hall are highly intelligent and cultured ladies, but it must be mentioned that they are quite inexperienced in independent voice phenomena. This rare form they have had little opportunity to study.

II

The sitters were, in addition to the medium, Valiantine, my wife, Mr. Hannen Swaffer, the three S.P.R. members, Una, Lady Troubridge, Miss Radcliffe Hall, and myself.

Valiantine was not introduced to either of the two new sitters, nor did he see their faces until we walked into the study, when the lights were switched off within a few seconds.

Within about ten minutes the spirit voice of Dr. Barnett gave us a greeting, and a few minutes later Bert Everett spoke to us in his shrill voice, high in the ceiling, and gave me the password which I had arranged should be given if the conditions were good.

During the evening several of the spirit guides materialized their voices and spoke to us. The loud voice of Kokum vibrated through the room, and Pat O'Brien spoke to several of those present.

Feda came through and spoke to us in her usual manner, in the independent voice.

I shall not record with any attempt at detail the supernormal physical happenings. I will confine myself rigidly to the mental evidence that was given.

To Una, Lady Troubridge, and to Miss Radcliffe Hall, three different spirits came through, giving their Christian names and surnames, and identifying their surviving personalities.

Both of these ladies were perfect sitters, and were quite excellent in the way they encouraged conversation and extracted evidence of value.

They know how to talk to the spirit voices when they manifest. Most people do not.

Using the luminous trumpet to amplify the sound, the voice of one of the spirits volunteered the Christian and surname of "Arthur Herbert," and spoke with both of them.

Lady Troubridge and Miss Radcliffe Hall were sitting on opposite sides of the circle, and when the spirit spoke to one the trumpet would, on occasions, flash across the room in a second and address the other.

When this spirit was asked to give the name through of a person it knew, the name was given, and this name was correct.

Another spirit giving its name was recognized by Lady Troubridge. The name sounded to me like "Lowther." The spirit conversed with her for some time. During the conversation, this spirit asked that her love should be given to her daughter.

Very carefully and gently Lady Troubridge asked this spirit to give through the name of her daughter. The name was given, volunteered by the voice, and the most unusual one of "Toupie."

A spirit voice spoke with Miss Radcliffe Hall, announcing itself to be her father. He announced himself in a very unusual way by saying: "It's Father Radcliffe." This, we ascertained later, was absolutely correct.

Hawk Chief came through and, in addition, Lord Northcliffe spoke in clear and distinct tones, in the independent voice, without using the luminous trumpet. He spoke for a little time with Mr. Swaffer, and he spoke with me.

My sister also came through, speaking independently in her gentle tones to me and to my wife.

During the evening, on one occasion the luminous trumpet whirled round the room at lightning speed, and was taken outside the circle. It was therefore whirled round over a foot behind the heads of the six sitters and of the medium. It was also taken up towards the ceiling. This is, of course, a remarkable physical phenomenon, but as I have repeatedly said, we do not base our evidence of survival upon any physical movement. It would, however, stagger many of the researchers who are chiefly interested in physical phenomena.

At the close, Dr. Barnett talked for a considerable time, and answered philosophical questions which were put to him by Lady Troubridge and by Miss Radcliffe Hall.

Since this test, which provided irrefutable evidence for the Society for Psychical Research, was agreed upon by Dr. Woolley and myself, I am pleased to place upon the records its complete success.

III

Intelligent minds must, of course, immediately understand that it is only mental evidence which can be considered, and whether mental evidence is collected in Mrs. Osborne Leonard's cottage, or in Whitechapel, or in Timbuctoo, or Los Angeles or Dorincourt, does not matter one pin's point, for established mental evidence wherever it maybe obtained can neither be refuted nor disturbed.

24

Valiantine asks to hear the jazz band—Notes compiled from Mrs. Bradley's report—The spirit of an Italian drummer—Dr. Barnett gives news of Valiantine's family in USA—HDB's impressions outside the room—A stupendous effort.

I

Saturday, March 14, 1925.

ON this evening I had not intended to hold a séance, but Valiantine had heard of the physical phenomena of the musical jazz instruments, which had taken place at Dorincourt under the mediumship of my wife and myself, and was anxious to hear the spirits play the instruments. He also said that he wished to have a little talk with Dr. Barnett, in order to ask him how his wife and family were getting on in Williamsport.

I have endeavoured to be careful with regard to overtaxing Valiantine with too many sittings, but it is interesting to observe that Valiantine always wants to sit. In fact, he seems to regard an evening as wasted if we do not sit. Despite all his experiences he is still as keenly interested in the spirit conversations and manifestations as the newest recruit might be.

On this evening I had some literary work which I wished to complete. My son Anthony had arrived down from Cambridge for the Easter vacation, and as he also was anxious for a sitting, I suggested that he, my wife, and Valiantine should sit together.

The jazz band set was placed in the centre of the circle, with the luminous painted drumsticks and sleigh bells, etc.

I give the following report from the notes which were taken by my wife.

II

After sitting for some little time longer than is usual, without anything happening, my wife remarked what a long time Dr Barnett (who almost invariably opens the séance) was in coming through. Immediately one of the bells sounded. A jazz record was then put on the gramophone, and the bells, triangle, and tambourine were played in accompaniment. A little later the luminous drumsticks were taken up, and the drum was played suddenly with a loud tattoo. The drum was played at first with slow beats, which became quicker and quicker, and louder and louder, until a tremendous volume of sound in syncopated time was heard.

The gramophone was then stopped, and a solo was played on the drum in the most perfect manner. Whilst this was proceeding, Anthony gave a jump as Warren Clarke's voice was heard speaking at the same time as the drum was being played. Anthony was startled at this, because he did not expect to hear a voice whilst the drum was being played. He asked Warren Clarke who it was playing the drum solo, and he replied Camarano," and added that he was the spirit of an Italian drummer, who was a wonderful expert.

After this exhibition, Dr. Barnett spoke with them, and Valiantine talked with him of his family, saying he was a little disturbed because his letters from America had been so delayed. Dr. Barnett told him that they were all quite well, and that he would receive a further letter from them very shortly—which he did.

Mrs. Bradley asked Dr. Barnett whether he would suggest a title for Gonnoske Komai's book in accordance with Mr. Komai's request. Dr. Barnett asked for particulars of the new book—as to whether it was written in English or Japanese—and said that he would endeavour to suggest a title when he knew more about it.

Dr. Barnett then said that the sitting must be closed, as on the following evening there were several fresh sitters coming to Dorincourt, and it was necessary for them to conserve the forces.

III

This account is made from Mrs. Bradley's impressions inside the room. My impressions outside the room are, I think, even more remarkable. I sat in the drawing room, at least twenty feet away from the circle, with closed doors, with a very thick separating wall dividing.

I must record that never in my life had I heard such magnificent drumming. The drum as an instrument does not appeal to me. It was played without any accompanying music, and every conceivable form of tattooing was played for at least a quarter of an hour, brilliantly and enthrallingly. It was a stupendous effort.

During the time that the jazz band was being played I heard Valiantine roaring with laughter. Apparently he was thoroughly enjoying the experience of a form of phenomena entirely new to him.

25

Pat, aged eight, sits with Valiantine—He tells how his aunt spoke to him, also Bert Everett and Bobby Worrall—Attention is drawn to the perfect conditions produced by a child—Miss Constance Collier's dead mother makes a significant remark—The late Lily Hanbury speaks to Dame Clara Butt—Mrs. Hilton Philipson, M.P., is greeted by a spirit friend—Mr. Ivor Novello meets an old acquaintance who had passed out—Clara Butt's singing—The spirits compliment a great artist.

I

Sunday, March 15, 1925.

MY young son Pat, to whom spirit communication is just as natural as the telephone, had been continually asking me if he could be allowed to sit up at night and attend one of the séances. This is, of course, quite impossible, because the sittings usually continue until about eleven p.m., which is too late for this eight-year-old boy.

On this evening, however, I was alone in my room enjoying a cocktail when Pat trotted in, and said that he had just had a five minutes' sitting alone with Valiantine.

Valiantine is very fond of Pat, and Pat of Valiantine. In fact, this kindly American man has all the fine simplicity of a child; that is why they get on so well together.

They played no music—did nothing. They just sat there together, and within a minute they were able to talk with the spirits.

Pat told me how his aunt talked with him. He said, "I recognize her voice at once now when she speaks." He also said that Bert Everett and Bobby Worrall spoke to him. The voices, he stated, he knew at once. Bobby chatted on with Pat about his games, and Pat told me that he laughed when Bobby told him how he had held the trains on the lines for him, whilst Pat was playing on the previous Sunday.

PAT(to me): Won't you please let me stay up one night and talk to them all again with you?

I promised Pat that one evening he should, and a few weeks later I redeemed my promise.

Scientific observers should note the effect of the perfect conditions obtained with Pat and Valiantine. Pat is a perfect sitter.

II

8.30 pm Sunday, March 15, 1925.
Sunday I usually keep for members of the theatrical profession. I know many of them, and before I embarked upon these psychic studies Dorincourt was the home of informal Sunday parties. When the spirit voices come through actors and actresses as a rule speak up very well; they keep the vibrations going, and they are not self-conscious or stilted in their conversation.

Present this evening: Dame Clara Butt, the famous contralto; Miss Constance Collier, one of our most cultured actresses; Mrs. Hilton Philipson, M.P., whose stage name was Mabel Russell; and Mr. Ivor Novello, a young genius, possessing the art of composing, writing, and acting. Also Mr. Swaffer, my wife, Valiantine, and myself.

Of the four guests, Mr. Novello and Mrs. Philipson had had no previous experience of any description, Dame Clara Butt had never sat at a direct voice séance. Miss Constance Collier had made a few experiments in various forms of psychical phenomena.

Within about ten minutes Dr. Barnett gave us a greeting. Then Bert Everett spoke to us in his shrill voice, Kokum, in his loud tones, and Pat O'Brien, Bert Everett gave me the code word.

Feda spoke to Mr. Swaffer, to my wife, and to me.

A voice was suddenly heard speaking just above Miss Constance Collier's head. We could not catch what was said, and I asked the spirit to endeavour to speak through the trumpet, as that might make it easier for us to hear.

The luminous trumpet was lifted and directed to Miss Collier. The voice was then quite distinct. It was the spirit of Miss Collier's mother, and together an affectionate conversation was carried on. Among other things the voice said to her: "I am so glad to see you both here together." And then went over to Dame Clara and spoke to her. This, Miss Collier tells me, was a very significant remark, because the conversation applied to a certain incident known to Clara Butt and to her.

A voice spoke to Dame Clara Butt, announcing itself to be Lily Hanbury (the well-known actress who died in 1908), and they talked together for a while. Dame Clara Butt was a very close friend of Miss Hanbury's before she passed over.

In the independent voice, within about a foot of Mrs. Philipson's head, a voice addressed her. I caught the name given, but Mrs. Philipson did not. I was careful to avoid volunteering any suggestion, and in a minute or so the trumpet was taken up, and the voice came through announcing itself to be "Hubert." Recognition was then immediate, and they talked on together for some time. Mrs. Philipson was addressed as Mabel. Here it should be mentioned that the other new sitters were addressed by their correct Christian names by the voices which spoke. The spirit which spoke to Mrs. Philipson was killed at Loos; a personal suggestion was put to him which had been worrying Mrs. Philipson for some months, and the answer was given. Hubert said he wanted Hilton to sit, so that he might be satisfied. In fact, Mr. Hilton Philipson had wished for an opportunity of sitting, but there was no room for him on this occasion.

A voice using the luminous trumpet addressed Mr. Novello, calling him Ivor. The voice announced itself as "Bertie Austin." Recognition was established, and together they talked on for a while, speaking of some of the characters they had known in Toronto. This spirit talked of its own accord, and volunteered the names of certain people. Mr. Novello mentioned one particular name, and asked the spirit how this person was getting on. The spirit of Bertie Austin in replying said: "He has not passed over yet."

Speaking to me in clear and dignified tones there came through the spirit of Dr. Ellis Powell. He referred to my work, and together we had an interesting talk on the development of spirit communication. He then asked me if I would be good enough to ask his wife to Dorincourt as he would like to talk to her. This I did at a later date.

Bert Everett and Dr. Barnett spoke with us on several occasions, Bert Everett giving a statement regarding a remarkable case of cross evidence. Bert said: "Mr. Bradley, I spoke in my own voice during a séance with Evan Powell in Hampshire a few days ago." It will be remembered that Captain Astley Maberley notified this fact to the Society for Psychical Research and called upon me and informed me of this. The incident is recorded in Chapter 21.

Towards the close, Dr. Barnett came through and asked whether there were any questions which we might wish to put to him, and several interesting questions were asked by Mr. Novello, Dame Clara Butt, and other sitters. Each question was answered in Dr. Barnett's usual fluent manner.

III

The sitting was a very good one although I felt that there was slightly too much tensity amongst the sitters.

It was perhaps a more remarkable evening than this record shows. Afterwards Miss Constance Collier said: "I could not sleep for hours that night, thinking of the beauty of it all." And Ivor Novello said: "It was the greatest day of my life."

When we walked out of my study, it appeared that five people had been sitting outside the door during the latter half of the proceedings, and had distinctly heard the various spirit voices speaking with us.

During the evening Anthony was in another room, entertaining some friends of the sitters. They were Dame Clara Butt's daughter and a girlfriend, Miss Madeline Cohen, and Mr. Hilton Philipson. These four and my son had left the drawing room, and had sat outside the door for some considerable time.

They all told me afterwards that it was an extraordinary experience for them.

It was a far more fluent evening than these notes convey. It must be remembered, however, that after an evidential name is given by a spirit, and recognition takes place, the conversation that ensues is usually of too intimate a character to be printed.

The first record that I usually put on the gramophone at a séance is that of Clara Butt's singing "God Shall Wipe Away All Tears" to Sullivan's setting. I placed this record on one side as Mr. Novello had told me that Dame Clara did not like to hear her own records, because the experience embarrassed her.

During the evening, however, I asked Dame Clara's permission to put the record on. She consented. I then asked her if she would mind joining in with the music and she kindly assented. It was good of her to do so, for she had recently been very ill. The effect was wonderful, as we had the two Clara Butt's singing at once, the waxen one on the gramophone, and Clara Butt herself, in the same room.

It was towards the end of this beautiful melody that the voice of Lily Hanbury was heard whispering to her. Later, Dame Clara Butt sang to us again, but this time without the gramophone accompaniment.

Feda came through and said: "Clara Butt has a very great voice."

BERT EVERETT: You have a marvelous voice.

This must be the first time that England's finest contralto has been complimented on her singing by spirits.

It was interesting to hear Constance Collier's mother talking to Clara Butt, because when Miss Collier's mother was dying almost the last thing she asked for was that Dame Clara should come and sing to her.

26

An official S.P.R. test sitting—Lady Troubridge receives an evidential communication—Dr. Woolley agrees—Lady Troubridge draws attention to a spirit speaking at the same time as Valiantine—Plain words from Dr. Barnett to Dr. Woolley.

I

Monday, March 16, 1925.

IT had been arranged during the preceding week with Dr. Woolley that after the first test sitting with Una, Lady Troubridge, and Miss Radcliffe Hall, both representing the Society, he should join this identical circle and note what transpired.

It was agreed that the sitting should take place at Dorincourt, where the conditions had been proved to be good for phenomena.

Meanwhile, the London press had given much publicity to the various experiments which were being conducted. The excess of publicity at this stage in the experiments was at times irritating.

Somewhat to my annoyance, there appeared in the *Daily Sketch* and other papers a statement to the effect that Dr. Woolley had said that these private sittings could not be regarded as official as far as the Society was concerned, as they were not being held on the Society's premises.

Dr. Woolley dined at Dorincourt, and before the sitting he told me that the statement had been made because he thought that I would prefer not to have the proceedings recorded as official. I replied that such was not my attitude, and that as I was inundated with requests for sittings it would be impossible for me to continue to hold exclusive sittings for the chief members of the Society, unless these sittings were regarded as the official tests and the proceedings placed upon the records of the Society.

Dr. Woolley agreed at once with me on this point, and said that the proceedings would be regarded as official and reported as such.

There were present four of the chief investigators of the S.P.R.: Una, Lady Troubridge, Miss Radcliffe Hall, Dr. Woolley, as the research officer, and myself.

The additional sitters were Mr. Hannen Swaffer, Mrs. Bradley, and Valiantine.

The keenest possible observation was kept upon all the phenomena which occurred.

The gramophone was played, and after about ten minutes the deep tones of Dr. Barnett gave a greeting, his voice coming from the centre of the floor.

A little later the shrill voice of Bert Everett spoke from high up near the ceiling. In reply to the question from me, he did not give me the code word. This meant that conditions were not good.

Pat O'Brien, in his Irish accents, spoke to us, and shortly afterwards Kokum gave us a greeting in his usual loud tones.

These three voices spoke, as usual, independently without using the trumpet, and from space.

Feda spoke to several of us. She also spoke independently and in her childishly feminine tones. The voice appeared to float round the room as she was addressing the various sitters.

Of the personal spirits, a voice spoke to Lady Troubridge and Miss Radcliffe Hall, announcing itself as "Arthur Herbert." Lady Troubridge and Miss Radcliffe Hall were sitting opposite each other whilst this voice was speaking, and the luminous trumpet was moved with considerable rapidity across the room whilst each of these ladies was being spoken to in turn by the voice.

The trumpet was lifted in the air, and taken towards Dr. Woolley, the spirit voice announcing itself to be that of his father. A few phrases were exchanged between them, but nothing of evidential value could be recorded.

Dr. Woolley is a comparatively young man. I did not know and I am quite certain Valiantine did not know, that Dr. Woolley's father had passed over.

Another spirit addressed Miss Radcliffe Hall, announcing himself to be "Father Radcliffe." Together they talked for a little while.

A voice addressed Mr. Swaffer, announcing itself to be a brother of his, but the voice was quite indistinct and weak, and nothing of an evidential nature was given. Mr. Swaffer had a brother who had died.

Another spirit addressed Lady Troubridge, giving the name of Mrs. Lowther, and spoke to her for some time. In answer to a question the voice, in replying, volunteered the names of two people, one being, I understand, the name of Mrs. Lowther's daughter.

Later, another spirit voice addressed Lady Troubridge, saying: "It's Harry—father." This appeared to me to be peculiarly significant, and after the sitting Lady Troubridge told me that it was evidential, because she always called her father "Harry." A conversation ensued between Lady Troubridge and this spirit.

During the evening, one of the luminous trumpets was lifted and whirled round the circle, and taken high up in the air. On several occasions, when the luminous trumpet was lifted and taken well away from the part of the room in which Valiantine was sitting Valiantine was called upon to speak whilst this phenomenon was taking place, and he did so.

Dr. Woolley's attention was drawn to the fact that Valiantine was speaking whilst the luminous trumpet was in the air, and well away from him. Dr. Woolley agreed upon this fact.

During the time that the spirit voice of Mrs. Lowther was speaking with Lady Troubridge, Valiantine spoke at the same time. The attention of Dr. Woolley and the other sitters was also drawn to this fact.

Dr. Barnett had said at a previous sitting that he would discuss with Dr. Woolley the conditions and the mentality at the two sittings held in the séance room of the S.P.R.

He did. For over ten minutes, in loud and determined accents, Dr. Barnett's powerful voice rang through the room.

Again I state that this characteristic and dignified voice spoke from space. It was the voice of the spirit of Dr. Barnett, and not the voice of anyone in the room. This was agreed to by Dr. Woolley; it was agreed to by Lady Troubridge; it was agreed to by Miss Radcliffe Hall; and it was agreed to by myself—four of the most experienced investigators of the Society for Psychical Research.

It was also agreed by my wife and by Mr. Hannen Swaffer, both of whom have heard Dr. Barnett on dozens of occasions. In addition to this, at the same time that Dr. Barnett's tones were ringing—literally ringing, for his voice was pregnant with determination—through the room, Valiantine suddenly interposed by asking a question, and the two voices were speaking simultaneously.

At the time when Valiantine was speaking simultaneously with Dr. Barnett, and the two voices were heard by all speaking together, Lady Troubridge immediately said: "I wish to state that the medium was speaking at the same time as Dr. Barnett."

II

I give a brief abstract of the conversation:

DR. WOOLLEY: Can you tell me, Dr. Barnett, why we were unable to get results at the S.P.R.?

DR. BARNETT: It was because the conditions there are not good.

DR. WOOLLEY: Can you tell me why that is?

DR. BARNETT: It is because of the tricks and contraptions which you have there.

DR. WOOLLEY: I really do not know what you mean, Dr. Barnett.

DR. BARNETT (immediately and in very firm tones) Don't be childish, you know perfectly well what I mean. You have there a great wire cage. What is that for? Do you think that a psychic is a kangaroo or a gorilla?

DR. WOOLLEY: Yes, doctor, but the cage was not for Mr. Valiantine—it was for another physical medium.

DR. BARNETT: The very fact of having things there of that description makes the atmosphere entirely wrong. You must approach the study of spirit communication with love and with reverence.

DR. WOOLLEY: I do try, doctor.

DR. BARNETT: You do not understand, sir. Your father spoke to you here tonight, and he says that it is very difficult to approach you, as you have built around yourself a rampart which it is almost impossible to penetrate. Let me tell you, sir, that you must change your mentality. This great truth is being spread throughout the world by people who are convinced that spirituality is the only thing that will stop wars. When people realize that life cannot be destroyed, then wars will cease. How do you account for the spirits who have been speaking here tonight, sir? Did you not hear them talking to their friends?

DR. WOOLLEY: Yes, I did.

DR. BARNETT: Well, how do you account for it?

DR. WOOLLEY: I am afraid I don't know.

DR. BARNETT: Well, sir, are you convinced?

DR. WOOLLEY: Yes, I think I am, doctor.

DR. BARNETT: No! You are not, sir. Your mind does not yet grasp this great Truth. We, on our side, are doing our best to convince you, and to convince the world. We are all working very hard, and very soon some wonderful proofs are to be given.

During the time that the conditions of the S.P.R. were being discussed by Dr. Barnett, I joined in the conversation, and said that I felt that it was an insult to intelligence to be asked to sit in a room filled with mechanical contrivances which were devised because of a suspicion of fraud. That was why I said that I would not agree to sit there again.

In reply to Miss Radcliffe Hall, Dr. Barnett said that women were much better sitters than men, as they were more spiritual and men were more material.

Dr. Woolley, as chief officer of the S.P.R., agreed that the physical phenomena—that is, the lightning-like movements of the luminous trumpet, were supernormal. When this occurred I deliberately asked Dr. Woolley "Do you agree that to be supernormal." He replied "Yes." It must also be noted that he agreed, as did every other sitter present, that Valiantine never moved from his chair. It must also be noted that eleven distinct and individual spirit voices spoke to us; that Dr. Woolley agreed that he heard these spirit voices, and that in answer to a question put by a spirit he said that he could not account for it.

It was an interesting and an electric evening, and Dr. Woolley was considerably impressed. In the London press there appeared on the following Sunday a statement from Dr. Woolley that he was perfectly satisfied with the conditions under which the sitting was held.

At the same time, I yet feel that Dr. Woolley's psychical studies are still inclined towards over estimating the supernormal faculties in man, whilst I am only interested in proving to the world the fact of man's spiritual survival.

27

Anthony and Valiantine experiment in the daylight—Anthony's account of Warren and Annie coming through—Mrs. Bradley's daylight experiment—A séance in a strange room without trumpets—"I regard this as a very remarkable test."

I

12.30 pm Tuesday, March 17, 1925.

I HAD arranged that this should be a day of rest from psychic studies, but apparently it is impossible to stop the sequence of remarkable events. Whilst I was in town during the morning, my son Anthony and Valiantine experimented in the daylight.

I give Anthony's account of what took place.

"At twelve-thirty on this very sunny morning of March 17, I partially drew the curtains in the study where the séances are regularly held. There was still plenty of light clearly to distinguish the various objects in the room, and also to study the expression on the face of George Valiantine. Valiantine held one end of the trumpet; I put the narrow end to my ear, and we waited a few moments. I could see Valiantine's face throughout the sitting. After some taps I heard a voice inside the trumpet whispering: 'Dennis!' I welcomed the voice, and asked whose it was. Clearly the answer came: 'Warren.'

"'I am so glad to see you here,' the voice continued. I remarked on the achievement of getting a voice through in the daylight. He replied that it was 'very difficult.' His voice, though not loud, was quite distinct. My uncle (Warren) then said: 'Your Aunt Annie is here,' and departed.

"The clear sounds of my aunt's voice then came through and greeted me by name. 'I am helping you in your work,' she said. 'And I am helping Herbert, too.' We talked for a minute or two, and then I asked her if she would be able to speak to my mother in the same manner. She replied that she thought she could. I then bade her goodbye, and fetched my mother to take my place.

"Mother told me afterwards that she sat, as I had done, with the small end of the trumpet to her ear. Both Valiantine's hands were holding the larger end of the trumpet, and in so doing he obscured his face from my mother's vision. His face, however, was reflected in a bookshelf on one side, so that she was able clearly to watch his face. His lips never moved.

"After some moments a voice whispered: 'This is Warren Clarke.' He then said something that was quite incomprehensible. Mother asked him to repeat it, but all she could make out was the words 'very difficult!' Then the voice became clearer. 'Tell Herbert not to get too impatient,' came through distinctly. (I may mention that my father, who through an excess of work, has lately been living almost entirely on his nerves, is inclined to spasmodic periods of irritability when attending uncongenial sittings.) Mother then got up and parted the curtains, allowing a flood of light to enter the room. She resumed her position, and again the voice of my uncle came through and continued the discussion."

The phenomenon of obtaining the voices in the daylight represents a tremendous leap forward in psychical research.

II

5 p.m. Tuesday, March 17, 1925.
On the afternoon of this day my wife, Valiantine, and myself were invited to tea with the Hon. Mrs. Fitzroy Stanhope at 49 Onslow Square. The Countess Ahlefeldt Laurvig was there and also another lady.

We had tea, and chatted. About five o'clock Mrs. Stanhope asked whether we would consent to hold a séance in her sitting room there and then. This proposition came as a surprise. No suggestion whatever had been made of it beforehand, and the call was purely a social one. I was irritated by the suggestion, as Valiantine had no trumpets with him, and it meant sitting on the spur of the moment in a strange room.

The position was rather delicate; I felt that a refusal might create a wrong impression. I did not feel that it was likely that we should obtain any result, and I do not care for the mental disturbance of negative sittings, as they always create an atmosphere of suspicion in the minds of new sitters. Anyhow, I felt the situation was one which would have to be faced, so I agreed.

The curtains were drawn to exclude the daylight.

The six of us sat around on a couch and easy chairs. No trumpets were used.

A gramophone was played, and in five to six minutes, whilst I was making certain remarks, there came through, high up in the room, the loud laugh of Bert Everett.

A little later, there came through Pat O'Brien, speaking in his broad Irish brogue, and giving us a greeting.

Later, Bobby Worrall. He spoke with a little difficulty, but his childish accents were quite clearly and distinctly heard by all of us. He talked for a little time with me, with the Countess Ahlefeldt Laurvig, and with Mrs. Fitzroy Stanhope. To the Countess he said, "Your brother is here."

A little later on, just near the Countess, a heavy breathing sound was heard, as though someone were trying with great difficulty to speak. Eventually the voice managed to say: "Oscar!" That was all. Oscar was the name of the Countess's brother who had passed away.

Bert Everett spoke to us in his shrill tones for a while, and the sitting then closed.

I regard this experience as remarkable. Suddenly, in a strange room, without trumpets or amplifiers, we were asked to sit, and four spirit voices were able to materialize and to speak with us.

The room was quite a suitable one, and the atmosphere was very good. During the sitting several luminous spirit lights were seen.

28

The author refuses the theory of telepathy and gives his reasons for so doing—The late Albert Chevalier speaks to his widow—Sir Arthur Conan Doyle's sister—The wife of E. W. Hornung—A conversation in Japanese—Evidence which greatly impresses the author—No wars in Mars—"I know my dead husband spoke to me," says Mrs. Chevalier.

Wednesday, March 18, 1925.

This sitting took place at Dorincourt at about eight forty-five p.m. Present, Sir Arthur Conan Doyle and Lady Doyle; Mr. Gonnoske Komai; Mrs. Albert Chevalier, the wife of the great comedian; Mr. Swaffer, Mrs. Bradley, Anthony Bradley, myself, and Valiantine.

After a few minutes the voice of Dr. Barnett gave us a greeting. A little later Bert Everett came through and gave me the code word signifying that the conditions were good.

The other guides who spoke were Pat O'Brien, Kokum, Hawk Chief, and Bobby Worrall.

In speaking to my son Anthony, Bobby said: "I saw you and Pat today in the garden playing with a ball." I mention this because it is representative of a series of extraordinary incidents, for whilst my wife and I and Valiantine may perhaps have been in town during the whole of the day, Bobby will come through and talk to us in the evening, telling us all that Pat has been doing throughout the day. The relation of these incidents, simple as they may appear, has a very considerable value, since no possible theory of telepathy can be applied to these subsequently proven facts.

Of the personal spirits, the first voice to manifest itself addressed Mrs. Chevalier. The luminous trumpet was lifted, coming close to Mrs. Chevalier's face, and, announcing itself as "Albert," said: "I am so glad to see you here, dearie Old Dutch; I am always with you." They talked together for some little time, Albert Chevalier's voice being distinct and characteristic. The identity of Chevalier was established beyond all question through the evidence volunteered. To Mrs. Chevalier he said: "Annie is here." I learnt afterwards that "Annie" was Mrs. Chevalier's mother. Mrs. Chevalier asked the following question of the spirit: "Do you know what next Saturday is?"

ALBERT CHEVALIER: It's my birthday anniversary.

Afterwards Mrs. Chevalier said that she recognized his voice immediately; it was characteristic, and could not be imitated. She told us that her husband's voice was one of the few that the famous mimic, Cissie Loftus, could never imitate, and that during his life Chevalier had tried to teach her to imitate it on several occasions, but without success.

A voice addressed Sir Arthur and Lady Doyle, announcing itself as "Kingsley," the son of the Doyles who passed away some little time back. A conversation between this spirit and the Doyles continued for some little time, and Kingsley volunteered the statement that "Annette is here."

Sir Arthur told us that Annette was a sister of his who had passed over thirty years ago, and that during the whole of his experiences at séances this name had never come through before, nor had the name ever been mentioned in public. Therefore, the volunteering of the name by a spirit must be regarded as of evidential value.

During the conversation between the Doyles and Kingsley, the luminous trumpet came quickly over to me, and said: "You are doing a very great work, Mr. Bradley," and then it flashed across the room to Sir Arthur, saying: "And so are you, father."

Through the luminous trumpet another personal spirit addressed Sir Arthur and Lady Doyle, announcing itself to be "Connie." The voice said: "We're here together—Willie and I." The spirit Connie was the wife of E. W. Hornung, the famous part-author of the play *Raffles*."

Another spirit talked with Lady Doyle, announcing itself to be "Lillie." Recognition was established, and together they talked for a short time.

The most dramatic event of the evening was when a voice addressed Mr. Gonnoske Komai in Japanese. Twice the luminous trumpet was dropped before the spirit could gain sufficient power to materialize the voice. Then, through the luminous trumpet which came close to Mr. Komai's face, touching him two or three times, the voice called: "Gonnoske, Gonnoske." This impressed Mr. Komai for reasons which will be explained later.

The voice gradually obtained more power, and then gave the name of "Otani." Identity was established, and a conversation was carried on in Japanese. It was not very long, but during the time references were made, to the children of Otani.

Afterwards Mr. Komai informed us of a very important point. The spirit addressed him as "Gonnoske," and in Japan only an elder brother, mother, and father are allowed to address a man by his first, or what we term Christian name.

Mr. Komai stated that the spirit who had been speaking was that of an elder brother who had passed away some time ago.

Almost immediately after this spirit had departed, Bert Everett spoke to Mr. Komai, saying: "Both your mother and brother are here tonight."

Mr. Komai is a youngish man, and it is essential to mention that no one in that room knew that he had an elder brother who had passed away, neither did anyone know that his mother was not alive. Nor could anyone else in the room speak Japanese.

I regard this incident of a conversation in Japanese, together with the striking evidence volunteered by the spirit voice, as one of the finest and most incontrovertible evidences that has been given of survival.

At the close Dr. Barnett spoke with us and talked about the title of a new book which Mr. Komai has just written.

Dr. Barnett then discussed with Mr. Komai the political situation. He spoke of the terrible possibility of further wars in the very near future. He said that Japan was building aeroplanes at a tremendous pace, and in very great numbers, and that the Japanese were preparing as fast as they could for a great war in the air.

The American situation was touched upon, and Mr. Komai said: "But America is a great country—far greater than Japan."

DR. BARNETT: That maybe so, but Japan's preparations are far greater and far more advanced than those of America.

KOMAI: The Japanese people do not want war; they wish for peace.

DR. BARNETT: I know that is so, but the political leaders of the country are those who are responsible. You are a great writer, and your writings will have great influence. Unless the whole world becomes more spiritual there will be a terrible upheaval of civilization. You can do great work.

In answer to another question, Dr. Barnett replied "In Mars war has been exterminated for a very long time. The inhabitants there are far more spiritual than those on this Earth. The Earth is a much younger planet."

After the sitting Mrs. Chevalier was overcome with joy. Her married life with Albert Chevalier had been one of ideal love. "It was Albert's own voice," she said. "I detected in his voice tonight that little something you cannot describe. There was a certain little tenderness in it that made him so popular, and it had an emotional quality that I recognized at once. You can tell the world that I did not only believe it was my husband—I know it was."

Then she went on to say "my life has been so empty lately. You do not know what you have done for me. It is the greatest day of my life."

29

A sitting devoted to S.P.R.—The author confesses that his irritableness is not improved—Feda discusses a curious mistake in the identity of two ladies—Advice to psychic researchers—A second sitting on the same evening.

I

Friday, March 20, 1925.

This was another evening devoted to the Society for Psychical Research. There were present, Una, Lady Troubridge, Miss Radcliffe Hall, Dr. V. J. Woolley, and myself (being representatives of the Society); and Mrs. V. J. Woolley, Mr. Swaffer, Mrs. Bradley, and Valiantine.

The time had been altered.

At a sitting, which had been held by Lady Troubridge and Miss Radcliffe Hall with Mrs. Osborne Leonard on the preceding Wednesday, Feda had suggested that it would be better for the voices if we sat at about six-thirty instead of after dinner, as this might improve the conditions.

Whether it improved conditions or not remains to be seen, but it did not improve my irritableness. My appetite seldom interests me, since I do not usually possess one, but I do not like taking an early cocktail without the antidote of food to follow.

The sitting was held at Dorincourt and it should be mentioned that Miss Walker—Sir Oliver Lodge's secretary—had arranged to be present. At the last moment, however, she was unable to attend, and Mrs. Woolley took her place. This fact, as I told Dr. Woolley, had not been mentioned to Valiantine, but Dr. Woolley said that he thought as they entered the hall Mrs. Woolley's name had been mentioned in Valiantine's presence.

This sitting was negative from the point of view of volunteered evidence; nevertheless, four of the guides spoke in their independent voices.

Dr. Barnett greeted us; Bert Everett and Pat O'Brien spoke to us. Although Bert Everett said that the conditions were quite good, I did not feel comfortable. I was nervy. I felt bored and tired at these somewhat prolonged S.P.R. "investigations."

Feda came through and after greeting us she seemed to me to call the name of "Miss Walker." I interrogated Feda as to why she volunteered the name of Miss Walker, and added: "You can see who are sitting here. Will you tell us why you mentioned her name?"

Feda did not reply, but said: "Raymond is here and wants to give a message to Miss Walker."

I then said to Feda: "If Raymond can see Miss Walker here, take the trumpet over and touch her." Almost immediately following this remark of mine the luminous trumpet was lifted and touched Mrs. Woolley.

Having experienced one comparatively negative sitting with the S.P.R. and not liking the mental conditions there, the suspicion immediately flashed across my mind that it was possible that Mrs. Woolley (whom I had never met before) was Miss Walker, and I called out: "Is that Miss Walker?" It was, of course, not Miss Walker, and it appeared to me that some peculiar mistake had been made. This rather depressed me, since Feda, through Mrs. Leonard, has given some of the most remarkable mental evidences that have been obtained through a spirit control.

In her independent voice Feda came over to me; her voice had an anxious tone, and in an agitated manner she said: "Mr. Bradley, that was another spirit who lifted the trumpet. It was not Raymond." Feda continued talking for some little while, impressing upon me and insisting she had not made a mistake.

By the tones of her voice, she was quite upset and I am inclined to think some extraordinary mistake had been made.

I wish to emphasize, however, that Feda's voice was clear and distinct, and that she was speaking from space. This can be verified by all of those who were present. Immediately after this Lady Troubridge said: "I wish to state that Valiantine knew that Miss Walker was not here and that Mrs. Woolley had taken her place, because before Mr. Bradley and Dr. Woolley came into the room in the presence of Mrs. Bradley we told him (Valiantine) of this." This point is a very important one.

The incident was upsetting. Dr. Barnett came through saying: "I wish to speak to Mr. Bradley." He said that Feda was absolutely right in what she had said, and that just after my question had been put to her the trumpet had been lifted by another spirit and taken towards Mrs. Woolley. Dr. Barnett added that it was the spirit of a lady who wished to talk to Mrs. Woolley.

After a minute or so Dr. Barnett said: "We must close this sitting."

II

During the week preceding this sitting, extraordinary evidences were volunteered of the survival of the spirit.

Spirit voices were easy and fluent, and astoundingly evidential.

The mental tests have been ten times greater than anything which could be evolved by the official mind of any research officer.

I announced afterwards that I should not bother to sit again as an investigating member of the S.P.R.. It was paradoxical for me to act as an initiate investigator of a new science, upon which I possessed an advanced knowledge. The Slade School would hardly request Augustus John to pass a primary examination.

At two S.P.R. test sittings incontrovertible evidence of survival had been given in the independent voices of recognized spirits. I could not feel, however, that by continuing this particular circle any longer the atmosphere was such that any fresh leaps towards knowledge would be made.

Again I wish it to be understood that, so far as Dr. Woolley and myself are concerned, he and I get on extremely well together, and I like to meet him and discuss various problems with him outside these circles. Inside the circles—although he is certainly a very good and attentive sitter—I feel a cross vibration of a cold, unresponsive, and non-comprehending attitude. This vibrates against my established knowledge. I have proved so much during the last two years, that any cold or theoretical attempt to explain materially the marvelous phenomenon of the independent voice becomes laughable.

Although this sitting maybe regarded as negative, the establishment of Valiantine with the S.P.R. was achieved on Monday, March 16. That was quite enough for me, and I could not concede any further time to these experiments with the Society, whilst many of the great intellects of Great Britain were kept waiting for their personal experience.

III

After the sitting we had supper together, and were quite a merry party. Later on, Dr. and Mrs. Woolley, Una, Lady Troubridge, and Miss Radcliffe Hall motored back to London; Mr. Swaffer remained.

Valiantine suddenly said: "Let the four of us sit together." So, at ten forty-five pm, Mr. Swaffer, my wife, and myself sat with Valiantine. No music was played, and within thirty seconds the spirits came through, and talked with us fluently and quickly for half an hour. We discussed any subject we wished with them. It was an extraordinary contrast in the difference of conditions.

Anthony was sitting in the adjoining room and heard the voices, loud, clear and distinct, talking with us.

My advice to psychic researchers of the future is this; The first essential of all is to learn how to approach the study in the proper mentality, and beyond all else to remember that to achieve progress spirit communication must be approached with love and with reverence.

Here is an odd fact: throughout the whole of the Valiantine series of séances Feda never came through again. Some few weeks afterwards I met Lady Troubridge at a P.E.N. Club dinner, and during our conversation she told me that at a sitting she had had with Mrs. Osborne Leonard Feda said she had not made a mistake on the evening in question. Lady Troubridge then said to Feda that, rather than there should be any possibility of a mistake being made, it would be better if Feda did not endeavour to get through at these voice séances again. Apparently Feda took this advice, for it is very significant that she has not been through since.

Lady Troubridge offered the opinion that it was quite possible it was not Feda at all who came through and spoke, but that it might have been an entity impersonating Feda. This contention I should not accept, as Feda has been through on dozens of occasions, speaking in a characteristic manner both at the Valiantine sittings and at the private sittings held under my own and my wife's mediumship. She has an unmistakable personality, and in addition to this, I have a remarkable accumulation of cross evidence through Feda in the direct voice, confirmed by sittings with Mrs. Osborne Leonard, when Feda has spoken through Mrs. Leonard in her trance condition. Not only have I and my wife had this, but many others who have sat with us have had the same experience of cross-evidence, including Mr. Swaffer, Mr. Newman Flower, and Mr. Harold Wimbury, Mrs. Gibbons Grinling, Mr. Denis Grinling, and Mr. Osborne Leonard; and even Mrs. Osborne Leonard herself has spoken with Feda at length at the direct voice séances held at Dorincourt. We all know her and every intonation of her voice.

Lady Troubridge's contention, therefore, cannot possibly hold. The very fact of Feda not having come through after this request was made proves that it was her individual self.

I am extremely sorry that Feda appears to have dissociated herself for a time from us, but this peculiar fact is of evidential value, as it proves that spirits are sensitive to any suggestion of disharmony with those with whom they are communicating.

30

A sitting by Pat's special request—Pat makes Dr. Barnett laugh—The spirit of Camarano performs a fine drum solo—An encore performance for Pat—Bobby Worrall blows the siren—Kokum is glad to see the "little papoose in his moccasins and kimono" —A child's attitude towards death.

I

Saturday, March 21, 1925.

A SITTING was held on this evening especially for Pat. I did not attend as I was not feeling very well, but I sat in the next room; and heard the spirit voices speaking.

There were present Valiantine, my wife, Mrs. Robert Graham, Anthony, and Pat.

Pat was anxious to hear the jazz band, the instruments of which, together with the siren and the sleigh bells, had been painted with luminous paint.

The following is Anthony's account.

"The jazz band set was placed, with the trumpet, in the centre of the room. Pat was thrilled at the thought of staying up late. He had sat only once before for a full night séance. That was a year ago.

"Bert Everett was the first guide to come through. He expressed joy at seeing Pat, who immediately recognized him by his voice. The conditions were 'exquisite,' for Bert Everett spoke within about thirty seconds after the lights had been put out.

"Dr. Barnett said he was pleased that Pat had come. In answer to a question of mine, Dr. Barnett said that for hundreds of centuries Mars had been free from war. Pat interrupted the doctor with: 'Excuse me, I hope you won't think this is rude, but I think you sound like a 'philosipher'. (Meaning, of course) philosopher.) Dr. Barnett boomed with mirth. He went on to deal with war on this planet, and spoke of the possibility of a devastating war in the air between 1926 and 1927. England, America, Japan, Germany, Russia, and France might be involved.

"When Dr. Barnett had finished, there was a movement in the drum. We played a jazz record, and soon perfect time was beaten by the luminous drumsticks on a cymbal, and afterwards on the drum itself. When the record was finished, Camarano (Dr. Barnett supplied the name) played a remarkably fine drum solo with unusual strength. We encored this, and, to please Pat, the drum was played to represent a horse galloping from a distance, growing louder and louder, then dying away, softer and softer. This was quite wonderful.

Annie spoke to Pat. She said she was helping me in my work. She welcomed Mrs. Graham, and said that she had twice visited her. Annie told my mother that she was helping my father, and that he should avoid too much excitement during his present work.

"Then Bobby Worrall talked to Pat, and said he had seen Pat and me playing tennis that afternoon. (Quite true.) Pat asked Bobby to blow a siren which had been placed on the floor, which he did; Pat then asked him to ring the hoop of bells which had fallen on to the floor. 'Yes,' said Bobby Worrall, 'if you'll hand them to me.' Pat picked them up and held them out. 'Oh, I felt a hand,' said Pat, unafraid and delighted, as they were taken out of his grasp. The bells moved quickly round the circle (they could be seen by the luminous paint on them). They then dropped. Pat picked them up, held them out, and again felt the hand take them from him.

"A spirit came through and spoke, without using the trumpet, to Mrs. Graham. 'Alice,' it said, 'it's Bob!' They talked together, and discussed a title for Winnie's new book. Then Mrs. Graham's father, with the aid of the trumpet, spoke to his daughter. He thanked Mrs. Bradley for bringing Mrs. Graham to the sitting, and he thanked Valiantine for the great work he was doing.

"Kokum was glad to see 'the little papoose in the moccasins and kimono.' (Pat was dressed in slippers and a dressing-gown). Beating an accompaniment on the drum, Kokum sang a short Indian song, which was encored.

"Finally, Warren (my uncle) speaking very clearly, talked to Pat, to my mother, and to me. This wound up a short sitting, where the power was exceptionally strong "

II

My young son Pat and I are very great friends, and often go for walks together, when we talk on all sorts of subjects. Pat's attitude towards death, since he has spoken with the spirits, is impressive. He said to me "Daddy! Before I used to talk to the spirits I was very frightened of death. Now I don't mind the thought of it a bit. Of course I don't want to die yet; I want to live on here, but I know that when I do die I shall have a splendid time."

Here is the new wisdom. If all the world could think like this it would be a much better place to live in.

31

Lovers reunited— "Give my love to Vivian" in German—Miss Violet Loraine's father is proud of his daughter's career—The spirit of Minnie, Miss Loraine's maid and dresser, comes back to her mistress: "I was with you, but I am not in the grave" —Miss Loraine's impressions.

I

Sunday, March 22, 1925.

The circle on this evening was a particularly good one. Some of us had enjoyed a strenuous afternoon's tennis at Dorincourt with Randolph and Joan Lycett (the English Internationals). The party at dinner was a merry one. The harmonious mentality of a mixed gathering is always conducive to the best psychic results.

The Lycetts had to return to town, and I did not go into the séance room, as I had some literary work which it was essential for me to complete. At odd intervals, however, from the next room, I heard the spirit voices talking.

My son Anthony, who, it maybe mentioned, is Editor of *The Cambridge Gownsman*, recorded what took place. The following are his notes:

"There sat—including Valiantine—Mr. Edward Joicey; Mrs. Joicey, formerly Miss Violet Loraine, one of our most brilliant revue actresses; Mr. Jack Baines, Cambridge University L.T.C.; Mr. George Prins, Mr. Hannen Swaffer, Mrs. Bradley, and myself. After one record had been played Dr. Barnett said, 'Good evening, souls' from the bottom of the luminous trumpet.

"Then the high-pitched voice of Bert Everett came from the top of the room, and said that the conditions were good.

'Kokum greeted us in loud Indian.

"Then Mr. Prins felt a touch on his head. 'George!' It was a strong voice, speaking without the trumpet. 'Yes, dear, who are you? Do try and speak to me.' The spirit picked up the trumpet and spoke through it. The voice throbbed with emotion. 'I'm your wife Viva.' There followed the usual delighted remarks that are exchanged when lovers are reunited. At Mr. Prins' request his wife (who was English) then spoke in German to him.

"We played another record on the gramophone.

"The trumpet swung round and stopped in front of Mr. Joicey. A voice spoke through it, but for some moments we could not make out whose it was. At last it became clearer. 'It is Laurence!' Mr. Joicey cried, surprised and delighted. 'Laurence' was a great friend of Mr. Joicey's. 'Clive is here, and will speak,' said Laurence, after they had spoken some time.

"'The trumpet was replaced in the centre of the room, and after a few seconds it was again lifted, this time by a spirit who announced himself as 'Clive.' Clive was Mr. Joicey's brother. 'I'm alive—tell them all at home that I'm alive!'

"The next spirit to come through addressed itself to Mrs. Joicey. 'Father,' announced a slightly husky voice through the trumpet. 'I am so glad to see you here,' said her father. 'I have been watching you, and I am so proud of your career. I am always with you. ... 'I see you've brought your husband,' and then the trumpet went over to Mr. Joicey for a moment.

'Yes, he's very satisfactory!' sentenced her father.

'Send my love to mother, dear.'

"Then a quick, jerky, very distinctive voice came through and said 'Vi.' Mrs. Joicey responded. 'It's Harry Wall,' the spirit announced. Harry Wall was an uncle of Mrs. Joicey's. The short, jerky voice conversed for a while. After he had gone, Mrs. Joicey exclaimed, 'That was exactly his way of speaking —in quick jerks! ' Certainly it was a very unusual voice.

"Pat O'Brien came through with his characteristic 'To be sure!' and spoke to us.

"Then a soft voice came through the trumpet, which Mrs. Joicey recognized with delight as belonging to Minnie, who for years had been her devoted and sympathetic maid and dresser. 'Call me by the name you used to call me,' said Miss Violet Loraine. 'I am so glad to speak to you, my child.' This was Minnie's name for her mistress. Mrs. Joicey said she had recently visited Minnie's grave. 'I was with you, but I am not in the grave.' Minnie said she was also with her mistress when she visited her old dressing room at the Alhambra. She also said how proud she was of her mistress, and that she was frequently with her. In response to a question she told Mrs. Joicey that the latter was holding in her hand, at that moment, a handkerchief and a letter. This was quite true; Mrs. Joicey had in her hand a handkerchief, and also the last letter that her maid had written to her. Before the spirit left she spoke also to Mr. Joicey, whom she had known in life. Minnie gave a tender farewell, and replaced the trumpet.

"Then a forceful spirit came through and poised in front of Jack Barnes. 'Grandfather,' it said. 'Yes, your mother's here, but I want to speak to you first.' Mr. Barnes said the voice was quite typical of the vigorous personality of his grandfather. 'He died in 1905,' he added. Quickly the trumpet was lifted again. 'I'm not dead!' said the voice.

"Then Mrs. Barnes came through and spoke to her son, saying how happy she was, and that she did not want to come back. Saying 'Goodnight' the sound of a kiss came through the trumpet.

"Mr. Prins was addressed again; he distinguished the word 'Oscar'—his brother. 'How is your ear?' said Oscar. 'Do not worry about it, it will be all right.' This was evidential, for Mr. Prins afterwards stated that he had recently had an operation on his ear.

"Finally Lord Northcliffe spoke in his independent voice to Mr. Swaffer, and said he would talk again about a matter in connection with the *New York Times.*

"William Archer, talking independently, and high up in the room, said that this was a great work we were doing here.

"The spirit of my mother's Aunt Carrie also spoke without using the trumpet, and announced herself clearly. She spoke for a while to my mother and to me.

"Dr. Barnett exclaimed that he was ready to answer any questions; but the habitual sitters had apparently exhausted most of their stock, and the new sitters seemed too overcome at the time to think of anything to ask. They thought of them as soon as the séance was over. So Dr. Barnett closed the sitting. It had only lasted an hour and a half, but each new sitter had been given undeniable evidence and proof of survival."

II

This was, apparently, a successful and evidential séance.

Sixteen distinct and characteristic personal spirits spoke to the sitters, including four of the guides.

All the new sitters told me personally that they thought the evening was wonderful.

We discussed what had taken place for some little time afterwards, and it is amusing to relate that, although it was a cold night, Mrs. Joicey, who was motoring back to London in a closed car, went off forgetting her hat and coat.

The next day Mrs. Joicey wrote me a charming letter, in which she said "I was so enthralled. My husband and I are grateful to you—we are both so happy about it, and are both quite convinced—after last night I have no doubts whatsoever."

32

*Miss Radcliffe Hall attends a daylight sitting with Valiantine—
Una, Lady Troubridge, joins the circle—"This has established
Valiantine in an exceptional way."*

Monday, March 23, 1925.

AFTER the S.P.R. sitting at Dorincourt which took place on Friday last, we had discussed the extraordinary phenomena which had transpired on two or three occasions when first Pat and then Anthony and my wife had obtained the voices in the daylight with Valiantine.

Una, Lady Troubridge, and Miss Radcliffe Hall were enormously interested in this, and it was arranged that they should come down on the following Monday, during the afternoon for an experiment.

Miss Radcliffe Hall sat alone with Valiantine for the first experiment.

The curtains were partly drawn to obscure the full strength of daylight.

Miss Radcliffe Hall could clearly observe Valiantine's face and lips, which never moved.

After a time, a few rappings were heard inside the trumpet, and then Miss Radcliffe Hall heard her father's voice speaking, and giving the name of her mother, who, he said, was with her in the house. He also gave a short sentence which Miss Radcliffe Hall could not quite decipher.

Lady Troubridge then joined them both and more rappings were heard. Just at this moment the telephone rang and interrupted the sitting.

After this, Lady Troubridge sat alone with Valiantine, when rappings were heard again from the inside of the trumpet, and also on the bookcase.

Then a voice was heard saying: "Arthur Herbert." A little later a voice announced itself as "Lowther," saying: "I wish Toupie was here." Lady Troubridge said: "She is away." Then the voice of Mrs. Lowther volunteered: "I was often with you in Stirling Street."

Lady Troubridge was extremely impressed by this unique experience. She stated that she had watched Valiantine's mouth, and noticed that it was closed, the lips not moving. She said, "I consider that this has established Valiantine in an exceptional way."

Afterwards Valiantine told her that he had no objection to sitting in the S.P.R. séance room, but Lady Troubridge said that, if she were he, she would not sit there again on any account, as the guides seemed to object to it, and she thought they could get finer results outside.

33

A medical séance—Dr. Barnett's prescriptions for tuberculosis, cancer, syphilis—Dr. Barnett is questioned by doctors as to his formulae—The author discourses on the pros and cons of these suggested treatments.

I

Tuesday, March 24, 1925.

THE records of the supernormal events contained in this book are set down in the precise order and date upon which they occurred. The sequence of these medical sittings which extended from March 24 to April 17, is, however, maintained in the following chapter. Meanwhile, other sittings were interspersed, and the chapter to follow this will continue the personal record from March 25.

Those who have read *Towards the Stars* will recall that Dr. Barnett said (Chapters XVIII and XIX of that book) that he would give through to us at a later date the treatments for certain human ailments.

He had told us that we must be careful in our selection of the qualified medical men who should be present to take down the formulae.

We had discussed this matter with Dr. Barnett on several occasions, and had made arrangements to hold the first sitting for this purpose on the above date.

The two doctors who were invited to be present were Dr. Abraham Wallace of 1 Park Crescent, Portland Place, and Dr. T. Moore O'Donnell, of Oxted.

There were present Valiantine, my wife, Mr. Swaffer, Dr. Abraham Wallace, Dr. Moore O'Donnell, and myself.

We all sat with writing pads on our knees to record what was said, and, in addition, Anthony was seated outside the door at a table on which was a red lamp, in order that he might also record and check all statements.

Only one gramophone record had been played, when the voice of Dr. Barnett greeted us with "Good evening, souls."

Dr. Abraham Wallace has had considerable experience of psychical phenomena. He was for some time on the Council of the S.P.R., but resigned.

Dr. O'Donnell has studied psychics for over thirty years, but had never before sat at a direct voice séance.

I introduced the two doctors to Dr. Barnett.

II

Tuberculosis

DR. BARNETT (to the two doctors): Are you both qualified to receive this great Truth for the sake of humanity?

An answer being given in the affirmative, Dr. Barnett proceeded.

DR. BARNETT: We have been rather disappointed with some of the Earth souls. I will now give you a treatment for tuberculosis.

After the two formulae, I desire to state the proportions, what to use, and what not to use.

The first is Squill, to strengthen the bronchial tubes and stimulate the bronchial mucous membrane.

Next, for the lungs.

Datura Stramonium in smoke form should be given to the patient. Enclose the patient in a room where he can inhale the smoke.

If the patient is not very badly afflicted, the first application should be used.

You must give the patient one cup of very strong Malva Tea to flush the bowels. When the bowels are flushed, give one cup of Blood Root Tea. Blood Root Tea stimulates the arteries and so helps to circulate the blood through the system.

Then you must give a bath with medicated Guava Leaves, and add to the bath one half-pint of Flowers of Sulphur. Put your patient in the bath as hot as he can stand it, by letting the hot water flow in gradually. Do not keep the patient in too long. Five minutes will be enough.

Then, the patient should be given plenty of fresh air and sunlight. If you can get artificial sunlight it would be better.

Now I must rest a little.

Doctor Barnett's voice was very loud and distinct and it is, of course, difficult for a spirit to materialize the voice and continue talking for some length of time without a pause. A record was played on the gramophone and then Dr. Barnett resumed.

Dr. BARNETT: You must try and eliminate fatty foods or rather fatty meats. Give the patient broth of beef or chicken.

The patient must not smoke; smoking will injure. And no alcohol of any sort—only when the patient rallies may he take a little.

Physical exercise is quite important, but do not overdo it.

Watch your patient very carefully while you are giving him the treatment. I mention this because it is very important that the patient should be under observation. A nurse should guard over the patient, as often he will try to get tobacco, drugs, or liquor, which would affect him. It would be beneficial for the patient to practice deep breathing.

(*A slight pause.*)

Take this down very carefully. This is where we introduce Antimony as part of the treatment.

An injection of Antimony is to be given once daily.

(A pause.)

Massage the chest and back daily with the following application: One drachm of turpentine, one drachm of alcohol, one ounce of olive oil, and one drachm of liquid camphor.

That is the treatment.

Dr. Barnett then went on to say that he could not continue to speak any longer on this evening, but that he would continue the instructions at the next sitting.

He asked whether we would like one or two of the other guides to speak with us, and, of course, we acquiesced.

Bert Everett came through and spoke with us for some little time in his shrill tones.

Kokum, in his wonderful powerful tones, spoke with us and told us how pleased Pat (my son) had been to talk with him at the séance on the previous Saturday.

Pat O'Brien spoke for quite a time, staying longer than he usually does. He talked with Dr. Wallace, and for some little while with his compatriot, Dr. O'Donnell.

Whilst Kokum was there he lifted one of the luminous trumpets, and it flew round the room, going up to the ceiling and rapping it.

Feda chatted with several of us. The sitting then closed.

III

Saturday, March 28, 1925.

This sitting was held specially for the purpose of taking down the formulae for the treatment of diseases. It had been arranged that Dr. T. Moore O'Donnell should attend to take down the formulae, and that he should consult Dr. Abraham Wallace afterwards.

There were present Valiantine, my wife, Miss Madeleine Cohen, Mr. Hannen Swaffer, Dr. T. Moore O'Donnell, and myself.

As before, Anthony was seated at a table outside the room taking down verbatim notes of the proceedings by the light of a red lamp.

After a few minutes the voice of Dr. Barnett came through and when greeting us said: "I want to say a few words to the doctor. With regard to the tuberculosis treatment, which was given earlier in the week, I heard you doctors saying that some of the remedies were old-fashioned. Have you improved on nature's way of producing your Earthly babies? I am giving you nature's remedies—what nature has provided for your physical body."

IV

Cancer

DR. BARNETT: The cancer treatment is very simple and easy. That which I am giving you now is a preparation that has never been investigated by human doctors; it is Syrup of Wild Cactus Fruit, which is called "Prickly Pear." Of course, you have heard of Wild Cherry. These two should be mixed together in a syrup form and three ounces given daily to the patient who is afflicted with cancer.

For the other medicine a teaspoonful of sugar—that is, cane or beet sugar—with four drops of Spirits of Turpentine. Take morning, and evening, on retiring.

The next is Enaculate of Phosphate, Strychnine and Calcium Phosphates, and Hypophosphate of Iron.

I desire to state that Antimony and Chaulmoogra Oil must he injected.

(A pause)

The patient must be treated with Red Rays. The bowels of the patient must be thoroughly kept open. Your patient must have an Epsom salt bath; one half-pound of Epsom salts in the bath. The patient must lie there for ten to twelve minutes. The body should not be rinsed off or dried thoroughly. The room must be of a fairly good temperature.

You should understand that the Syrup of Cactus will eliminate the cancer in people who have a slight attack. Syrup of Cactus is a blood purifier that will check the disease.

If you have cases such as sores—cancerous sores you must use Potassium Bromide and Sulphate of Zinc, and Petroleum. Mix these ingredients together with Flowers of Sulphur and Pulverized Alum, and apply it to the afflicted part with a very hot iron (place some cotton wool over the top before putting the iron on). This should be done twice daily, and if it is possible, manipulate (massage) the spinal column from the cerebellum to the lower extremities with the friction of the hands.

Now I shall give you the diet. Meat of any kind should be eliminated. Vegetables, eggs and milk are very good. The milk should be boiled and cooled before giving to the patient, and the drinking water also. Give plenty of water to the patient.

(In answer to a question put to him.)

In the case of advanced cancer, such as cancer on the breast, the remedy should be applied locally, between medicated cotton, by means of a hot iron.

During the time that Dr. Barnett was prescribing the treatment for cancer, on several occasions he replied to odd questions put to him by my son from outside the door.

After Dr. Barnett had gone, Bert Everett spoke to us for some little time; Kokum also. At the request of Mr. Swaffer he took up both the trumpets and whirled them round the room. Mr. Swaffer had asked Kokum to do this for the observation of Dr. O'Donnell who was very much impressed by this physical manifestation.

Pat O'Brien came through and spoke to us, carrying on a short conversation with Dr. O'Donnell.

Annie spoke in her independent voice to me and to my wife, saying that she would like to hold a private sitting as there were certain things she wished to discuss with me.

On retiring to rest on the evening previous to this sitting, the pillow on my bed was moved and placed in a more comfortable position for my head by unseen hands. Prior to this I had had one or two similar experiences, but not nearly so impressive as this. On this occasion I lifted my head quite clear of the pillow and half raised myself from the bed—my head being several inches clear of the pillow. My pillow was then lifted and placed about my head.

When my sister was talking to me on this evening I asked her whether she was with me the night before when I had gone to rest, and she told me that she had been with me, and that she had made my pillow more comfortable for me.

Warren spoke for a little while.

V

Monday, March 30, 1925.
This sitting was held at eight-thirty p.m., for the purpose of receiving the formulae for the treatment of diseases given by Dr. Barnett.

There were present Valiantine, my wife, Dr. O'Donnell, Miss Madeleine Cohen, Mr. Swaffer, and myself. Anthony sat, as before, at a table on which was placed a red lamp, taking down a verbatim account of the proceedings.

After one record was played on the gramophone, Dr. Barnett came through and gave us his usual greeting.

Syphilis

DR. BARNETT: You understand that this remedy is for syphilitic purposes. Now, doctor, I prescribe the Squill tea for the patient to vomit. Next you should use the bark of the Areca Root. That is the tonic after you have brought the patient to a vomiting point.

The next treatment you should give the patient is one grain of Mercury. Then another is Anchita—that is the purgative, also for the skin disease. The next is Glycerophosphate-Strychnine and Lime.

The next remedy to take inwardly is Magnesium Charcoal and Sulphur. Pulverize them very fine, and give a teaspoonful three times a day, in between your other remedies.

The next. You should give a treatment with oil, Sulphur and Petroleum. Mix these together and rub over the body. If there are running sores on the body, use Sulphur and Borax powdered. Use a little Sulphurated Zinc and apply dryly on the sores. The patient must be bathed also.

Now in each and every one of these treatments the patient must have a vomiting spell, and you must use a purgative to move the bowels freely; you must use these remedies according to my directions.

These remedies are very simple, the treatment lies in applying the different formulae in the order prescribed.

The doctors from this side of life shall guide and help you through with your work. I am very glad that I have been able to give you these formulae so easily and so readily, and I shall speak to you later.

After Dr. Barnett had gone there came through the spirit guide, Bert Everett, who conversed with us for some considerable time. His voice was very powerful on this occasion, and he was extremely humorous. He referred to having seen Valiantine at the first night of "Tarnish" at the Vaudeville Theatre. Bert Everett and Valiantine carried on a conversation together regarding happenings of the previous evening.

Kokum also came through, and spoke to two or three of us.

Of the personal spirits, the luminous trumpet was lifted, and Miss Cohen was addressed by her mother, and they talked with each other for a short time.

The luminous trumpet was again lifted, and a spirit voice talked with Dr. O'Donnell. Dr. O'Donnell told us that it was the spirit of his sister Mary.

A spirit voice using the luminous trumpet, speaking from high up in the room, announced that it was "George Kates," saying that he was the secretary of the N.S.A.—presumably the American Spiritualist Society. This spirit had a very loud voice, and he also announced that George Warne—the president was with him. George Kates, in speaking to Mr. Swaffer and to me, said that we were doing splendid work in this country.

Warren spoke to my wife, to Mr. Swaffer, and to me.

At the close Dr. Barnett said that he would be prepared to answer any questions which might be put to him by the doctors at the next sitting, after they had considered the formulae which had been given through.

VI

Monday, April 6, 1925.

This evening was devoted to the medical communications. Dr. Abraham Wallace and Dr. T. Moore O'Donnell had studied the formula given through for tuberculosis, cancer, and syphilis, and had formed the questions they wished to put to Dr. Barnett on the various points.

There were present Valiantine, my wife, Dr. T. Moore O'Donnell, Miss Madeleine Cohen, Mr. Swaffer, and myself. It should be noted that the circle has not varied during the last two sittings for these medical communications. Anthony, as usual, was outside the door taking notes.

One gramophone record was played, and from the time of his greeting Dr. Barnett's conversation went on without cessation for an hour and a half. He spoke at considerable length on the various points, but only the chief points which maybe of value are recorded. It must be understood that the questions of Dr. Wallace and Dr. O'Donnell were called out by my son sitting outside the room, and he recorded the replies as they were spoken directly from the loud and impressively distinct voice of the spirit of Dr. Barnett. The questions were tabulated beforehand, as this was the clearest way of putting them.

Tuberculosis

DR. O'DONNELL: Why eliminate fat and meat from the diet?

DR. BARNETT: When I say fat I mean fatty meats, not milk, butter, olive oil, etc. Your milk and water should be boiled and cooled before giving to the patient.

DR. O'DONNELL: What effect has Antimony on T.B. bacilli, and how does it limit their lethal effects—if any—to diseased tissues only?

DR. BARNETT: It is according to the way you give it. The disease in the lung tissue causes the patient great distress by becoming clogged. The Antimony will clarify —the tissues and build up the cells. After the antimony you must give the tea I prescribed; that will eliminate any disturbance of the healthy parts of the lungs.

DR. O'DONNELL: how much Antimony and Chaulmoogra Oil to be injected?

DR. BARNETT: Half a grain of Antimony and one drachm of Chaulmoogra Oil once daily.

Cancer

DR. WALLACE: Is the prickly pear wild cactus the Opuntia vulgaris, or what genus of cactus?

DR. BARNETT: It is a spine cactus; the pears have very small spines, and they have a purple flower. You can get them in France, in Italy, and America.

DR. WALLACE: Is the wild cherry the Primus serotina?

DR. BARNETT: The ordinary wild cherry.

DR. WALLACE: Spirits of turpentine. For what symptoms and at what stage of disease?

DR. BARNETT: Turpentine is for the cleansing of the blood, and to eliminate the secretions that the irritations are caused from. It can be used at any stage.

DR. WALLACE: What does the term "enaculate" mean?

DR. BARNETT: It means phosphate of iron and strychnine.

DR. WALLACE: At what stage should the red rays be used?

DR. BARNETT: At the very first. Electric red rays. The red rays are something entirely different to the violet rays. They should be used once daily, and, if possible, should be used in the presence of sunlight or artificial sunlight. Exposure from ten to fifteen minutes.

DR. WALLACE: Why Epsom salts baths?

DR. BARNETT: The Epsom salts bath is to clarify the pores of the skin, and to penetrate the delicate tissues; and also to remove from the body aches or pains.

DR. WALLACE: What is meant by a slight attack?

DR. BARNETT: Slight attack is the first stages.

DR. WALLACE: Can you tell if cancer be of bacterial nature, or is it primarily a change in the nuclei, and a change in the cell contents; or is it a perverted physiological process or diminished vitality in the nerve elements—especially the sympathetic nervous system or is there a combination of causes?

DR. BARNETT: It is a complication of affections of the secretions of the blood caused by certain foods and infections, through inoculation.

DR. WALLACE: What are the predisposing and exciting causes of cancer in its various situations?

DR. BARNETT: It is caused by skin eruptions; the slightest skin affliction may exist, and then take a cancerous turn. Some people are predisposed to cancer, and an irritation that may heal up in some maybe cancerous in others. It is not hereditary.

DR. O'DONNELL: How does your cancer treatment compare with the radium treatment?

DR. BARNETT: There is no comparison. Your radium can heal, but it does not eradicate the disease from the system. The disease must be brought through channels by the purification of the blood.

DR. O'DONNELL: How will your treatment reach, say the liver? Will Chaulmoogra and Antimony be sufficient?

DR. BARNETT: The application of the treatment with Antimony and Chaulmoogra Oil will be sufficient, and will reach the liver.

Syphilis

DR. O'DONNELL: In what way is your treatment an improvement on Jonathan Hutchinson's of forty or fifty years ago?

DR. BARNETT: There is no comparison. I am only giving a mild dose of mercury daily. It is the collective treatment that will have the effect, and not the mercury alone.

DR. O'DONNELL: How is the spirochaete destroyed, especially in the cerebro-spinal fluid?

DR. BARNETT: I desire to state that it can be treated by softening the bones by phosphates. I desire to give the doctor here the penetration by Antimony on the spinal column once daily, and by the phosphate of lime and strychnine you shall be able to penetrate the marrow of the bone.

DR. O'DONNELL: Is the Antimony the chief factor in the treatment?

DR. BARNETT: The Antimony is not playing a very large part—the other remedies which follow have the great effect. The secret is the combination. We have greater doctors here than on your physical plane. For thousands of years we have been trying to help humanity, but have been disregarded.

HDB: You are acquainted, of course, Dr. Barnett, with the treatment of syphilis by 606, which is a discovery of the last fifteen years. Can you tell us the ultimate effect of this treatment?

DR. BARNETT: We have great doctors on this side. We desire to state that these milder treatments are more efficient than the modern methods you are using now. Although you have been able to help your patients to a certain extent, you have not been able to eradicate the disease.

With regard to 606, you have been able to help your patient, but you have not been able to eradicate the disease from the blood. There is a possibility of a recurrence after 606, and it might be serious for the patient.

DR. WALLACE: Can you say anything of the electronic reactions of Abrams? Can you get into connection with him?

DR. BARNETT: Yes, we have discussed that on this side of life, and it is very efficient. Yes, we have met Abrams, and we have discussed the matter.

I can express no opinion as to whether the formula which have been given will prove of value or not. The attempt is worth making. In any case there is established beyond doubt the amazing phenomenon of a spirit voice, speaking in loud tones, giving through methods of treatment, many of which are beyond any preconceived thought in the minds of those who are listening. The telepathic theory cannot apply to this phenomenon. It is a discarnate intelligence, volunteering information in its own voice. It should be noted also that the replies which came through in the tones of Dr. Barnett were given in an intelligent, determined and authoritative manner. His voice was wonderful throughout. There was no pause, neither was there the slightest hesitation. To me, and also to Dr. O'Donnell, the fluency of this sitting was extraordinarily impressive.

VII

8.30 p.m. Friday, April 17, 1925.
This evening was arranged for the last sitting with the doctors on the formulae which had been given by Dr. Barnett. There were present Valiantine, my wife, Dr. T. Moore O'Donnell and his wife, and Dr. Abraham Wallace.

On this occasion, Anthony had gone up to Cambridge. I therefore took his place and sat outside the room with a table in front of me—on which was placed an electric lamp and a writing pad in order that I might record what transpired.

Within about one minute I heard Dr. Barnett speaking, and the following are my abbreviated notes of the conversations which ensued.

DR. BARNETT: Good evening, souls. I am very glad to see you here tonight.

DR. WALLACE: I am sorry I could not come before, but I have read and enjoyed your statements. May I ask you some questions?

DR. BARNETT: I shall be very pleased to answer you.

DR. WALLACE: I am interested in the causation of cancer. Can you tell me the predisposing causes, and are they modified by meat eating?

DR. BARNETT: Yes, but they are sometimes caused by vegetables also, owing to the Earth-decaying substances.

DR. WALLACE: You mean the causes are absorbed?

Dr.. BARNETT: Yes, by the infusion of the Earth to the vegetables.

DR. O'DONNELL: You mean by the decaying substances entering into the vegetable matter?

DR. BARNETT: Yes. Both mix with the gastric juices and are absorbed together. You know animals get cancer as well.

DR. WALLACE: Will you state the pathology? Is it more or less a blood disease? And will you tell us also what is the determining cause of locality?

DR. BARNETT: As you know, sometimes it is upon the heart, sometimes on the liver, and sometimes upon the breast.

DR. WALLACE: What causes it to locate upon the liver?

DR. BARNETT: It is caused through the transfusion of the blood through various organic localities.

HDB (interposing from outside the room): You mean by that, Dr. Barnett, that it is therefore likely to attack the weakest organs?

DR. BARNETT: Yes, it will attack the most sensitive part of the organization.

DR. WALLACE: Suppose there are local indications of an attack upon the female breast? How should one treat this? If the woman's breast is swelling and one is not certain, but may assume that it is cancerous, how should this be treated?

DR. BARNETT: I have given you this. The treatment should be made through the iron with local applications in order to scatter the blood.

DR. WALLACE: When should one apply the treatment of the red rays?

DR. BARNETT: The red rays should be used from the first stage until the last. You must follow the directions which I have given.

DR. WALLACE: Suppose the disease is in an ulcerated stage. Should the iron then be used?

DR. BARNETT: Yes. It will enrich the surrounding tissues, and protect the other parts of the body.

After these few questions had been answered Dr. Barnett said that the treatments which had been given through for the various diseases were evolved from the combined intelligences of the doctors on their side. He said with him on this night there were Dr. Gustave Geley and Dr. Peebles, who had passed over in California. At this remark Dr. Wallace asked Dr. Barnett to convey to Dr. Peebles his regards.

Reverting back to the various treatments, Dr. Wallace asked Dr. Barnett a question regarding the use of Antimony, and said: "Is it injected into the blood vessels?' Dr. Barnett replied: "Yes, the disease must be treated as a blood disease, and you must get to the seat of it."

After a few further questions had been dealt with Dr. Barnett called out to me in a loud tone: "Mr. Bradley, you can now come into the room." I therefore put my notes to one side and joined the circle.

The sitting then continued. The circle was a really good one, and the power was particularly strong.

Kokum and Bert Everett came through and talked with us at some length, and Pat O'Brien also spoke for a while to most of the sitters, and, in addressing me, was quite jocular, saying: "Mr. Bradley, you said you would only write one book on psychics, but now you have nearly completed another, and you will find it very difficult to escape this subject once you are drawn into it. You will write more books than these two."[142]

Bert Everett was humorous and fluent in his talk, and the voice of Kokum rang through the room.

Bobby Worrall spoke of Pat, saying he saw Pat playing with the tadpoles, and riding a bicycle, and so on, describing Pat's actions during the day.

Of the personal spirits there came through to Dr. O'Donnell the spirit of his sister Mary, who spoke with him for a little time through the luminous trumpet, and then, flashing across the room, spoke to Mrs. O'Donnell.

To Mrs. O'Donnell there also came a spirit giving the name of "Ray," and speaking with her for quite a while.

To Dr. Wallace there came the spirit of his mother, who spoke with him and, a little later, the spirit of Dr. Peebles—using the luminous trumpet—spoke in clear and distinct tones to Dr. Wallace. He (Dr. Peebles) said, during the conversation, "You remember there was a banquet held in my honour, when the empty chair was left for me. I was present at the banquet, and I appreciated it very much, and I enjoyed the gathering."

This remark was certainly of evidential value because none of us, with the exception of Dr. Wallace, knew of this incident. A banquet had

---

[142] I sincerely trust not. The subject is so inexhaustible that it exhausts the writer. I desire to refresh myself with satiric fantasy, as a dissipation from this cosmic reality.

THE WISDOM OF THE GODS

been arranged to be held in the honour of Dr. Peebles on his hundredth birthday in—I believe—California. Dr. Peebles passed over just prior to the banquet, but the banquet was held just the same, and an empty chair was placed there in appreciation of him. This Dr. Abraham Wallace told us afterwards.

Annie spoke to me and said that she would like a private sitting held so that she might talk to my wife and to me about Gertrude.

The sitting then closed.

It will be seen that five evenings were specially devoted to the taking down of the suggested treatments for diseases from Dr. Barnett. These treatments were all given in the presence of doctors, and I publish the communications as they were received without offering any opinion whatever as to their value. It is necessary, however, to record the phenomenon of a spirit voice speaking from space for such a considerable length of time, and conversing at least intelligently upon medical matters for hour after hour during five long sittings.

That the methods prescribed will be adequately tested is problematic.

The medical profession is, of course, the most conservative trade union in the world. It is unlikely to accept psychical supersight, and may discard and even endeavour to ridicule the formulae given. That is no concern of mine. But first it must prove its knowledge and submit its proven and efficacious remedies of these scourges before its criticism will bear weight.

If the medical profession possesses the knowledge by which cancer can be cured, then a suffering world will acclaim it. If it does not, then it has no ground for condemning any suggested treatment, from whatever quarter it may come, until that treatment has been scrupulously tried, and proved to be valueless.

If certain parts of the treatment may appear to be given in a simple and unveiled expression, that is no reason for off-hand condemnation of the whole, if the complete combination, in the particular and specific order given, has never been tried. If only one clue is provided in the formulae which leads to one subsequent discovery, that alone would be invaluable.

There is, however, another point of view which I am bound to state as a very experienced psychical researcher. I do not for one moment accept every communication which comes through as inspired by omnipotent wisdom, for I am quite aware that the spirit of man, when he passes over, does not become infallible.

Dr. Barnett lived on Earth some sixty or seventy years ago.

The spirits tell us that their time is occupied in acquiring knowledge of the vast spiritual spheres of the Universe.

We have therefore to consider whether Dr. Barnett has progressed in medical intelligence on questions appertaining to the Earth.

As a counter argument, however, since I have for two years received direct communications in his own voice from Dr. Barnett, I am capable of judging whether he is an intelligent spirit on the majority of other matters discussed by him. This he has most certainly proved himself to be, and he has confounded in discussion many men of considerable intellect. But even this fact does not conclusively prove his medical intelligence.

I state these points in order to show that I wish to be perfectly fair in my analysis of these experiences.

Considering the remarkable communications, and the astounding evidence of survival of intelligence which have been established, I should in no circumstance feel justified in omitting to publish Dr. Barnett's opinions and his methods of treatment of diseases. Until they are tried it is impossible to say whether they are likely to prove efficacious or not. And surely this is only the method of the faculty.

Whether the treatments given prove efficacious or not does not affect the wonderful phenomenon of the resonant, distinct and fluent voice of Dr. Barnett, speaking from space, in tones which rang through the room. His voice was clearly heard from outside the closed door, where these records were taken down as he spoke. He was also heard from time to time by various servants at Dorincourt, who happened to pass by the room at the time.

All those present, including Dr. O'Donnell and Dr. Abraham Wallace, can vouch for the supernormal facts as they are stated. Both doctors were there to observe and to act as witnesses, and as impartial recorders of what took place. Their opinions upon the communications must, of course, be reserved. Dr. O'Donnell, however, has stated that he considered the phenomenon of the voice, the actual materialized voice of an unquestionably intelligent spirit, was the most marvelous experience of his life.

34

An amazing development of incalculable value—Mr. Swaffer's account of a daylight sitting—No trickery possible—"We have removed the fear of death."

3.30 pm Wednesday, March 25, 1925.

On this day Mr. Hannen Swaffer traveled down to Dorincourt in the early afternoon. As an investigator he was intensely interested in the new phenomenon of obtaining the spirit voices in the daylight. This is an amazing development of incalculable value. I append Mr. Hannen Swaffer's report.

"Last week, most convincing proof of all, I heard voices in the daylight.

"Valiantine sat facing me, so that I could see him perfectly in the bright light of day, holding a trumpet (or amplifier) eighteen inches from his face, but covering the broad end with his hand, so that enough darkness was made inside. Then, one after the other, I heard the voices of Lord Northcliffe, Warren Clarke, and Dr. Geley, the distinguished French scientist who was killed in an aeroplane disaster last August.

"The voices were faint; but I heard their messages. It was proof positive, for the bitterest skeptic, that there could happen in light what happens much more easily in the dark.

"No ventriloquism could place a voice right inside the trumpet. Besides, the medium did not move. No trickery was possible.

"In every way, now, during these frequent sittings, we have made every test; Valiantine's mediumship has survived them all. Una, Lady Troubridge, and Miss Radcliffe Hall, two expert members of the Society for Psychical Research, heard these voices, in just the same way, last Monday. Mrs. Bradley and her elder son have heard them also.

Her younger son, Pat, aged eight, hears them, almost every day, in like circumstances. He talks to his aunt and uncle as a matter of course.

"When we have removed the fear of death, we shall have taken from humanity its greatest dread. Yes, We shall have reshaped all the philosophies and made life explainable."

35

A spirit hand touches Mr. Beverley Nichols—Lord Chancellor Westbury gives advice to one of his descendants—Pat Raymond Lodge thanks Mrs. Bradley for her courtesy to his father—A spirit treats a fractured wrist—The Hon. Mrs. R. Bethell's impressions.

I

Thursday, March 26, 1925.

THIS sitting was held at Dorincourt at eight-twenty p.m. As I was not feeling well I did not attend, but sat in the adjoining room. Here is Anthony's account.

"There were present Viscountess Molesworth, the Hon. Mrs. Richard Bethell, Mr. Beverley Nichols (the author), Mr. E. P. Hewitt, K.C., Mr. Swaffer, Mrs. Bradley, Valiantine, and myself.

"Perhaps the conditions were not quite so good as Bert Everett maintained they were; for it was not until after four records had been played that Dr. Barnett greeted us with his customary 'Good evening, souls!' and Bert Everett spoke his welcome.

"Then Mr. Beverley Nichols felt a touch, and clearly a voice said, 'Beverley, Beverley!' He answered it, and asked who it was. But there was no further sound. A spirit hand again touched his; and he complained of feeling very cold and somewhat faint. The sitters urged him to wait, and not to break the circle. But, half fainting, he got up and asked to be taken out. 'Give me some light,' he said. He stumbled out, and sat for some time on the stairs; after some brandy he recovered his nerves, but he did not re-enter that sitting.

"The spirits were remarkably quick in coming through again after the break. The trumpet was picked up, and a hoarse voice spoke to Mrs. Bethell. 'Grandfather Westbury' was made out with some difficulty. 'Are you the Lord Chancellor? ' asked Mrs. Bethell. 'Yes.' Westbury, the Lord Chancellor, was Mrs. Bethell's husband's great-grandfather. He said that he was interested in Mrs. Bethell's son. 'Should he go to the Bar?' asked Mrs. Bethell. 'Yes, dear, if he wants to.'

"Mrs. Bethell's grandmother also came through and sent her love to Mrs. Bethell's mother.

"The luminous trumpet was then taken to Lady Molesworth. 'Charlie Molesworth,' the spirit announced itself. 'Oh, yes,' said Lady Molesworth, to her son. 'Ronnie is here,' volunteered the voice, 'and Raymond as well.'

"When the trumpet had been placed in the centre, it was picked up by a firm, powerful spirit. 'Pat Raymond Lodge,' came through clearly. Hannen Swaffer, for evidential reasons, asked who was Ronnie? 'Ronnie Morgan,' said Raymond distinctly. 'You are doing a great work,' he said to Mr. Swaffer. 'You and Bradley. I heard you discussing the attitude of my father. I'm sorry.' Raymond put down the trumpet, and Mr. Swaffer explained to the other sitters that there had been a controversy between Sir Oliver Lodge and my father on the question of "control."[143] For the second time Raymond came through and the trumpet was raised. Raymond again repeated the view that he had just previously expressed, and added: 'I disliked the suggestion very much. It's not like him.'

"Then Raymond's voice addressed Mrs. Bradley.

'Thank you for your courtesy to my father,' and then with Mr. Swaffer he continued to discuss this incident.

"After this interesting interlude, the luminous trumpet was lifted and the spirit of Mr. Hewitt's father spoke to his son. A little later the spirit of Mr. Hewitt's mother spoke.

"The questions answered by Dr. Barnett were illuminating. He discussed for a moment the cure for tuberculosis that he had given through. He said that the cure was not his own individual remedy, but one of combined knowledge and was given to alleviate the suffering

---

[143] See Chapter 12. Book Two.

of humanity on Earth. Mrs. Bethell asked him a question about Tut-ank-Amen's tomb; but Dr. Barnett replied that he was not interested in such matters. In answer to another question, Dr. Barnett said that all inspiration comes from the spirit world. The spirits tried to impress people on Earth, but they were left with free will as to whether to act according to those impressions. In answer to two questions, Dr. Barnett said that his Christian name was Franklin, and that he was on the fifth sphere.

"Mrs. Bradley thanked Dr. Barnett for some advice he had given that morning through Valiantine.

"My mother had that morning slipped on the parquet floor of her bedroom and fractured her wrist. (The fracture was discovered later by an X-ray photograph.) She was in considerable pain and it was impossible to obtain a doctor, as they were all out on their rounds. She motored to Putney but was not successful in obtaining a doctor, and eventually a chemist bound up the wrist. She was still in great pain, and when she returned Valiantine held a special sitting, when Dr. Barnett came through and told him to get some boiling vinegar and to bathe it in the vinegar and bind up the wrist until the doctor came along. This was done, and the pain was relieved and the swelling diminished almost immediately.

"Dr. Barnett went on to say that he would supply Hannen Swaffer with good material for his articles, and thanked him for the work he was doing. He said that Mr. Swaffer had developed enough power from his frequent sittings to start a séance himself.

"Dr. Barnett told Mrs. Bradley that he would try and come through and talk to her, and also to Mr. Bradley, after Valiantine had gone. He also said that during the daylight sittings it would be better to cover the trumpet with some dark material. As long as there was some dark place—such as the covered mouth of the trumpet—for them to talk into they could communicate in the light."

As will be seen from my son's notes, after a little time Mr. Beverley Nichols was brought out of the room. I looked after him and gave him brandy and applied hot towels to his head, and he remained with me until the end of the sitting.

When Mr. Nichols had recovered we both went to the door of the study and listened to the voice of Dr. Barnett discussing various subjects. From outside the door I called out to Dr. Barnett and asked him whether we could continue the sittings to obtain certain treatments on the following Saturday with only one doctor present, and he replied loudly—from inside the room: "That will be all right, Mr. Bradley."

The Hon. Mrs. R. Bethell wrote to me afterwards saying: "I wish I could tell you half of what the joy is that you have given me by your great kindness."

In an interview which appeared a few days later in one of the London newspapers, Mrs. Bethell said:

"I regard spirit communication as something very sacred and not as a Society stunt. Probably something terrible would happen if it were taken up in that way, and I totally disagree with people who want to regard it in the light of social amusement."

36

A sitting of many artists—Mr. Oliver Baldwin is spoken to by dead relative—Miss Margaret Bannerman's ring is recognized by a spirit—The author smashes a gramophone record—Mr. Oliver Baldwin's account of the sitting.

I

Sunday, March 29, 1925.

The circle on this evening was extremely interesting. It was composed almost entirely of artists. We all knew each other well, and the atmosphere was consequently responsive and harmonious.

There were present Valiantine, Mrs. Bradley, Anthony Bradley, Mr. Swaffer, Miss Margaret Bannerman, the well-known actress, Mr. Donald Calthrop, M. Vladimir Cernikoff, the Russian pianist, Mr. Oliver Baldwin, son of the Prime Minister, and myself.

My guests arrived quite early in the evening, and the dinner party was a jolly one. Cernikoff played to us both before dinner and afterwards, immediately before we entered the séance room.

At the last moment, a lady who had been invited was unable to attend on account of illness. It will be observed, therefore, that there were only two ladies present and seven men, which in a large circle forms a wrong proportion of the sexes, and is occasionally liable to make manifestations difficult.

Although there was pleasant harmony amongst the circle, I did not feel that the psychic conditions were by any means perfect.

Early in the evening the spirit voice of Dr. Barnett gave us a greeting, and the spirit voice of the guide, Bert Everett, came through and spoke with us for a while.

Pat O'Brien also spoke a few sentences.

Of the personal spirits, the first to manifest was a voice addressing Mr. Oliver Baldwin. The luminous trumpet was lifted, and a voice calling "Oliver" announced itself to be "Uncle Harold." The power did not appear to be very strong, and whilst a conversation was being conducted between them the trumpet was lifted and dropped six times. Certain personal questions were put by Mr. Baldwin to the voice, and were replied to. Afterwards Mr. Baldwin explained that this was not really an uncle, but his father's first cousin, Harold Baldwin, who died about five years ago. "He was so much older than we children were, that we used to call him uncle." In the use of certain words Mr. Baldwin said he recognized the Worcestershire accent.

The trumpet was again lifted, and a voice addressed Miss Bannerman in a very emotional manner. Miss Bannerman cried, "Is it W——?"[144] The voice answered in the affirmative, and continued to address her in a somewhat agitated manner. Miss Bannerman was affected, and during the conversation that ensued, said to the voice: "I have something with me tonight which you gave me. Can you tell me what it is?" The voice immediately replied: "Yes, you are wearing the ring I gave you." Miss Bannerman said that this was quite correct.

A voice addressed M. Cernikoff in French, but was very indistinct, and the identity of the spirit was not established.

I was feeling a little impatient at the paucity of voices and the slight incident of the discordance of a scratched gramophone record having annoyed me, I took the record off, smashed it up and threw it on the floor. This, I am afraid, was not quite the right mental vibration to throw out. Incidentally, it amused me very much when I threw the record on the floor, because Dr. Barnett came through and gave a loud, understanding laugh, but shortly after this he came through again, and said that we should have to close the sitting.

In view of the astounding psychic results that have been obtained recently, I have become hypercritical, and the sitting therefore appeared to me to be relatively poor. It did not, however, strike the three new

---

[144] This character had been killed by an accident on board ship some years back.

sitters in this way, for Miss Margaret Bannerman, Mr. Oliver Baldwin, and M. Cernikoff all regarded the evening as remarkable.

After the séance Cernikoff played to us very brilliantly, and though to me there had been a comparative poverty of psychical phenomena, the entire evening and the company were a delightful relaxation.

II

Mr. Oliver Baldwin afterwards sent me his own account of his experience at this sitting, which I append.

"In all, I think the luminous trumpet through which the voice addressed me raised itself five times. The intervals are marked with an (X).

"VOICE: Oliver.

"O.B.: Yes.

"VOICE: Oliver.

"O.B.: Yes, who is it?

"VOICE: Uncle Harold.

"O.B.: Yes.

"VOICE: I am very glad to see you here.

"O.B.: Yes. (X)

"VOICE: How's your father?

"O.B.: Very well, as far as I know. How are you?

"VOICE: Very well. Can't you hear?

"O.B.: Not very well. Can you speak louder? (X)

"DR. BARNETT: Will the gentleman not touch the trumpet.

"VOICE: Oliver.

"O.B.: Yes.

"VOICE: Can you hear me?

"O.B.: Yes, what is it?

"VOICE: You are doing work. Tell them to stop these terrible wars. (To the other sitters) Stop these terrible wars.

"O.B.: Can I do anything for you?

"VOICE: I am always near you.

"O.B.: Can I do anything about the money?

"MR. BRADLEY (addressing a remark to me): Don't ask a material question.

"O.B.: It isn't material. (X) (To the Voice) Can I do anything for your wife?

"VOICE: Let her have the money. Don't forget.

"O.B.: No.

"VOICE: Don't you forget.

"O.B.: I won't forget.

"MR. BRADLEY: Ask him his wife's name. Speak to him.

"O.B.: Can you tell us the name of your wife?

"MR. BRADLEY: We want it as a test. Dr. Barnett will explain to you. If you don't mind, we should so like to have it.

"O.B.: Will you tell us your wife's name?

"VOICE: I have said it before.

"MR. BRADLEY: I'm sorry we didn't hear.

"VOICE (to O.B.): Why do you ask. You know her name quite well."

I lunched with Mr. Baldwin on the following day, and he said that to him the experience was wonderful, and that he regarded spirit communication as the greatest thing in the world.

37

A sitting at the request of a spirit—Health advice from Dr. Barnett—Kokum plays a joke upon the medium—Irrefutable evidence from a child spirit—The author's Uncle Michael comes through for the first time—Messages from Mars—An experience that would stagger the average psychical researcher.

I

Wednesday, April 1, 1925.

ON Saturday Annie had expressed a desire that we should hold a private sitting.

So in accordance with her request no guests had been invited, my wife and I sitting with George Valiantine.

The conditions were perfect since the three of us are voice mediums, and there were no extraneous vibrations. We did not trouble to play any music; we knew that we should get into touch with the spirit voices without the slightest difficulty.

The lights were turned off, and within thirty seconds Dr. Barnett greeted us. We had a very long discussion with him on all sorts of personal subjects. He discussed at considerable length certain minor points of health with me, and gave me very valuable advice. He also gave advice to my wife, and his statements displayed an intimate knowledge of her. He spoke with Valiantine on certain points regarding his family in America.

Kokum came through on several occasions. He sang Indian songs in a wonderful manner, and lifted one of the luminous trumpets which had been placed in the centre of the room, and upon which he loudly tapped whilst he sang. During the singing of one song he kept time by patting the trumpet on my knee. He touched me several times with his materialized hand on my head and on my shoulder. To Valiantine, who is somewhat bald, he gave two or three resounding pats on the top of his head.

Bert Everett came through several times.

Warren spoke to us in the independent voice on personal matters for a quarter of an hour. He mentioned his children—Phyllis and Betty—and his wife, and expressed the wish for an opportunity to speak to her. I explained to him the difficulties of arranging this, since his wife is nervous of spirit communication. He sent this message to his father:

"Tell him that I am always near him, and that my love remains with him."

The spirit of my sister Annie's son, Georgie, speaking independently, talked with us for a little time, giving irrefutable evidence of surviving personality by mentioning certain incidents which, since their intensely personal character would be likely to affect a living person, it is quite impossible to publish.

Annie, speaking in her independent voice, discussed at length some family matters. Her conversation with me was of an intimate nature.

The luminous trumpet was lifted, and a somewhat powerful voice addressed me. The voice announced itself as "Michael—Uncle Michael." A lengthy conversation followed between us, and Michael also spoke for a while to my wife. It was a pleasure for me to welcome this spirit, for I had a great affection for this Irish uncle of mine, as on Earth he was one of the kindliest old souls I have ever met. He passed over twenty years ago at the age of about seventy.

During my two years' experience I had often wondered why it was that Michael had not come through to me. I asked him the reason for this, and he replied that although he had wished to speak to me he had not managed to materialize his voice before.

BERT EVERETT (after Michael had left): He is a fine spirit, and has a face very much like your father, Mr. Bradley.' There are always so many spirits round you, when you are holding your sittings, who wish to speak to your friends. Michael has stood aside to let others get through.

The luminous trumpet was taken straight in front of Valiantine's face, and the voice addressed him, saying 'This is Cousin Lulu.' Valiantine and this spirit talked together for some time. I emphasize this in order to point out that on many occasions the medium himself converses with the spirits. Lulu then added to Valiantine: "Your Uncle George is here."

Later Uncle George spoke in a strong, independent voice to Valiantine, to me, and to my wife. He told Valiantine not to worry because he did not come through very often to speak to him, the reason being that he was so much occupied with other work in the spheres.

At the close of the sitting Bert Everett talked with us at great length about life in the planet Mars. He told us how much more advanced they were than those on the Earth plane, and he said that in the near future they would be able to communicate with us; that they were endeavouring to do so now. He said that later they would be able to send a message enclosed in a dart, which would be dispatched through the air on the ether waves.

Bert Everett insisted, as Dr. Barnett always insists, on the necessity for us to endeavour to stamp out wars on the Earth plane before we can arrive at any proper spiritual development.

II

This sitting lasted for two and a half hours without a pause.

The conversations were long and absorbing. The voices were strong and powerful and, as I know, were heard by the servants of the house, at various times, when they were passing by outside the room.

It was a wonderful evening—one which would stagger the average psychical researcher.

38

An obstinately skeptical sitter—Dr. Barnett rebukes Mr. Allan Miller—Mrs. Gordon Craig talks with her son who was drowned—Miss Rebecca West spoken to by spirit voices—Lady Malmesbury explains a tragic delay in her journey to her dying mother.

Thursday, April 2 1925.

THERE were present Valiantine, my wife, Mr. Swaffer, Mr. Allan Miller, of New York; Miss Rebecca West, one of the few women writers whose work impresses me; Mrs. Gordon Craig, the wife of the artist son of Ellen Terry; Susan, Countess of Malmesbury, and myself.

Miss Rebecca West and Mrs. Gordon Craig had had no previous experience of direct voice séances, and Mr. Allan Miller had had one previous experience only in New York last year.

A few days prior to this sitting I had received a Marconigram from Mrs. Grace Rodems, saying that Mr. Allan Miller would be in London during the weekend, and asking me to do the best I could to find a place for him at a sitting with Valiantine.

In Chapter 6 of Book One it will be seen that Mr. Miller was one of the sitters at the séance when Mr. De Wyckoff unjustly accused Valiantine of fraud.

After about ten minutes Dr. Barnett gave us his usual greeting. Bert Everett also greeted us, his shrill voice coining from high up, near the ceiling. I asked Bert Everett the usual question as to the conditions that evening, but he made no reply, this being the signal that communication would be difficult. A little later, during the time that an Irish melody was being played upon the gramophone, Pat O'Brien spoke in his Irish brogue.

The luminous trumpet was lifted, and floated in the direction of Mr. Miller, a voice calling "Allan." The voice was not very distinct, but Mr. Miller would not in any way encourage the voice.

The luminous trumpet was again taken close to Mr. Miller's face, and, as far as I could make out, the voice said something about "Judge Morris." At any rate, that is how the name sounded to me. The voice said to Mr. Miller: "You knew my son," and went on to refer to San Bernardino. It gave the full address of a certain place, to all of which Mr. Miller replied only in monosyllables. His attitude appeared to me to be obstinately skeptical—if not actually antagonistic.

During one of the pauses, when the voices were addressing Mr. Miller, Dr. Barnett came through and said: "Mr. Miller, you must encourage your spirit friends if you wish them to speak."

After a voice had volunteered certain names and places, and the trumpet had been dropped, my wife said "Surely, Mr. Miller, you got some evidence there?" I interposed and said: "We do not know whether it was evidence or not." Immediately I made this remark the luminous trumpet was lifted and the same voice came straight over to me and very firmly said: "I gave him evidence."

During the conversation the voice had made reference to Mr. Miller's father. This voice did not, however, make any remark from which we could gather whether Mr. Miller's father was alive or had passed over.

HDB (to Mr. Miller): Is your father alive?

MR. MILLER: I would prefer not to say.

The voice, addressing Mr. Miller, said deliberately, "Your mother is here." This, of course, was a direct statement that she had passed over. None of us knew whether Mr. Miller's parents were alive or dead, so he alone could say whether this was correct or not.

A great deal of the power was used in the attempts made by the spirits to speak to Mr. Miller.

DR. BARNETT (to Mr. Miller): It will be some time before you will be able to understand this great truth.

MR. MILLER: I am anxious to be convinced.

DR. BARNETT: You have not approached this subject in the right spirit. I have heard your conversation with Mr. De Wyckoff, and I have heard you holding this subject up to ridicule.

The luminous trumpet was lifted and came over to Mrs. Gordon Craig. A voice said to her: "It's Peter." The voice spoke with very great emotion. There were tears in it, and during the conversation it broke down and cried. I do not think the voice was crying from pain, but at the joy of speaking with her. The voice was that of Mrs. Craig's son, Peter, who was drowned nearly two years ago while trying to save a girl from the sea at Selsey. Fully dressed, the boy had plunged into the sea, but so weak was he after his long illness from shell shock that he was drowned in his mother's presence.

Mrs. Craig was also crying. After a while the trumpet dropped to the ground.

I then turned the gramophone on again, and whilst Galli-Curci was singing Solveig's song from *Peer Gynt*, the trumpet was again lifted and came to Mrs. Craig.

MRS. CRAIG: Peter, do you know who used to sing that?
PETER: Yes, Katherine.

This, Mrs. Craig told us, was perfectly true, and it maybe regarded as of considerable evidential value.

After the séance Mrs. Craig said: "The voice was intensely characteristic of my son, not so much in what was said, as in the personality, which was unmistakable. The circumstantial points you have heard, and my son's personality and sympathy with me were present, unmistakably and exactly as when he was here."

A very strange incident then occurred, for the trumpet was again lifted, and a voice spoke to Mrs. Craig. At the same time the other trumpet was lifted, and another voice addressed Miss Rebecca West, calling "Rebecca!" The two trumpets were in the air at the same time, and the two voices were speaking simultaneously. The voice addressing Miss Rebecca West was indistinct, but I certainly thought I heard it say something like "Grandfather West." In this case some mistake may have been made, for her correct name is not West but Fairfield.

Later on a spirit addressing Miss West announced itself to be her mother. This voice was a trifle more distinct, and together they talked for a little while.

They discussed certain matters which Miss West had to attend to with regard to her mother's affairs after she had passed away. Whilst conversing with this spirit Miss West was somewhat emotional.

Two distinct spirit voices spoke to Lady Malmesbury. The first spirit was that of her father, and the second that of her mother, both of whom carried on short conversations with her. During the war, when her mother was dying, the train by which Lady Malmesbury was traveling to her was held up during an air raid for five hours in a tunnel. When she arrived at the bedside her mother was dead. Lady Malmesbury referring to this said: "I could not get to you, you know, dear." Her mother's voice replied, a little pathetically: "I waited for you as long as I could."

During the evening Kokum also spoke in his great voice, and taking up one of the trumpets (the less luminous of the two) whirled it round the room. Then, dropping it, he took up the other one, which was more luminous, having luminous stars on it, took it up to the ceiling, whirled it round and hit the ceiling.

Bobby Worrall talked with us in his childish tones.

HDB: What's today, Bobby?

BOBBY: Pat's birthday. I saw Pat this morning when he woke up in the dark.

This was correct, as we ascertained later that Pat had awakened at six o'clock in the morning when it was dark to look at his presents, which had been placed on his bed.

At the close Dr. Barnett spoke to us for some considerable time, and an interesting discussion on various philosophical and scientific questions took place. The conversations were carried on by various of the sitters, and some very interesting questions were put to him by Miss Rebecca West, by Lady Malmesbury, and Mr. Swaffer.

39

The investigator invites certain members of his household to a sitting with Valiantine—The results are chronicled by his chauffeur, A. Huntley.

Friday, April 3 1925.

DURING the time that these sittings were being held at Dorincourt it was only natural that certain members of my household should have become extremely interested. I therefore arranged a sitting for them, at which neither I nor my wife were to be present.

The names of those present, in addition to George Valiantine, were A. Huntley, my chauffeur; Mrs. Huntley, his wife; H. North, my head gardener; E. Boler, my butler; and Mrs. Walker, who is on the domestic staff.

Apparently they formed quite a good circle, and obtained fairly good results.

Five of the guides spoke during the evening Dr. Barnett, Bert Everett, Pat O'Brien, Bobby Worrall, and Kokum, who at one time whirled the trumpets in the air.

Of the personal spirits, five manifested during the sitting and I append herewith an account exactly as written that night by A. Huntley.

"I should like to give my impressions on a sitting which was held tonight at Dorincourt.

"The circle consisted of some of the staff at Dorincourt, and was kindly arranged by Mr. H. Dennis Bradley.

"The meeting started at eight forty-five p.m., and after a little music the illuminated trumpet gradually rose up and stopped in front of Mrs. Walker. A voice spoke to Mrs. Walker and said: 'I am your sister Emm. I am very happy here; will you give my love to my sister.' Mrs. Walker was very nervous and was at a loss as to what to say to the spirit voice. The trumpet then dropped to the floor.

"The gramophone was again played and the trumpet arose, slowly going round the circle and stopping at Mr. North, who inquired: 'Who are you?' The spirit voice answered: 'Harry—I am your grandfather; give my love to your father.' No one in the circle knew his name was Harry.

"We again played the gramophone, and after some little while one of Mr. Valiantine's spirit guides, Dr. Barnett, said: 'Have patience, souls.'

"Soon after the trumpet went to my wife, who asked" 'Who is it trying to speak to me?' The spirit voice was not very distinct, but my wife heard the words 'Give my love to Aunt Helena,' and then 'Mother.'

My wife became very excited and exclaimed 'Mother, is that my mother?'

'Yes,' the spirit voice answered, also excited. 'I am very happy, but your father is not.' My wife's father had a very bad habit which is causing my wife great anxiety. My wife asked her mother what she could do to help him. The voice answered, but my wife did not understand.

"The trumpet immediately came over to me and said: 'Alec, you can help him.' The trumpet, returning to my wife, said: 'Give my love to Aunt Helena.' Aunt Helena is my wife's father's stepmother who brought my wife up after her mother had passed over.

"My wife was then touched on the head and the trumpet fell to the floor. One of the spirit guides (Bert Everett) then said: 'That was the lady's mother who touched her.'

The trumpet then came over to me and a voice addressed me, saying: 'Alec.' I recognized the voice as that of my father, but asked: 'Who are you?' The voice immediately replied: 'Your father.' I said:' 'Are you happy? ' and the reply cane back: 'Yes, are you?' I said: 'Yes' to which he added: 'Not very. He then went on to speak about my private affairs, and certain domestic troubles. He went over to my wife and said: 'My girl, you must do better—I am Father Huntley.'

"I then asked my father: 'Are you with my brother?' and he replied: 'Yes.' I then said: 'What is his name?' and he replied: 'Owen William,' (This was the correct name of my brother who passed over seventeen years ago.) My father gave me a message for my mother saying: 'Tell her I am always with her and I am doing all I can to help her. I am glad she is getting well again.' (My mother has been ill for the last two months.) My father again said that he was very happy and added something which I could not catch. I was then touched on the hand and the trumpet fell to the ground.

"After a while the trumpet moved towards Mr. Boler, but the voice speaking was very weak. He understood that it was 'Hilda Boler.' The voice talked considerably, but I could not make out what it was saying.

"Another of Mr. Valiantine's spirit guides—Bobby Worrall—came through. He told us that he had been watching my little daughter, Doreen, playing with the doggie and the little car; also that she had broken a milk jug (which was true).

"Dr. Barnett then talked with us for a while.

"After attending this sitting tonight with Mr. Valiantine I am convinced, and the others who were present are also convinced. We gave no information away, but received it all from the spirits themselves. No one here knew my wife's mother was dead, or that she had an Aunt Helena, or knew anything about her father. Neither did anyone know my mother had been ill, or anything about my own affairs.

"I can only say it is a great Truth, and truly wonderful."

40

"I am a researcher and not a missionary" —The author discourses on a certain type of mentality—Miss Gladys Cooper asks for a sitting—Self-invited guests who anticipated a sensational entertainment—An unknown spirit speaks to Mr. Somerset Maugham—Mrs. Dudley Coats's sharp retort—An appallingly dull evening—"Sensitiveness is a culture of polarity."

I

Sunday, April 5 1925.

THE events recorded in this chapter are of interest only in the retrospect. In experience they were drab, and dull, and dreary.

There is no easy path to knowledge, and in psychics, as in all things, the danger of success is satiety. An evening of poverty, therefore, may prove a healthy stimulant. And should the subtle student be also a psychologist, he will, upon occasion, batten on his boredom, and, if it amuses him, create an interest where none had hitherto existed.

The series of psychical experiments and investigations conducted at Dorincourt had by this time aroused considerable comment. Many well-known people were publicly recounting their experiences. This publicity was impossible to avoid. My letters ran to many thousands, and the majority came from people sincerely anxious to inquire and to learn.

I am, however, a researcher and not a missionary. I have adhered rigidly to the principle of never discussing spiritualism or psychical research with anyone unless the desire has first been expressed for me to do so. Let me emphasize also that I have never asked anyone to a séance. The sitters have asked me to allow them to be present, and there were so many of my personal friends in the literary, artistic, theatrical, and scientific circles, whose requests could not be refused.

Of the rest, it was a matter of selection. It was obviously necessary to limit the number of sitters. My house is not a public institution; my drawing room is not Olympia; and my spirit of hospitality is finite.

In the selection my emotions were mixed. I determined to study the psychological as well as the psychical aspects, but the last thing I desired was that my house should be used as a public peepshow. One does not pander to the jaded palate of society sensation hunters. If they have exhausted all forms of titillation of the senses, they must suffer the bankruptcy of their ingenuity. The study of psychics, involving the establishment of the actual possibility of direct communication with the surviving spirits in another sphere, is the most important discovery in the history of the world. To regard it merely as a new sensation is an insult to intelligence.

My prolonged investigations have proved that the mental attitude and harmony among a circle of sitters are of paramount importance to the necessary vibrations for "voice" manifestations. It is not essential for a sitter to be a believer in psychic phenomena. An utter skeptic will not disturb, so long as he, or she, is open-minded and willing to be convinced, for no one has been, or is, more keenly critical than I myself. But it is necessary that one should feel that one is assisting at a serious attempt to explore the unknown. To attend in a mood of sheer curiosity, in order to be "in" the fashionable craze of the moment is to pervert a supreme subject.

Fortunately, except in rare instances, I was spared personal contact with such types of mentality. On the rare occasions that I met them, however, they provided me with an ephemeral mental exercise.

II

Some little time before the séance I am about to record, I received a letter from Miss Gladys Cooper. Using Mr. Ivor Novello's name as an introduction, she begged for an invitation to a sitting with Valiantine. In her letter she asked vaguely if she might "bring three or four friends." I replied that it was impossible to find room for so many, but that I would arrange for her to come with one friend.

Miss Cooper and I had not met personally for some seventeen years. At that time she was a chorus girl, and I was a struggling young writer. She applied for a part in a play of mine, which was then being produced in the West End. The leading part was played by Charles Bryant, an exceptionally fine actor, who had previously played in Mr. John Galsworthy's "Justice" and was the original Lawrence in the first production of Sir Arthur Pinero's "Iris." After Miss Cooper had rehearsed in my play for a week, the producer, Mr. Clifford Brooke, decided that it would be unwise to take the risk of her inexperience in comedy, and Miss Nina Sevening was engaged for the part.

Since that time Miss Cooper's praiseworthy determination has achieved its reward, and during the last two years she has played the leading parts in the revivals of Pinero's "Iris" and "The Second Mrs. Tanqueray," and has given successful interpretations of these two crudely neurotic but typically Victorian ladies of easy virtue.

In spite of my letter requesting her to bring only one friend, on the Friday prior to this sitting she wrote me again, begging me to allow her to bring a third guest, whose name she mentioned, Mrs. Dudley Coats. She did not vouchsafe the name of the first friend. I replied that another sitter would make the circle rather larger than was useful or comfortable, but that if she wished, she was at liberty to bring Mrs. Coats.

A short time previously Mr. Hannen Swaffer had asked Mr. W. Somerset Maugham, the dramatist, if he would like to join one of the circles; and, through Miss Margaret Bannerman, a request was made to me that Mr. Maugham might bring his wife.

In accordance with the usual procedure of my Sunday evening sittings, I sent a formal little note of invitation, asking my guests to arrive in time for a light dinner to be taken at seven so that the sitting might be held about eight.

Miss Cooper arrived, accompanied by Mrs. Dudley Coats, and her second friend proved to be Miss Olga Lynn. Mrs. Dudley Coats, whose leg had been broken in a hunting accident, was carried in on a chair.

As a psychologist my psychical studies have sharpened my powers of observation, and human character is easily stripped of its decoration and veils.

There existed a curious atmosphere. It was irritating to me, because it was obvious that my self-invited guests had come anticipatory of some sort of sensational entertainment. Apparently they assumed that at a given moment the curtain would rise upon a psychic cabaret show of unexpected daring. The role of mediumistic impresario was one that did not appeal to me.

When Mr. and Mrs. Somerset Maugham arrived dinner was served. Mrs. Dudley Coats, who was confined to her chair, preferred to remain in the drawing room. Miss Cooper solicitously insisted on keeping her company. Miss Olga Lynn accompanied the rest of us to the dining room, rising at odd intervals to look after her friends. Their needs were, I trust, adequately attended to.

By this time I was ineffably bored with the entire atmosphere. I had before this realized that my hospitality had been requested simply because these séances had become "fashionable." But to regard a great scientific, philosophical and phenomenal study merely as a "vogue" was uncomplimentary to my intelligence, as a writer of international repute. None of my guests had the faintest knowledge or conception of psychics, and they exposed their ignorance of modern research and literature.

As an experienced investigator I felt that any psychic experiment carried out under such conditions would inevitably prove negative, and that any serious attempt at research could at once be abandoned.

I therefore decided that I would not waste my time by joining the circle, and the sitters consisted of Valiantine, my wife, Anthony Bradley, Miss Gladys Cooper, Mrs. Dudley Coats, Miss Olga Lynn, Mr. Swaffer, and Mr. and Mrs. Somerset Maugham.

I append Anthony's account of what took place.

III

"There was evidently some lack of harmony at this sitting, for it was not until the fifth record had been played on the gramophone that Dr. Barnett's deep voice opened the séance.

"Bert Everett soon followed, with his high-pitched greeting: 'Good evening, souls.' He was asked whether the conditions were good, but preserved silence. Some more records were played.

"An independent voice, speaking apparently with some difficulty, exclaimed: 'Gladys! Gladys!' Miss Cooper asked for the name of the speaker, but no answer came.

"After another attempt at speech, the luminous trumpet was picked up, and the voice again addressed Miss Cooper, and the only words which could be deciphered were 'Gladys,' and what sounded like, 'Phyllis is here.'

"There seemed to be repeated efforts to speak through the trumpet to Miss Cooper (whose first sitting it was), but soon the voice, meeting with little response, ceased, unidentified.

"From somewhere in the room came a noise like a slight groan; but it is by no means certain that this was due to psychic phenomena. Miss Olga Lynn then seemed excited, and expressed the desire that she should not be touched.

"The guide, Dr. Barnett, speaking through one of the trumpets, remarked that the conditions were not hypostatic, and, in answer to a question, explained that he meant that there was a lack of unison.

"Then the trumpet was lifted towards Mrs. Maugham, and almost instantly fell to the ground.

'You must behave yourselves,' said the voice of Bert Everett. Through excitement, one of the sitters had impulsively touched the trumpet. 'The spirit was going to speak to your husband,' Bert explained to Mrs. Maugham.

"With great difficulty, it seemed, the trumpet was lifted, and a voice addressed Mr. Maugham. All that could be distinguished was: 'Hullo! Hullo! Somerset.'

"'Why do you call me 'Somerset'?' asked Mr. Maugham.

"The trumpet was again raised, and the voice made one more attempt to speak, but the conditions were apparently too adverse.

"Mrs. Dudley Coats then expressed the wish that someone would talk to her. After a short interval the trumpet was lifted laboriously to the level of her face.

'Coats' was the only word that could be distinguished.

'Are you a relation of mine or of my husband's?' asked Mrs. Coats, whose maiden name was James.

'Your husband's,' replied the voice.

'I don't know any of my husband's relations,' she observed.

"There was no further communication. The 'conditions' or 'atmosphere' seemed quite wrong, and further communication seemed unlikely.

'We must close now. Goodnight,' said the voice of Dr. Barnett.

"Compared with others, this was certainly the most unsatisfactory sitting ever held at Dorincourt."

IV

The evening was an appallingly dull one. Yet it provided my satiric sense with fresh fuel. In addition it was of value in proving how futile it is to attempt to establish communication with the spirits merely to satisfy the feverish desire for a new emotion.

It is absurd to imagine that all that is necessary is to enter a room, press a psychic bell, and a spirit will appear to order. Such an impression is an utter perversion of all psychical research and study. Spirits are not the servants of our will, nor are they likely to manifest in order to satisfy a casual curiosity. It is the individual mentality that raises or depresses the seeker after Truth in the psychic scale, and the mentality that coldly discards all unnatural cravings for the sake of new excitement, and declines to pervert whatever laws govern these mysteries, is the only one likely to achieve results of value to human knowledge.

V

Sensitiveness is a culture of polarity. It may swing to the supreme psychical heights, or to the physical depths.

My intensive studies may have illustrated a fourth dimension and a sixth sense, and certainly they have provided me with a knowledge of the hidden human faculties.

That the intelligentsia of the world are alive to the psychic discoveries of today maybe evidenced in the fact that my works have been translated and are published in France, Germany, Poland, and Italy. This statement is not a blatancy on my part; it is an irrefutable proof of the trend of the studious mind.

The personal powers of mediumship that I have developed have been of value to me. I can now read the mentality of any man or woman within a few minutes. That reading is not my predisposed conception of people, nor does it regard their egoistic conception of themselves.

The development of a mediumistic sensitiveness provides one with a weapon of subtlety.

41

S.P.R. officers at a Dorincourt daylight sitting—The first experiment: answers given by taps—The second experiment: Mr. Dingwall hears a voice through the trumpet—The third experiment: A voice saying, "Father Woolley" —A scientific advance.

I

Tuesday, April 7, 1925.

HAVING been informed of the results of the experiments of Una, Lady Troubridge, and Miss Radcliffe Hall, who had obtained the voices in the daylight with Valiantine, I received a letter from Dr. V. J. Woolley, asking me whether I could arrange a daylight sitting for him and Mr. Dingwall—another research officer.

This I arranged for the afternoon on the above date. The first attempt was made shortly after three-thirty p.m. in my study.

Dr. Woolley and Mr. Dingwall sat together with Valiantine. Valiantine held the trumpet up—some distance away from his face—and placed his hand over the broad end in order to obscure the daylight. The trumpet is held in the daylight in order to conserve all the power for the materialization of the voices. The ear of the sitter can also be placed to any part of it in order to catch the faintest sound. Valiantine's face could be observed both by Dr. Woolley and Mr. Dingwall. It should be noted that Valiantine made no movement, neither did his lips move during this experiment.

Taps were heard on the trumpet. A code was given three taps for yes, and one for no. Questions were put, and the answers given by taps. One of the sitters asked whether six taps could be given inside the trumpet, and six taps were given. No voices were heard.

After this they each tried the experiment of sitting alone.

The next experiment was made a few minutes afterwards with Mr. Dingwall sitting alone with Valiantine. Raps were heard inside the trumpet, and, at the request of Mr. Dingwall for a rap to be given at the end of the trumpet and in the middle of the trumpet over which he placed his ear, such raps were given.

During this short sitting, raps were heard in another part of the room. A voice materialized and spoke to Mr. Dingwall through the inside of the trumpet. The particulars of what was said I cannot give; I do not know. The words which were heard by Mr. Dingwall may or may not be given in the reports of the S.P.R.. All I can say is that when Mr. Dingwall came into the drawing room after this sitting he told me that he had heard a voice through the trumpet.

It must be carefully noted that a voice from inside the trumpet spoke to Mr. Dingwall in the daylight, and he spoke back to it—a conversation consisting of two or three sentences being carried on.

The third experiment was made by Dr. Woolley, sitting alone. He afterwards told me that many raps were given in answer to questions, and that a voice was heard from the inside of the trumpet, saying it was "Father Woolley."

Dr. Woolley and Mr. Dingwall were very interested in this experiment, and asked whether I could arrange for another daylight sitting for them. I said that if it were possible for me to do so I would.

II

I had not experimented to see whether I could get the voices in the daylight, and I therefore asked Valiantine at five forty-five pm whether he would try this with me, to which he immediately consented.

Valiantine sat in a lounge chair, resting back comfortably, and holding the trumpet away from him at arm's length—placing one hand over the large end. I could observe his face throughout the sitting. He did not move in any way, neither did his lips open at any time, except to ask a question when he addressed a spirit.

Several taps were made inside the trumpet, and in less than a minute I heard voices whispering to me. I did not catch what was said, and asked: "Is it Annie speaking to me?" The reply came immediately and distinctly, saying: "No, it's Warren." We carried on a conversation of a few sentences, and then he said, "Annie is here, and she would like to talk to you." Within a few seconds the voice of Annie came through. It was fairly clear and distinct. She said, amongst other things: "I have been helping you to straighten things out."[145]

During the conversation with her, I referred to the many little chats which Pat had had with her in the daylight, and she replied with a little laugh, saying "Yes, I always try to encourage him." She also told me to tell Dennis, my son, that she was trying to impress him. Later she said: "I am glad Valiantine is coming to this country." (This referred to Valiantine having said that he would endeavour to come to this country in the autumn.)

This phenomenon of obtaining the direct spirit voices in the daylight is a great scientific advance. It represents, perhaps, an advance with more striking possibilities than any form of phenomena yet recorded.

III

Mr. Dingwall is a very interesting person, and possesses a mercurial mind on psychical phenomena. He described to me, and to the others present, some of his recent experiences in America, when, on behalf of the English Society for Psychical Research, he was present at various sittings held under the mediumship of Margery. He said that she is a very remarkable medium, and that he is convinced of the genuineness of the phenomena which took place.

In a letter to Baron von Schrenck Nofzing, which was reproduced in the January issue of the *Paris Revue Metapsychique*, Mr. Dingwall said, among other things "I saw (teleplasmic) fingers and felt them in a good light. The control was irreproachable."

The strange thing, however, is that when referring to these same experiments with Margery in one of the recent issues of the English

---

[145] This is perfectly true, and referred to business affairs which had required a considerable amount of my attention.

Journal of the Society for Psychical Research he wrote: "The conditions, therefore, of the sittings, are such that I cannot at present affirm my belief in the authenticity of these phenomena." And I understand that since making this complete contradiction he has further stated "that he cannot come to any conviction as to the genuineness of the phenomena, and that nothing will induce him to say that he will admit their supernormal nature." Mr. Dingwall is evidently a man of varied opinions.

I am left wondering if he is an admirer of the methods of the old or the new regime of Russian diplomacy.

42

Mr. Harry Price records this sitting—Bert Everett uses the code word—The gramophone stops for no apparent reason—An Italian conversation—The circle reproved for talking too much—Mrs. Ellis Powell speaks to her husband—Lord Northcliffe speaks to Louise Owen—The controls put the gramophone out of order—Mrs. Vlasto's impressions.

Wednesday, April 8, 1925.

This sitting was held at Dorincourt at about eight-thirty p.m. There were present Valiantine, Mrs. Erato Vlasto, a personal friend of Sir Edward Marshall Hall;[146] Mrs. Ellis Powell, Miss Louise Owen, Miss Lilian Walbrook, Mr. Harry Price, the Honorary Director, National Laboratory of Psychical Research; the Rev. Walter Wynn, and Mrs. Bradley.

I did not attend the sitting, but sat in the adjoining room. During the séance I heard the voices of several of the spirits.

Unfortunately, Mr. Wynn had to leave early to catch a train to the country, and his early departure disturbed the circle.

---

[146] Sir Edward Marshall Hall, whom I have known for some years, was anxious to attend a "direct voice" sitting as he had never experienced this phenomenon. Unfortunately, however, about this time, through strain of overwork he had undergone a severe illness and was unable to attend.

VALIANTINE AND THE VOICES

From the account given to me by the sitters afterwards it appears that four of the guides spoke, and of the personal spirits, Dr. Ellis Powell spoke on two occasions with Mrs. Ellis Powell; Lord Northcliffe spoke in the independent voice to Miss Louise Owen, and the spirit of Lester spoke with Miss Walbrook on three or four occasions.

A relative of Mrs. Vlasto's, named Panny, spoke to her.

The spirit of Mr. Harry Price's mother spoke on two occasions to him, and the spirit of his son Rupert spoke to Mr. Wynn.

I had asked Mr. Harry Price, who is a very experienced investigator, to take careful notes during the proceedings, and I append herewith his report.

"The séance commenced at eight twenty-six p.m., the circle being composed of the following ladies and gentlemen, who sat in the order here given, commencing from the left of the medium: Mrs. Dennis Bradley, who attended to the gramophone; the Rev. Walter Wynn, author of *Rupert Lives*, etc.; Miss Lilian Walbrook, authoress of *The Case of Lester Coltman*; Mrs. Ellis Powell, widow of the late Dr. Ellis Powell; Mrs. Vlasto; Miss Louise Owen, for many years confidential secretary to the late Lord Northcliffe; and the medium, George Valiantine.

"Mr. Dennis Bradley asked me to take notes of the proceedings, and generally to take charge of the séance should anything untoward happen. This report was compiled the morning after the sitting from about twenty pages of notes written in the dark as the events occurred. Mr. Anthony Bradley (Mr. Bradley's son) was outside the door of the séance room, recording the names of the controls as they came through. The sitters did not link up hands, but sat quite free, and chatted with one another.

The sitters having taken their allotted places, two telescopic (usual aluminium type) trumpets were placed upright on the floor in the centre of the circle; the lights were then turned out. The trumpets had been made luminous at their bell ends, one having a row of luminous dots, extending from the luminous band at the mouth to nearly the top of the first section. The position of both trumpets was thus apparent during the entire sitting. I will remark *en passant* that the luminous paint used for marking the trumpets appeared to contain either radium, bromide, or mesothorium both radio-active substances which appear to become brighter the longer one beholds them in the dark. Ordinary luminous paints, composed of phosphorescent sulphide of zinc or similar substances, rapidly lose their energy in the dark and need further excitation in order to become luminous once more.

"The lights having been turned out, a request from the medium for music was met by Mrs. Dennis Bradley starting the gramophone and putting on the record of Clara Butt's 'There shall be no more Death.' This was followed by a hymn and the Lord's Prayer repeated by Valiantine. These vocal endeavours upon the part of the circle seemed to stimulate the forces at work, for immediately afterwards several of the sitters felt a cold breeze blowing from that part of the room to the right of the medium. A minute after Dr. Barnett (the medium's principal control) in a loud, rich, round voice said: 'Good evening, friends!' The sitters suitably responded. The doctor's voice appeared to come from the right-hand trumpet, which, however, did not move. A moment later the other trumpet was lifted by some unseen agency and the mouth placed within two inches of my face. At the same time a voice whispered 'Harry, Harry!' I acknowledged my name, but the trumpet dropped back to its position on the floor. A request for more music was met by the playing of Clara Butt's 'Abide with Me,' and a song by Galli-Curci. Left trumpet moved again. I then asked if the conditions were good, and immediately, Bert Everett, a control who usually makes himself heard at these sittings, shouted in a high-pitched falsetto voice, which appeared high up: 'Splendid, exquisite!' This last word was, I understand, a code word arranged by Mr. Bradley with Bert. Kokum, the medium's Red Indian guide, then gave a war-whoop which shook the room. I could not help being struck by the almost exact resemblance of Bert's voice to that of the elder Fratinelli, one of the two famous clowns who for years have amused Paris at the Cirque Medrano, Montmartre. Every time Bert spoke I was reminded of the curious squeaky voice of Fratinelli, ainé, when talking broken English. The resemblance was really startling, but the Fratinellis are, of course, very much alive.

"It was at this juncture that a curious thing happened. Mrs. Dennis Bradley informed us that the gramophone had 'jammed' and could not be started. Valiantine (who does not become entranced, and chats throughout the sittings) said he would try and 'fix' it, but he, too, could not start the machine. Miss Louise Owen then asked her friend, Miss Lilian Walbrook, to sing. Miss Walbrook, who has a charming voice, obliged by singing a number of songs which included 'Il Bacio.' Upon the conclusion of this song the right-hand trumpet rose into the air, approached Miss Walbrook (who was on my right hand) and a voice said: '*Ringrazio assai-La ringrazio tanto e tanto*' (Thank you—thank you very much). It was then asked if it were the composer (Luigi Arditi, 1822-1903) speaking. The trumpet was lifted again and a voice said 'Si, si signora!' Other phrases I caught were '*Canta a meraviglia* (sings charmingly); ... *Briganti*[147] ... *Piedmont*[148] ... *Frequentate it teatro?* (Do you visit the theatre?) and his last words were as far as I could catch them ... *l'esecuzioni di questa attrice e stupenda ... di nuovo ... felite notte!* Which seems to imply that the entity who was speaking thought Miss Walbrook's singing very charming and wanted an encore! I am informed that Valiantine does not know a word of Italian.

"Immediately after this interesting Italian conversation, the deep voice of Dr. Barnett, speaking from the trumpet (not raised) said: 'I am very pleased to see you here tonight, Mr. Price.' I suitably responded. The left trumpet was then levitated, went round the circle and stopped at Mrs. Ellis Powell. A voice said: 'It's Ellis speaking,' and greetings were exchanged between the voice and Mrs. Ellis Powell. Dr. Barnett from the other trumpet then reproved the circle for talking too much: 'Do not converse with one another when the spirits are speaking!' We promised we wouldn't. The left trumpet was then raised to quite near my face and a voice said: 'Harry, can you hear me?' This was repeated twice, and I endeavoured to answer, but the voice stopped and the trumpet was lowered.

"It was at this point that an amusing incident occurred. Bert's shrill little voice told me that I was not to 'reach out for the trumpet.' I replied that Mrs. Dennis Bradley had asked me to pick up the trumpet which had fallen over, and that I understood it was their usual procedure. Mrs. Bradley confirmed this. Dr. Barnett then said: 'He means you are not to touch the trumpet which is standing up.'

"Mrs. Ellis Powell then had a few more words with her husband, after which there was a lull. We then sang 'We are waiting just now,' a tuneful little ballad which seemed to have the desired effect, for Bert's piping voice at once exhorted us to 'sit up straight.' A moment after several of the sitters stated they could feel a cool breeze. Then we all sang 'We shall wear the white robes,' after which a voice said: 'Good evening, Louise!' which Miss Owen at once recognized as Lord Northcliffe's. 'Good evening, Alfred,' responded Miss Louise Owen, who held quite an animated conversation with her old 'chief.' During the period of their talk I heard the words: 'Tell Swaff to keep it up'—a very pointed reference to the work which Mr. Hannen Swaffer (for many years on the staff of Carmelite House) was doing. Mr. Swaffer was often called 'Swaff' by Lord Northcliffe when alive. I was informed that Lord Northcliffe detested the trumpet (which he did not use). He came through via the direct voice.

---

[147] Briganti was an opera composed by Arditi in 1841.
[148] Arditi was born in Piedmont, 1822.

"Before Northcliffe departed, Miss Walbrook asked him if her relative named Lester was with him. The voice replied that he was, and almost immediately the right trumpet was raised and 'floated' over to Miss Walbrook who at once recognized Lester's voice. After some greetings and kisses, the entity departed.

"A voice then tried to make itself known to the Rev. Walter Wynn, and all the sitters distinctly heard the words: 'It is your father who is speaking,' but the trumpet dropped before any questions could be asked. Bert's shrill voice then shouted again: 'You are not sitting up straight in our chairs!' —and we admitted the soft impeachment. The left trumpet was again lifted up towards my face and a voice said 'Harry, your mother is speaking.' The voice was very weak and indistinct, and I regret that I was unable to hear all that was said to me. But the words 'God bless you, my boy,' were quite distinct and several kisses were given me. Then the trumpet dropped.

"A new control was now heard. He was greeted as Pat O'Brien, a Hibernian with a rich Southern Irish brogue. He spoke a few words and said he was 'pleased to see Mr. Price with us this evening.' We all welcomed Pat, who did not stay long.

"Mrs. Vlasto then had a message and kisses from a relative (daughter?) named Panny (pet name for Pansy), who said that Grandpa, Jimmy and William were with her. The trumpet then moved round to Mr. Wynn and we all heard the voice saying: 'It is I, father, it's Rupert speaking,' and a touching conversation ensued between father and son.

"Again there was a slight lull in the proceedings, so we whistled some lively tunes (the gramophone being still *hors de combat*). To the strains of the 'The Campbells are Coming' the right trumpet suddenly jumped up (if I may use the term), and commenced dancing a jig, keeping time to our whistling. The dancing trumpet then sidled over to the stationary one and tapped itself against its companion, the metallic 'clicks' making a not unmusical accompaniment to our whistling. Suddenly, and without a word of warning, Bert shrieked out in a threatening voice: 'Sit up straight and keep your knees in,' and I am sure we all trembled as much as the inhabitants did in 'Alice in Wonderland' when the Queen kept on shouting 'Off with their heads!'

Dr. Barnett then asked me if I lived at 31 Scot's Avenue, and I replied that I had never heard of the address. He then said there was someone who had lived at that address waiting to speak to me, but as I could not identify him, the doctor would not let him through. At this juncture (ten-twelve p.m.) the Rev. Walter Wynn informed us that he had to leave, and Dr. Barnett at once shouted that the sitting was over. After the departure of Mr. Wynn we hesitated a few moments, but the doctor thundered out: 'I have closed the circle'—which left nothing to the imagination as to what he meant! He was obviously annoyed at the unorthodox ending of the séance—and this should be an object-lesson to those persons who prematurely break up the circle.

When the lights were at last turned up, Mrs. Bradley found to her astonishment that the gramophone was quite all right and had fixed itself! It was suggested that the 'controls' had put the machine out of gear in order that Miss Walbrook might be given an opportunity of giving us some songs. The circle now dispersed after a most interesting evening. For hours after I fancied I could hear Bert admonishing us to 'sit up straight'; and I shall never forget the commanding voice of Dr. Barnett, the rich Irish brogue of Pat O'Brien, or the trumpets dancing a jig to the strains of 'The Campbells are Coming.'"

Mrs. Vlasto sent me the following account of her experiences. The evidence as to the names seems to me of value.

"This only relates to my own personal points, but should you like some others verified I think I remember most of what took place.

"Almost as soon as we sat I saw psychic lights in the room and was touched quite definitely on the knees and then on the face.

"The gramophone was started and I heard the voice of my little girl on the other side joining in; she was not using the trumpet and the voice was low, but quite clear and absolutely true. Once more in the evening I heard her; this time she raised the trumpet, holding it high and firmly. 'Hullo, hullo! (Question: Is that Grandpa?) No, Mummy, it's Panny. I've got through at last. Grandpa is here and will try later. Jimmy and William have not come in, there is such a crowd of us, that's what's making it so difficult. (Then I missed something she said and I told her I could not quite hear.) No, Mummy, it's awfully difficult tonight; I can't make it loud or clear. Goodbye, Mummy, must stop.' Pan put the trumpet down quite quietly and I did not get any more from her or the promised talk from her grandfather, who constantly communicates with me. The other names are correct. Jimmy is a nephew and William a boy I never knew this side but know very well on the other as he is a great friend of Pansy's. At a trance sitting in the afternoon Pan had mentioned that she would bring Grandpa, William and Jimmy through."

43

This experience, during which the spirit of Michael Bradley established his identity, prompts the following comment: "Such an incident shows how natural and normal spirit communication can be made in perfect conditions."

Good Friday, April 10, 1925.

A WEEK or so previously an old uncle of mine Michael Bradley, had come through and had spoken to me for the first time, expressing the wish that he might have an opportunity of speaking to his brother—my father.

My father, who is eighty-five years of age, was spending Easter with us, and on this evening a sitting was held. I did not attend, as I was confined to bed with a chill. The sitters were therefore George Valiantine, my wife, and my father.

No music was played, and the spirits spoke to them within a minute or two.

Four of the guides, Dr. Barnett, Bert Everett, Kokum, and Pat O'Brien, spoke several times at considerable length.

Michael came through, using the luminous trumpet and speaking in loud and distinct tones. He addressed my father as "Dan"—the name by which he was accustomed to address him. Together they conversed for quite a while, my father asking many questions which called for evidential replies.

Michael spontaneously volunteered all the information which was required of him. He mentioned the place of his birth, near Galway, his age when he passed over, and many details of his career on Earth, thereby clearly establishing his identity. That is what invariably happens under harmonious conditions.

Annie spoke to my wife and to my father for some time. She referred to her mother and to the illness of Gertrude.[149]

Dr. Barnett and Pat O'Brien spoke fluently on various subjects during the sitting. Anthony, who was in another room at the time, happened to pass the door when Dr. Barnett was speaking. He called out a greeting to Dr. Barnett from outside the room, whereupon they two carried on a conversation. The door of my bedroom (which was on another floor and some distance away) was ajar, and I heard the various remarks made by my son, but I did not, of course, at such a distance away, hear the replies which were made.

---

[149] My father passed away during the July following this sitting. Although an Irish Roman Catholic, he told me that he considered the comfort and the philosophy of spiritualism to be magnificent.

44

Miss Winifred Graham's daylight experiment—Her comment: "It seemed so marvelous and far nicer than sitting in the dark."

Saturday, April 11, 1925.

On the afternoon of this day my wife and George Valiantine were taking tea with Miss Winifred Graham and her mother at their charming old house in Hampton. During the afternoon they were discussing the phenomenon of obtaining the voices in the daylight. Miss Graham expressed great interest, and said that she had a trumpet which had never been used for the purpose of a séance. Valiantine offered to make an experiment.

Both Miss Graham and her mother spoke to the spirit of Bob Graham. Here is Miss Graham's account of what took place.

"Quite casually, to our delight, Mr. Valiantine suggested to my mother that she and I should listen through the trumpet in broad daylight to see if the spirit voices could be heard.

Mr. Valiantine had said that the atmosphere quite good for the vibrations.

"To our surprise, we heard whispering voices, speaking faintly through the trumpet.

My mother and I heard my father speaking.

"It seemed so marvelous, and far nicer than sitting in the dark. I noticed with pleasure the calm and detached look on Mr. Valiantine's face."

45

This sitting is described by Jessica Sykes, the wife of Charles Sykes, the famous artist—The whispering spirit voice that was not encouraged—My husband's aunt and father manifested their voices—A loud voice calls me by name, announcing itself as 'Mother.'

∼

I

Saturday, April 11, 1925.

THIS sitting was comparatively poor. Present: Valiantine, my wife, Mr. Charles Sykes, Mrs. Sykes, Mr. T. C. Cannell, and Mr. Alfred Johnson.

I sat in the drawing room, during which time I heard, on occasions, the voices of the various guides. Neither Mr. Cannell nor Mr. Alfred Johnson had had previous experience.

During the evening four of the spirit guides carried on conversations with the sitters.

The supernormal lifting of the trumpet occurred on several occasions was lifted and taken into the direction of Mr. Cannell, a voice speaking to him, but he did not succeed in establishing any recognition.

The trumpet was lifted to Mr. Alfred Johnson, and a very indistinct voice spoke to him. Here again recognition could not be established.

To Mr. Sykes a spirit came, addressing him by his name, and calling herself 'Charlotte'—an aunt of his. This spirit also spoke to Mrs. Sykes. Charlotte spoke to Mr. Sykes of another relative of theirs, named 'May,' and said that he should inquire after her.[150]

Mr. Sykes' father also spoke to him for a while, and also to Mrs. Sykes.

To Mrs. Sykes there also came through her stepmother, who passed away in November, 1924. This spirit spoke to her for a short time.

I append Mrs. Sykes' account of what took place.

II

"We sat in the dark, chatting of things relevant and irrelevant, to the accompaniment of various selections from opera and jazz, which were played upon the gramophone. Meanwhile, we were gazing from time to time for any signs of movement from the two luminous trumpets with their luminous bands, which stood in the centre of our small circle.

"It was three-quarters of an hour before any manifestation of any description occurred.

"Then we saw one of the trumpets lean to one side, and the voice of Dr. Barnett greeted us. Another spirit guide (Bert Everett) spoke from high up in the room, and to a question as to whether the forces were weak, no reply was given.

"A little later the same high, squeaky voice, speaking from somewhere near the ceiling, called out 'Good evening, Mr. Sykes, glad to see you here tonight,' and after a slight pause— 'and you, Mrs. Sykes.'[151]

"Some little time elapsed, and then one of the trumpets made a direct ascent and a decided turn towards Mr. Cannell, who appeared somewhat surprised and affrighted, demanding if someone wanted to speak to him, and asking who it was. The whispering voice made several attempts to pronounce the name loud enough for Mr. Cannell to hear, but Mr. Cannell was not encouraging in his attitude, and nothing of a satisfactory nature seemed to be forthcoming.

"At this stage Dr. Barnett rebuked Mr. Cannell, telling him that he was rather excited and should calm himself. Mr. Cannell asked

---

[150] It was ascertained later that this relative had had, during the last day or two, a slight stroke, and this was not known to Mr. Sykes at the time.

[151] It was over a year ago since we had heard this same voice speak at a séance at Mr. Bradley's.

Dr. Barnett whether he could tell him the name of the spirit, and Dr. Barnett replied that he thought the name was 'Chanwell,' but that the spirit would have to identify himself. Several subsequent attempts, however, failed entirely, and the forces weakening, the trumpet fell with a rattling noise to the floor. The trumpet was then replaced by the sitter nearest to it.

"The music was resumed, and a powerful voice shouted out something which was incomprehensible, but those of us who had sat before knew it to be another of the guides who calls himself 'Kokum.' Music was continued, and after a short interval one of the trumpets rose and swept towards my husband. The gramophone was stopped and a loud whisper announced: 'Aunt Charlotte,' saying: 'How are you, Charlie? I am pleased to see you here again.' My husband asked if his father were there, and the voice said, 'Yes.' A little later his father came and greeted my husband, who asked: 'Is Hannah with you, and do you think she is strong enough to speak?' The voice said: 'I think so.' but the trumpet began to descend, and failed to establish further communication. The music was restarted, and in a short time a trumpet made a decided movement in my direction, and stopped within ten inches from my face, and a voice called me by name 'Jessica'—announcing itself as 'Mother.' I had lost my devoted stepmother in the previous autumn, and had nursed her during the last sixteen days of her ebbing life. I asked if she knew that I was with her at the end, and she said: 'Oh, yes.' The trumpet, without descending, then swept across to my husband and greeted him. We then heard a sound of kisses, and the trumpet fell to the floor again. Again the trumpet was raised, and Aunt Charlotte said: 'Have you seen Aunt May? You should see her.' My husband's Aunt May is alive, but having heard nothing of her for months, we rang up one of her daughters on the following day, and were told that she had been the victim of a slight stroke, and had been ill with influenza for a month, from which she was slowly recovering.

"A voice, using one of the trumpets, then tried to speak to Mr. Johnson, but was unable to make itself understood, and shortly afterwards the voice of Dr. Barnett announced: 'We shall have to close now. Goodnight.'"

46

Five spirit voices talk with Pat in the broad daylight.

Sunday afternoon, April 12, 1925.

DURING the afternoon of this day Pat had a short sitting with Valiantine in the daylight.

Five distinct spirits spoke to Pat. He spoke to Annie, with Warren, with Bobby, with Bert Everett, and with Pat O'Brien.

Bobby discussed the various things he had done during the day; he talked with him about the tadpoles which Pat had taken from the pond in the garden, and told Pat how he had seen him riding his bicycle, and how he had seen him fall and break the bell of the machine.

Pat talks to the spirits and they to him as quickly and as naturally as to any one of us on Earth.

47

A sitting that stands out in vivid contrast—An illustration of the negative and positive in psychics—Leon Quartermaine, the distinguished actor, has a conversation with his brother—The spirit of a friend puzzles Mr. P. G. Wodehouse—Harry Pelissier says he will welcome Miss Fay Compton on the other side—Billie Carleton recalls her death, and her friend, Jack Marsh, recalls an incident—"No jealousy on the other side," says Dr. Barnett—Miss Compton writes her impressions.

I

Sunday, April 12, 1925.

This sitting stands out in pleasant contrast to the boring proceedings of the previous Sunday. It was held in the evening at about eight forty-five p.m., and there were present, in addition to George Valiantine, my wife, and myself, Miss Fay Compton, her husband, Mr. Leon Quartermaine, one of our few really brilliant English actors; Mr. P. G. Wodehouse, the famous novelist, whose wit has cheered two continents; and Miss Leonora Wodehouse.

My guests were all charming and clever people. They arrived in the late afternoon, and we all dined early and held the sitting afterwards. The atmosphere created by the entire party was responsive, natural, enjoyable, sincere, and devoid of affectation. I emphasize this because I have learnt that such a mentality is of inestimable value when pursuing psychic studies with a mixed assembly. As a point of psychological interest I draw attention deliberately to the mentality which was exhibited on this evening in vivid contrast to that shown on the previous Sunday, which was certainly its antithesis. These two evenings illustrate the effects of the negative and positive in psychics.

Six of the spirit guides spoke to us. Dr. Barnett opened the sitting with his usual greeting, and then Bert Everett spoke. Pat O'Brien came through and spoke a few sentences in his rich Irish brogue. Kokum gave us a greeting, and Hawk Chief spoke a sentence or two and, in response to a request, gave a very loud war whoop.

Bobby Worrall also came through, and referred to Pat's doings through the day, telling us how he had seen Pat fall from his bicycle in the garden and hurt himself.

The luminous trumpet was lifted and taken close to Mr. Leon Quartermaine. The voice announced itself as "Harold." Apparently Harold was a brother of Mr. Quartermaine's, and together they conversed for a short time.

To Mr. P. G. Wodehouse a voice volunteered the name of "Ernest Wodehouse." This apparently was a cousin of Mr. Wodehouse's, who had passed away during the war. In answer to a question the spirit said he had passed over a few years ago, and it also volunteered something about being with Mr. Wodehouse when he was in Harrogate about a year ago. When the voice had gone, Mr. Wodehouse said it was true that he had been in Harrogate a year ago, but he could not understand why the voice had referred to this incident. The voice of Dr. Barnett then came through and said, "There is no confusion; the spirit is quite correct—he said that he was with you in the spirit when you were in Harrogate a year ago."

The trumpet moved over to Miss Wodehouse and, said: "I am so glad to see you here, Leonora."

I have been convinced, as I have said before, that Miss Fay Compton is exceptionally psychical. I am of the opinion that she could, if she wished, develop into a very powerful medium. She would, I believe, be able to obtain the voices herself in time.[152] To me, her psychic faculties are apparent, both in her personality and in much of her stage work. Her performance in Barrie's *Mary Rose* was one of the most remarkable impersonations I have ever seen, and it impressed all London. Not only was her acting inspired, it even suggested to me that she was controlled.

---

[152] I assert this belief with deliberated confidence—HDB

VALIANTINE AND THE VOICES

It was not merely her beauty; the ethereal character which she played was conveyed by her in a poetic manner which was beyond even the conception of the author. I mention this in order to illustrate why it is that Fay Compton at a sitting appears to attract the spirits.

Four individual spirits came through to speak to her on this night. The first was Harry Pelissier, her first husband. Pelissier is a very virile and determined spirit. He spoke to her in a voice which vibrated with love. He is apparently as much attracted to her now as he was whilst he was on Earth. Not only did he speak to her, but he spoke to Leon Quartermaine with an understanding of the changes which had occurred in Earth conditions. Pelissier told Fay that when she passed over he would be there to welcome her.[153]

Miss Fay Compton's father spoke to her.

Billie Carleton announced herself by her full name to Miss Compton.

FAY COMPTON: Billie, do you remember the time when you passed over?

BILLIE CARLETON: Yes, it was the day after the Victory Ball.

Billie Carleton was an exceptionally beautiful girl, but on occasions she had been known to take drugs. The assumption was that on the morning after the ball she took an overdose of some drug to give her sleep.[154]

FAY COMPTON: Is Jack with you?

BILLIE CARLETON: Yes, he is here, and he is going to speak to you.

A little later there came through a voice, addressing Miss Compton, announcing itself to be "Jack Marsh." They two talked for a while, and I then said quietly to Fay: "Will you ask him if he knows me?" Miss Compton asked the question, and the luminous trumpet came over to me and said: "I am glad to see you here, Mr. Bradley!" We talked in what to the others must have appeared to be a very enigmatic manner. I referred to an incident of which Jack Marsh alone could possibly have known, and which had occurred some years ago. I referred to this occurrence in very veiled terms, but Jack Marsh knew exactly what I meant, and laughed with me over this matter.

The incident in question was a peculiarly dramatic one, in which both Jack Marsh and I were concerned, and each of us had seen a certain humorous phase of it.

---

[153] I can only give a vague indication of the conversation which took place.

[154] I do not see why Billie Carleton should not take a material drug. Most persons are drugged throughout life by their own appalling mental stupidity, which is infinitely worse.

I knew Jack Marsh quite well in life. He was a unique character. On the day that Billie Carleton died I was lunching with him and a few other people at a house in Bruton Street. After lunch the conversation turned upon Billie Carleton, and Marsh had talked much about her. At about three to four p.m. in the afternoon he left us, saying that he was then going to see Billie. At this time he was entirely unaware that she was lying dead. Jack Marsh was a very close friend of Billie Carleton's.

At the close of this evening, Dr. Barnett answered several questions which were put to him. In answer to one, be said that jealousy did not exist upon the other side, and in answer to a spontaneous question of mine as to whether sexual perverts found progression difficult when they had passed over, he replied that although it retarded them for a time, they were afforded an opportunity of developing when they had recovered from this condition.

After the sitting I asked Miss Compton if she would write her impressions in her own particular style, just as she felt them.

Here are Miss Fay Compton's impressions of this sitting.

"I have only had two experiences of séances in my life. Both of these were at Dorincourt, and both were, to me, equally remarkable.

"It is very difficult for me to write my first impressions of a séance, chiefly because I was so intensely worked up and excited about the whole idea. I don't quite know what I expected, certainly not the rather 'matter of course' atmosphere that existed at Dennis Bradley's house on that first Sunday evening in March.

"I shall not try to give a description in detail of what happened. Mr. Bradley has already done that much better than I can. It was jolly to find such a congenial atmosphere when I arrived; one always expects people to put on a 'manner' in unusual circumstances, but we had a talk and a very happy dinner together before the séance began, and I was pleased to find the medium—Mr. Valiantine—such a simple, charming man. I would like to say that he has a very strong American accent. This, to my mind, is important, as so many unbelievers think that a medium is a brilliant ventriloquist. If so, Mr. Valiantine must be a super ventriloquist! None of the spirits who came through at the sitting were American, barring Bobby Worrall, and perhaps one or two of the guides.

"I am rather amused when people tell me that mediums are conjurors and ventriloquists. If they are, they have only to adopt the stage as a profession, and I guarantee they will make fortunes—certainly Mr. Valiantine would!

"I am an extremely nervous person, and I confess that on the first occasion when I was sitting in the dark—waiting—I was thoroughly frightened. The gramophone was played—I was told that sound helped the spirits to come through—and after about two records had been put on, Mr. Valiantine asked us to say the Lord's Prayer together. I was glad to do this. It gave me a sense of comfort and reality. We sang together, and some more records were played. I was told that I might feel a touch, and was to acknowledge it by saying a word of thanks, or anything that would suggest I was not indifferent. I was terrified at this, but when, a little later, someone shook my knee quite forcibly, I felt rather happy about it, and said my 'Welcome, friend' with real sincerity, and quite forgot to be frightened any more.

"You will have read in Mr. Bradley's account what happened, and what was said. I think he only wants me to give my impressions—not an account of what happened.

"On the first occasion, as I remember, one of the first guides who spoke was Bert Everett—in such a strident, telling voice, high up in the room, that I nearly jumped out of my chair, but after a moment I thought his was such a jolly voice that I was anxious to talk to him myself. I was astonished to find that the medium did not speak at all, except to ask occasional questions. I had always imagined the spirits spoke through the medium—that is, using the medium's voice as an instrument.

"These guides spoke from all parts of the room, and one was conscious of a presence in each place that they spoke. Also I was tremendously aware of the spirits that had learnt to come through more often, such as Warren Clarke and Mr. Bradley's sister. They seemed to be walking about, and with us in the room plainly. It is impossible to put into words the effect they gave, even with the spirits who had never tried to speak before, and who spoke at this séance, with the aid of the luminous megaphone. I was aware of a personality as well as a voice.

"People have asked me if I could recognize the voices of the particular spirits who spoke to me—my father, my first husband, Harry Pelissier, and Billie Carleton. It was impossible to recognize intonations as they spoke scarcely above a whisper. I understand it is difficult for them to speak clearly at once; they have to learn, as I should think we on this side have to learn to encourage them. But the personality of each was very distinct.

"I was touched several times during the séance, and was aware of a great force that seemed to be surging through me. Mr. Bradley thinks

I am psychic, and that I am able to give the spirits help in coming through. This may account for this strange feeling.

"I am not going to write of the personal things that were said to me; Mr. Bradley has recorded what took place, and it is all quite correct. I have only tried to explain a little of what I felt.

"I am very grateful to Mr. Bradley for letting me attend the two séances, and I have found them a most wonderful and enthralling experience."

48

Miss Winifred Graham records her impressions of her second daylight séance.

Monday, April 13, 1925.

ON the afternoon of this day Miss Winifred Graham and Mrs. Graham were at Dorincourt and experienced their second sitting in the daylight.

The following is Miss Winifred Graham's account:

"My mother and I were asked to Dorincourt, and during the afternoon we heard the direct voice again in the daylight.

"The clearness of the messages was greatly increased on this occasion by using Mr. Valiantine's trumpet, which had played so important a part in many séances. My father spoke to me and to my mother. Whilst he was talking to me, I mentioned the abbreviated name of a very dear relative, entirely unknown to the medium. Later on my father brought this relative through to talk to me. The voice of this spirit was most characteristic. Bright, quick, and young, insisting that there was no death! The voice of this younger spirit was in contrast to that of my father's, which was purposely deliberate as he had more to say, and wished to make it clear and strong.

"My father was emphatic in his thanks to Mr. Valiantine.

"When the trumpet was placed in the cupboard afterwards it was glowing with a strange purple light."

49

*A poor sitting—Spirits speak to
Miss Constance Collier and Mr. Ivor Novello.*

~

Wednesday afternoon, April 15, 1925.

THIS sitting was held at the house of Mrs. Arthur Bendir, at 43 Grosvenor Square, London, W.

I was not present and the sitters consisted of Valiantine, Mrs. Bradley, Mrs. Arthur Bendir, Miss Constance Collier, Mr. Ivor Novello, Mr. W. B. Purefoy, and another gentleman whose name I do not know.

The two luminous trumpets were placed in the centre of the circle. There was considerable difficulty in excluding the daylight from the room.

It was some three-quarters of an hour before any phenomena of any description took place. The sitting was comparatively poor, but four of the guides spoke a few words: Dr. Barnett, Bert Everett, Kokum, and Bobby Worrall.

Supernormal movements were manifested and various of the sitters were touched on occasions.

The spirit of Miss Collier's mother came through and spoke to her for a short time and, in addition to this, a spirit named Bertie Adams (who had spoken to Mr. Novello on a previous occasion) came through and spoke for a short time with him again.

50

*Mr. P. H. G. Fender receives a spirit message for his father—
An old servant speaks to Mrs. Arthur Bendir—Mrs. Theodore
McKenna talks to her son, Justine—"You must stop these wars"
—Mr. Oscar Hammerstein, the dramatist, receives valuable
evidence.*

***

Thursday, April 16, 1925.

This was held at eight forty-five p.m. There were present Valiantine, Mrs. Arthur Bendir, Mrs. Theodore McKenna, a sister-in-law of Mr. Reginald McKenna, ex-Chancellor of the Exchequer; her sister, Mrs. Hannen, Mr. Oscar Hammerstein, the author of *Rose Marie*; and his wife, Mrs. Hammerstein; Mr. P. H. G. Fender, the famous cricketer, and myself.

The majority of those present had had no previous experience of séances, and as usual on all occasions except my Sunday experiments, none of the guests was introduced to Valiantine.

The conditions appeared to be good. After two gramophone records had been played, Dr. Barnett gave us a greeting, and Bert Everett spoke in his shrill voice from high in the room. In answer to a question of mine, he gave me the code word which told me that the circle was a harmonious one.

Twice during the evening the loud voice of Kokum spoke in tones which startled some of the sitters. Pat O'Brien spoke in his rich Irish brogue to me and with two or three of the others. Bobby Worrall referred to Pat's movements during the day, remarking that he had seen Pat at the dentist's.

To Mr. P. H. G. Fender a voice spoke, using the luminous trumpet. It was indistinct at first, and it was only on the second or third attempt that it managed to establish its identity. It announced itself to be Mr. Fender's grandfather, and during the conversation Mr. Fender asked the spirit where he had lived and the voice replied: "Dundee."[155] The name of "Percy Fender" was volunteered and the voice referred to Mr. Fender's father, and sent a message to him. Mr. Fender asked if, in certain circumstances, he should take this particular message to his father; the voice was quite insistent in saying that he should.

A spirit voice spoke to Mrs. Arthur Bendir, announcing itself to be "Harry Bendir." During the conversation which ensued with Mrs. Bendir certain references were made to his brother Arthur.

Later in the evening another voice spoke to Mrs. Bendir, using the luminous trumpet and announcing itself as "Ellen." Strangely enough, this spirit appeared to be quite surprised that Mrs. Bendir was in the circle, saying: "Fancy seeing you here," and then went on to refer to certain meetings. It appears, as Mrs. Bendir told us afterwards, that this was an old servant of hers who was very attached to her when she was a young girl, and this servant had been in the habit of regularly attending religious meetings.

When this spirit had gone, Dr. Barnett's voice was heard in the centre of the room, giving a laugh and saying: "The spirit was talking of her Salvation Army Meetings." This, I understand, was an evidential remark, as at one time this servant did attend Salvation Army Meetings.

During the evening a voice was heard speaking independently—not using the trumpet—just near where Mrs. McKenna was seated. The voice was a little faint, but I managed to get the surname. We all heard the voice and I thought I heard the words "just beginning." A little later I heard the voice say "McKenna." This is somewhat extraordinary, because a very short time afterwards the trumpet was lifted and taken close to Mrs. McKenna, and a voice spoke to her, announcing itself distinctly as "Just McKenna"—a peculiar forename. We learned later that this was the spirit of "Justine McKenna," a son of Mrs. Theodore McKenna's, who had passed away when he was, I believe, twenty-one years old. He was addressed by the family as "Just." Together mother and son talked

---

[155] This was afterwards ascertained to be correct.

for a while, and in answer to a question from Mrs. McKenna as to what he was doing in the spirit world he replied that he was studying the war records. Mrs. McKenna could not quite understand this reference, and said: "That is a peculiar thing for you to be doing." The voice replied very firmly and decisively: "You must stop these wars." This, I may mention, is the insistent desire expressed by nearly every spirit. It appears to be of paramount importance to the world that wars must be stopped; otherwise our present civilization is in danger of collapse. While the voice of Justine McKenna was speaking to Mrs. McKenna on two or three occasions he addressed his remarks to her sister, Mrs. Hannen, saying how pleased he was to see them both together.

To Mr. Oscar Hammerstein the spirit of his mother came through and spoke to him for a little while on two occasions. During the time that she was talking to him she mentioned something about "Aunt Annie." Mr. Hammerstein did not quite catch the name, but Mrs. Hammerstein—who was seated opposite—heard the name and said: "She is speaking of Aunt Annie." The voice then went over to Mrs. Hammerstein and said: "I was talking of 'Mousie.'" This is a point of considerable evidential value, as the "Aunt Annie" referred to was known by the nickname of "Mousie," and this name was volunteered by the spirit voice.

During the evening the luminous trumpets were moved in all parts of the room, and on one occasion both of them were lifted together, and on another, Kokum lifted the trumpet and whirled it round the room, touching the ceiling with it. These physical manifestations are remarkable to observe.

51

The wonderful daylight experience of two strange ladies.

4 p.m. Friday, April 17, 1925.

ON this Friday afternoon my wife received a call at Dorincourt from two ladies who were strangers to her. They had motored from Camberley (in Surrey) in order to see if there was any possibility of obtaining a sitting with Mr. Valiantine. My wife told them it was impossible to arrange this, as every evening had been booked up. She, however, asked them to take tea with her, and during the conversation she referred to the many incidents which had occurred at the sittings, and also to the phenomena which had been produced in full daylight with Mr. Valiantine.

Valiantine spontaneously offered to give them a daylight sitting.

The two ladies are Mrs. D. F. McKenzie and her daughter, Mrs. Theo Uzielli.

Mrs. Uzielli took the first sitting, and through the trumpet, in the daylight, the voices of both her father and her brother came through and spoke with her.

Their names, which I understand were volunteered, were Donald and Charlie. Whilst Mrs. Uzielli was speaking to them, her father told her that he would like her to call her mother in.

Mrs. McKenzie then came into the room, and she spoke to her husband and with her son.

This was quite an exceptional test when one considers that two strange ladies, within a very short time of their appearance at Dorincourt, were able to speak in the daylight to some of their dead relatives.

52

Countess Ahlefeldt-Laurvig joins in a conversation in French and Russian with the spirit of her brother Oscar in full daylight.

~

5.45 p.m. Saturday, April 18, 1925.

DURING this afternoon the Countess Ahlefeldt-Laurvig paid a social call at Dorincourt upon my wife. This call was paid without the slightest intention of holding a séance.

Both George Valiantine and I were present, and various points psychics were discussed.

My wife told the Countess of the daylight sittings which had taken place, and she was so extremely interested that Valiantine offered to give her an immediate sitting if she wished.

The Countess and Valiantine sat in my study in the daylight, and almost immediately the voice of Oscar (brother of the Countess) came through and spoke to her. The first part of the conversation was carried on in Russian, and then the Countess suggested that it should be continued in French.

The sitting lasted for about a quarter of an hour, and on returning to the drawing room the Countess said that the experiment was quite a marvelous one, and that her brother would have gone on talking for a long time, but that she had to stop the conversation as she had to motor back to town and change for a dinner engagement.

53

The author's mother, a devout Roman Catholic, speaks to the spirit of her daughter—A blue bird comes into the circle—Mr. Noel Jaquin's experiment—The imprints of a hand and of the feet of a bird—The smear of sexual perversion—HDB calls for a public exposure.

I

8.30 p.m. Saturday, April 18, 1925.

ON this evening, at the request of the spirit of Annie, I had asked my old mother to come to Kingston for a sitting. My mother, who is in her eightieth year, had never sat before, and although, through reading my writings, she was quite convinced of the actuality of spirit communication, yet being a devout Roman Catholic, she was not entirely sure in her own mind as to whether the study was the right one.

There were present only four sitters: Valiantine, my wife, my mother, and myself. Within a few minutes Dr. Barnett came through and greeted us.

Shortly afterwards the voice of Annie came through, speaking independently, and addressing herself to her mother at once. Together they two conversed for some little time. Annie also spoke to my wife and me. She referred to Gertrude's health, and appeared to be somewhat doubtful as to her condition.

Annie's son Georgie came through and talked with my mother. My mother loved Georgie perhaps as much as anyone on Earth, and he was very fond indeed of her. The conversation between them vibrated with love and emotion. The various conversations had lasted perhaps some three-quarters of an hour, when, as my mother was feeling tired, I took her out of the room. As I opened the door, and the light from the hall streamed into the room, the voice of the guide, Bert Everett, was heard in strong light calling out in sympathetic terms: "Goodnight to you, Mrs. Bradley."

My mother then went to bed, and afterwards told me that she thought it was a most marvelous experience.

After she had gone the three of us continued the sitting. It is necessary here to mention that another purpose of this sitting was to make an experiment of perhaps paramount importance, the nature of which I will explain.

Mr. Noel Jaquin—who is one of the greatest experts on hand prints in Great Britain, and has diagnosed diseases and character in an extraordinary manner asked me a few weeks previously to make an experiment during the Valiantine sittings with some of his smoked paper nailed in a box, the box to be placed in the centre of the circle at a séance, with the object of seeing if it were possible to obtain the fingerprints of a spirit. His idea was unique, and this experiment had never before been attempted, except upon one occasion, under our own private mediumship at Dorincourt, when the result was negative.

Noel Jaquin's contention was that if alleged spirit hands had touched various of the sitters, then these hands could be placed upon the smoked paper, and the imprint obtained.

Therefore Mr. Jaquin's box—which I opened—was placed in the centre of the circle upon a stool.

During the time that the spirit of Georgie had been speaking to us, the trumpet had been lifted very carefully, and the voice had spoken through it, but although the trumpet went all round the circle, it did not touch the stool.

Warren came through, and he talked for some little time with my wife, and with me, and also with Mr. Valiantine. It is useless for me to retail the context of my conversations with Warren and Annie. They are intimate and fluent, and masses of evidential points were spontaneously volunteered.

Bert Everett spoke to us for some time, Pat O'Brien for perhaps some ten minutes or so, and I carried on a lengthy conversation with Dr. Barnett.

I asked Dr. Barnett about sexual perversion. I had asked this question on the Sunday before, but I explained to Dr. Barnett that I knew he could not answer it at length then, as the subject was difficult to discuss in the presence of others.

Dr. BARNETT: Sexual perversion has a very grave effect upon the development of character, and especially on the development of the spirits when they pass over to the other side. When sexual perversion is cultivated or fostered it is infinitely worse than in the cases where it is inherent or instinctive. The cultivation of such ideas is a curse [and those] who practise their vices on Earth live in darkness for some considerable time when they leave their physical bodies, until such time as they can learn to develop out of their mental condition.

Reverting to the experiment of the fingerprints towards the end of the sitting, there was a silence for some ten minutes to a quarter of an hour, during which time we all felt a considerable amount of power being drawn from us. Throughout there was a fluttering around the room, and then a strange but attractive sound of a bird "tweeting" all round the circle. We all remarked upon this.

Dr. BARNETT: There is a blue bird attracted here. (A little later) The bird is sitting on your case (meaning the case containing the smoked paper).

There was a further pause of some ten minutes, and then Dr. Barnett said: "We are drawing the power to obtain the ectoplasmic impression of a hand."

After another pause of a few minutes Dr. Barnett told us that we should close the sitting. The lights were then turned on, and to our astonishment there was the imprint of a hand with the four fingers, part of the thumb, and also part of the palm, and, on another sheet, there was the imprint of the two feet of a bird.[156]

I informed Mr. Noel Jaquin of this on the following Monday, and he regarded these impressions as of the utmost importance.

It maybe shown that it was utterly impossible for the imprints obtained to be produced by any of the sitters who were present.

Mr. Noel Jaquin's carefully studied report appears in a subsequent chapter.

---

[156] Photographic reproductions of the "ectoplasmic hand" and the "bird's feet" are shown below.

II

I had particular reasons for asking Dr. Barnett these questions upon sexual perversion. I know the West End of London as well as any living man. Not only am I a psychologist, but I have far greater knowledge of the inner lives and habits of those whom I meet either casually or socially than they imagine. The rotten "smear" of sexual perversion is a thousand times more dangerous than the average man or woman realizes.

It is omnipresent—the "smear" exists in the arts, in literary circles, in the theatre, and in the Universities of Great Britain. It is more blatant now than ever before. It is more apparent than it was in the time of Oscar Wilde, and what is needed is some great public exposure which will loosen these perverts' strangle-hold upon a certain section of the public.

These decedents imagine for the moment that they are secure, but they are fearful cowards at heart, and determined efforts should be made to suppress and smash their evil influence.

I am no hypocritical moralist. My forty years have been lived completely and at electric pace, but the constancy or inconstancy of my passions have been controlled by natural instinct. I am unconcerned and uninfluenced by man's invention of any moral code, but I realize that the whole universe can only be governed by natural laws. Perversion is rebellious to creation, and is a crime against nature. Its affects upon the scheme of the universe maybe insignificant and ephemeral, yet it represents a cancerous growth which may destroy a nation.

54

Three voices speak to Mrs. Gibbons Grinling—A spirit addresses Mr. Dennis Neilson-Terry—Miss Mary Glynne is reminded by her father's spirit of a visit to Penarth—The late Lord Curzon speaks to Mr. Oliver Baldwin—A message to Lord Birkenhead—Lord Curzon met by his first wife on the other side—The impressions of Mr. Denis Grinling and Mr. Oliver Baldwin.

∼

I

Sunday, April 19, 1925.

THIS séance was a fairly fluent one. We had all dined together, and amongst the guests there was a pleasant sense of harmony. The sitters were Valiantine, my wife, Mrs. Gibbons Grinling; her son, Mr. Denis Grinling; Mr. Dennis Neilson-Terry; his wife, Miss Mary Glynne, the charming young actress; Mr. Oliver Baldwin, and myself.

Within a few minutes the voice of Dr. Barnett greeted us, and during the evening spoke to us at length on two or three occasions on several subjects.

Of the other guides, Bert Everett spoke in his shrill tones, Kokum and Hawk Chief manifested and spoke a few sentences, and Pat O'Brien also came through on two occasions, speaking with the various sitters in his rich Irish brogue.

Of the personal communicators, there came through, using the luminous trumpet, three individual spirits who spoke to Mrs. Gibbons Grinling and Denis Grinling. One was Cedric, a son of Mrs. Grinling's, who passed away some little time back, who volunteered his name; another was Godfrey, a friend of Mr. Denis Grinling's, who was killed in the war; and the other, Raymond, a younger brother of Denis Grinling's.

To Mr. Dennis Neilson-Terry a voice spoke—not very distinctly—giving the name of "Emily," and saying that she was his grandmother. This spirit referred to Maria, her sister.

To Miss Mary Glynne there came a voice, using the luminous trumpet, saying it was her father. During the short conversation which ensued the voice said, "I was with you in Penarth." This, Miss Glynne told us afterwards, was correct, as she had been acting in Cardiff in a new play the preceding week, and during the time she was there she had visited the house in which her father had lived in Penarth.

Oliver Baldwin was spoken to by a spirit, announcing himself as "Harold Baldwin," his uncle. A little later the luminous trumpet was lifted and Mr. Baldwin was addressed by a voice announcing itself as "George Curzon." This was the spirit of Lord Curzon of Kedleston who had passed away a few weeks before. During the conversation Lord Curzon asked him to tell Lord Birkenhead he had spoken to him, and he also sent his love to Lady Curzon, adding: "Tell them of this great Truth." All these names were volunteered by the spirit. During his conversation with us Lord Curzon told us that his wife (his first wife) had been there to meet him when he passed over. She had been a great help to him in his new condition.

Later another voice addressed itself to Mr. Baldwin, announcing itself as "Admiral Madden," and during the time that this voice was speaking it said to Mr. Baldwin: "Will you say that I did my duty?"

During the evening there came through, using the luminous trumpet, the spirit of Harry Pelissier, who spoke in exactly the same manner and tones as on the occasions when he had spoken to Fay Compton. Once or twice he gave his peculiar laugh. He spoke also to Mr. Dennis Neilson-Terry, and to me. In speaking to Mr. Terry, he referred to the conversation that he had had on the previous Sunday with Fay, and also referred to having spoken to Leon Quartermaine. He told Mr. Terry some of the things he had said to Fay. He spoke to Mrs. Bradley of his son Anthony Pelissier, who had come down to Dorincourt on the Friday before, and he spoke in terms of great affection of his wife, saying: "She is my soul mate and the mother of my child."

During the time the spirit of Harry Pelissier was speaking to Mr. Neilson-Terry, they two held a little conversation on affinities. The conversation was quite light, and on certain points Mr. Terry did not entirely agree with him. Pelissier said: "It is no use arguing with me; I am now on this side and I know better than you do." Pelissier also went over and spoke to Mary Glynne, during which he said, in a jocular manner, "You are not jealous of him (referring to Dennis Neilson-Terry) are you, my child?"

Just preceding and immediately following Pelissier's talk with us, whilst the gramophone was playing with the lid closed down, the time was changed and on two occasions some weird and peculiar noises were made from inside the box.

Late in the evening the spirit of Arthur Playfair came through, and spoke to Mr. Neilson-Terry and to me. Again he referred to Phyllis Monkman, saying that he wanted to talk with her.

After talking to us all for some little while, and answering a few ethical and philosophical questions put to him, Dr. Barnett closed the sitting.

II

In a letter which I received from Mr. Denis Grinling two days later, in referring to the séance, he said:

"Cedric, my brother, spoke first, giving his name unaided. My mother gave away the names of Godfrey (a very great friend killed in the war) and Ray, my younger brother, who spoke immediately after Cedric. Their few remarks were natural and kindly, and their way of expressing themselves was familiar. Godfrey had an eager way of speaking, which was reproduced faithfully.

"When I asked Ray to lift the trumpet up to the ceiling, he said: 'I'll try.' A moment later he raised it quickly from the floor to the ceiling, thumped the ceiling hard, and then let the trumpet fall with a clatter.

"The etheric force must have failed before he had time to return the trumpet gently to the floor. This struck me as a crucial piece of evidence of the genuineness of Valiantine's powers, as I made the suggestion to my brother spontaneously without any previous warning. Also, the medium would have to perform noisy gymnastics to achieve the same result."

III

The following are Mr. Oliver Baldwin's notes:

"A spirit voice, using the luminous trumpet, announced himself as George Curzon, and addressed me as Mr. Baldwin. He said that he was pleased to see me there, and that he knew my father (Stanley Baldwin) very well. He said also that he had a tremendous amount of important work to do as he had left so much undone.

"He asked me to tell Birkenhead, and also to tell his wife (Lady Curzon) that he was well and happy. In answer to a request made by Mr. Bradley, George Curzon said that he would try and come through on the following Wednesday night, April 22.[157]

"The second spirit which spoke to me was my Uncle Harold, who thanked me for what I had done about the money, and he also repeated his entreaties regarding the catastrophic wars. In answer to a suggestion of mine as to whether he would like to send a message to my father, he replied that he would like to speak to him, but that he did not think he (my father) would.

"The third spirit which spoke to me gave the name of Admiral Madden, saying that he was pleased to speak to me. I was uncertain of the identity of this spirit, but amongst other things he said: 'I did my duty.' Regarding this spirit, I have not been able to find out anything about an Admiral Madden; some say he is still alive. I believe, however, there was also an American Admiral of that name. ... I think Mrs. Grinling 's conversation with the spirits one of the most beautiful things I have ever heard."

---

[157] This he did. See Chapter 58.

55

*Valiantine sits with two of his friends in the daylight—
Bobby Worrall speaks to his grandfather.*

∼

Monday, April 20, 1925.

ON this day two friends of Mr. Valiantine's were guests at luncheon at Dorincourt. They were Mr. Harry Worrall and his daughter Maud.

After luncheon a short sitting was held in the daylight. Miss Worrall sat first, speaking with four individual spirits. The first was her mother, the second was her grandmother (who volunteered the name of "Grandmother Hooper"), and then with a brother of hers, who had passed away over forty years ago. This brother she had never met in life as she is the youngest of quite a large family.

Miss Worrall is the aunt of the little spirit guide, Bobby Worrall, who had spoken to her on one previous occasion at Dorincourt—last year—but he had never met her in life, as although of English parents, he was born and passed away in America.

Bobby Worrall spoke to his aunt for quite a while.

After this Mr. Harry Worrall[158] sat and spoke to Bobby for a short time.

---

[158] Mr. Worrall is the grandfather of Bobby Worrall.

56

*Mrs. Maurice Hewlett unable to keep her appointment—
The author makes a characteristic outburst—The secret of the
blue bird revealed.*

I

Tuesday, April 21, 1925.

AMONG the many thousands of applications begging for an opportunity of attending one of the Valiantine sittings, I received a letter from Mrs. Maurice Hewlett, widow of the distinguished writer, who passed away a little time back. I regard Maurice Hewlett as one of the finest English writers of the twentieth century. He was a master of literary style, a subtle psychologist, a delicate ironist, a fine and sensitive artist. Mrs. Hewlett was engaged on a work of his life and letters. As it appeared to me that it would be of absorbing interest if we got the spirit of her husband through to talk to her, in which case he would be likely also to talk to me, I acceded to her request, and invited her to be present. Unfortunately, it appears she had suddenly to undergo an operation, and I received a telegram saying that Mrs. X. (for reasons which will appear later I omit this lady's name) would arrive in her place.

The telegram was not from Mrs. Maurice Hewlett, it was from Mrs. X., and it did not ask for permission to come, but simply said that the lady would be present.

VALIANTINE AND THE VOICES

There was no time for me to reply, but I was, frankly, annoyed at this procedure, as there were many persons with greater claims than this lady.

The lady, who was entirely unknown to me, arrived just after eight o'clock. Directly I saw her, I felt instinctively that we should get no good results. It was not a question of my resentment at her self-invitation; it was an intuitive and indefinable feeling of mine.

This feeling was so strong that I told Valiantine within a few minutes of her arrival that I should prefer not to go into the sitting. He, however, persuaded me to sit, and eventually I agreed.

I had invited Mr. Noel Jaquin in order that we might make a further experiment, in his presence, to see if we could obtain other spirit imprints.

Mr. Jaquin prepared two sheets of smoked paper, which were placed on a stool in the centre of the room.

The sitters consisted of Valiantine, my wife and myself, Mrs. Ayres whom I felt to be quite a good sitter; Mr. Noel Jaquin, and Mrs. X.

Within two minutes I knew we were in for a blank evening. Several records were played upon the gramophone, and I then said that I should prefer to leave the room. The other sitters persuaded me to stay on. After three-quarters of an hour the voice of Dr. Barnett spoke. All he said was: "It is very difficult tonight." Then, after a pause of a few minutes, he said: "We shall have to close."

II

We then adjourned to the drawing room, and a little later the two ladies motored back to town.

Both Mr. Valiantine and Mr. Jaquin were very anxious after they had gone to make a further experiment. The four of us therefore sat again.

The atmosphere was amazingly different, and within one minute Dr. Barnett came through and spoke. He continued to talk at great length, and had a most interesting discussion with Mr. Jaquin. For over an hour, without cessation, we continued our talk with the spirits. Only once during that hour was the gramophone used, and then only for a quarter of a record, whilst a spirit was endeavouring to gain a little more power for materializing his voice.

Bert Everett spoke with us for a long time, as did Kokum, in his tremendous tones.

Pat O'Brien also talked with us on various subjects.

Whilst Dr. Barnett was discussing the ectoplasmic fingerprints with Mr. Jaquin, he said, referring to the feet marks of the bird, that Annie had brought this blue bird with her.

To Mr. Noel Jaquin there came through, using the luminous trumpet, a spirit announcing itself as "George Gregory"—a brother-in-law who has spoken on another occasion at Dorincourt.

Warren came through, speaking clearly and distinctly in the independent voice to my wife, and Valiantine, and myself. Warren remembered having seen Mr. Jaquin at a sitting at Dorincourt and they discussed how Warren had said what an excellent idea it was of Mr. Jaquin's that the endeavour should be made to get a spirit imprint.

The voices throughout were wonderful, but at the close Dr. Barnett said that they could not manage to materialize a spirit hand, but that they would make a further trial at some future time.

The contrast in the results of these two sittings on one evening was very striking.

57

Pat Bradley asks an impartial question about a boat and is given a satisfactory answer—An Alsatian wolfhound hears a spirit voice in the daylight.

Wednesday, April 22, 1925.

PAT had asked a few children to Dorincourt on this day, and they had arranged for some games in the garden.

The rain was coming down in torrents in the morning, and his mother suggested that it would be better to postpone it until the next day.

Pat, however, did not want to do this, and said that he would like to talk to the spirits and ask them about the weather. He found Mr. Valiantine, and they had a sitting together in the full daylight. Little Bobby Worrall came through, and Pat asked him about the weather.

BOBBY: I should let your friends come, because I think the weather will clear up later on (which it did, about midday).

Bert Everett spoke to Pat, and in the room was my Alsatian wolfhound—Mike. Whilst Bert Everett was talking he called out in a jocular tone, "Good morning, Mike." The dog leapt up and looked at the point in space from which the sound of the voice came. They say that a dog can see spirit forms, but whether the dog saw or not, he heard the voice.

Pat, who was then expecting a new boat, asked Bobby when it was coming.

THE WISDOM OF THE GODS

BOBBY: On Friday.
And it did.
Bobby promised to be one of Pat's guides during life.

58

An anonymous statesman's experience at Dorincourt—Lord Curzon says he is alive—Lord Northcliffe reminds HDB of an important omission—The statesman receives a warning.

Wednesday, April 22, 1925.

IT had been arranged some few weeks back that this evening should be reserved for a certain gentleman who must remain anonymous. I can only say that he is one of the few really great men of intellect in Britain.

He has occupied one of the highest positions in the State, but there are political reasons why his name should not be mentioned.

We all dined quietly before the sitting, and there were present Valiantine, my wife, myself, and the anonymous gentleman, whose first experience of a séance this was.

The conditions appeared to be quite good, as after the first record had been completed upon the gramophone Dr. Barnett came through and spoke.

Bert Everett spoke in his shrill tones; Kokum spoke, and also Pat O'Brien, who stayed for some little time, addressing each of the quartette. Bobby Worrall spoke with us, and referred to Pat's doings during the daytime.

The first of the personal spirits which manifested was that of George Curzon (Lord Curzon of Kedleston), using the luminous trumpet. He spoke on two or three occasions to the anonymous sitter and to me. He referred to certain well-known characters in the political arena whom he wished to be informed that he (Lord Curzon) was alive. During the conversation he was insistent upon the point of the possibility of a coming catastrophe, which would be likely to have a terrible effect upon our civilization, saying: "You must use every endeavour to stop those wars. Tell the——Tell——"[159]

Lord Curzon referred to his last illness, and he then volunteered the name of Dr. John Everidge, and made a reference to an operation which had been performed on him.

The reference to Dr. John Everidge I omitted to record in my notes at the time, although the name was, of course, heard by the four of us. My attention was drawn to this important omission by the spirit of Lord Northcliffe, speaking in his own voice at a séance held on the following Friday, and this extraordinary incident is recorded in Chapter 61.

I asked the anonymous sifter, who knew Lord Curzon quite well, if he knew whether Dr. John Everidge had attended Lord Curzon. He replied that he did not know, and added that he had never heard of Dr. Everidge. Neither had any of us.

A little later, using the luminous trumpet, another spirit addressed the anonymous sitter. This voice spoke to him in tones which vibrated with emotion. It was the spirit of a very near relative. The sitter could not hear what was said very distinctly—he is a trifle hard of hearing—but he continued the conversation throughout with delicate sympathy. Personal messages of love were given through, and although little of what might be termed an evidential character was volunteered, the correct date of the passing over of this spirit was given.[160] Using the luminous trumpet, the spirit voice spoke on several occasions, but at times, apparently, it found it difficult to sustain the power.

After she had gone, the voice of Dr. Barnett came through, and confirmed her actual relationship.

Later, speaking in the independent voice, Annie spoke to me and to my wife. She said that it had been a little difficult for the previous spirit which had spoken to materialize her voice, as it was the first time she had attempted to do so.

At the close Dr. Barnett spoke to us all for some considerable time. During the discussion, it suddenly occurred to me to put a question

---

[159] The names, which I must not publish, were, of course, volunteered.
[160] An evidential point this.

to him upon suicide. I asked him in what degree the crime of suicide, as practised in Europe, was regarded in comparison with the rite of "hari kari" as practised in Japan. Dr. Barnett replied that mentality was regarded, and that when the mind conceived "hari kari" as a sincere sacrifice, it could not be regarded in the same light as the crime of suicide, which was the revenge of body upon soul, through despair.

Dr. Barnett discussed with us various subjects, but in particular dealt with a catastrophe which was likely to happen within the next one or two years. Speaking in very determined tones to the anonymous sitter, he said that unless a great wave of spirituality should sweep over the world, the next war, which would be waged from the air, would destroy our civilization. He said that the crucial years were from this very moment until 1927, and he impressed upon us the urgent necessity of spreading spirituality as the only possible means of averting this disaster.

59

A sitting for the purpose of obtaining supernormal imprints, Mr. Noel Jaquin assisting—Mr. Christopher Marlowe, M.A.— Mr. Jaquin discusses the ectoplasmic hand with Dr. Barnett— Imprints of a signature and of a butterfly—Mr. Charles Sykes' view of the butterfly—Mr. Marlowe's impression—Mr. Jaquin's analysis of the imprints—The author: "These imprints will confound the criticism of the great scientists."

I

Thursday, April 23, 1925.

THIS sitting was held for the specific purpose of endeavouring to obtain, if possible, some more supernormal imprints.

Mr. Noel Jaquin took the precaution of taking the impressions of the hands of Valiantine, of each member of my family, and of all the servants at Dorincourt, in order to see if there was any similarity in outline to the imprint of the hand which had been taken on the previous Saturday. None bore any resemblance.

The number of sitters on this occasion was slightly larger than usual. In addition to Valiantine, my wife, and myself, there were present: Mrs. Robert Graham, Miss Winifred Graham, Mr. Charles Sykes, Mrs. Sykes, Mr. Christopher Marlowe, M. A., of St. John's College, Cambridge, and Mr. Noel Jaquin.

It should be mentioned that Mr. Sykes, as an artist, is greatly interested in the impression which had been obtained on the previous Saturday.

Mr. Jaquin prepared the room, and placed various sheets of smoked paper in different parts of the room. Two sheets were placed upon a stool in the centre of the circle. Sheets were also placed on the mantelpiece, on the bookcase, and on the carpet underneath the stool.

After one record had been played Dr. Barnett gave us a greeting.

Bert Everett spoke to us, and gave me the code word indicating that the conditions were satisfactory.

Kokum spoke in loud and vibrating tones. He lifted one of the trumpets, and whirled it round the circle at lightning speed, taking it high in the air, and tapping the ceiling with it.

The spirit of Mrs. Graham's husband, announcing himself as "Bob," spoke to his daughter, and to his wife.

The voice of Mr. Charles Sykes' father spoke to him. He only spoke a sentence or two, and said to Mr. Sykes "We are working on the imprint."

To Mr. Christopher Marlowe a voice came through which was very indistinct at first, but on the second attempt it announced itself by name as a relative of his. Only a few sentences were spoken, during which Mr. Marlowe mentioned something about her being dead. The voice replied very firmly: "I am not dead."

After this a voice, using the luminous trumpet, announced itself as "George Gregory," and spoke for a very short time to Mr. Jaquin. The voice said: "We are doing our best to help you"; meaning, presumably, that they were doing their best to get some impressions upon the smoked paper.

Warren spoke for a short time in the independent voice.

All these conversations were very short. It was apparent that the power was being conserved for another purpose.

Dr. Barnett at one time made the somewhat significant remark: "We are doing our best to help you through." The remark was significant in the respect that, as a rule, he would say: "We are doing our best to help them through."

At the close there was a very interesting discussion between Mr. Noel Jaquin and Dr. Barnett in reference to the ectoplasmic hand, the imprint of which had been given a few days previously.

Towards the end Dr. Barnett said: "We have done our best," and then bade us goodnight.

The lights were then turned on, and on one of the two sheets which had been placed on top of the stool there was the signature of "O. B.

Everett." On another there was the imprint of what might be assumed to be ectoplasm, and on a sheet, which had been placed on the carpet underneath the stool, there was an extraordinary imprint of a butterfly.

With regard to these remarkable impressions I must leave Mr. Noel Jaquin (who is an expert) to deal with the first two, and Mr. Charles Sykes to deal with the imprint of the butterfly.

Mr. Sykes said that it was utterly impossible for this butterfly to be drawn, that it could only be the imprint of the body of a butterfly, and that there was that peculiar quavering of a butterfly's body which could only be rendered by an impression, and not by a drawing.

II

Mr. Charles Sykes' Report:

(Mr. Sykes is not only one of the greatest sculptors, in England, but he is a fine painter. His works have been exhibited in the Royal Academy and in the Paris Salon.)

"I had the good fortune to be present at a very interesting séance, to which Mr. Bradley invited my wife and me, at Dorincourt on Thursday, April 23, 1925.

"It had been Mr. Bradley's desire to obtain, if possible, imprints of materialized hands upon some smoked sheets of paper placed within and without the circle of nine sitters, including Mr. Valiantine, the medium.

"When the room was again in full light there were quite other surprises for us on the three sheets of paper in the centre of our circle. On one was inscribed a large signature, another showed a cloudy form, and the third the distinct imprint of a butterfly which had evidently been impressed back downwards, and measuring nearly two inches across from tip to tip of its opened wings.

"The imprint of this butterfly bears all the appearance of some roguishness (not roguery; it is much too well defined for that). It is an accomplishment in two extremes, which is shown in the first case by the delicacy in which the smoked surface of the paper has been disturbed by the very soft texture of the wings, and in the second case by the relatively great force expressed by several distinctly embossed impressions of the corners of the wings, the two eyes and the antennae, which becomes clearly visible while holding the reverse side of this firmly made paper edgeways to the light.

"Someone asked if it would be possible to draw it so well by hand. In full daylight it might be possible to copy it, laboriously, after the lithographic fashion, but to invent it—well, it is too exact.

"It has been suggested that a rubber stamp might render a like effect. A rubber stamp would not be fine enough. It has also been suggested that it might be done by the model of a butterfly made in metal—but where would be the velvety impression of the wing surface?

"It should be mentioned also that there is an obvious drag action, mostly left at the serrated edges of the lower portions of the wings, and a very slight drag at the shoulders and top edges of the upper wings, yet all appears steady at the body, the eyes and the antennae.

"It is difficult to determine whether this drag was caused on being impressed or released, or by a flutter of the wings only.

"The piece of paper on which the butterfly appeared had been laid upon the soft carpet, underneath a leather seated stool which had crossbars to its four legs. These crossbars were less than a hand's width from the floor, and close to the crossbar nearest to my feet was the imprint of the butterfly with its abdomen pointing in my direction. This description of its position is made to explain how difficult it would have been to make the impression with a stamping device, when the crossbar would have halted the natural action of the hand returning towards the body, which is the direction of the dragged effect. Even if this could have been done, the solid body of the person would have had to pass between me and the illuminated trumpets, and I should have seen the luminant crossed sharply by the passing of the solid form, for during the sitting I had easily been able to notice the shape of one trumpet cutting sharply in front of the glow from its companion on rising from the floor whenever some voice wished to use it."

Mr. Christopher Marlowe's Note.

"On Thursday, April 23, 1925, owing to Mr. Dennis Bradley's kindness, I was enabled to attend the first séance in my experience. Being naturally open-minded and entirely ignorant of all such phenomena, I did not expect very much to happen, but the results absolutely staggered me. The genuineness of the voice of a relation, who communicated a private and personal message, which would be perfectly unintelligible to the other sitters, is incontrovertible, and the comment of Dr. Barnett to sit up and not cross my legs—I was leaning forward at the time in the dark—appears also inexplicable by human means. I was certainly amazed by the reality and power of the spirit-forces and by the wonderful clearness of the imprints. Seeing that all the power was concentrated on making these imprints, the fact that a special message was communicated to me takes on a new and deeper significance."

Mr. Noel Jaquin's Report.
Mr. Noel Jaquin's report deals with the supernormal incidents of Saturday, April 18, Tuesday, April 21, and Thursday, April 23, 1925.

"Being a specialist on the human hand, it was only natural that the idea of obtaining an imprint of these solid substances which materialized in the darkness of the séance room, was to my mind, of the utmost importance.

"In this Mr. Bradley agreed, but he thought it was much more likely that results might be obtained if I were present. This did not appear to me to be entirely reasonable. If the spirits of the dead are able under certain conditions to materialize a hand so that persons sitting can be touched, it seemed to me but a simple matter to place the hand upon smoked paper.

"On Monday, April 20, I was asked to see Mr. Bradley in London, and he informed me that on the previous Saturday evening at Dorincourt the imprint of such a hand had been made. I had given Mr. Bradley a cork lined case which I use for carrying smoked sheets of paper; the paper was ready for the making of impressions and secured by means of drawing pins. In order to take the imprint of the human hand the paper must always be removed from the case, and laid upon a folded duster, so that it is perfectly flat, in order that the pad beneath ensures an impression of the hollow palm surface being taken. This Mr. Bradley did not know, so he had simply placed the case as it was upon a stool in the centre of the circle. The carboned surface of the paper is so delicate that the least touch will mark it, and the imprints are fixed afterwards with a solution of gum and spirit.

"On Tuesday 21, I went down to Dorincourt to examine the imprints. One was that of a hand, the other the two feet of a small bird. I then took the imprints of the hands of the sitters, but there was no resemblance between the spirit hand and those of the people in the house. In the two imprints made at the Saturday night sitting there was one baffling point of difference. The imprint of the man's hand was quite clear, and devoid of lines, not even the skin ridges were marked, yet in the imprint of the bird's feet there were clearly the cell-like markings of skin. These cell-like formations both in size and in shape are those of a small bird. In addition the claw markings are clearly defined.

"After dinner on this evening, a sitting was held which was a negative one. This ended at eight forty-five p.m. Two of the guests then returned to town, so that at nine o'clock Mr. and Mrs. Bradley, George Valiantine and myself returned to the study. Almost at once we were greeted by the deep voice of a man. This was Dr. Barnett. Mr. Bradley introduced me and told him that I was impressed with the imprints. I then proceeded to ask one or two questions as to the imprints, and in a very deliberate manner Dr. Barnett concisely answered. Some of these questions and answers were very involved and scientific, and I do not think that anyone without a deal of scientific knowledge could have answered them, certainly not as the Doctor replied. He explained that the first imprint, that of the human hand, was an ectoplasmic hand; that is a hand covered or built up of ectoplasm, whereas the imprints of the bird's feet were made by an actual materialized bird held loosely together with ectoplasmic forces. In answer to a question as to the lines in the hand imprint, he explained that at the base of the thumb these were not nerve lines, but were made by the joint of the thumb causing a natural creasing of the ectoplasm. This was a point that I had observed when first examining the imprint, and in this I knew that the answer was correct.

"I asked Dr. Barnett if he agreed with the theory that disease was caused primarily by mental attitude and that bacterial infection and the consequent symptoms were only the material expressions of this deeper cause.

"In slow and measured tones he explained that this was only partly correct, that a lack of balance in the chemistry of the physical body could be equally responsible for the development of disease. In answer to further questions he explained that this was the explanation of inherited predispositions.

"I then asked if he did not agree that scientists were working on wrong lines in concentrating on the materialistic aspect of disease, disregarding almost entirely the mental aspect. To this he replied: 'Your scientists, sir, are babes.'

"During the sitting we heard voices coming from various parts of the room, some from our own level, some from high in the air, and others from the trumpet. The voice of Bert Everett, I must admit, caused me to jump, not that I am a 'nervy' type, but the effect of the unexpected, high-pitched voice coming from high in the air was most weird.

"Dr. Barnett, Bert Everett, Kokum, George Gregory (a brother-in-law of mine), and Warren Clarke all spoke, each without the aid of the trumpet, with the exception of George Gregory.

"A further experimental sitting was arranged for Thursday, April 23, and we asked these spirits to assist us to the best of their ability. This they promised to do.

Thursday, April 23, 1925.
"On Thursday I arrived at Dorincourt at five-fifteen p.m., bringing with me fresh paper, which I smoked in the study myself. As a scientific investigator I took every necessary precaution; I regarded it as essential to work upon the assumption of the possibility of trickery somewhere. I took the fingerprints of all the servants, including the gardener and chauffeur. None of these in any way resemble the imprint of the ectoplasmic hand made on the previous Saturday.

"There is no need to give again the names of the sitters. The study and the chairs around the circle were prepared in my presence. I had placed sheets of prepared paper round the room; upon a stool in the centre I had placed two sheets side by side, I placed another on the mantelpiece, and one upon a bookcase, and underneath the bars of a leather seated stool, upon the carpeted floor beneath, I placed one other sheet. In addition to these articles, there were two trumpets standing.

"All having taken their places, Mr. Bradley was about to switch off the light when I asked him to wait one moment, and, under the pretence of rearranging the papers, I marked them A B C, noting exactly the positions in which I had placed them. The lights were then turned off. Mr. Bradley was sitting beside the gramophone, and I was on his left hand, exactly in the doorway, so that no one could enter or leave the room without my knowledge.

"One record only had been played, when from near the floor came the voice of Dr. Barnett, saying 'Good evening, souls.'

"Bert Everett spoke to Mr. Bradley, then the trumpet was lifted and went over to Mr. Charles Sykes (the famous artist) and he spoke for a moment or two with his father. This voice ended by saying: 'The others are working on the imprint.'

"Soon after the trumpet was again lifted, and came over to me, and without any hesitation the following words came through, clearly and strongly, 'Noel, it is George Gregory. We are doing all we can to help you.'

"The trumpet resumed its position upon the floor before I had time to reply in any way.

"During the sitting there were short conversations by various spirits with everyone sitting. In the case of Mr. Christopher Marlowe, who had never sat before, it was remarkable that the voice of Dr. Barnett should suddenly say: 'Would the gentleman sitting next to Mrs. Bradley uncross his legs and sit up straight.' This Mr. Marlowe at once complied with. Who could have known that he was sitting thus?

"I remarked in a whisper to Mr. Bradley: 'When the show is over, would you ask everyone to retain their seats until I have examined the 'papers?' No sooner had the word 'papers' left my lips than the voice of Bert Everett remarked: 'He calls it a show. He will be eating popcorn in a minute.' I am convinced that the nearest sitter could not have heard my whisper.

"At the end of the sitting, Dr. Barnett said that they had done the best they could for us. I then asked if they had made the imprint of an ectoplasmic hand, or of a materialized hand. He replied: 'Neither, we have used a mixture of both and we have done the best we can for you.'

"At the end of the sitting Mr. Bradley asked that everyone should remain seated until I had examined the papers. When the lights went up, I at once went over to the stool and examined the papers, which were exactly in the same positions that I had placed them. On one was the impression of some soft substance and the imprint of a thumb, but with no trace of the skin's ridges. On the other paper the signature 'O. B. Everett,' and some smear-like marks. Upon the paper which was beneath the stool was the delicate impress of a butterfly. These impressions were at once fixed by me with a solution of gum and spirit before I allowed them to be handled by any of the sitters.

"I stayed the night at Dorincourt, and early next morning went into the study with Pat Bradley, who is aged nine. I asked him to let me have a look at the trumpet used the night before. I then held it in my right hand, and asked Pat to put his ear to the smaller end. It must be understood that the morning was bright and clear. The sun was streaming into the room, and within two seconds there were distinct raps from the inside of the cone. Just after this Valiantine entered the room, and I requested him to hold the trumpet while I listened. This he did, holding it at arm's length while I placed my ear to the smaller end. Within three or four seconds there came the whispered greeting from the voice of my brother-in-law, George Gregory. I then asked him why they had not given the imprint of a hand; the reply was indistinct. After a pause he remarked: 'There is the impression of my thumb upon the paper at the lower edge.' Here I should mention that the thumb mark referred to is, like the imprint of the hand, an ectoplasmic impression.

"I then asked George Gregory some personal questions, which were satisfactorily answered.

"It was certainly impossible for Valiantine to have answered these questions had he the knowledge with which to reply, as I could see his face the whole of the time, and furthermore, the sound came from inside the trumpet.

"I am convinced that had there been trickery I should have detected it in these impressions. The imprint of the hand is not complete, and the thumb was not fully materialized. This Bert Everett knew, as he told me on the Tuesday evening. Since then I have tried to reproduce, by means of kid gloves and rubber, an imprint like the one given on Saturday, but without success. This incomplete thumb is important. The second joint of the human thumb is generally hollow, and it is very difficult to get it impressed, certainly without the top phalange.

"The imprint of the butterfly is most fragile, and it must have laid upside down upon the paper. Had this been done with an actual fly I should have detected the scales from the wings, which come off at the slightest touch. A rubber stamp would have rendered the outline hard, and taken away most of the carbon particles. I asked Mr. Sykes if an artist with the most delicate brush could reproduce a like impression of a fly on smoked paper. His reply was decidedly in the negative. Then, apart from the imprints, there are the voices; no one man could have given such a dramatic display.

"I am convinced that these are supernormal imprints. How they were made we cannot be quite certain. In the matter of the butterfly the opinion of an artist like Mr. Sykes must count before mine."

Imprint of spirit signature obtained on April 23, 1925.

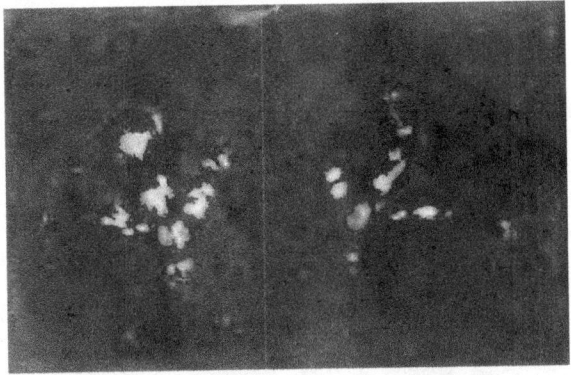

Imprint of materialised bird's feet obtained on April 18, 1925.

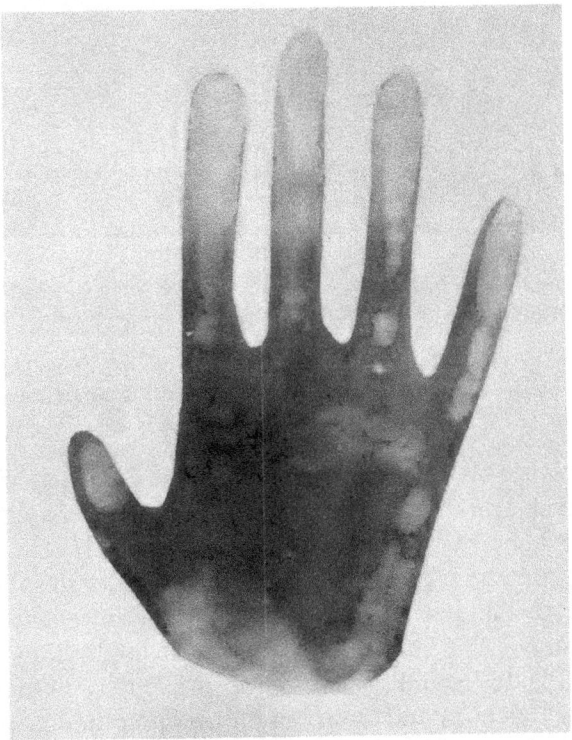

Imprint of ectoplasmic hand obtained on April 18th, 1925. To obtain a clear reproduction this imprint has been cut and mounted by Mr. Noel Jaquin.

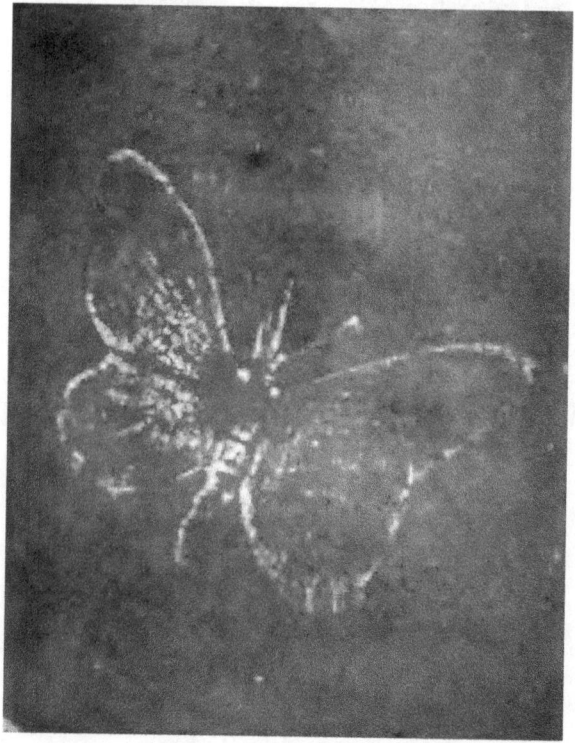

This super-normal imprint of the materialised form of a butterfly was obtained under rigid test conditions arranged by Mr. Noel Jaquin on April 23rd, 1925. The actual size from wing to wing of the original is two inches. The reproduction is enlarged for clearness.

Thus the reports of two distinguished experts. One, that of one of the greatest experts on imprints, and the other that of a very great artist. These reports show that these are proved to be supernormal imprints. To me they are remarkable because of their wonderful subtlety. Even if the butterfly had been a drawing, and not an impression, it would have been impossible for any living human being to draw a butterfly in the dark, and it would be just as impossible for a human being to take a butterfly's body and force its imprint upon the smoked paper.

We asked for a material sign and proof of spiritual phenomena, and the sign is given by the impression of a blue bird, and that of a butterfly. The cry for the material was answered by poetic symbols. These impressions will confound the criticism of the great scientists.

60

Mr. Charles Sykes' record of a daylight sitting—He discusses the butterfly imprint with the spirit of his father—Mrs. Sykes' notes.

I

Friday morning, April 24, 1925.

MR. CHARLES SYKES was so impressed by the experiment on the previous evening that he was extremely anxious to have the opportunity of hearing the voices in the daylight. He and his wife therefore motored down from London early the next morning.

In the full daylight, with the morning sun flooding the room, Mr. Charles Sykes spoke first with his father and then with his mother.

Mrs. Sykes then sat, and she spoke for a while with her mother.

Because of its supreme importance, one must reiterate the fact that Valiantine's face at these sittings can always be clearly observed, and that the voices are heard away from him.

I append Mr. Sykes' account.

II

"On Friday, the following morning, I had my first experience of a daylight sitting.

"It was twelve forty-five midday, summer time, with sunlight in the room. Mr. Valiantine took for himself the most comfortable upholstered chair, resting his elbow upon its soft arm, and, holding the wide end of the trumpet in his left hand, he invited me to put my ear to the narrow end, and to squat in front of him on a leather-seated stool which sank at my weight, and stuck its corners into my early middle-aged flesh.

"However, I could swivel about on this, and see his complete figure.

"In a few seconds there were tappings within the trumpet in ones and twos, and some hilarious rattlings.

I made several attempts to find out who was tapping, and then asked if they could speak. I was answered by two taps. I expressed my patience, and very shortly afterwards was addressed by a familiar name. Asking who spoke, I was answered that it was my father. Remembering that his voice had spoken to me on the evening before, saying: 'We are working on the imprint now, Charley,' I discussed the production of the butterfly impression. My father was an artist, and he explained that the embossed effect was caused by the force from below drawing the butterfly downwards on to the paper, and not by the wet fixative blown on to the paper by Mr. Jaquin. It had been a difficult work. He had been employed, with others, in this production, and they were very pleased with their success. He was very jocular and gay in his manner, and even gave me some tender and fatherly advice, which was just what I deserved, though I am not quite so young as when we last met together at his home.

"He also brought my mother's voice to speak to me. I changed ears on the trumpet, swiveling on the stool, and taking a fresh view of Mr. Valiantine, who was by this time beginning to look tired and pale.

"My mother's voice and manner were characteristic, undemonstrative, but deeply affectionate. Hoped I would come again to speak with her. Wished me to speak to her at my own home. Rejected my suggestion that I might be heavy and loutish in such a case, and begged me to try. Told me what had passed between her most intimate sister and me within the few days just elapsed.

"Mr. Valiantine afterwards showed me the phosphorescent parts of the trumpet—how they had gained in luminosity during the sitting, in contrast with the other trumpet which had not been in use since the night before. I must have been a little tiresome—I had kept the conversation up so long."

Mrs. Sykes' Notes

"At the conclusion of my husband's sitting I entered the room which Mr. Valiantine had not vacated.

"Seated on the stool in front of him, and holding the trumpet to my ear as instructed, I had not a minute to wait before hearing my name called.

"My astonishment was so great that my presence of mind seemed to desert me. On asking who spoke, the voice replied: 'Mother,' and said, 'Father and Cecile (my sister) are here, and wish to speak.'

"I trembled violently, feeling I could not control my mind sufficiently to hit upon questions that would lift the conversations above the merest commonplace, and knowing how quickly gone are these voices, and how remote was my chance of getting in touch again.

"The sitting yielded no more than greetings and statements of happiness. But that was entirely my fault since it was the trend of my conversation."

61

The last of a wonderful series of séances—The fine friendships of this life kept intact and immeasurably strengthened in the next—The great Truth of Survival established, not upon myth or upon belief, but upon the solid foundation of knowledge.

Friday, April 24, 1925.

VALIANTINE was due to sail back to his home in America on the following morning. This is therefore the record of the last of this wonderful series of séances.

Towards the end, supernormal events had crowded one upon the other with supernormal rapidity, yet despite the strain I was feeling of the long and varied experiences, I could not help feeling a little sad, knowing, since a rest was imperative, that it would probably be many months before I heard the audible voices of my friends speak to me again.

I should have preferred an entirely private sitting, but this was impossible, as some of my friends were anxious to be present. Unfortunately, on this evening I had a racking headache, and at one time thought it would be impossible for me to sit. Valiantine, however, treated my head and eyes by massage with his fingers and thumbs, and succeeded in relieving the pain enormously.

Pat had begged to be allowed to sit up so that, as he said, "he might say goodbye to the spirits."

The circle consisted of Valiantine, my wife, Pat, Miss Madeleine Cohen, Miss Louise Owen, Mr. Hannen Swaffer, and myself.

We did not trouble to play any music, and Dr. Barnett came through within less than a minute and spoke with us.

At frequent intervals the other guides, Bert Everett, Kokum, Hawk Chief, and Bobby Worrall spoke.

Young Pat was simply wonderful. He chatted away with them all joyfully, without pause. Pat is easily the best sitter I have ever known. He is far better than the most experienced student of psychics with whom I have sat, and he is ten times more intelligent and interesting in his conversation with the spirits than the majority of spiritualists. All that so many can say when they have achieved the miracle of speaking with a voice on another plane is some fatuous remark such as, "Are you happy?" or else, "Have you any message?" This is such a silly greeting; it is not the welcome that should be accorded. It is as if when I walked into a drawing room in Mayfair, my hostess, looking askance at me, inquired: "Have you any message?" in which case I should immediately walk out again. Pat seems to create a continuous vibration, which attracts an immediate and fluent response from the spirits with whom he is talking. He would be invaluable as a tutor to some of the scientific investigators, in order to teach them how to become good sitters. All the guides were charming to him, and the tones of their voices evidenced the love they felt for him. It was intriguing to hear Bobby Worrall talking to Pat on his childish doings. These two are firm friends, and the friendship is quite as firm as any that might exist between two children living together on the Earth plane.

Bert Everett laughed and joked with Pat. Kokum and Hawk Chief both came through and spoke to him, and, at the same time the voices of these two spirits joined each other, and on more than one occasion they were both speaking simultaneously.

The spirit of Miss Madeleine Cohen's mother spoke words of love to her. Lord Northcliffe, in the independent voice, spoke to Miss Louise Owen, to Mr. Swaffer, and to me. Whilst he was talking to me he referred to Lord Curzon coming through. Northcliffe stated that he was also present on the previous Wednesday and had heard what had taken place. He then volunteered the following statement: "Don't forget, Mr. Bradley, that Curzon mentioned Dr. John Everidge when he was talking to you." (See Chapter 58.) This is quite a remarkable statement because I had forgotten to record that on the previous Wednesday Curzon had mentioned Dr. Everidge, and made certain references to him and to his last illness. None of those present on that night—not even the anonymous sitter (I asked him at the time), who knew Lord Curzon personally—knew that Dr. Everidge had attended Lord Curzon. In fact, none of us knew his name, and it was only at the precise moment of dictating this paragraph that my secretary ascertained by the directory that there is such a doctor, and also ascertained over the telephone that he had attended Lord Curzon.

Georgie spoke to me and to my wife, and was awfully pleased to see Pat sitting in the circle. This was the first time that Pat had spoken to his young cousin. Georgie had passed away before Pat was born, so he had never heard his voice before. He spoke to Pat in a charmingly natural manner.

Annie spoke in her quietly modulated tones, and together she and I talked with that intimate understanding which has always existed between us. There was great love and perfect sympathy in her tones, and just before she left me she placed her hand affectionately on my forehead. It was a most tender action. The hand was fully materialized, and I could feel the warmth of her fingers. She told me that she would always be with me, and that she would help me with all her power throughout life. I spoke to her of our own private voice séances, and she said that it would be quite all right for us to resume holding these in the coming autumn, after I had taken the necessary rest.

Warren spoke with us in his usual cheerful manner. He thanked Valiantine for the great work that he had done. To my wife he spoke in terms of great affection in the same terms of affection with which they had always regarded each other, for they were great friends on Earth, and this friendship has not only continued intact, but has become immeasurably strengthened since he has passed over. To me he spoke about my work and of the many experiences which have been recounted in this book, which he said would have an infinitely greater effect upon the world than I imagined. I told him that I should miss the sound of his voice, and that of Annie during the period of rest which I was about to take. He said that they would both be able to get into mind communication with me whenever I wished. Before Warren left he placed his hand—fully materialized upon my head, and then said goodnight to each of the sitters in turn.

In the records contained in this book I feel that I have failed to do justice to the wonderful characters of my sister and of Warren Clarke. I have purposely refrained from giving details of their stimulating and encouraging talks to me on account of the mass of other experiences which it has been necessary to publish. Yet both of these characters have done great work, and have given marvelous evidence of survival. Together, they represent the foundation, not of my belief, but of my knowledge.

The sitting by this time had lasted for over an hour, and it was long past Pat's bedtime. It was arranged, therefore, that he should slip quietly from the room, and, after calling goodnight to the spirits, he went out.

The breaking of the circle certainly affected the vibrations, and the sitting did not last very much longer.

I thanked Dr. Barnett for his brilliant discourses, telling him that it was impossible for me adequately to convey them in the published records, since I could only briefly indicate a small part of all that he had said.

I also thanked each of the other guides in turn for the phenomenal work which they had done, and for the help they had given us in bringing through the spirit friends of the numerous people who had sat with us at Dorincourt.

Whilst Pat O'Brien was talking with me he placed his materialized hand upon my head.

Dr. Barnett closed the sitting, and thus ended a series of the most remarkable séances which has ever been held. A series which represents probably the greatest advance in knowledge that has yet been achieved in the history of psychical research, or in the annals of spiritual communication.

THE LAST CHAPTER

In which the author reviews that which he has done—Exploring the depths and climbing the heights—Defying the scientist and the Churches—The divine law of evolution—The spirit of wisdom.

I

June, 1925.

WHAT is the extent of man's conception?
Blinded by materialism man has barely evolved from a condition of barbaric mental ignorance. And not as yet has he shed the mask of his primitive conceit, nor has he yet begun to realize the magnitude of the eternal spirit.

The insignificant planet man inhabits he imagines to be the apex of existence. When he looks towards the stars, his physical range of sight is far beyond his mental vision—for in his stupendous arrogance he can comprehend no other form of life beyond his own. Before his eyes is stretched the reality of a vast universe, beside which this tiny world is the fraction of an atom—a dancing mote in a sunbeam; yet in his limited perception man conceives human life as all of life, his puny world to comprise the cosmos.

A conglomerate, distorted and hypothetical history of a few thousand years is presented to him, and he imagines that it represents the history of the universe. He is content to assume that his primitive conception

THE LAST CHAPTER

constitutes a cosmic knowledge. He accepts without question a barbaric philosophy; he is chained to tradition, thwarted by convention; he allows his future, physical and spiritual, to be determined for him by the rules and systems of a mediaeval order of thought. As a result he has become either a blatant pro-Earth materialist or a weak superstitionist, vaguely fearing a nebulous heaven and a disgusting hell.

Can any thinker accept these conceptions? All about us is an immense universe, which we can actually see, but of which we know practically nothing. We live upon a planet infinitesimal in relation to space, and our human history has occupied the fraction of a second in relation to time. Is it logical to imagine that the universe is meaningless: a chaotic, irresponsible, unintelligent, and uncontrolled mass of lifelessness? Such a contention is absurd. The universe is a magnificently ordered scheme, controlled by an Intelligence infinitely beyond the Earthly.

Eternity is beyond mathematical reasoning; we must accept eternity in the terms of the boon of time to enable us to acquire knowledge.

We have barely arrived at the infancy of human understanding; yet we stand on the threshold of a great Truth.

The material discoveries of the twentieth century are above the wildest dreams of our fathers. We have conquered the air by defeating gravitation; our wireless communications have conquered distance; scientists have produced poison gases that can annihilate civilization, should the governments incline towards international suicide.

Despite the amazing material progress in invention and discovery—unprecedented in the history of mankind—it is a moot point whether that progress has tended towards good or evil. When the philosopher glances at the chaotic unrest existent everywhere—mental, physical, spiritual—he is not readily reassured by the materialistic argument.

The obsession of materialism is the death of the finer spirit of man. The Divine Intelligence concedes to man the priceless gift of free will. He is afforded limitless opportunities to advance materially and spiritually or to remain lethargic and stagnate and decay.

God made us free and gave us free wills. It is only man who forges chains around man. It is only man who restricts, restrains, cripples, and blinds.

We are living in the most materialistic age this world has known. The miracles of yesterday are the material facts of today. It is significant and symptomatic that the inexplicable material discoveries of our modern age should be counter-balanced by our recent psychical or spiritual discoveries. It is so that a magnificent new channel of thought is opened, offering possibilities beyond conception.

II

The key to wisdom is within man's reach.

The extent of man's knowledge hitherto has been confined to one small material Earth.

We have made a tremendous leap. We have established actual communication with the people of another world—a people of a higher and more refined intelligence than ourselves. This epoch-making—this proven fact must be accepted by the physicist, the priest, and the poet.

And I assert, after studied deliberation, that this fact never before has been indisputably proved. Religions have preached survival, but have relied upon faith and myth. Modern psychic literature has established proofs of supernormal phenomena of a physical character, but has failed to collate the reiterated sequence of volunteered mental evidence necessary to convince the dispassionate investigator.

The fact that by some strange and unexpected chance I spoke to the spirit of my sister in America did not lead me to imagine that the world would or should accept this personal incident as an all-sufficing evidence of a colossal reality.

The first revelation of two years ago was vivid and impressive, but subsequent revelations have become even more vivid, and my knowledge has advanced.

For two years I have collected evidence in order that the unprejudiced student of the future may form a proper—a just—opinion of the actual presentation of proved facts.

I shall write no more books of evidence of survival: I am surfeited with evidence; I am weary of it.

I have no wish to dissipate more time on dreary recollections of the "evidential" names, the dull places and the mundane events which happened on Earth. Spirits possessing a high intelligence despise these questions about their primitive and physical existence. Such are offensive to their intellects, yet they have answered, and have given irrefutable evidence of their surviving personalities.

We and they have established the fact of spiritual communication beyond dispute. Further development must be of a philosophical nature. We must conserve our opportunities and refine our minds in tune with the spirits of a higher plane.

There are ten thousand things I desire to learn.

Since this work has achieved its purpose of presenting irrefutable evidence, before analysing the considerable advance it represents in

THE LAST CHAPTER

psychical research, it would be interesting to consider the attitude of the pseudoscientific critic.

III

During June, 1925, the *Morning Post* printed a debate on spiritualism between Sir Arthur Conan Doyle and Sir Arthur Keith. Doyle was the advocate and Keith the antagonist. Doyle won on points. This was inevitable, for Doyle was armoured with knowledge, whilst Keith was handicapped by ignorance.

Now, Sir Arthur Keith is an exceptionally clever man, and brilliant in his own particular branch of science, but he is a baby in psychics. He is a good-humored opponent, but in his *Morning Post* articles he fell into every psychical pitfall.

Obviously he has never read one scientific work on psychics, and confessed he has never experienced one séance, yet had the audacity to assert: "There is no method of investigation used by spiritualists which we have left untried. They have no means which are not accessible to us." Such a statement, after his confession of ignorance, can only be taken humorously. But it would be interesting to know whether Keith would desire us to accept it in the ironic, the satiric, the comic, or the mediaeval sense. I incline towards the "comic" definition, since that is the more logical, and the more obvious.

Sir Arthur Keith's views, however, do represent a considerable section of unsophisticated opinion, which is nineteenth century in knowledge and ideas. He says, "The messages are seldom instructive."

I detest the word "messages," but he is ill-read, for many of the recorded "communications" are brilliant, and are accepted as such by many men of letters and of science.

Sir Arthur Keith assumed that any inexplicable phenomena could be accounted for by the gullibility or susceptibility to illusion of "spiritualists." He advanced the loose contention that all phenomena were the product of heated imagination. Such an argument is merely foolish, and has been disproved by facts.

The most scientific, psychological and intellectual minds are now applied to this study, and phenomena which would stagger Sir Arthur Keith, if he experienced them, are coldly analysed and reduced to their relative degree of insignificance or importance.

But despite the somewhat time-worn, feeble, and infantile arguments used by Sir Arthur Keith, he did touch on some interesting points.

It must be understood that he knows nothing whatever of the research work which has been conducted during the last two years. Keith stated that "the human brain can only accept what it sees, and what it infers has been checked over and over again, and the scientific man will not believe anything is true until independent witnesses, at chosen times, have verified it time upon time." This is sound, and forms a legitimate basis for accepted knowledge. Knowing the density of man's intelligence, that is precisely the principle I have worked upon in my investigations.

I have proved this colossal miracle of actual communication with the living spirits of another world in the presence of hundreds of independent witnesses, and upon hundreds of occasions. The witnesses have all heard the voices, have all talked with them, and the great majority have received intimate and personal proofs of the surviving personalities.

It is in no spirit of arrogance that I insist that never before in history has such a deliberate series of psychic experiments been conducted. In no other branch of science has it been deemed necessary to reiterate so frequently a proven fact before it is accepted. But this fact, which we conceive to be a miracle, is in reality normal and natural, although it necessitates an added comprehension in the undeveloped human mind. That is why it has been necessary to establish it a hundred times before the world could be expected to accept it.

IV

It is natural that any new and rare discovery should be received with skepticism by the average human mind. The mid-Victorian would have ridiculed the idea of telegraphing without wires, just as a hundred years ago smug old admirals derided steam. A scientist, upon hearing the sounds emanating from one of the first gramophones, became indignant at what he believed to be an attempt to deceive him, and stated angrily that he was certain it was a ventriloquial trick. Until the twentieth century, every advance in knowledge was made in the teeth of an uncomprehending opposition and a blind conservatism. The gigantic strides made in material knowledge during the last twenty years have negatived any number of traditional theories, and only recently has bigotry towards physical or material progress ceased to exist.

THE LAST CHAPTER

The modern progress of psychical knowledge is astounding. Communication in the actual, audible voice with the occupants of another world is infinitely more miraculous than the scientifically inexplicable discovery of wireless.

Gradually the scientific and religious bigotry towards psychics is diminishing, and soon those who adhere to their mediaeval ideas will be relegated to the mental dust heap.

The loose and unintelligent assumption that all spiritualistic phenomena have been and are produced by fraud, must be dismissed. This obvious contention has been disproved by an accumulation of ascertained and tested facts.

I assert with confidence that no student of psychics and of spiritualism will fail to obtain a firm conviction of survival, provided he goes about the study with a critical and an open mind. No knowledge is attained without toil.

There are ten thousand and more degrees in psychics, as there are in love and in philosophy. There are as many frauds posing as mediums as there are false mistresses and treacherous friends.

There are many forms of mediumship, and the charlatan invariably takes the easiest course. The simplest method for the fake medium to adopt is to pose as a clairvoyant. No attempt at physical phenomena is necessary; the medium merely talks through his or her own lips, fishes about for names and information from the visitor, and manages, upon occasions, by vague and general references, to impose upon a considerable number of credulous inquirers. This type of charlatan is more vicious than the silly professional fortune-teller or palmist, engaged to occupy a secluded corner and amuse the jaded guests at rag West End supper-parties.

Mrs. Osborne Leonard is a clairvoyant medium, but she is in a class by herself. She stands unique as the best clairvoyant medium the world has known. She enters into, and remains throughout, in a condition of complete trance, and the caliber of the evidence obtained through her is remarkable. There are a few others who are genuine, but with whom the results are found to be variable. There are many others whom I have met who are simply pitiful, and the alleged communications received are an insult to intelligence. I should prefer to anticipate obliteration to survival, if such manifestations represented any indication of an afterlife.

If the critics of psychical phenomena base their judgment upon the lowest form which they may have experienced, they are justified in their satiric censure, but in no form of science, art, or philosophy is it justifiable to base one's opinion upon the lowest degree. It is only fair to judge from the heights, and to base opinion on the summit of acquired knowledge.

Automatic writing is another form of mediumship. It is the favourite and comparatively easy form of individual development.

In rare cases, some very remarkable evidence of survival has been obtained, and occasionally some brilliant philosophical essays have been volunteered. These emanate from the few well-developed automatic writing mediums. As for the rest, I would estimate that 99.99 per cent are either absolute nonsense, or else represent the subconsciously coloured expressions of the mind of the writer. Personally, as a psychical researcher, I would accept nothing as supernormal without veridical evidence, and though I might be intrigued by a philosophy expressed, I should require a confirmation of it in the independent voice of the spirit before I should feel justified in proclaiming any statement as coming from a discarnate entity.

In my study I have deliberately chosen the rarest and most difficult branch. The direct voice is the one really great phenomenon. All other forms of mediumship are subsidiary and insignificant in comparison. It is rare; I have said there are only about a dozen known mediums in the world through whose instrumentality it can be obtained, and with many of these the "voice" phenomena are variable and poor, and the results are often negligible.

The last series of experiments conducted under Valiantine's mediumship is unique, and represents the most amazing development on record.

V

A complete record of the experiments conducted by me with Valiantine is contained in *Toward the Stars*. In this volume there is the record of a further sixty séances held during a period of twelve weeks. A few were negative, but at ninety percent. of them voice phenomena occurred of an amazing character.

These experiments I made with the purpose of studying psychological aspects in connection with psychical phenomena. That is why I have mixed my assemblies. Between two and three hundred persons have sat with me, many of them famous people whose repute is such that their testimony must be accepted. Mentioning the professions—not

THE LAST CHAPTER

necessarily in the order of merit—of those who have been present at the Dorincourt sittings, they are science, medicine, authorship, art, stage, journalism, law, army, sea, politics, and butterflies from the social wheel. Any other profession that I may have omitted to indicate must be put down to inadvertent delicacy.

My choice was not indiscriminate—it was deliberate, The conditions of various mentalities have varying effects upon the production of psychical phenomena. It was valuable to observe these, and to a psychologist, interesting after to note the various mental viewpoints.

It is unnecessary for me to summarize the results obtained; the complete work, and each coldly recorded experience, provide the material for individual study. As a philosophical student, I present effects and facts, and leave the reader to form his own opinion.

To refresh the mind, it should be remembered that at the recorded Valiantine sittings, some hundreds of entirely different spirits spoke in their own "direct voices." The voices have been those of both sexes: men and women, boys and girls, young children. Each voice has been characteristic and has represented a distinct individuality. The evidence volunteered by these spirits of their surviving personality must be accepted by any logical mind.

During the last series of experiments, spirit communicators have spoken in most European languages and in Chinese and Japanese. Certain of the sitters have, on several occasions, in the course of conversation, changed the language from, say, German to English, or Danish to Russian, or Italian to French, and the conversations have been carried on without pause.

Then there is the advanced development of obtaining the spirit voices in full daylight. This represents a further leap forward in psychical phenomena. It has rendered criticism impotent.

The accumulation of mental evidence of the survival of the spirit after bodily death has now established the fact so incontestably that a new criterion of intelligence will have to be accepted, and the man who does acknowledge his belief in spirit communication will be regarded as wise, and the man who does not will be called a fool.

In addition to all the mental evidence given, an exceptionally peculiar illustration of physical phenomena was obtained. The imprints obtained in the smoked paper test of Noel Jaquin are remarkable. Naturally, on this occasion I was an acute observer, but Noel Jaquin, the fingerprint expert, and Charles Sykes, the sculptor, were equally acute.

The most delicate imprint of a butterfly was obtained under test conditions, and in such a way that it was proved to be supernormal.

I defy any scientist in the world to account for this phenomenon by any human material theory.

The scientists, on occasion, become tiresome by their demand for physical proof of phenomena. Here is a material phenomenon presented to them in an artistic form. It is left for them to explain. The symbol is splendidly poetic, and its artistry suggests an ironic sense. That is its quality, and, to me, it is a physical evidence of the fine truth of a surviving sense of humour.

I await with interest a scientific material explanation.

VI

Hitherto, when the skeptical scientists have been presented with the accounts of spiritual phenomena which they cannot explain, they have fallen back upon the feeble theory that they maybe written down and accounted for as "hallucinations." Sir Arthur Keith and many others have advanced this argument. Such a contention is not only illegitimate in serious debate, but it has no basis in fact. Excluding all question of the mental evidence volunteered—though it is conceivable that one person might imagine he heard "voices" speaking, it is not conceivable that a dozen people would, at the same time, also imagine they heard these same "voices." Is it logical to concede the absurd theory that not only was one person hypnotized into this imagination, but that all the sitters were undergoing hypnotic suggestion? But as a scientific investigator, anticipating this contention, I took precautions during my last series of experiments to disprove the argument of this remote possibility. On several occasions I arranged for persons to listen outside the door. Those outside the door heard the "voices" as clearly as those inside the room. Many have heard the spirit "voices" quite distinctly whilst sitting in an adjoining room.

I have answered and disproved in this book every materialistic contention that has been advanced; it is now my privilege to challenge the antagonistic scientists to answer me and nullify my facts if they can.

THE LAST CHAPTER

VII

The establishment of direct communication with the spirits on another plane is not only a wonderful new branch of knowledge, it portends a new philosophy, and a new confirmation of religion.

The somewhat bitter antagonism of the various Churches, and the Roman Catholic Church in particular, is easily understandable, even though it is intellectually silly. The Churches preach survival, but they cannot prove it; their fundamental doctrine depends absolutely upon an afterlife, and yet they endeavour to discredit those who are proving this fact. Why is this? The reason is that they fear actual communication with those who have departed from this life lest they may refute the manufactured ideas and beliefs which the Churches have imposed upon their followers. They are timid lest the reality may disturb the ritual, threaten the autocracy and weaken the powers of government.

The Roman Catholic Church is the most powerful autocracy in the world. It is a very subtle and brilliant organization. It has evolved a fine artistry and has encouraged the arts. It has always ruled the herd with a rigid discipline, and finessed with the intelligentsia with cultured tolerance. I appreciate both these methods. The Church controls newspapers all over the world. This lower branch of the Press has been violent in its abuse of spiritualism. In June, 1925, one of the leading English Catholic weekly papers contained the following statements:

"We have never known man or woman who touched spiritism seriously, who did not suffer mental, moral or physical deterioration."

"Spiritualism is not all fraud. At the back of all there is a reality and that is diabolism."

"It is from hell, beyond all doubt."

"There is no evidence whatever that any spirit is that of a deceased man or woman."

"The whole record of the cult reeks of lies, blasphemies, filth, immorality, and vice."

Such statements as these are contradicted by facts, and intelligent persons do not lay themselves open to obvious contradiction.

Is it evil that nearly every spirit to whom we have spoken is anxiously impressing upon us the necessity of preventing war, lest we destroy our civilization? Is it evil that the spirits tell us they are endeavouring to impress and inspire in us the developments of art, literature, and a more beautiful conception of life? Is it evil that the spirits exude a degree of love and sympathy towards us, infinitely purer than that we experience on Earth? Is it evil that they speak of Christ as the greatest spiritual philosopher that has lived on Earth? If these expressions are evil, and come from hell, then I prefer hell to their nebulous heaven, with its effortless hereafter which they do not even attempt to describe. But neither I, nor anyone else, will go to the mediaeval hell of flames they have invented, nor will I, nor anyone else, pass to the eternal perdition and eternal punishment which, by a barbaric doctrine of fear, the Church holds as a threat to ensure the subjection of the uneducated masses.

The violent bigotry of this section of the Church must not be taken as representative of its intellect. I was educated as a Roman Catholic. I have a respect for the Church, and am on intimate terms with several of its leaders, who have discussed my psychical studies with me at considerable length, and who are greatly impressed by the evidence of progress.

There is in spiritualism no refutation of Christ, or of His principles. He was the great Spirit, and the effect of His work can never be destroyed.

He was the greatest medium that has lived. That is the explanation of all the miracles accorded to Him, and the resurrection of His body maybe assumed as His spiritual materialization.

I am an historian and a psychologist, and will venture a forecast. Within this twentieth century the Roman Catholic Church will accept the fact of direct spirit communication, and will adapt her religious philosophy to embrace this new discovery.

There are nearly a million spiritualists in England alone. There is no need to build new churches; nor invent new religions. There should be only one religion.

An international institution, such as the Roman Catholic Church, moves warily, and whatever iniquities she may have committed in the past by thwarting psychical development, she has been right in not accepting spirit communication until the value of the fact has been proved.

No established religion has been able to offer the proof of survival, nor has it suggested any eternal occupation beyond "resting in peace" on a billowy cloud.

What we have now learnt from the direct evidence of the spirits who have communicated with us is that our physical span on Earth is relatively a mere second of our existence, and the shedding of the bodily chrysalis is our first flight towards a limitless vista of learning, in which omniscience is still beyond conception.

The Churches talk loosely of God, and they reduce Him to a finite level.

It would be wiser to assume that no man departing from his first Earthly stage is fit to approach God. The higher spirits can conceive and reverence the Omnipotent Intelligence, which is the God of the Universe, but countless millions of years may elapse before they are qualified by gradual stages of acquired knowledge to enter into the condition of the Godlike Ones.

VIII

Only the really great man is humble enough to own the scantiness of his knowledge. The material scientific progress, remarkable as it may appear, is only initial, and few of our intellects have advanced beyond finite conceptions. It is only an exaggerated ego that disputes immortality. Mr. Bernard Shaw has conceived a material Methuselah and prolonged the physical beyond human patience. He expresses an aversion from spiritual immortality when he says: "A man may believe that he has a soul without believing anything so monstrous as that he is going to live forever." But what might appear monstrous to a Shaw might appear alluring to another. It is a matter of individual philosophy. To retain my own personality after leaving this speck of dust, and then to explore the knowledge and magnificence of the universe, to commune with minds beside which the greatest intellects here are relatively those of puking infants—that represents to me a faint conception of the magnitude of eternity.

It is to Shaw's credit, however, that after going back to Methuselah he resuscitated Joan of Arc. And, incidentally, he is the only man who has made a fortune out of the voices, though Joan's were merely clairaudient and entirely unauthenticated.

There is a divine law in evolution. Man is given free will and opportunities on Earth in order that he may develop his mentality by his efforts. The purpose of his physical existence is that of a preliminary examination to lay the foundations for his next stage. His intellect maybe judged by the difficulties he has overcome. To illustrate the standard in a material sense, it is now an insignificant feat for a man to take an aeroplane from London and fly to Paris, but it was an astounding feat for Wilbur Wright to fly the first twenty yards. So in psychics are we making our first precarious flights, which will, in the future, enable mankind to leap to a greater ascendancy in thought. At a not far distant date, when audible communication with the spirits becomes a normally accepted and practised activity throughout the world, these first few efforts may appear as primitive. But they will mark an epoch in history.

I have proved the adamant fact that mediumistic powers are a latent and not an abnormal faculty in man. That is a discovery of paramount importance. The simple formula; by which I and my wife developed as mediums maybe followed by all who wish to develop this faculty.

All the scientists who have studied psychical phenomena in the past have made one great omission. They have confined their studies to the few reliable mediums who have haphazardly developed. They have regarded these as rare and abnormal types. No scientist has as yet attempted to develop personal mediumship himself.

Since my own development, at my suggestion three different people have started experiments. One was not successful, the second obtained supernormal physical phenomena, and the third, a very cultured woman, obtained remarkable physical phenomena immediately, and at the twelfth experiment obtained the voices.

The first recorded instance of modern psychical phenomena occurred only about seventy years ago. I have no wish to disparage the work of the mediums of the past, but it must be realized that the great majority of genuine mediums have not been of the intellectual type. I respect their work none the less for this, and recognize that, but for the exhibitions of their faculties, I might not now be occupied in the study. Yet as a student I am bound to state that the phenomena produced, and the "direct communications" spoken, have hitherto been of a low order of intelligence, which is the precise reason that the obvious opportunity has been so often given to the material scoffer.

Like attracts like. Intelligence attracts intelligence. And to arrive at progress, mediumship must now be developed on the highest and not the lowest plane. It is a colossal study, and a great science. It can, and must be directed on the intellectual plane. The future of psychical knowledge will depend upon personal development.

THE LAST CHAPTER

IX

For two years, night after night, and often for hours upon end, I have conversed with my dear sister and with my fine friend Warren. Intimate as I was with them when they were on Earth, they are both far nearer to me now than ever before. Closely connected as we were, I have actually spoken with them more intimately, and at greater length, since they have passed over than during the whole of their lives on Earth. Together they have been magnificent to me. They have guarded my material interests, they have tended my physical health during stress, they have provided me with the certainty of survival, and they have been the means of spreading a spiritual knowledge, the development of which maybe beyond our dreams.

We are no longer in the realms of physical imagination. We are living in a world of psychical reality. Literally, hundreds of people have heard Annie and Warren speaking to me, who will all come forward and testify to this fact.

I say with cold deliberation that if Annie and Warren are not two vivid, intellectual, and living personalities, then the many ephemeral characters whom I know on Earth and meet and idly chat with in Mayfair, at first nights, at the theatres, or at the Embassy Club, are either all dead people, or they are mere figments of my imagination. My spirit friends have given me far more impressive evidence of their existence than the various social cyphers have given me of theirs.

There is no death. I have taken pains in the compilation of two big books to prove that. I have succeeded in establishing direct and practically regular communication with another world, and this discovery is the greatest step towards knowledge in history.

It is a new form of wireless.

At present it is dependent upon the most delicate vibrations, the laws of which are still only imperfectly understood. But the difficulties are gradually being overcome, for we have learned that under carefully studied conditions these voice communications can be obtained with amazing fluency.

It is impossible to offer any material explanation of the method by which the voice phenomenon is accomplished. Neither is there any necessity why it should be explained, since no scientist in the world can explain electricity; no scientist can explain wireless, and no scientist may ever be able to explain audible spirit communication. None of these three forms of phenomena is an "invention." They are all modern and progressive discoveries. An "invention" is something material, and usually ephemeral. A discovery is fundamental. It is eternal. Electricity had always existed before it was "discovered." So also did the means for wireless exist before the process of usage was discovered.

The means for the usage for these three forms of phenomena have always existed, and will always exist. They represent parts of the elements of the Universe.

Psychical research today is the Cinderella of the sciences, but tomorrow it will be the magnificent mother of progress. And as it is the youngest of the sciences, so is it the most sensitive. To approach the study without the utmost delicacy and care is courting failure, which is precisely where so many pseudoscientists and investigators have exposed their ignorance. They have taken spasmodic plunges into experiments, with only the clumsiest conception of the subtle forces, too often with a clumsy bluster. To use an analogy, such an attitude maybe likened to a bully with a bludgeon storming the heart of a goddess who can fly, and imagining that she can be carried to the cave of his ideas.

The latent forces of the medium, whoever he or she maybe, represent the instrument for communication.

Are not our human bodies the medium of every known sense and perception? Are not our eyes the medium of our vision, and our ears the medium of all sound? So is the ectoplasmic force we possess the instrument through which the discarnate spirits can communicate with us on Earth.

The path towards development is easier than it was a year ago. We have tested, and have found a formula to work upon.

None of us dare to assume to explain the existing mysteries and miracles of the Universe before our eyes.

All that we can do is to make the endeavour to comprehend. Who can explain creation? A speck of protoplasm may either dissolve and disappear, or, with conception, may fructify and become a great poet or painter.

We are learning that the physical and the mental, and the material and the spiritual, are not so indivisible as we had imagined. To arrive at knowledge, we must exercise our mental capacity to its fullest extent.

Man must discover for himself. That is the divine law. It is the law of the Universe, and it is the law to which even spirits must adhere. It is a wise and equitable law, for if all knowledge were given to us without

THE LAST CHAPTER

individual effort, interest and emotion would cease, and we should be the poorer and not the richer for our experience. We should remain undeveloped entities.

The actual mentality and personality we possess survive when we enter the next sphere of existence. It is for us to strive to develop our minds and our spirits to the fullest extent during our Earthly life. And by the strength of his endeavour man may evolve from his abysmal crudity, and the Earth may hail the coming of the superman.

To arrive at wisdom the heights and the depths of experience must be explored; and Truth must be established, not upon myth, nor upon belief, but upon the solid foundation of knowledge.

As man evolves of his own effort and initiative, so will he arrive at greater comprehension, and, shedding his insularity, so may he approach towards the wisdom of the gods. Then before him will open a limitless future of philosophy, of art, and of culture, and from the spirit we shall discover the sources of knowledge, of genius, of inspiration.

End.

APPENDIX A.

Munnings Séances: The 1929 Edition

*I*n a later 1929 edition, HDB having appeared to have decided that Munnings was a fraud, and rewrote the summary of the second sitting (probably after the third sitting). Ed.

He wrote:

"An interesting point to note is that no fraudulent medium prolongs a "voice" séance beyond an average of one and a half hours. The strain of such performances is considerable, and the risk of possible detection is ever present. This particular séance, however, got completely beyond any control from Munnings. Phenomena occurred, physical and mental, entirely apart from him. The first half was composed of badinage of an indifferent character, but the last hour was definite in interest and personality. During this latter period Munnings was compelled to remain sitting—over an hour beyond his usual time—merely as a cipher, or a "listener in," to phenomena beyond any he had hitherto been able to evolve.

"When the sitting ended he was bemused and timid, and far more puzzled than anyone present."

In the 1929 edition HDB also replaced chapter 24: THE THIRD EXPERIMENT WITH MUNNINGS, with this extended chapter relating to subsequent events concerning Munnings. Ed.

THE THIRD EXPERIMENT WITH MUNNINGS

Munnings again fails—After this final experiment his claims to mediumship are dismissed as valueless—His subsequent exposure by HDB—His effrontery in bringing a libel action—The Moseley Munnings articles and their sensational headings—HDB's effective reply in the Press.

January, 1925.

IT was in the latter part of January that this third and final sitting with Munnings was held at Dorincourt. There were present, in addition to my wife and myself, Dr. V. J. Woolley, Honorary Research Officer of the Society for Psychical Research, Mr. P. G. Wodehouse, Miss Leonora Wodehouse, and the Baroness Kakucs.

Mr. Munnings informed me before the sitting that he was feeling unwell, and had been suffering from a bad cold.

Of the sitters the Baroness Kakucs and Miss Leonora Wodehouse had had no previous experience of séances.

I explained to Dr. Woolley beforehand I had found at previous experiments with Munnings that it was seldom one received any actual evidence of personal identification of the communicating voices.

Dr. Woolley also understood that this was not a case of test research work, but that it was to be regarded merely as an experiment to observe any supernormal phenomena which might occur.

Dr. Woolley was sitting next to Munnings.

I placed my own illuminated trumpet in the centre of the circle, and, on this occasion, Munnings having observed the striking effect of the movement of my illuminated trumpet at the two previous sittings, had painted his trumpet with two vivid, luminous stripes in a similar manner. The effect of this was very good as both trumpets could be clearly seen. The two trumpets were placed about a foot apart.

Four records were played on the gramophone before anything transpired.

During the time that the fifth record was playing my illuminated trumpet was suddenly lifted into the air, and moved all round the circle—touching each of the sitters. It was then taken higher into the air, and I asked whether it could be taken to the ceiling. It was taken to the ceiling, which it rapped several times.

Whilst my trumpet was lifted to the ceiling I engaged Munnings in conversation, so that there could be no doubt in the mind of anyone

APPENDIX A.

that either he or I or anyone else was moving. I do not know whether Dr. Woolley happened to observe this fact.

The movements of my trumpet were supernormal.

A little later the voice of Emanuel came through, using Munnings' illuminated trumpet.

Emanuel said that the power was rather weak, and that the spirit communicants would have to draw a certain amount of power from me and from Mrs. Bradley. I replied to Emanuel, saying that I did not wish him to draw very much power from me, as I had been advised to be careful of the strain of mediumship.

Emanuel said that they would be careful as to how much power they took from us.

The few voices which came through during the evening were weak and disconnected, and they seemed unable to hold the power for more than one minute or so at the time.

A spirit purporting to be that of Dan Leno sang the verse of a song, but the voice was not very good.

A spirit voice came through announcing itself to be that of Lord Grenfell, whose funeral had taken place on that day. Lord Grenfell, I learned later, was interested in spiritualism, but the voice did not volunteer any information which could be regarded as evidential.

Husk talked to my wife and me on our mediumship. Husk seemed to be disturbed; his voice was not very distinct, and although I asked certain questions which might have been of considerable value, I obtained no evidential replies.

It is significant to note that neither Annie nor Warren have attempted to speak at a Munnings' séance.

The sitting was devoid of any evidential proof of the personality of the communicating spirits.

That supernormal phenomena occurred is, however, indisputable.

After these three sittings, which took place within a week or two of each other, and during which no mental evidence of any value whatever was forthcoming, I dismissed Munnings and wasted no further time.

As a result of my writings I receive on an average, between one and two hundred letters each week from various correspondents. All of those who requested my opinion upon Munnings I strongly advised not to sit with him nor have any dealings with him.

In February,1926—fifteen months after my three experiments with Munnings—a friend of mine attended a sitting under his "mediumship," during which Munnings was discovered in an obvious attempt at trickery. My friend immediately wrote to me at Monte Carlo, where I was then staying, describing the incident. On my return to London I at once got into communication with him and told him that Munnings must be exposed in the Press and the public warned against him. I arranged a luncheon with Sir Arthur Conan Doyle and the two gentlemen who were concerned with the incident in question, and that evening a letter bearing the joint signatures of Sir Arthur Conan Doyle, Dr. Abraham Wallace, Mr. R. H. Saunders and myself, was dispatched to the Press.

My satiric senses were aroused by the fact that although the three experiments I made and recorded with Munnings were of a minor character, and completely negative in result, yet, when the exposure of Munnings' detection in fraud was published—bearing my signature— enormous publicity all over the country was given to this letter, because it contained evidence of mediumistic fraud; while, on the other hand, practically the whole of the English Press ignored the innumerable, genuine, and incontrovertible evidences which had been obtained at the George Valiantine "voice" sittings, and at the sittings held under my own and my wife's mediumship. Apparently a discovery of fraud is regarded as of more importance than the discovery of genuine supernormal phenomena.

After my public exposure of Munnings his career as a fraudulent medium was ended. He endeavoured to justify himself by bluffing statements. When interviewed by one of the English Sunday papers, Munnings said that he was consulting his lawyers with a view to vindicating his honour at the Courts. This same paper interviewed me, and I informed him that Munnings could take any action he liked, and that I should be only too pleased to defend my allegations and prove the exposure.

After this, nothing more was heard in the Press regarding Munnings for considerably over a year. Then, in January,1928, Munnings brought an action against the proprietors of the *Daily Sketch* and the *Sunday Herald*, claiming damages for alleged libel. The libel consisted in the publication of the letter to the Press bearing my signature, exposing obvious fraud on the part of Munnings, and warning the public not to have any dealings with him.

When the case was down for hearing on January 20, Munnings had not the pluck to appear and face the issue. Judgment was entered for the Defendants with costs, and Mr. Norman Birkett, K.C., who appeared for the *Daily Sketch*, said at the hearing: "To bring an action for libel in circumstances like these is a piece of effrontery, the like of which is without parallel."

APPENDIX A.

The action was dismissed.

The case was reported in practically every newspaper in England, and Munnings' career as a "medium" was finished. Since he was unable to obtain a further living by practising his so-called "profession," and not being inclined to provide for his livelihood by honest labour, he at once proceeded to raise funds by selling what he called his "Confessions" to a popular newspaper. The rapidity of this change of front, or perhaps one should say effrontery, was remarkable. On February 5, 1928, in the weekly newspaper, *The People*, there appeared the first installment of his so-called "Confessions." These were not written by Munnings, but by a Mr. Sydney A. Moseley, the journalist mentioned in Chapter 14, from interviews with Munnings. These Moseley-Munnings articles were served up in a sensational form to attract the public interest, but they failed to arouse any serious attention, since with Munnings' character already exposed it mattered little what he said, either one way or the other.

It appears, however, he and his interviewer, Mr. S. A. Moseley, who wrote the articles, were not in perfect concord, for in another interview with Munnings, which appeared later in the March issue of the *International Psychic Gazette*, in the course of questioning regarding the references made to a series of séances at which messages from G. R. Sims were purported to have been received, and which the Moseley-Munnings articles on February 5, stated to be fraudulent, Munnings was asked by a representative of the *International Psychic Gazette*

"Are the messages that have come from you through him all false?"

"Of course they are not," he declared; "that is what I have come to see you about."

"Then, if they are not false, why are you saying," I asked him, "that your whole psychic career has been a fraud."

"I have not said so," he replied emphatically. "I have not said anything about the Sim's messages. They (referring to the writers of his alleged confession) have not had authority to say anything about Sims. It was stipulated that they should show me a proof of the article; they did not do so. You know, as well as I do, that I could not have given the messages that Sims has given."

"But, nevertheless," I said, "for some consideration or other you have betrayed those who have befriended you, and are saying that everything you have done has been a fraud."

"I am not," he declared. "All that I have given them is a story of my life. They are writing it. I am not. You know I couldn't write it."

The articles appeared in each issue of *The People* for several weeks. On February 19, my name was used, and one of the insignificant instances of a trifling character which had taken place at one of the Munnings sittings at Dorincourt was commented upon. There was nothing in this reference to which I could take objection. On Sunday, March 11, however, on which day I was lecturing at the Queen's Hall on "The Evidence for Survival," *The People* published a Moseley-Munnings article, with the following heading in thick type"

Inner History of Famous Séance.

This was an absurdly sensational heading, since each of the sittings I had with Munnings were recorded by me as being negative. The article which appeared was garbled, and sentences from my records were transposed in such a manner that an entirely different meaning was given to them, and many of the statements made by Munnings were absolutely false. I immediately wrote to the editor of *The People*, acquainting him of these facts, and he then asked me whether I would make a reply in article form when the Moseley-Munnings series was ended. To this letter I replied as follows":

"I have your letter of March 16, and will certainly make a reply to the Munnings articles when the series is finished.

"But in the meantime, I must insist that my name is not again used in the manner it was in your issue of March 11, or I shall be compelled to take immediate steps to protect myself. You will, of course, understand it is quite impossible for me to permit a convicted criminal, and a self-convicted liar, such as Munnings, to use my name week after week for the purpose of casting aspersions upon me. Sir Arthur Conan Doyle and Mr. R. H. Saunders must adopt whatever course appears best to them, but so far as I am concerned, any repetition of this action on the part of Munnings will compel me to take immediate legal proceedings."

After this, although the series continued, there was no further reference to my name.

On May 18, 1928, *The People* published my reply, and the following is a verbatim reprint:

"The article published in the issue of March 11, 1928, contains statements made by Mr. Munnings, in reference to a séance held at my house.

APPENDIX A.

Many of the statements of Mr. Munnings are false, and I am able to prove their falsity by witnesses who were present.

"The statements published and the implications made are calculated to convey an entirely wrong impression of what took place. Sentences in this article are quoted from a book of mine and are deliberately transposed so that they are given such an erroneous meaning that they cannot fail to mislead the reading public.

"Towards the end of 1924 I held three experimental sittings with Mr. Munnings, and after the third I dismissed his claims to mediumship as valueless. These three sittings are recorded in my book, *The Wisdom of the Gods*. The first sitting held on December 18, 1924, is summarized by me in the following verbatim quote:

"The séance was peculiarly mixed: there was an absolute scarcity of actual evidence end personal identity. I could not claim any recognition of the purported spirit of my 'grandfather,' and Mr. Hannen Swaffer does not claim that he could recognize the 'voice' of Lord Northcliffe, or that any evidence whatever was offered proving it was Northcliffe."

"At the second sitting, held on December 31, 1924, my summary is:

"My analysis of this sitting is that nothing occurred which could be regarded as being of a personal evidential nature."

"At the third and last sitting, held early in January, 1925, my analysis is as follows:

"The sitting was devoid of any evidential proof of the personality of the communicating spirits."

"Upon each of the three occasions that Munnings was at my house—Dorincourt—two other powerful mediums were present. That certain supernormal phenomena took place is indisputable, but these phenomena had taken place upon many occasions, in the presence of witnesses, before Mr. Munnings had ever entered my house. I have distinctly stated in my book that when these phenomena were happening, Munnings was the most astonished man in the room, and exclaimed that he had never seen anything like it before.

"Two years ago Frederick Tensely Munnings was caught in a deliberate fraud at a séance held at which a personal friend of mine was present. Immediately after that, a letter addressed to the Press, signed not only by myself, but by Sir Arthur Conan Doyle, Dr. Abraham Wallace and Mr. R. H. Saunders, was published in March, 1926, warning the public of the fraudulent behaviour of Mr. Munnings. From the moment this letter appeared Munnings' career as a fraudulent medium was ended, and he was effectively prevented from obtaining further money from the public by false pretences.

"It is essential that the public should clearly understand that the exposure of fraud was first made, not by Mr. Sydney A. Moseley, and not by Munnings in his "Confessions," but that it was made several years ago by myself, Sir Arthur Conan Doyle and others.

"During the whole of my psychical research work I have personally conducted and attended many hundreds of sittings, all of which—with the incontrovertible personal evidence obtained by the various sitters in German, French, Italian, Russian, Spanish, ancient and modern Chinese, Japanese and idiomatic Welsh—have been recorded by me in detail in my published works.

"It is interesting to compare these records with the three sittings which I held with Munnings, at which, despite all his pretensions, he was unable to produce one solitary point of evidence, and it is of paramount importance that the public should realize that the fraudulent medium can never produce incontrovertible mental evidence.

"Mr. Sydney A. Moseley was warned over two years ago, by a letter bearing my signature, that Munnings was fraudulent; he was also notified in my books that Munnings entirely failed to produce any evidential matter. The credit, therefore, of preventing Munnings from pursuing his nefarious career is due to the determined action of Sir Arthur Conan Doyle and myself."

The publication of the Munnings articles in *The People* has this value. The articles may have served to illustrate to the public the crude attempts of the fraudulent medium, in comparison with the remarkable discoveries that have been achieved through genuine mediumship, to produce incontrovertible personal evidence. Does any intelligent man imagine that the case for psychical phenomena, which is now internationally accepted, is based upon the promiscuous culling of such banal facts and obvious information obtained from registers, directories and "Who's Who"? They would be immediately disregarded

APPENDIX A.

and discounted by any expert. Unless a medium can produce evidence of such a character that it can be proved to be entirely outside his knowledge, and also, at times, outside the knowledge of any of his sitters, it is impossible for him to establish himself as possessing any claims to recognition by experienced psychical researchers.

My reason for dealing at such length with the Munnings case is that during 1928 long, sensational, misleading and deliberately false statements have been made in articles which have appeared all over the United States of America, purporting to be Munnings' "Confessions." It is essential, therefore, to expose the whole circumstances in detail.

APPENDIX B.

Thoughts and Extracts from *And After*

In 1931 Bradley published *And After*, where he documents his thoughts on Valiantine during the last sittings he did with him, where fraud was detected, not in any of the evidential communications, but during the Noel Jaquin imprint experiments.

In chapter one Bradley shares his thoughts on Valiantine:

"Valiantine, at the height of his mediumistic powers, was, to my mind, the greatest "voice" medium the world has ever known. In view of the subsequent chapters in this book, a brief resume of the records of his mediumship under my personal supervision, in my own house, may be given.

"On the first occasion that Valiantine visited England, in 1924, he stayed with me at Dorincourt for five weeks. During this time I held twenty-eight "direct voice" séances. Of these, one was entirely unsuccessful, four might be regarded as negative in evidential results; the remaining twenty-three were remarkably successful.

"In 1925 Valiantine stayed with me again at Dorincourt, from February 13 until April 25, and during these ten weeks I conducted sixty-one séances. Only two of these were complete failures; five were what I should describe as negative in results, although phenomena occurred, and fifty-four were successful.

"Valiantine visited me again in 1927, staying with me at Dorincourt, a few records of which are published in this book.

"Up to, and including, 1927, I had conducted considerably over one hundred experiments with Valiantine, 95 per cent. of which were successful. Between two and three hundred people witnessed the phenomena which took place, the majority of whom were men and women of established reputation in various paths of life.

Valiantine has stayed with me for periods of months on end, and I have had ample opportunities of studying his character. He is a man of instinctive good manners, but it is essential to state that he is semi-illiterate. He possesses no scholastic education whatever, beyond the ordinary simplicities; he is ill-versed in general conversation and ideas. I mention these facts because many of the communications which have been made in the "direct voice" under his mediumship have been brilliant in their expressions and culture.

"Fluent conversations have been carried on by various "voices" in nearly every language, and in many dialects. French, Basque, German, Spanish, Italian, Sicilian, Russian, Dutch, Danish, Portuguese, Arabic, Ancient and Modern Chinese, and idiomatic Welsh have all been spoken. Of the many hundreds of "voices" (feminine and masculine) which have spoken, the great majority possessed distinct character and individuality. The *timbre*, accent, and manner of delivery, and, beyond all, distinctive personality, were recognizable in innumerable instances. There was also a considerable number of cases recorded by me in which communicating "voices" gave valuable cross evidence of communications made by them at other sittings at which Valiantine was not present. There were also several cases of information given by "voices" of facts which were proved to be not only outside the knowledge of the medium, but outside the knowledge of any of the sitters present in the circle.

"In 1925, I recorded a series of sittings held in full daylight, during which the closest observation of Valiantine's face was made, and many evidential communications were given by the various "voices" which manifested under these conditions.

"A number of official sittings were held by representatives of the Society for Psychical Research, during which supernormal evidences were recorded in the Proceedings of the Society. It was established by corroborated evidence that Valiantine and a spirit voice were speaking simultaneously.[161] Una, Lady Troubridge, and Miss Radcliffe Hall were two of the representatives of the S.P.R. present, and referring to the

---

[161] This has happened on innumerable occasions.

APPENDIX B.

daylight experiment, Una, Lady Troubridge, wrote, in the Proceedings: "I consider that this has established Valiantine in an exceptional way."

"During the year 1925, in my opinion, Valiantine's mediumship was at its pinnacle, and the complete records which were published by me at this time are unique in the history of psychic science."

And After has not been widely available since its first publication. According to Weiser Antiquarian, "Bradley ... included a chapter on his dealings with another American Medium, Mrs. Hamilton, whose cause was being championed by a London accountant, Robert Sproull. Sproull took exception to Bradley's comments and sued him for libel, apparently winning £500 damages. The book was then withdrawn from circulation by the publishers."

It's clear from his writing that Bradley had become more than disillusioned by his experiences with Spiritualism, as can be seen in "The Last Chapter" of *And After* which we have included here. *Ed.*

THE LAST CHAPTER / AND AFTER

THE rise and fall of Valiantine presents an intriguing psychological study.

The records of his phenomenal mediumship prove that at the time he was at the height of his powers he could be accounted as the most remarkable physical medium in history. Later, when his mentality developed a materialistic outlook, decay set in. His reason for attempting these imprint frauds will remain incomprehensible. He was receiving no money from me, and for him to imagine that in the presence of imprint experts he could commit palpable fraud and escape detection was a sign of sheer lunacy, with the actual personal imprints of famous men in our possession, only a madman would offer his big toe for comparison. Yet Valiantine, despite his illiteracy, is by no means a stupid man.

Powerful objective mediums, such as Valiantine, possess a strain of abnormality. From my observation of him, from the first moment of his last-and final-visit, it was certainly apparent that he had developed a form of megalomania. Flattery, adulation, and the gifts of large sums of money had led him to imagine himself a man of super importance. Since adopting professional mediumship Valiantine became unquestionably the highest paid living medium. In these hard times there are few men who can command the sum of four or five hundred pounds a week for their services. Considering the marvelous accumulation of subjective phenomena i.e., incontrovertible mental evidence given in the "direct voice" on matters completely outside his knowledge- it remains an enigma that he should have attempted such palpable and stupid objective fraud. No man in his right senses would destroy a brilliant reputation br. imbecile and meaningless acts, with the distinct possibility-even probability-of a ruinous discovery.

The fact of Valiantine's fraudulently produced toeprint cannot negative or explain the fact that, under the mediumship of this imperfectly educated and semi-illiterate American provincial, Archaic Chinese was spoken by the "voice" of "K'ung-fu-T'zu" on several occasions, during which this "voice" discussed abstruse problems in Chinese literature. Here again is an example of the heights and depths.

In my intensive study of psychical research, and my observations of the cult of spiritualism, I have discovered that there are deeper problems to be considered than those which are outwardly apparent.

I have been careful to record meticulously the facts of my experiences, irrespective of their tendencies towards good or bad. The deeper problem is one which I have weighed and considered during the last few years.

Taken scientifically, psychical research represents an absorbing study. In its present state, it is a subject which should be studied only by those who possess a sound knowledge of its various intricacies. That supernormal phenomena do occur, and that genuine communication with "spirit entities" is, in certain cases, possible and practicable, has, in my opinion, been definitely scientifically proved.

As a result of these proofs, a vast multitude, totaling millions, in all parts of the world, have branded themselves as "spiritualists," and, with the herd instinct, many sections have sought to found a new religion.

There exist also, in practically every country, certain sections which label themselves "psychical researchers." These sections consider themselves superior in intelligence to the spiritualists; and the spiritualists consider themselves, often by reason only of some alleged communication from "Black Eagle," or "Pink Feathers," as infinitely more ethereal than mere mundane-minded researchers.

As an impartial student, I have had ample opportunities of observing both sections. As for the so-called Societies for Psychical Research, I have found that no research whatever is made by them, but that their activities are chiefly devoted to bitter and prejudiced attacks upon all forms of supernormal phenomena, which they happen to find inexplicable.

APPENDIX B.

So far as the English S.P.R. is concerned, it would certainly appear only logical and dignified for it to cease to pretend to function, since its present officials deny all existence of supernormal phenomena. From its own publications it is obvious that its *raison d'être* is at an end. The jaundiced attitude exhibited towards the carefully compiled work of scientists might be regarded as vicious, were it not discounted by fanaticism. Strangely enough, many of these antagonistic types are so peculiarly constituted that they hang on to the subject, just as a jealous lover will hang on to a mistress for the perverse pleasure of tormenting her. They hang on viciously, in the hope of gaining an opportunity to Injure or destroy.

Any such opportunity for harm provides them with a sadistic mental emotion.

There is also a very considerable section of "half and halfers." This section forms itself into further Societies, and endeavors to obtain the respect of the populace by adopting high-sounding titles, such as the "International Laboratory of So-and-So," or the "British Empire Institution of This and That." Such societies, whilst posing as scientific, flirt with the spiritualistic sections, and are thus enabled to attract more members to their Associations. And when one studies the faces of the ordinary members of these so-called Psychical Research Societies, one observes the unattractive signs of their obsession. Their worried expressions are, if anything, more disturbing than the vacuous stupidity of the simple-minded, enthusiastic, and credulous spiritualists.

Spiritualistic societies, during the last decade, have sprung up all over England, and all over the world.

International Unions are being formed by propagandists, and vulgar demagogues, seizing their opportunities, are surging forward to lead the mob.

My experience during the last eight years of my studies of the various forms of mediumship in many hundreds of séances, in addition to the development of my own personal "direct voice" mediumship, qualifies me to judge and express a considered opinion upon values and upon tendencies.

Spiritualism is now being foisted on the public as a new religion. I assert deliberately that, as a religion, it is a farce. Tinpot little churches are being erected all over the country; irresponsible spiritualistic tub-thumpers are appointing themselves as preachers of a new gospel; dud clairvoyants are giving banal exhibitions at their church services under the blasphemous guise of spirituality. Boring and ill-written hymns are sung; hypocritical prayers are intoned by vulgar and crafty mediums; and the name of God is dragged into abysmal mud.

Bemused enthusiasts proclaim that because "White Feathers," speaking through the mouth of some alleged Medium in Lancashire accents and pidgin-English, has announced to the world that reincarnation is a fact, we must all at once prepare ourselves to be reincarnated.

Obsession becomes so fixed that every word spoken by an alleged spirit communicant is accepted as fundamental and omnipotent truth. "White Feathers," having lived his life as a Red Indian on the prairies, is, of course, qualified to know; even though, being a particularly "happy" soul, he has not yet decided when to make his second appearance in the flesh on earth.

Reincarnation, says White Feathers, is necessary for man's development. "Every time, in every way, man gets betterer and betterer." It would be dull to reiterate "White Feathers" or "Black Tomahawk's" solemn pronouncements, but "reincarnation" is accepted as a belief by very considerable sections of the credulous. It has no scientific or logical foundation. There exists certain evidence of man's survival as a "spirit entity" in some other sphere, the proofs of which are the retention of his memory.

But no evidence has ever been produced of anyone existing on earth who has been able to prove that he remembers his previous existence. The argument that man arrives at perfection by innumerable reincarnations on earth is singularly inept today. One scans the horizon in vain for some signs· of these supermen.

I have stated earlier in. this book that I have resigned my membership or the various Research and Spiritualistic Societies to which I belonged. The reason for my resignation was that these Societies suppress the truth.

Personally. I see no need for any of them. They exist only to keep a few officials, or as institutes to which wealthy spinsters may leave bequests. The majority of the Spiritualist Churches all over England are perpetually begging for money. I receive hundreds of letters asking me for contributions. I have found the same thing with the London Societies-the eternal begging for funds. When I say that from no Psychical Research Society nor from any Spiritualistic Society have I ever gained one solitary suggestion of value in my studies one may realize the extent of their futility.

As for the Spiritualist Churches, their services may offer some appeal to the illiterate mind, but as a form of worship I regard them as deplorable and subversive.

APPENDIX B.

Their ritual is on a low plane, and is uninspired and ignorant. The platitudinous banalities of their preachers, so often tinged with the suggestion of pseudo-mysticism, are repulsive to any developed intelligence.

The theory of man's survival was accepted long before the fact was ascertained. Survival is the fundamental basis of all the finely evolved religions that have existed for centuries. An intuitive acceptance of faith is more refined than a tardy recognition of fact. Those who are attempting to form a new religion of "Spiritualism" should realize that naked facts-unclothed by sound philosophy-can be extremely vulgar.

I have stated that in the study of "spirit communication" a deep problem is involved. From the thousands of letters I have received I am fully aware of the tremendous desire which exists in the minds of most human beings to communicate again with those whom they have lost. With considerable patience and perseverance such communication, in some cases, can be achieved.

When such proof has been established to the satisfaction of the ordinary man and woman, I would then advise them to leave all experiments with professional mediums severely alone; if they wish to continue their psychic studies they should do so privately, and in the sanctuary of their own homes. In my own research I have been fortunate enough to achieve the purpose upon which I set out. I have proved, with considerable toil, to my own satisfaction, that man survives bodily death. So I believe can this fact be proved by any scientist who is prepared to sacrifice the time, and endure the pains of the labor involved.

So far as the promiscuous study of this vast subject is concerned, and the important question as to whether it is advisable for the majority of those who are compelled to provide for and live their lives on earth to enter upon it, my answer must be reserved. It depends entirely upon the individual. In "direct" voice communication, when one is in contact with intelligent and personally known entities, conversations can be held which are beautiful and inspiring, but it must be realized that when once the channels of communication are opened, lower and less intelligent entities are also, at times, afforded opportunities.

It is because of this danger that if I were asked "is the tendency of spiritualism in its present public form towards good or evil?" I would reply that it is so often misused and abused, that the general tendency is towards evil.

"Spirit communication" is not a religion; it is a scientific discovery which is in the stages of infancy.

The searcher after knowledge must inevitably meet with setbacks, accidents, and handicaps. The fraudulent actions of certain professional mediums no more affect the value of the science itself than the fraudulent action or a banker affects the practice of banking. But fraud and imposture, when practised under the cloak of religion, become blasphemy.

The established religions have been founded and built upon a fine and cultured philosophy. So far as this country is concerned, the Church of England and the Roman Catholic Church are based upon a solid foundation, and their services are conducted with dignity and reverence. Throughout the many years of my psychic studies my attitude towards the Spiritualist Churches has remained unchanged. The conclusions expressed in my previous psychic books regarding the religious aspect remain unaltered. I was educated a Roman Catholic and I remain a Roman Catholic.

The attitude of the Roman Catholic Church towards spiritualism is antagonistic. She has been wise enough not to deny that communication with spirits is possible, but she has discounted and discouraged it by the contention that only evil spirits communicate with human beings. Although this broad contention is incorrect, as I have proved by personal communication with many individual spirits, yet, at the same time, it is unquestionable that in the lower grades of mediumship there are innumerable evil, lying, and impersonating entities seeking channels of communication, with the result that many séances which are held are of a degrading character, and in such cases the practice is unhealthy and morbid.

It has also to be considered that even when brilliant phenomena take place, they evolve a great mental strain, and a dominating aftermath of mental occupation, which can only be borne by the strongest of minds.

For nearly two thousand years, despite her rigid autocracy, the Roman Catholic Church has furthered an artistic culture which survives. Her very sensuality is creative, and makes a wondrous appeal. Beethoven, Weber, Haydn, Mozart, Gounod, and other great composers have given to the Church the divine inspiration of their music, just as many of the world's greatest painters and sculptors have paid tribute with their art.

Gorgeous vestments and jewelled caskets are made to adorn the interior of wonderful cathedrals and stately chapels. To seek to replace such artistry and beauties by banal services conducted by ignorant and illiterate mediums and preachers, with confused ideas and a smattering of knowledge, is absurd.

APPENDIX B.

I am on intimate terms with several of the leaders of the Catholic Church and the Church of England. They have discussed my psychical studies with me at considerable length. An international institution, such as the Roman Catholic Church, moves warily, and considers very carefully the forms of government by which the unintelligent mass may be led.

There are at present very few mediums of any value in England, but there are innumerable undeveloped mediums of a low order, through whom spirit entities of a similar low order may endeavor to communicate. Like attracts like. There are deceptions and vulgarities among these entities just as there are among the many living beings whom we meet in life. It is only logical to assume that relative good and evil exist in all the many spheres of existence beyond the planet upon which we are now living. Therefore, I am in accord with the wisdom of the Roman Catholic Church in not encouraging indiscriminate psychic experiments, until such times as the means of communication are more fully developed, and the value and integrity of the communications are more critically analyzed.

I am neither insular nor bigoted. As I respect the dignity of the Catholic faith, so do I respect the dignity of the Church of England, and the dignity of the Jewish faith, the solid foundations· of which have withstood the tests of time. But I have no respect for the spiritualistic so-called Churches, based on a mushroom foundation of sporadic phenomena. Such phenomena, whether true or false, are not the worship of God, and do not supply the place of any serious religion or historic creed.

Psychical research is a science, the study of which, in Its present stages, should be undertaken only by the few.

It is a science in which there are many pitfalls, and at times, considerable danger. Dangers exist, both physical and mental, which are imperfectly understood.

Spiritualism, as a modern belief, has attracted the imagination of millions of people of all nationalities. It has become a "cult." That supernormal phenomena do exist is unquestionable. That the cult of Spiritualism is widely contaminated by fraud is also unquestionable.

The scientific researcher must impartially appraise the value of all that is genuine, and rigidly discard all that is false. He must be coldly impersonal in the knowledge that falsity pulsates with truth. He must be a physicist and a psychologist. He must realize that, whilst falsity may often lead to the discovery of truth, so also will truth be the means by which falsity is unmasked.

In psychics, the great unscientifically minded mass, who have made a few trifling and indiscriminate experiments, expose themselves to the dangers of obsession.

This engenders a narrow perspective, and is liable to have a detrimental effect upon the healthy living of life.

The condition of the world today, politically, economically, socially, and morally, does not exhibit encouraging signs of man's progress. Our so-called civilization is still barbaric. Only a glimmer of intelligence is to be observed here and there, and the majority of those inhabiting this speck of a planet have still to learn the alphabet of the Universe. Our conceptions are limited, and the processes of evolution are slow.

The psychologist seeks to discover the purpose of life, and the possibility of an afterlife.

My faith in man's survival is now immutable.

That faith has been confirmed by knowledge.

In the course of the acquisition of knowledge I have become familiar with the contrasting--and sometimes intermingling-shades of good and evil.

All creation pulsates and alternates in the throes of good and evil.

All that I have attempted in these pages is to present with Justice, sincerity, and truth, a summary of my psychic studies.

It remains for those who read to draw their own conclusions.

They may then discover that the most difficult word for man to write is FINIS

APPENDIX C.

In 1931, after Valiantine had returned home to Williamsport in the USA, news had spread about the Bradley séance in London and his local paper the *Williamsport Sun*, interviewed him. Subsequently, The *International Psychic Gazette* published a booklet titled *Exposure of Dennis Bradley* which included Valiantine's rebuttal published in the *Williamsport Sun*. We have included it here. *ED.*

The original cover

Tom Charman's Impressions of the Psychic Pictures on Smoked Papers.

No. 1.—The Lanky-haired Fellow. No. 2.—The Antiquated Lean Lady. No. 3.—The Swan. No. 4.—The Laughing Lady. No. 5.—The Old Man. No. 6.—The British Officer. No. 7.—Mr. Lloyd George. No. 8.—The Comical Cat. No. 9.—The Old Turk. No. 10.—The Donkey's Head. No. 11.—The Lady's Profile (between 5 and 8). Nos. 12 and 8 represent what Mr. Bradley calls "The Alleged Doyle Imprints," and No. 7 represents what he calls the "Alleged Lord Dewar Imprint." And all four he suggests were made by George Valiantine's toe in the dark! Could absurdity go further?

EXPOSURE OF DENNIS BRADLEY

～

Being an Account of his Efforts to Discredit a Famous Direct Voice Medium and "Smash Spiritualism." With GEORGE VALIANTINE'S REPLY

Reprinted by special request from
THE INTERNATIONAL PSYCHIC GAZETTE
for November and December.

CHAPTER I.

MR. H. DENNIS BRADLEY, author of *The Wisdom of the Gods, Towards the Stars* and other notable works, has just launched a new book bearing the enigmatic title of *And After* (T. Werner Laurie, Ltd., 10/6).

A NEWSPAPER'S PRELIMINARY PUFF.

Even before its publication its sensational character was proclaimed by a " Daily Express Special Representative " in an article, based on an interview with Mr. Bradley himself, which had the following scare headings: -

"Tricks of a Famous Spiritualist Medium Exposed."
"Finger-prints of the Dead Faked."
"Big Toe used as 'Spirit' at a Séance."
"Medium Caught in Act of Fraud."
"Mr. D. Bradley's Exposures."

The writer of the article is probably the same scribe who a few days before had made a virulent anti-Spiritualist stunt for the Express out of an alleged medium's alleged confession with the following attractive titles:–

"Medium's Amazing Confession."
"Hundreds Duped by Pretence of Spirit Guide."
"Séance Frauds."
"His Own Voice in the Trumpet."
"Séance Quackery Revelations."

Our contemporary *Light* promptly and cleverly identified the subject of this article, a man named Beare, with an unnamed medium who had already made a similar "confession" in the *Catholic Times*, which paper described him as "a Catholic who strayed and now repents," wishing "to return to the faith of my fathers, trusting God will forgive me for being an arch-deceiver for thirteen years!" The Catholic connection with this virulent attack on Spiritualism should not be overlooked.

Similarly Mr. Dennis Bradley reveals in his new book:– "I am on intimate terms with several of the leaders of the Catholic Church," who "have discussed my psychical studies with me at considerable length." He says further that "to seek to replace such artistry and beauties (as those of the Catholic Church) by banal services conducted by ignorant and illiterate mediums and preachers, with confused ideas and a smattering of knowledge, is absurd." His leanings, therefore, like Beare's, are at present distinctly away from Spiritualism and towards "a return to the faith of my fathers."

THE PURPOSE OF THE BOOK.

The *Express's* flattering recommendation of Mr. Bradley's book reveals its intention thus:–

> "Spiritualists the world over will find their faith shaken to its roots by disclosures which are made in a book to be published in England at the beginning of next month. The author is Mr. H. Dennis Bradley, one of the leaders of the Spiritualist movement in this country" (sic).

But was he ever a Spiritualist leader? We have never heard of his following. He was not, however, denied an ornamental place at the tail of the movement.

The article continues:—

> "George Valiantine, an American, hitherto regarded by Spiritualists as the greatest medium of all—a man beyond reproach—is exposed as a trickster."

Few Spiritualists in this country have ever seen Valiantine, who was always strictly reserved by Mr. Bradley for the entertainment of himself and his distinguished friends. Other Spiritualists had no chance of witnessing his phenomena, but they had no reason to believe that Mr. Bradley's glowing descriptions of his superlative gifts and personal honesty were untrue.

A SIMILAR "EXPOSURE" RECALLED.

As for his now being " exposed as a trickster " by Mr. Bradley and his two clever confederates, Noel Jaquin and Charles Sykes, we believe that is probably no more true than that honest William Hope, the famous psychic photographer, was "exposed as a trickster" by Harry Price, with the assistance of Eric Dingwall and James Seymour. Just as Hope's character was triumphantly vindicated by a critical analysis of the crafty one-sided story of his accusers, so we predict will Valiantine's, when Bradley's bold assertion of guesses as facts, and his own admitted guile and craft during the experiments, are subjected to the same process. It strikes us that this whole story of Valiantine's " decline and fall," when carefully read in the book, smacks much more of the nature of a cunning Jesuitical plot than of a fair-minded and impartial inquiry.

"SPIRIT IMPRESSIONS."

The Express report continues:—

> "At a series of séances held at Mr. Dennis Bradley's house, with George Valiantine as the medium, a number of 'spirit impressions' were produced. These spirit impressions were found to have been produced by Valiantine himself."

Now it is not true to say that these impressions, whatever they were, "were found to have been produced by Valiantine." If they were actual "spirit impressions" he had, of course, nothing whatever to do with them, beyond providing (along with the other mediums present) the essential element of his mediumistic organisation for their production by spirit entities. Dr. Alfred Russel Wallace once defined a medium as " a person in whose presence psychical phenomena happen." They do not happen without the presence of mediums, and when they do happen it is not because the mediums have indulged in pranks or conjuring tricks with hands or toes or elbow joints !

If, on the other hand, it is claimed that the imprints were "physical impressions" produced by George Valiantine's or anybody else's toes, Mr. Bradley must first prove that that was **physically possible** in the circumstances under which they were produced.

THE CIRCUMSTANCES OF THE EXPERIMENTS.

Let us try to visualise the scene from the particulars given in the book.

There is a small circle in Mr. Bradley's house on February 20, 1931, consisting of Mr. and Mrs. Bradley, Mr. and Mrs. Charles Sykes, Mr. Noel Jaquin, and Mr. Valiantine. (It is just as well to mention here that Valiantine was a guest in Mr. Bradley's house, and was giving his services in a long series of séances without a penny of reward) :-

"The circle was a carefully chosen one," says the author, "because each of the sitters was experienced, and one could rely on meticulous observation, and also on expert knowledge of imprints.

> "We all dined together, and immediately prior to the sitting, which began at 8.50 p.m., Mr. Jaquin carefully smoked two sheets of blank foolscap paper.
>
> "One of these sheets was placed on top of a small, but heavy, old oak coffin stool, and the other on the carpet beneath the stool.
>
> "The sheet on the top of the stool was placed on a blotting pad, measuring 14½ inches by 9½ inches.
>
> "The coffin stool has four bars, 2 inches thick, at the bottom between each of the four legs, and standing 1½ inches from the floor.
>
> "The four legs are 2½ inches square in thickness.
>
> "The sheet of smoked paper on the floor was placed underneath two of the legs of the stool.

"The sitting was, of course, held in darkness, with the exception of the distinct luminosity from the spots on the diagonal wires on the celluloid trumpet."

WERE PHYSICAL IMPRESSIONS POSSIBLE?

No particulars are given as to the position in the room or the height of the coffin stool, and these may be of consequence. Was the stool, for example, within easy reach of Valiantine's toes or not? That should have been stated.

Was there space for a man's foot to pass between the bars of the small stool and so reach the paper under the legs of the stool?

Assuming that there was, a barrier 3½ inches from the floor all round the stool inhibited free access to the floor. Would it be possible for anyone to curve his foot over this 3½ inches high barrier so as to enable him to reach the smoked paper lying on the carpet with his big toe, and make such an impression of its delicate lines and ridges that it could afterwards be identified?

A CHALLENGE TO MR. BRADLEY.

If Mr. Bradley thinks that feat is possible he ought to demonstrate it himself before independent witnesses. We challenge him to do it.

As for the paper on the blotting-pad on the top of the stool, to make a toe imprint on it would, it seems to us, be still more difficult. Even if the paper lay no higher than the seat of the medium's chair, he might perhaps get an impression of the back of his heel by stretching forth his foot, but it is difficult to see how he could curve round his big toe to the paper to make any sort of imprint at all. But again Mr. Bradley will perhaps oblige by himself showing its possibility?

Then, even if these feats could be successfully accomplished by some extraordinary mobility of foot, no skin impressions could be made unless the experimenter's shoes and socks were off, and there is no evidence at all that Valiantine's were ever off. He was carefully guarded by three meticulous observers, who were only too ready to pounce on him and catch him flagrante delicto, had he made the slightest suspicious movement.

Also, if his toes had been pressed on the smoked paper, surely some sign of the carbon would have been found when Valiantine was afterwards stripped and examined, but no trace of any carbon was found on his toes or anywhere else.

THE "ELBOW JOINT" EPISODE.

There is also a question of Valiantine having made an impression of his elbow joint in a tin of melted wax, though it is difficult to see what purpose there could be in doing so, for it would prove nothing. Had he wanted to do so he would have had to pull up the sleeves of his coat, shirt, and vest in the presence of his watchful guard, make his mark with his elbow joint, and pull them down again, without arousing suspicion, but there is not an atom of evidence that he did any of these things. It is true that a green stain was afterwards found on his elbow, but that can be perfectly explained in the light of psychic science without concluding that his elbow was ever near the wax.

Looked at from the purely physical point of view the misdeeds attributed to Valiantine by his accusers seem not only silly and purposeless but also impossible.

It is incumbent on Mr. Bradley to prove that they were physically possible in the circumstances under which they are supposed to have been done. If he fails to prove that possibility then his whole case falls to the ground.

He will then have to withdraw his book and his cruel aspersions, which have been broadcast throughout the world, against Valiantine's probity. As a man of honour it would also be his duty to apologise to the hitherto inoffensive and honest medium he has so grossly wronged.

IF SUPERNORMAL NOTHING IMPOSSIBLE.

If, however, the imprints on the paper were genuinely super-normal—that is, made by spirit operators—then nothing is impossible. Physical barriers could not prevent them from impressing smoked paper either on the stool or under the stool, and these impressions could be whatever they pleased, whether a butterfly's wing or a bird's foot, or the thumb of a disembodied spirit, or the facsimile of any living person's heels or toes or elbow joints. Neither the medium nor the sitters would have any part in making such psychic impressions, and they would not be responsible for whatever happened. Their guides, controls and psychic operators would alone be responsible.

It is inconceivable that Valiantine's long-tried, faithful, and honest guides would have impressed a facsimile of his toes to imitate existing impressions of thumbs, whether of Sir Arthur Conan Doyle, Lord Dewar, or anybody else, and thus destroy the good name of their medium. Mischievous or mal-intentioned spirits might do so, to gratify the wish of their own particular mediums.

WHOSE MEDIUMSHIP?

Now Valiantine's phase of mediumship is for the "direct voice." He makes no pretensions to "physical mediumship," such as would be required for the kind of psycho-physical phenomena produced. But Mr. Dennis Bradley does. He writes (page 303):—

"On certain occasions, physical phenomena, and also voice phenomena of a distinctive nature, have occurred at the private sittings held under the mediumship of my wife and myself, when Valiantine has *not* been present, or even in this country. These distinctive phenomena have, later on, taken place similarly while Mrs. Bradley and myself have been sitting under the mediumship of Valiantine. On one occasion when Valiantine was visiting England, a family sitting was held, especially in order that Valiantine might observe *certain phenomena which had not occurred under his own mediumship.*"

The italics are Mr. Bradley's own, and they emphasise a point that is important, namely, that certain phenomena sometimes occurred during séances for which neither Valiantine nor his guides were responsible, but for which Mr. and Mrs. Bradley and their guides were. It seems hardly fair that the Bradleys should appropriate all the kudos when things go right and that Valiantine should be shouldered with all the responsibility when curious unexplained physical phenomena happen.

THE 1925 EXPERIMENTS.

Let us now give a history of these so-called "experiments," that have all taken place in Mr. Bradley's own house, with a summary of the results. We here quote from page 296 of the book:—

"When Valiantine was in England in 1925, when discussing with Mr. Noel Jaquin the phenomena of materialised hands, which occasionally touch sitters during séances, he suggested that if the spirit hands touched various of the sitters, then these hands could be placed upon smoked paper and an imprint could be obtained.

"The first experiment was made on April 18, 1925, with only Mrs. Bradley, Valiantine and myself present. At the end of the séance, when the lights were turned on, it was discovered that on one sheet there was the imprint of a hand with four fingers and also part of the thumb. On the other sheet there was the imprint of the two feet of a bird. Now these imprints have never been scientifically explained. They have been studied by many experts, who have not to this day been able to determine how they could have been produced by normal means."

A BUTTERFLY'S "DRAGGED" EFFECT.

A further experiment was made on April 23, 1925, when Mr. Jaquin and Mr. and Mrs. Sykes joined Mr. and Mrs. Bradley and Valiantine. Two further imprints were obtained, namely, the signature of O.B. Everett and the delicate velvety imprint of a butterfly lying on its back. There was no suggestion then that these imprints were made by Valiantine's toes, although it is admitted there was a "dragged" effect in the butterfly impression. It was a similar effect in 1931 that suggested to Mr. Bradley that the smoked paper must have been "moved" and by Valiantine's toes; *hinc illae lacrimae!* Mr. Sykes in his report stresses how difficult it would have been for any human hand to have made this butterfly impression with an India rubber stamp owing to the cross-bars at the foot of the stool, and Mr. Jaquin says:– "I am convinced that these are supernormal imprints."

COLLECTING THUMB-PRINTS.

There were no further experiments of this nature until February, 1931, about six years later. Mr. Bradley had in the interval been taking thumb-prints from famous men, including Sir Arthur Conan Doyle and Lord Dewar, in the hope that after their death they might be able to give identical impressions as proofs of their survival. Valiantine was quite willing to sit in experiments with this intention. Mr. Bradley says "the series of imprint sittings were devoted to materialistic attempts to obtain physical phenomena." Valiantine's mediumistic gifts are not adapted for securing such "physical" phenomena, but as we have seen above Mr. and Mrs. Bradley's are. That is very important, and should be kept in mind.

THE 1931 PHENOMENA—A WARNING!

Now we give a summary of the essential facts in the first two of the 1931 series of sittings:–

February 19, l931—Valiantine sits with Mr. and Mrs. Bradley for "voices" only. "Thirteen different and distinct spirit voices manifested," and among them that of Mr. Bradley's own sister Annie, who said, "as if endeavouring to give him some urgent warning":– "Herbert—it's Annie. Be *careful*! Be *careful*!" Mr. Bradley could not understand this warning, but it is not unreasonable to believe that it was a warning to be careful of his own conduct in the "experimental" sittings he was about to begin, and it is a pity he did not take this warning, though it "remained stamped upon his mind."

EXPOSURE OF DENNIS BRADLEY

"THE DOYLE VOICE!"

February 20, l931—First experimental sitting for imprints.

Present:-Mr. and Mrs. Bradley, Mr. and Mrs. Sykes, Mr. Jaquin, and Valiantine. Conditions obviously not good. Communications few and short. "A voice, speaking in a light and somewhat husky whisper, said, "Bradley—Doyle … Arthur Doyle." And a little later, "I am trying to give an imprint." Bradley says he could not recognise this husky whispering voice as Sir Arthur's. It claimed, "This is the first time I have spoken in this way," which he knows cannot be true of Sir Arthur's.

It was obviously an impersonation. Nevertheless, "for the purposes of the prosecution," he calls it hereafter "The Doyle Voice." "George Gregory" told his brother-in-law Jaquin that "he would endeavour to help in obtaining a supernormal imprint." "Pat O'Brien" said, "You know, Mr. Bradley, Doyle has been trying to get his imprint through."

MR. JAQUIN'S OPINION.

The sitting closes. Impressions are found on the two pieces of paper, placed on and under the stool. Mr. Jaquin "fixes" them with a solution and takes them away to "compare them with the original imprint of Sir Arthur Conan Doyle's hand, which he had in his possession."

Next morning Jaquin telephones to Bradley that "he had studied the imprints, and so far as he could see, they corresponded with Doyle's!" This "expert" opinion should be noted for these imprints later become part of the dossier convicting Valiantine of fraudulently making them with his toes!

MISLEADING LABELS.

Photographic reproductions of them appear in the book with the following labels:–

> "*Exhibit No. 1.*—A photograph of the smoked paper as found and fixed after the séance held at Dorincourt on Friday, February 20, l931. During this séance a 'voice' alleged that Sir Arthur Conan Doyle was 'trying to get an imprint through.'"

> "*Exhibit No. 2.*—A photograph of the smoked paper placed underneath the stool at the séance on February 20, 1931.The curious indentation may have been caused by uneven pressure."

The *suggestio falsi* of these labels will be obvious.

SPIRIT ARTISTS AT WORK.

Not being experts we can only speak of these imprints as they appear. We find no sign of any visible imprints of either a thumb or a toe, but we do see curious markings which suggest that spirit artists have been having quite a game with Bradley and his expert associates! There is, for example, on No. I, a swan's long neck with head erect, which may signify that this was the occasion of Bradley's Spiritualistic swan song! Close beside it, under Bradley's signature, there is a laughing lady's face, well thrown back, as if she is enjoying the joke. And upside down there is a comical fellow with lanky hair and a pointed nose. On No. 2 there is, in the centre, an old man's white face, with a big nose, square jaw, and retreating forehead, and at the side what may be the back view of a group of children's heads.

CONTRADICTORY ACCOUNTS.

We think it well to quote in full the three contradictory accounts given of these first imprints:—

> (1).—BRADLEY writes on February 21 (page 319):— "At about 9 a.m. on the morning of February 21, Mr. Jaquin telephoned me. He told me that he had studied the imprints, and so far as he could see they corresponded with Doyle's."
>
> (2).—JAQUIN writes on February 21 (page 378):— "On the following morning I carefully examined the original imprints of the hands of the late Sir Arthur Conan Doyle, which were taken by me in 1925. I could find no point of resemblance to the séance prints, the origin of which I felt to be extremely doubtful."
>
> (3).—JAQUIN in his "Report on the Imprints, Deductions and Conclusions" (page 383) writes:— "On Friday, the 20th, the first imprint was later (sic) discovered to be a right toe.

Owing to the normal impression being blurred *it was impossible to obtain sufficient data to establish fraud."*

Our italics, to indicate that an intention to make an allegation of fraud against Valiantine was in the minds of his inquisitors from the very beginning!

MORE ARTISTIC EFFECTS.

We find later on in the book that it is the lanky-haired fellow who has been spotted as the alleged toe print! He has been very artistically enlarged and in the process has become transformed into an antiquated lean lady, with white goffered cap, ruffle round the neck, shawl over the shoulders, wearing dark spectacles, and—like Maggie Tulliver's famous doll and the very finest Greek sculpture—sadly battered as to the nose! This artistic production (the alleged fraudulent attempt to produce Sir A. Conan Doyle's thumb-print) is printed as Exhibit II page 340, alongside a "normal impression of the right big toe of George Valiantine."

The two companion pictures are no more resemblances than chalk is like cheese.

A REFERENCE REQUIRED.

All the same the *"Daily Express* Special Representative" says:– "Ex-Chief Detective-Inspector Bell, who examined as a finger-print expert the 'spirit' impressions secured at the Valiantine séances and the toe and finger prints of the medium, declared:– 'The resemblance between them is exact. In a court of law the resemblance would be sufficient to hang a man charged with murder.'"

We must call upon this *Express* journalist for his reference, for this pretended quotation is neither in Inspector Bell's Report, printed in full, nor anywhere else in the book! Nor anything the least like it!

EX-INSPECTOR BELL'S REPORT.

The Ex-Inspector's Report is almost entirely confined to one isolated item, namely, his search for "points of similarity" between what Mr. Bradley calls "the supernormal impression of one of the alleged Lord Dewar imprints" and a "normal impression" of Valiantine's left toe. There is no general resemblance between them, but the ex-Inspector was paid as "an expert" to find "points of similarity" in their lines and ridges, and professes to have found eighteen. He was not asked to find their "points of essential difference" and has, therefore, nothing to report on that head, but these are the crux of the whole matter, and some of them could have been pointed out to Mr. Bradley for nothing by any intelligent school child!

THE WISDOM OF THE GODS

"THE DOYLE VOICE" SAYS "I WILL TRY."

We now continue our summary of the séances:—

February 21.—Same sitters as last. The only new element in the conditions is that Sykes has brought a cigarette tin filled with modelling wax, which is placed on the stool beside the smoked paper. "Pat O'Brien," when asked if there would be further imprints, replied that "Doyle was trying to do so," and the alleged "Doyle Voice," slightly huskier than before, says "I will try and do so," in reply to a request by Jaquin that he should give an imprint of his index finger. A childish feminine voice, recognised as that of "Honey," one of Valiantine's guides, volunteered the statement, "I have put my hand on the paper." When the lights are put up "certain impressions" are found on the smoked paper which was on the top of the stool, but only "meaningless scrolls" on that underneath. Nothing on the modelling wax.

QUITE AN ART GALLERY!.

Mr. Jaquin took the sheets away for examination, but made no report on them—why not? They are printed as Exhibits 9 No. 3 and No. 4 in the book. Among the "certain impressions" we find an excellent picture of a British officer wearing his service cap, and immediately in front of him the profile of a lady, whose chin, nose, and front hair are touched with light. Then in the middle there is the face of an old Turk, whose headdress is half pulled off. Above him is a comical looking cat, which has perhaps done the deed, and has turned its face round in its flight to see whether it is pursued. The so-called "meaningless scrolls" are like a child's attempt to draw a donkey's head and jaw on a slate. It has quite a droll appearance. Valiantine's toes must be rather clever, to do such pretty sketches in the dark!

VALIANTINE BRINGS UP BLOOD.

February 22.—When Valiantine retired to bed the previous night be had coughed violently and brought up a quantity of blood. He wished to sit with Mr. and Mrs. Bradley alone on this date in order to consult "Dr. Barnett," one of his spirit-guides. The doctor told him there was no need to worry, as in the efforts for materialisation they were compelled to use not only his ectoplasmic forces but also his blood. The blood taken from him had not been properly re-assimilated by his body at the end of the séance.

"THE DEWAR VOICE!"

"One of the most fluent and remarkable voice séances I have ever known" is Mr. Bradley's description of what followed. Twenty-six different voices manifested. But near the end, a whispering husky voice (probably the same as impersonated Doyle), announced itself as "Dewar." It sounded in no way like that of the late Lord Dewar and pronounced the name as "Do-er" and not Dew-er. Bradley says this "may indicate impersonation." Of course it did. The speaker said he had "tried" to get his index finger on the wax on the previous evening, the 21st. He did not say he had succeeded, and no discernible impressions were, in fact, found on the wax.

February 23.—The Bradleys, Sykes, Jaquin, and Valiantine were the sitters. Besides the smoked paper, Sykes had brought a tin of softer wax. What Bradley now calls the "Lord Dewar Voice," this time "weak and muffled," said, "I have tried to give an imprint." The impersonator only said he had "tried." After the séance the two sheets of paper were "fixed" with solution and examined. Photographs of these are given in the book, and the labels attached to them are very carefully devised to cunningly suggest that the imprints were made by Lord Dewar himself, though Mr. Bradley knew very well that all the evidence indicated that the spirit claiming to be Lord Dewar was an impersonator.

VERY CURIOUS MARKINGS.

Mr. Jaquin makes no report on these, but this is how they appear to us:–

Exhibit No. 5.—This paper shows a very dark part and a much lighter part. On the dark part are two blobs of a medium shade, one of which is indefinite in shape, and the other is rather a good attempt at a likeness of Mr. Lloyd George, with his shaggy hair. On the top of the black part is the representation of an old man, with a well-rounded head, an enormous Punch-like nose, and a small projecting chin as if he had lost all his teeth.

Exhibit No. 6.—We see no imprint whatever on this smoked paper taken from under the stool, but the whole smoky mass makes a very curious picture. It portrays an old Hebrew prophet in long voluminous robes. He has abundant white hair and a long flowing white beard. His two hands are held up as if in remonstrance. His left foot is seen under the skirt of his robe, but his right foot is off the edge of the paper, the right leg being outstretched as if in the act of kicking someone outside the pale!

THE EXCUSE FOR BRADLEY'S CAMPAIGN.

This is the smoked paper which Bradley says "had been moved during the séance." He does not say so in so many words, but he means by Valiantine's toe! There were six pairs of toes in the circle, but it is Valiantine's he is after. This is the beginning of what may become known as "The Famous Bradley Toe Fiasco," and we must leave the dramatic story of its tragical development for another chapter.

It will be noted that up to this date there had been no signs of success excepting in the first imprints which Jaquin mistakenly thought "corresponded with Doyle's." Valiantine has taken no part in these séances beyond sitting in silence to help with his psychic power. He has made no claim that he could produce the thumb imprints of Sir Arthur Conan Doyle or Lord Dewar or anybody else. This was a series of experiments which might be successful or they might not. If not successful it did not matter a brass farthing to him. This was not his phase of mediumship and he was not being paid by results; he was, in fact, being paid nothing. If successful he would have been gratified because it would have pleased Bradley, and would have been a good piece of evidence of survival.

The impersonator of the "Doyle and Dewar Voices" was obviously none of his guides or controls, but a mischievous entity attracted by some sinister influence in the séance room. We shall see later how from such a small matter as the suspected "movement" of a smoked sheet Bradley found a starting point for his determined campaign to denounce his friend and guest, whom he had called the greatest medium in the world, as a fraud and a cheat. We shall also find the probable psychological reasons for his extraordinary change of attitude.

CHAPTER II.

INTRODUCTION.—*Last Month we mentioned cogent reasons for believing it was physically impossible for Valiantine to make toe prints on the smoked paper lying on and under the coffin-stool in Bradley's séance room. We challenged Bradley to himself perform the feat before independent witnesses if he thought it possible, out he has met our challenge with silence! We also called upon the DAILY EXPRESS to supply the reference to a pretended quotation from an alleged declaration by Ex-Chief Detective Inspector Bell, but again we are met by silence, though we called the Chief Editor's personal attention to the matter.*

The fair inference to be drawn is that Bradley cannot demonstrate the physical possibility of doing what he denounces Valiantine for having done, and that the EXPRESS cannot give the reference to a quotation which never existed.—ED., I.P.G.

OUR readers will recall that when the curtain dropped at the dose of the First Act in Mr. Dennis Bradley's ridiculous farce, as described in our last issue, two smoked sheets were taken from above and below the coffin-stool.

TWO FAINT BLOBS.

On the dark smoky part of the sheet on top of the stool were two faint blobs of a medium shade, the first of them indefinite in shape, and the second rather like Mr. Lloyd George, but neither of them the least like anybody's toe-prints! These two faint blobs are what Mr. Bradley hereafter calls "the alleged Dewar prints," on which he principally bases his allegations of fraud against his guest, George Valiantine, the American medium.

NO RIDGES VISIBLE.

We have carefully examined these blobs on the photograph of the smoked paper (Exhibit 5) with the most powerful microscope at our disposal, and can find no trace whatever of any skin ridges or lines of either thumbs or toes!

THE ADVENT OF THE RIDGES.

These blobs, however, when reproduced as Exhibit 9, are artistically enlarged, and are covered with a profusion of beautiful digital furrows and ridges, not visible in the originals! These enlargements are placed alongside a print of "George Valiantine's left big toe," also covered with furrows and ridges, and Mr. Bradley confidently announces on his label:– "**All of these digital impressions· are the same.**"

INSPECTOR BELL'S REPORT.

A still further enlargement of part of one of these blobs (with the artistic ridges and furrows), was submitted later to Ex-Chief Inspector Bell, along with an enlargement of **part** of the imprint of Valiantine's left big toe, and the Inspector reported:–

> "Both the impressions submitted to me are, without doubt, of the same type of pattern, and disclose skin ridge characteristics which agree not only m type, but also in the sequence in which they appear.
>
> **"In short, the peculiarities shown in one impression are to be found reproduced in the other.**
>
> "Eighteen of these clearly defined ridge characteristics, which are in agreement, are marked in each case by means of lines drawn and numbered."

THE PECULIARITIES REPRODUCED.

We have emphasised in black type what seems to us to be the essential part of this report, namely:– "The peculiarities shown in one impression are to be found **Reproduced** in the other," and again we lay emphasis on the· word **"REPRODUCED."** For the Inspector was not furnished with the original documents, as he should have been if an opinion of any true value was desired, but with "photographic copies" in which the lines on the one were "found reproduced on the other!"

INFERENCES THAT MAY BE DRAWN.

Is not the only inference that can be fairly drawn from this report, that some photographic artist had faithfully carried out the work entrusted to him of "reproducing" Valiantine's toe lines on "the alleged Dewar print"? Not, as Mr. Bradley would suggest, that Valiantine had taken off his shoes and socks in the dark and made a toe impression on the paper on top of the stool in the presence of Bradley, Jaquin, and Sykes, without their being cognisant of his clever and, indeed, impossible feat?

"THE PAPER HAD BEEN MOVED!"

The second smoked paper, the one lying on the carpet and underneath the coffin-stool, showed no sign of any imprint at all, but the whole smoky mass formed a strange picture of a Hebrew prophet in his voluminous robes. Bradley says on the label attached to this picture (*Exhibit No. 8*):—

"It will be seen by the distinct light patch that the smoked paper had been moved during the séance." By "the distinct light patch" he refers to the prophet's long white beard, which is naturally a little hazy in outline; but the sharp clear outlines of his priestly robe and left toe show not the slightest trace of movement.

Moreover, it is difficult to see how this particular piece of paper could have been moved, even if all the big toes in the room had made a combined effort to do it, for it was firmly pinned down on the carpet by two legs of the heavy coffin-stool, and it was guarded all round by a stout rail, 3½ inches high above the floor, which reached down to 1½ inches from the carpet! But this pretended evidence of a "movement of the paper" starts Bradley on his vigilant hunt for Valiantine's toe! It forms a picturesque episode in his play and we leave Bradley to describe it in his own words:—

BRADLEY'S OWN STORY.

SECURING VALIANTINE'S TOE-PRINTS.

"When Valiantine and the others had left the séance room Mr. Jaquin and I had a talk together, and we arranged that he should take the impressions of the big toes of Valiantine and of all those present in the circle.

"He therefore at once prepared fresh sheets of smoked paper. We then joined the others, and I told them it was absolutely necessary that every possible precaution should be taken, and that I would like them to agree to have their toe prints taken.

"When I made the suggestion, although I avoided looking straight towards Valiantine's direction, I could notice that, in his manner, he did not seem at all disturbed. ...

JAQUIN PERFORMS THE CEREMONY.

"The four men returned to the séance room, and Mr. Jaquin first took an impression of his own toes—right and left. Valiantine then took off his shoes and socks quite quickly and, taking a sheet of the smoked paper, was about to make the impression himself [as Jaquin had just done], when Mr. Jaquin intercepted him. Mr. Jaquin took hold of Valiantine's right and left toes, and took the impression of them in the manner he desired.

"In turn the toe impressions of the other sitters, Mr. Charles Sykes and myself, were taken, and then those of Mrs. Sykes and Mrs. Bradley.

AN ALLEGED DISCOVERY.

"After these impressions had been completed and the paper fixed, we compared Valiantine's toe-prints with the alleged spirit imprints which had been obtained during the evening.

[Why were all the other toe-prints ignored?] Mr. Jaquin at once observed the similarity. Just as he had done in the case of the earliest "imprints," which he first told Bradley "corresponded with Doyle's," and during the same morning wrote he "could find no point of resemblance"; and in his Report said:— "The first imprint was later discovered to be a right toe!" This finger-print expert marches rapidly from one extremity to another; first, Doyle's thumb imprint; second, not so; third, a toe!

J BRADLEY ALSO OBSERVES THE SIMILARITY.

"I had that day purchased two powerful magnifying ·glasses for the purpose of examination [this incident had evidently been prepared for], and on comparison I also observed the similarity.

[Though none to be seen!]

VALIANTINE ACCUSED!

"After the taking of the toe-prints Valiantine and the other sitters had returned to the drawing-room. I re-joined them, and asked Valiantine quite genially [sic] to come and glance at the imprints. He then joined Mr. Jaquin and myself in the séance room. Mr. Jaquin handed him the two smoked sheets, the one containing the impression obtained during the séance ["the alleged Dewar print"] and the other of Valiantine's left toe.

Mr. Jaquin, in a casual manner, remarked:— 'Have a look at this, George; they look rather similar to your left toe.'

"It must be understood that both Mr. Jaquin and myself, throughout the whole of this incident, were purposely very easy and friendly in our manner toward Valiantine.

VALIANTINE'S EMPHATIC REPLY.

"When Mr. Jaquin handed the two sheets to Valiantine for comparison, I watched Valiantine closely. As he took the sheets his hands trembled slightly. This was the first sign of agitation he displayed. He had hardly glanced at the imprints for more than two seconds when he said:– 'I can't see any similarity. They are not at all the same.'

CALMING VALIANTINE.

"We did not wish, at this period, to disturb Valiantine any further, so we laughingly endeavoured to calm him by telling him how curious similarities such as these do sometimes occur with skin imprints.

"Mr. Jaquin took away with him that night the séance imprints and also the toe imprints, and I asked him to have photographs taken of them as soon as possible the next day."

THE EVIDENCE TO DATE.

Now let us review the development thus far of the attempt to convict Valiantine of making dead men's thumb-prints by means of his toes! Three "imprint séances" have been held, on February 20, 21 and 23.

On February 20, there was obtained what Mr. Bradley calls "the alleged Doyle imprint," which looked like a lanky-haired fellow in the unenlarged photograph, and like an antiquated lean lady in the enlarged version, artistically touched up with a profusion of pretty lines! On February 21 another "alleged Doyle imprint" was spotted, which looks like a comical cat in the small photograph, but loses most of that resemblance in the touched-up enlargement.

On February 23, two "alleged Lord Dewar imprints" were found on the smoked paper, one indefinite in shape and the other rather like Lloyd George. They bear no resemblance to any mark that could have been made by anybody's toe, but later on, *mirabile dictu*, they are found in touched-up photographic enlargements to exhibit the identical ridges and furrows of Valiantine's toe!

THE FINAL SÉANCE.

We shall now resume our summary of the "imprint séances." There were to be three more, but the next was the last.

February 27, 1931.—Present, the Bradleys, the Sykes, Jaquin, and Valiantine. Few voices spoke and what they said "was practically of no account." "Bert Everett," in shrill tones, announced, "Segrave is here."

After a lengthy pause "Bert" said "Exquisite!" a word he frequently utters. Bradley asked—"What is exquisite? Do you mean that we have got an imprint through?"

"Bert"—"Yes." Bradley—"Whose?" "Bert"—"Segrave's." When the lights were switched on several "imprints" were found on the smoked sheet on top of the stool, "one of which was apparently a finger." Bradley's label on the photographed copy of this sheet says:– "There are several impressions of elbow joints, a finger impression, and also skin ridge markings.

During the séance it was alleged that an imprint has been given by the late Sir Henry Segrave."

"THIRD DEGREE" IN TORTURE CHAMBER."

The ladies at this stage left the séance room, and waited in the drawing-room until between two and three in the morning, while the three men worked their cruel will on the gentle, honest, unsuspicious Valiantine. This particular chapter in the book is entitled "The Collapse of Valiantine," and though it is an ugly story, it is narrated by Bradley with an air of personal triumph. We again think it well to let the author tell his tale in his own way:-

BRADLEY'S PRELIMINARY OBSERVATIONS.

"Mr. Sykes, Mr. Jaquin, Valiantine and myself then each examined the imprints closely in turn under the magnifying glass. I remarked casually, but with a purpose, that they were certainly quite different from those obtained at the previous imprint sittings, and added, also with design, 'If it can be proved that these imprints could not be made by anyone who was present in this room tonight, then it will be possible to assume that they are supernormal.'

IMPRINTS OF VALIANTINE'S FEET.

"I stated that we must take every precaution to ensure absolute proof. This afforded Mr. Jaquin the opportunity to suggest that he should take the impression of the whole foot of Valiantine. To this Valiantine readily agreed, and Mr. Jaquin took the impressions of both of his feet, including his heels. The object of this was to discover if there were any signs of methylene green . I did not anticipate that there would be. Assuming a very ordinary craftiness on the part of Valiantine, it did not appear to me logical he would be likely, in view of what had happened previously, to repeat the same type of fraudulent performance. [Up to now there had been no sign of any "fraudulent performance" on Valiantine's part.]

"FOR PURPOSES OF COMPARISON."

"It was useful, however, for Mr. Jaquin to obtain further imprints of Valiantine's feet for the purposes of comparison with the imprints which had been previously obtained. [A very different purpose for which they might be useful occurs to us!]

"While his feet imprints were being taken Valiantine showed a slight sense of resentment, and said that if his feet imprints had to be taken, then the feet imprints of every other sitter should be taken also. [Quite right too, but there is no mention of the others having done it!]

JAQUIN CONFRONTS VALIANTINE.

"While we were discussing this, and Valiantine was replacing his laced shoes and socks, Mr. Jaquin left the room for a moment or so. He then returned with the photographic enlargements of the séance imprints obtained on Monday, February 23, and also the photographic enlargement of Valiantine's big left toe.

[The prints referred to were "the alleged Lord Dewar prints."] He confronted Valiantine with them, saying, 'How do you explain this?' [Valiantine's reply, if any, is not stated.]

BRADLEY "A CALM OBSERVER!"

"In view of the happenings which had occurred at the sitting on this evening I consider that Mr. Jaquin was too precipitate in his action. I did not interfere in any way, because although Mr. Jaquin and Mr. Valiantine were both getting slightly excited, I maintained throughout the attitude and mentality of a calm observer. It was essential for me to record all the facts. [He has just burked what Valiantine had to say in answer to Jaquin.] Trivialities may occasionally excite me because of their irritation, but when the moment arrives for essentials to be considered the effect on me has always been to foster an aloof perspective in order to obtain a clearer and more penetrative survey. I interposed, and stopped the slight argument between Mr. Jaquin and Valiantine. I said it was necessary for us to consider the imprints which had just been obtained.

FINGER PRINTS TAKEN.

"We all examined them again, and in view of the fact that one of the séance impressions was that of a little finger, we suggested that impressions must be taken of Valiantine's little fingers. [Why not of all the others?] Valiantine assented to this quite readily, and Mr. Jaquin then took them and fixed the imprints.

"The imprints of Valiantine's fingers, as taken, were certainly shorter than those of the séance imprint. This, however, might have possibly been explained by the stretching of the joints. [Some new magical process!]

"EXPLAIN ·THE. RESEMBLANCE!"

"Mr. Jaquin then asked Valiantine whether he could explain the resemblance. Valiantine replied firmly and confidently, but with genuine heat, 'That is not my little finger.' Jaquin then remarked that it was suspiciously like it, to which Valiantine angrily replied, 'I bet you two hundred pounds that it is not my little finger.' Mr. Jaquin was slightly nonplussed by this, and did not pursue the point.

BRADLEY ADMITS "CONSIDERABLE DIFFERENCE."

"Valiantine was peculiarly emphatic when he made this remark; so much so that he really appeared confident that it was not his little finger, and that this could not be proved. I observed that there was a considerable difference between the length of the 'Segrave' séance finger imprint [the one in question] and that of George Valiantine's little finger imprints, taken by Mr. Jaquin.

JAQUIN'S IMPUDENT SUGGESTION.

"Mr. Jaquin then added to Valiantine, 'If it's not your little finger then probably you have a dummy finger in your pocket.' Valiantine became indignant at this, and said, 'You can search me.'

BRADLEY ADVISES HIS GUEST TO STRIP!

"This gave me [Bradley] the opportunity of suggesting to Valiantine that for his own sake the best thing for him to do was to strip and submit to being searched. Valiantine at once agreed, saying, 'You can strip me; I don't mind being searched if you agree that everyone else is stripped and searched afterwards.' To this we all assented.

VALIANTINE'S POCKETS SEARCHED.

"Valiantine then took off his jacket, waistcoat, and trousers, and I asked Mr. Jaquin to undertake a search of Valiantine's pockets. The pockets contained only the usual objects a man carries. [There is no mention of the three inquisitors stripping or letting Valiantine go through their pockets!]

AN OMISSION.

"I remembered afterwards, however, that Mr. Jaquin had omitted to examine Valiantine's pocket handkerchief, which, of course, might have shown traces of the wiping away of the marks of the smoked paper. This omission was unfortunate, because a search for all possible traces was particularly essential, having regard to Valiantine's emphatic challenge that the smoked paper imprint was not his.

A GREEN STAIN!

"Proceeding with his search, Mr. Jaquin then rolled back the shirt sleeve of Valiantine's right arm. There were no concealments and no markings. Rolling back the shirt sleeve of the left arm on the elbow was discovered *a large stain of the preparation of the finger-print ink and methylene green.*

VALIANTINE CANNOT EXPLAIN.

"The stain was pointed out to Valiantine and he was asked to explain it. He looked at it, appeared somewhat staggered, and then said, 'I just can't explain it; what it is I don't know, or how it got there? [This reply reminds us of William Hope's answer, when tricked by Harry Price and Co. We asked him what had happened and he said, "I have been tricked, but I don't know how." Had Valiantine examined his inquisitors' hands and handkerchiefs "for all possible traces" of finger-print ink and methylene green might he not also have discovered something? That was another unfortunate omission.]

BRADLEY'S "PROOF."

"I then told him that the tin of modelling wax had been specially prepared with methylene green, and that this was a proof that he had used his elbow to make the séance imprint.

[This was no proof at all, in view of another explanation much more likely to be true.] I told him to put on his clothes and we would discuss the matter.

THE INQUISITORS IN TURN BADGER VALIANTINE.

"In turn we asked him if he had any explanations to give of the smoked imprint, and of the stain. In reply to our questions he merely continued to insist [as any other man conscious of his innocence would have done] that he had never used his toes, and that the only way he could account for the stain on his elbow was that his ectoplasm must have absorbed the methylene green, and when it returned to his body had left the stain on his elbow.

[An explanation quite in accord with proved facts in psychic science, though it was possibly not the correct explanation in this particular case.]

"To the majority of questions which were put to him Valiantine had one stock reply, 'I can't explain.'

VALIANTINE BREAKS DOWN.

"We questioned him at considerable length, and he then showed signs of breaking down. Rising from his chair, he said in a broken voice, 'I can't stand it any longer. I can't stand it—let me go.' I told him quite gently, but firmly, that he must not go to bed until he had given us an explanation.

HE COLLAPSES AND BECOMES UNCONSCIOUS.

"He [Valiantine] still seemed to trust and rely on my help. He sat down again, but after a few more questions he collapsed utterly, and burst into a violent fit of sobbing. His whole body shook convulsively, and when the sobbing subsided he became unconscious. His eyes closed and his body shook with violent trembling ; he gasped for breath. It was apparently a fit of nervous hysteria.

SYKES AND JAQUIN APPLY BANDAGES.

"Mr. Sykes at once suggested that cold water bandages should be applied to his head. This was done: Mr. Sykes applying the bandages while Mr. Jaquin continued to re-soak the towels every few minutes.

"IN DANGER OF A STROKE."

"Valiantine remained in this condition for nearly two hours. During this time his heart beat was extremely rapid, and, by the signs of congestion shown in his face, his blood pressure was evidently high. His pulse was extremely rapid and intermittent. At one time, shortly before he recovered consciousness, Mr. Jaquin said that he thought his condition was such that he was certainly in danger of a stroke.

BRADLEY HELPS HIS GUEST TO BED.

"It was about 2 a.m. when he recovered, and then I took him up to his room. He was in a distressed condition, but was just able to walk upstairs with my help, hanging on to me with his arm round my neck.

He thanked me for helping him, speaking in heart-broken tones, almost like a child.

VALIANTINE'S SORROWFUL QUESTION.

"He sat limply on his bed, his eyes looking into space, and, not as if he were addressing me, he said, in broken tones: 'Why did they do this to me? Why did they do this to me?' These words were said in a manner difficult to describe. Strange as it may seem I do not think that he meant by 'they' to refer to Mr. Jaquin or to Mr. Sykes, to me, or to any of us.

BRADLEY'S "WORDS OF COMFORT."

"Valiantine was in such a distraught condition, and evidently so weak and ill, that it was only merciful for me to give him a few words of comfort. I told him to try and ease his mind and get some sleep. He threw his arms round me and embraced me.

THE LADIES EXONERATED!

"After leaving Valiantine I rejoined the others. Mrs. Bradley and Mrs. Sykes had remained in the drawing-room since the close of the séance at about 10.30 and, of course, they had no· part in any of the proceedings which had taken place since then."

"THIRD DEGREE" EXAMINATIONS.

Now has there ever been a story in real life so cruel, so merciless, and so inhuman as this of Valiantine's "third degree" examination by three educated men in the Torture Chamber of Dorincourt? The intention was obviously to extort by persistent bullying "a confession" from Valiantine that he had, as a medium, been guilty of a fraud he had never committed, a confession which would make a tremendous sensation throughout the world, to the great discomfiture of Spiritualists and to the great satisfaction of Bradley's Mother Church! But Valiantine, sensitive to a degree as he is, and brutally borne down as he was, held firm to the assertion of his complete innocence, and thereby baffled his inquisitors with their wicked trumped-up accusations!

Had the police subjected any suspected criminal, even a suspected murderer, to such a cruel ordeal, bringing him within an ace of a stroke of paralysis, if not of death itself, in order to extort a confession (even a just one) the whole country would have been roused to a storm of angry indignation.

POINTS OF PSYCHOLOGICAL INTEREST.

The most difficult part of the story to understand is why Bradley, still in the midst of his admiration for Valiantine's "voice" phenomena, should have rounded on him and denounced him in his book and through the Press as a fraud, without the faintest shadow of excuse.

BUSINESS ARRANGEMENTS.

A certain coolness and distance had apparently sprung up between the two men in connection with their business relations, which Bradley describes in detail in his book.

Briefly summarised, these were that for Valiantine's first visit to England he was paid the sum of £225, including expenses, of which Bradley paid one half and Mr. Joseph De Wykoff, an American admirer, the other.

On subsequent visits Bradley defrayed Valiantine's expenses, and "a present was made to him of about £200." He does not say whether anyone shared this expense, but we have ascertained that in 1925 Bradley himself paid £105 and other contributors £204 6s.

As Valiantine became more and more famous he received many big offers for his services. Bradley writes:– "One man whom I know personally offered him £300 for six sittings. I did not allow Valiantine to accept this offer because I detested the idea of mediumship being placed upon a definite commercial basis."

SÉANCES ON THE CHEAP!

On the second last occasion [1929] Valiantine came to this country, Bradley did not send him a cheque for his expenses as he knew that another client would treat him "in an exceptionally generous manner." He says:– "My expenses had been so heavy in connection with his previous visits that **I had no intention whatever of making a contribution on this occasion.** Valiantine, however, appeared to take it for granted that I should do so. His manner seemed to me to have become hardened and materialistic. He spoke in a somewhat conceited manner, and certainly had very decided views as to the monetary value of his services. He remarked to me casually that some people would pay a million pounds for such privileges. He apparently disregarded the fact that the translated publications of my psychic books in most of the European countries were largely responsible for his having become internationally famous."

A FIFTY-FIFTY MUTUAL INDEBTEDNESS.

Bradley on his part disregarded the fact that but for Valiantine he would never have soared "Towards the Stars" or glimpsed "The Wisdom of the Gods," or written books on these subjects. There was a 50/50 account of mutual indebtedness between them.

Bradley continues:— "There can be little doubt that the rapid accumulation of money did not have a beneficial effect upon Valiantine's character. As a man, I think it ruined him." So he generously refrained from helping in his ruin—by paying him nothing!

VALIANTINE'S TERMS.

It is only fair to state that Valiantine never charges any fees and relies for a living on the voluntary gifts of his clients. So Bradley was under no compulsion to pay anything for the two series of séances he asked for and obtained, though there was, of course, an implied contract to make him the customary gift.

"THIS SACRIFICE OF YOUR TIME."

For the last visit in 1931, Bradley sent Valiantine an offer from an English doctor of £200 for a fortnight's sittings and asked for a fortnight's sittings for himself (to be included in the same fee !). Valiantine replied that it would not pay him to come over for a month for £200 if he had to pay his own expenses, but should his other client also wish him he would come. Bradley replied:— "I think you should not consider whether it would pay you to come over for £200, but whether, in view of everything that has been done for you in the past you should not make this sacrifice of your time."

OTHER CLIENTS TOLD.

Arrangements were completed. to give the additional client a month's sittings, Bradley a fortnight, and the Doctor a fortnight.

The Doctor paid Valiantine a cheque for £200 in advance, which Bradley on making his charge of fraud against Valiantine demanded back! He asked whether Valiantine had yet been paid by his other client for his month's sittings and on being told no, told Valiantine to say nothing to this client until he had been told "exactly what had happened!" The Doctor and the other client were told Bradley's version of "exactly what had happened." The Doctor decided to take the sittings arranged for nevertheless; while the other client received Bradley "in a somewhat cold manner" and, says Bradley, "I am almost inclined to think that he believed Valiantine more than he believed me!"

BAFFLED AND THWARTED!

Thus Bradley's efforts to injure Valiantine in the eyes of his two paying clients were baffled. His desire to ship him off on the 4th of March, immediately after the so-called "exposure," instead of the 18th as arranged, was thwarted.

And all the satisfaction Bradley got out of his schemings was the knowledge that he had secured two series of Valiantine séances free of cost. To his titled friends he had, like some grand seigneur, been giving away the highly valued and exclusive privilege of attending Valiantine séances at his house, and they are not likely to be grateful to him to-day for having been made the unconscious sharers in his parsimony!

PARTING KICKS.

Bradley knew that he would never again get a series of sittings with "the greatest medium in the world" on such stingy terms. The parting of the ways had come, and it was celebrated in such injurious ways as we have seen, which may fitly be described as Bradley's parting kicks!

J. L.

CHAPTER III.

VALIANTINE'S REPLY TO THE ACCUSATIONS. DENNIS BRADLEY'S THREAT TO "SMASH SPIRITUALISM."

WE (the International Psychic Gazette) sent Mr. George Valiantine a proof of our November article on his so-called "Exposure" by Dennis Bradley and invited him to send us his own account of the affair, which has already been noised abroad to the most distant countries in the world.

The following is his reply, which confirms our faith in his absolute innocence, and our belief that he is the victim of one of the most wicked and disgraceful attempts to discredit an honest medium by crafty tricks and widespread slanders ever experienced in the history of the Spiritualist Movement:—

Williamsport, Pa., U.S.A.
November 7, 1931.

DEAR Sir,—I am in receipt of your letter of October 25, enclosing proofs of your review, for which kindly accept thanks.

I think it is a fine article and appreciate your kindness in taking so much interest in me.

I was very much surprised when the Editor of one of our papers here in Williamsport called me by telephone and told me that Mr. Bradley was writing a book denouncing me as a fraud, and he asked me what kind of a man Bradley was. I told him, as far as I knew he was all right.

I am perfectly innocent of the charges made against me. It looks to me as though it was a frame-up, as there were none of my friends present at the sitting, and, therefore, they had everything their own way.

As far as the weeping is concerned, they certainly did abuse me, which hurt my feelings very much. They tried to make me admit that I made them (the imprints) and I told them if they could explain it, to go ahead and do so, as I could not; and I told them it was beyond me, and that **I was perfectly innocent of any wrong-doing.**

The night before I left, Bradley urged me to have a sitting, which I did. Mr. and Mrs. Bradley and myself sat as usual, but we could not get any voices, only the movement of the trumpet, and **Bradley, after the sitting, became very angry because we did not get anything and said he was going to smash Spiritualism.**

The next morning I left for Southampton.

They threatened to denounce me to the world, by the International News, **that I was a fraud. I told them to do just as they liked, as I was innocent,** and he (Bradley) wanted me to leave London by the next boat, and for me to cancel the arrangements we made with Dr. Vivian, of Southbourne, which I did not do. He did not want the newspaper men to know when I left England, fearing that the reporters would interview me.

Noel Jaquin took my toe and foot prints, six times, and I would like to know why it was necessary to take them so many times, and as all the prints were mixed up, mine with those of the Spirit prints, which we had gotten, **they could easily have taken two copies of mine to Scotland Yard and said one was supposed to be that of Sir Arthur's.** At the first sitting we had for finger prints, the prints of all those present were taken, but after that, only mine were taken. Why was that? I could not understand why Dennis Bradley, after writing two books on Spiritualism and lauding me as one of the greatest mediums of to-day, would deliberately turn around and denounce me as a fraud; but since reading your article, I can clearly see what is back of it all: that he wants to return to the Catholic faith, and before doing so, he wants to make amends, and is taking this means to do so by denouncing me as a fraud and thus try to smash Spiritualism.

I am enclosing herewith an article which was printed in our *Williamsport Sun.* I was interviewed by a reporter here.

What seems so strange to me is that there was nothing in the New York papers about it; but it is my opinion that Bradley wanted the paper of the City in which I live to know about it.

In conclusion, I wish to state again, that I am perfectly innocent of the charges made against me.

Again thanking you for your interest in the matter, and trusting that everything will be all right, I am, sincerely,

GEORGE VALIANTINE.

AFTERWORD

Herbert Dennis Bradley, author of the 1924 book, *Toward the Stars*, concluded this first edition of *Wisdom of the Gods* published in 1925 on a very zealous and fervent note, stating that the spirits "have given irrefutable evidence of their surviving personalities." He contended that his two books set forth a series of psychic experiments unequalled in history. And he deemed George Valiantine "as the most remarkable physical medium in history." Many students of psychical research might very well agree with him. In the 1929 edition, Bradley, with egg on his face, made a few revisions admitting that one of the mediums mentioned in the book, F. T. Munnings, was supposedly exposed as producing fraudulent phenomena (see appendix A).

In his final book *And After*, published in 1931, Bradley seems almost distraught in admitting that Valiantine, the medium most mentioned and admired in his two previous books, was caught in what seemed certainly to be a deceptive act. Clearly, Bradley had the carpet pulled out from under him by this "deception," and while he didn't fall flat on his face, he apparently appeared to some as a stumbling fool.

In *And After* Bradley claimed that Valiantine's increasingly materialistic lifestyle and attitude, which he observed when Valiantine arrived in England in 1931, had permitted devious low-level spirits to influence him, thereby bringing about the deception. The "teachings" coming through some credible mediums from supposedly advanced spirits held that lower-level spirits, being closer to the earth frequency, were better able to communicate and influence mortals than more advanced spirits—those at a more distant frequency—and that some of these lower-level spirits were as deceitful as they were in the earth life. It was further taught that the more materialistic a person, the more likely he was to be influenced by low-level spirits. Bradley writes:

"As he [Valiantine] became more and more famous, when he visited this country he usually stayed with me at Dorincourt, although he often received many big offers for his services elsewhere. One man, whom I knew: personally, offered him £300 for six sittings. I did not allow Valiantine to accept this offer because I detested the idea of mediumship being placed upon a definite commercial basis.

On the last occasion he came to this country, prior to the 1931 visit, Valiantine brought with him his wife, and seemed decidedly changed in his outlook on life. He had meanwhile received large sums of money from wealthy patrons.

On this occasion I did not send Valiantine a cheque for his passage as he was only staying with me for a few days. I was not conducting a series of sittings at Dorincourt, and I knew that he would be treated in an exceptionally generous manner by Mr. X, with whom he had arranged to spend a month or so. My expenses had been so heavy in connection with his previous visits that I had no intention whatever of making a contribution on this occasion. Valiantine, however, appeared to take it for granted that I should do so. His manner seemed to me to have become hardened and materialistic. He spoke in a somewhat conceited manner, and certainly had very decided views as to the monetary value of his services. He remarked to me casually that some people would pay a million pounds for such privileges. He apparently disregarded the fact that the translated publications of my psychic books in most of the European countries were largely responsible for his having become internationally famous.

He was most passionately devoted to his wife—a woman a few years his junior and when they visited England together, he lavished every attention on her.

She brought with her far more clothes than the majority of women travel with, many of which she had never worn, and she took back with her considerably more.

She possessed, I should imagine, a wardrobe equal in size to that of society beauties. Valiantine's devotion to his wife is to his credit, and at this time he certainly had the means to gratify her wishes.

He told me that for four weeks' mediumistic services at Mr. X's house he received the sum of £1,500, in addition to his double travelling expenses, which amounted to a few more hundreds.

AFTERWORD

It is probably true that Valiantine, an ordinary uneducated man, finding himself catapulted into the limelight, like many people in that situation was influenced by his newfound celebrity status. But, it is also clear from Bradley's writing, that he was put out—his ego bruised—by being placed on the sidelines while others offered more money and in exchange, wanted more of Valiantine's time.

The alleged deception took place in late February 1931 when Valiantine held six sittings at Bradley's home, beginning February 19 and ending February 27. Some spectacular voice phenomena took place. Bradley reported that 13 different and distinct voices were heard in the very first sitting, as eight individual personal voices and five of Valiantine's guides manifested.

After "Dr. Barnett," one of the guides spoke, not using the trumpet, the trumpet was lifted and floated close to Bradley. "Herbert, it's Gert," the voice came. Bradley's sister, Gertrude, had died in 1928. "Although somewhat faint in tone, the 'voice' was quite distinguishable. The conversation which followed was on purely family matters, and answers to questions which were put were made without hesitation," Bradley recorded. "During the time my sister was talking to me, the trumpet several times wafted rapidly from me to my wife, to whom many remarks were also addressed."

Bradley's father, Dan Bradley, then spoke "in his direct, spontaneous and characteristic manner," providing abundant evidence of events that had happened since his physical death in 1925. He also spoke to Mrs. (Mabel) Bradley and to Valiantine, the trumpet floating from one to the other. Every sentence, Bradley stated, was delivered in the "attractive Irish accent" that characterized his voice when alive. "Every intonation was identical with his intonation when alive, as was that peculiar unmistakable 'voice' of his, which could be recognized among a million."

Bradley's sister, Annie, spoke, seemingly agitated. "Herbert, it's Annie. Be *careful*! Be *careful*!" Bradley asked for an explanation, but Annie said she could say no more, only that he *must* be careful. Mabel Bradley's father and brother then spoke with her, both providing evidence of their identify.

On February 25, Lady Doyle, the widow of Sir Arthur Conan Doyle, and Adrian, his adult son, visited Bradley's home at his invitation and sat with Valiantine and the Bradleys. Bradley reported that both Lady Doyle and Adrian recognized the voice coming through as that of Sir Arthur. The voice carried on a conversation with the two about personal and domestic matters. The sitting lasted for some 90 minutes with the Doyle voice dominating the evening. Bradley was impressed with the sitting, noting that there was a deepness in the intonation of the voice which was characteristic of the Doyle accent, though most of the personal and domestic matters discussed were unknown to him. However, they were meaningful to Lady Doyle and Adrian. Bradley further recorded that the voice said to Adrian, "I am ready to go in the 'chitty' any time with you," and went on to discuss the son's racing cars. Lady Doyle later mentioned that Sir Arthur had used much the same verbiage with Adrian two or three times when he was alive.

Toward the end, a voice came through announcing itself as "Fatty." Adrian Doyle recognized it as a friend of his named Duncan, who was killed in a motor vehicle accident a year or so earlier. A short conversation took place between the two, mostly about motor racing.

As impressive and convincing as the voice phenomena were to the Bradleys, the Doyles, and others during those February 1931 sittings, an experiment by Bradley failed badly and pointed to fraud on the part of Valiantine.

That same month at one of the sittings, Bradley had asked Doyle and another communicator claiming to be Lord Dewar, who had passed away 10 months earlier, to leave thumb or fingerprints on smoke paper with some waxing substance brought to the room by Noel Jaquin, the hand and fingerprint expert (who is featured in earlier chapters). Jaquin also sat in observing, and examining the prints. Although Bradley's report of what took place is difficult to follow, the bottom line is that prints supposedly left by Doyle and Dewar matched up to Valiantine's big toes. Bradley was shocked and demanded an answer from Valiantine, who claimed innocence and repeatedly said he had no idea how his toes were imprinted on the paper. Nor was Bradley able to get an answer from Valiantine's guides, one of them saying that the experiments were successful.

Bradley was unforgiving of this deception and ended his friendship with Valiantine before writing *And After*. In this third book, Bradley remained certain that Valiantine had produced genuine spirit voices and was adamant that as Valiantine's humble nature was gradually replaced by pride and hubris, mischievous, low-level spirits were able to influence him and cause him to cheat on the imprints. "In 'direct' voice communication, when one is in contact with intelligent and personally known entities, conversations can be held which are beautiful and inspiring," he wrote in the last chapter of the 1931 book, "but it must be realized that when once

AFTERWORD

the channels of communication are opened, lower and less intelligent entities are also, at times, afforded opportunities."

Bradley was certain that Valiantine could not speak the many foreign languages, if any, that came through him, especially the ancient Chinese dialect that Professor Neville Whymant heard (see Foreword for a discussion of this). Moreover, Valiantine would have had to anticipate questions put to him by Whymant about Confucius and recite without warning 15 verses of a Confucius poem in a Chinese dialect. One skeptical researcher, while not doubting the integrity of Whymant, theorized that because there were many Chinese living in America, Valiantine may have picked up a few Chinese words here and there, enough to fool Whymant, who then unconsciously filled in the blanks with his own knowledge of the Confucius poems. The fact that the Chinese voice offered ideas new to Whymant and other scholars was not addressed by the skeptic.

It was further observed by Bradley that at one sitting, three voices were heard speaking together, all overlapping, and in one case when a spirit was talking with Valiantine, the spirit voice talked over his voice, i.e., the voice began responding to Valentine before Valentine had finished his sentence.

Bradley was equally certain that Valiantine could not have known much of the personal information that came through for him, his wife, and many others over the years, and further that he could not have imitated their voices, accents, manners of speech, etc. Nevertheless, he faced the skeptical mindset that said, "once a cheat, always a cheat."

Blaming the toeprints on devious "earthbound" spirits was not going to fly with the skeptics.

Writing in the December 1931 issue of *The International Psychic Gazette*, Valiantine claimed his innocence and charged that it was a "frame-up" by Bradley. "I could not understand why Dennis Bradley, after writing two books on Spiritualism and lauding me as one of the greatest mediums of today, would deliberately turn around and denounce me as a fraud," he stated, going on to say that Bradley wanted to return to his Catholic faith and for him to do so he was required to make amends by denouncing him and smashing Spiritualism. In fact, Bradley ended his 1931 book by admitting that, even though such psychic research is valid, the danger is that it will be misused and abused, leading to a "religion" such as Spiritualism, which he says has a "general tendency towards evil." He further stated, "I was educated a Roman Catholic and I remain a Roman Catholic."

As discussed in the foreword, the controversies surrounding Valiantine's mediumship contributed significantly to the decline of psychical research and the birth of parapsychology, which focused on extrasensory perception (ESP) and telekinetic, now called psychokinetic (PK), phenomena, while avoiding any discussion of mediums, spirits, or of consciousness surviving death in an afterlife. The mediumship of Mina Crandon, aka "Margery," and Rudi Schneider, like Valiantine's, both taking place mostly during the 1920s, also resulted in considerable controversy and added much fuel to the fire. Crandon and Schneider were studied more for the physical phenomena produced than was Valiantine, but, like Valiantine, they were also known for the direct or independent voice—alleged spirit voices originating away from the medium and not from their voice mechanisms. The voices were often amplified by a cone or trumpet, but with some voices this was not always necessary. With Crandon, the voice was said to be that of Walter, her deceased brother, and with Schneider it was primarily an entity who gave her name as "Olga."

The spiritualistic claim with Crandon, Schneider, Valiantine and many other mediums was that spirits were actually involved and responsible for activity that observers claimed to be a trick of some kind, but since science did not recognize the existence of spirits, such an explanation was not acceptable. Therefore, fraud was the only scientific explanation. In fact, Valiantine had been charged with fraud several times before the 1931 toeprint fiasco, but they were dismissed as spirit activity by those who were open to the spirit hypothesis. Those who were not open to it remained stymied since so much of it appeared to be beyond conjuring. What conjurer, for example, could have anticipated questions about the poems of Confucius and then recited 15 verses of one such poem in a Chinese dialect, while also pointing out an error by scholars in interpreting one of the verses in another poem of Confucius?

Some researchers were more open to non-fraud explanations, while not necessarily endorsing the spirit hypothesis. Sir William Crookes, a pioneer in X-ray technology and president of the Royal Society, one of the early researchers, referred to a "force" and an "intelligence" accompanying the phenomena he had witnessed with medium D. D. Home. In his 1904 book, *Researches into the Phenomena of Modern Spiritualism*, he wrote:

> The theory of Psychic Force is in itself merely the recognition of the now almost undisputed fact that under certain conditions, as yet but

imperfectly ascertained, and within a limited, but as yet undefined, distance from the bodies of certain persons having a special nerve organization, a Force operates in which, without muscular contact or connection, action at a distance is caused, and visible motions and audible sounds are produced in solid substances. As the presence of such an organization is necessary to the phenomenon, it is reasonably concluded that the Force does, in some manner, as yet unknown, proceed from that organization. As the organization is itself moved and directed within its structure by a Force, which either is, or is controlled by, the Soul, Spirit, or Mind (call it what we may) which constitutes the individual being we call 'the Man,' it is an equally reasonable conclusion that the Force which causes the motions beyond the limits of the body is the same Force that produces motion within the limits of the body.

Crookes went on to say that the Force is seen to be often directed by Intelligences.

In the May and June 1926 issues of the *Journal of the American Society for Psychical Research*, Dr. Karl Gruber, a German physician, biologist, and zoologist, reported on his research of the physical mediumship of Rudi Schneider, explaining that 'synchronous movements' between the medium and an object out of the medium's reach resulted in movement of the object. "If this connection is broken by movements of the hand or other object across the field of activity, or if it is roughly torn away, either temporary or lasting bodily injury to the medium results," Gruber stated, noting that his research involved more than one-hundred experiments. "This fact has been repeatedly misunderstood by the skeptical, who have seen in it the unmasking of a frightened medium."

Gruber cited the reports of Dr. William J. Crawford, a mechanical engineer who carried out 87 experiments with Irish medium Kathleen Goligher between 1914 and 1917. Crawford concluded that the movement of a table or other object out of Goligher's reach resulted from invisible "psychic rods" extending from the medium to the object being moved. These psychic rods were made of what others called "ectoplasm" or "teleplasm," though Crawford referred to it as "psychic stuff." They originated with what Crawford referred to as "operators," which he took to be discarnate human beings, only after giving consideration to the "secondary personality" theory preferred by many researchers. "These particular mechanical reactions cause her to make slight involuntary motions with her feet, motions which a careless observer would set down as imposture," Crawford explained.

Crawford communicated frequently with the operators and stated that "the operators themselves do not seem to know much about the scientific aspect of the phenomena they produce." In his 1919 book, *Experiments in Psychical Science*, he went on to say that "many of the cases of fraud which have been brought forward against mediums I know to be untrue, and further, I know (which the authors of the fraud theory do not) exactly where the truth lies and in what way a genuine manifestation has borne the appearance of a fraudulent one."

While making a distinction between conscious and unconscious fraud, the latter taking place while the medium was in a trance state, and admitting that both exist, Crawford concluded that both had been much overestimated.

Even at séances, such as the Golighers', where everything is above suspicion, where all phenomena can be demonstrated with the greatest ease to be genuine to the last detail, things happen which to a superficial observer might appear fraudulent. ... The seeker after fraud (who by the way is usually a person with no knowledge of science) immediately puts them down to imposture. My experiments, conducted over a long period of time and more thoroughly than any ever carried out hitherto, have proved to me beyond all question that the medium's body is either directly or indirectly the focus of all the mechanical actions which result in phenomena. And not only is it the focus but it also seems to supply a kind of duplicate of portions of her body, which can be temporarily detached and projected into the space in front of her. Thus, things happen in the séance room which, from the nature of the case, sometimes bears a superficial appearance of fraud, though, in a properly conducted circle it is only superficial, and the true and genuine nature of the phenomena can always be discovered by a little investigation.

Before Goligher, Valiantine, Crandon, and Schneider were studied by scholars and scientists, Eusapia Palladino was the subject of extensive testing by researchers in Italy, France, Great Britain, and the United States. "Even if there were no other medium than Eusapia in the world, her manifestations would suffice to establish scientifically the reality of telekinesis and ectoplasmic forms," wrote Dr. Charles Richet, the French physician, professor, and researcher, who won the 1913 Nobel Prize in medicine, in his 1923 book, *Thirty Years of Psychical Research*.

Ectoplasm was described by Richet as "a whitish substance that creeps as if alive, with damp, cold, protoplasmic extensions that are transformed under the eyes of the experimenters into a hand, fingers, a head, or even into an entire figure." It was reported by many researchers, with various mediums it usually exuded from the medium's nose or mouth, but sometimes from the ears, pores, or vagina. It was vaporish with some mediums, including Palladino (and apparently with Valiantine), but denser and more substantive with other mediums.

Richet, who had more than 200 sittings with Palladino, reported that ectoplasmic arms and hands emerged from her body and did what they wished, independent of her will, as her consciousness had vacated her body. However, because light had a negative effect on the production of ectoplasm, darkness was usually required and it was not always obvious to others in the room what was taking place.

> It is also quite easy to understand that when exhausted by a long and fruitless séance, and surrounded by a number of sitters eager to see something, a medium whose consciousness is still partly in abeyance may give the push that (s)he hopes will start the phenomena ..."

Richet further explained

> There is a quasi-identity between the medium and the ectoplasm, so that when an attempt is made to seize the latter, a limb of the medium may be grasped. ... More frequently, the ectoplasm is independent of the medium, indeed perhaps it is always so; though I do not mean to imply that the severance or capture of the ectoplasm can be effected without danger to the medium.

Some of the those studying Palladino suggested that her "third arm," an ectoplasmic extension molded by her spirit control, known as "John King," was carrying out the activity which others saw as fraud. Moreover, some of the investigators reported on "rhythmic actions" of her fingers, arms and legs that were in accord with activity taking place some distance from her, apparently through the invisible or mostly invisible ectoplasmic rods extending from her limbs to the point of activity, as if she, or the spirit controlling her, had become puppet masters of sorts. "When [Professor Oscar] Scarpa held Palladino's feet in his hands, he always felt her legs moving in synchrony with ongoing displacements of the table or chair," reported Professor Filippo Bottazi, who referred to the action as "synchrony."

Sir Oliver Lodge, a world-renowned British physicist, collaborated with Richet and two other scientists in one study of Palladino. It took place on an isolated island, and the researchers were sure Palladino brought nothing into the room and had no opportunity to "prepare" the room in advance of the sitting. Lodge wrote that Palladino resented the charges of fraud and that he was willing to give her the benefit of the doubt, so far as morals of deception were concerned, referring to her as a kindly soul with many of the instincts of a peasant. "She wanted us to understand that it was not conscious deception, but that her control took whatever means available, and if he found an easy way of doing things, thus would it be done," Lodge explained.

Lodge also reported on a test involving a spring dynamometer, which, when squeezed, measured hand grip strength. It was Richet's idea that all the energy used at a sitting had to come from the medium or some of the sitters. Thus, Lodge recorded the grip strength of Palladino and each sitter before and after the two-hour sitting. In the test reading, Lodge scored the highest, followed by Richet, and the other two scientists, with Palladino's being much weaker than the four men. But after the sitting, Palladino was giving a feeble clutch when she suddenly shouted, "Oh, John, you're hurting!" and the men observed the needle go far beyond what any of them could exert. "She wrung her fingers afterwards, and said John (King) had put his great hand around hers, and squeezed the machine up to an abnormal figure," Lodge explained, noting that "John King" occasionally showed his hand, "a big, five-fingered, ill-formed thing it looked in the dusk."

As prominent in the field of science as men like Lodge, Richet, and many others were, mainstream science was unable to accept their countless experiments and observations. While Lodge gradually came to accept the existence of spirits and the survival of consciousness in a spirit world after death, Richet preferred the middle ground, accepting the reality of the strange phenomena he had observed with various mediums but concluding that they all originated in the medium's subconscious in ways not yet understood by science, or even by the medium. He occasionally flirted with the spirit hypothesis, but remained steadfast in resisting the idea of spirits. Indications are that most researchers of that era sided with Richet, while the majority of scientists steered clear of the field, considering it just so much humbug.

Since mainstream science did not then and still does not now recognize the existence of spirits, it follows that it makes no distinction between advanced spirits and "earthbound" spirits, or those at various levels between earthbound and the higher realms. However, those

AFTERWORD

who came to accept the spirit hypothesis generally concluded that there were many levels of consciousness in the spirit world, not simply the heaven and hell taught by some orthodox religions. Robert Hare, a professor of chemistry at the University Pennsylvania and another of the early psychical researchers, explained that, as he interpreted it all, one's initial place in the afterlife is based on a "moral specific gravity," and from that place the soul can advance to higher levels, or higher vibrations. This was the general belief adopted by those calling themselves "Spiritualists" and was based on "teachings" coming through mediums from supposedly advanced spirits.

But researchers came to realize that the teachings could be distorted by the medium's subconscious mind and beliefs embedded there. Also, many spirit teachings and various physical manifestation could be interfered with by low-level spirits, the lowest referred to as "earthbound." Such spirits, it was said, transitioned to the spirit life at a very low moral specific gravity and were slow to awaken, often not even realizing they had departed the physical life. In some cases, there was a divided consciousness, much like the person absorbed in a good movie. The low-level spirits continue their deceitful ways in the afterlife and because they are closer to the earth frequency are better able to communicate and carry out physical phenomena than more advanced spirits, who are at a more distant frequency.

French educator Allan Kardec, still another of the early researchers, put many questions to supposedly advanced spirits through mediums, including one asking why God permits low-level spirit to influence us. As set forth in his classic, *The Spirits' Book*, the response from spirit came: "Imperfect spirits are used by Providence as instruments for trying men's faith and constancy in well-doing. You, being a spirit, must advance in the knowledge of the infinite. It is for this end that you are made to pass through the trials of evil in order to attain to goodness. Our mission is to lead you into the right road. When you are acted upon by evil influence, it is because you attract evil spirits to you by your evil desires, for evil spirits always come to aid you in doing the evil you desire to do; they can only help you to do wrong when you give way to evil desires. If you are inclined to commit murder, you will have about you a swarm of spirits who will keep this inclination alive in you; but you will also have others about you who will try to influence you for good, which restores the balance, and leaves you of your decision."

All that seems in accord with the Christian Bible, which tells us in 1 John 4:1, to "test the spirits, as to whether they are of God," while 1

Thessalonians 5:21 also instructs us "to test them all and hold on to what is good." In 1 Corinthians 12:10 we are told to "discern" what the spirits have to say.

"Many of the teachings came from "group souls"—a number of discarnates or "spirit entities" speaking as one, or different discarnates taking turns communicating "higher truths" through a particular medium. One such group soul, called Imperator, communicated through the mediumship of William Stainton Moses, an Anglican priest, during the late 1800s. "Development in mediumistic power is accompanied by risk as well as by blessing," Imperator advised. "And when a strong hand does not surround the medium the risk of invasion by undeveloped spirits is increased. Care and prayer are requisite."

According to Imperator, deceptive spirits are attracted to circles in which the intentions are not pure, or are more materialistic. "They who evoke physical marvels to please wonder-seekers are too frequently the sport of spirits intellectually and morally on a low plane," the group added. "You cannot even rely that you are at different times conversing with the same spirit; for they will assume names and forms, and take pleasure in deceit."

So what can we believe about Valiantine and the whole story related by Bradley? Did Valiantine have telepathic abilities that permitted him to read the minds of others and then provide names and facts suggesting that deceased relatives and friends were communicating with them? Did this mind-reading extend to things not even on the minds of those sitting with him, or, in some cases, not even known to them? To tell of personal matters not even remembered by them? Did it permit him to simulate their accents and intonations? To speak fluently in many foreign languages?

At the same time, we have to ask if Valiantine was so stupid as to think his big toes would match up with the thumb of Lord Dewar and the finger of Sir Arthur Conan Doyle. It is not entirely clear from Bradley's reporting as to how much Valiantine knew about the planned imprints, but he had been happy to experiment with prints before in Noel Jaquin's smoked paper experiments, which are documented in earlier chapters, so even if he wasn't informed of the plan, why would he think his toes would be evidence of anything?

Or was Bradley right about low-level spirits somehow controlling Valiantine and carrying out the deception? Is that what Annie, Bradley's sister, was trying to warn him about? If so, was it conscious fraud or unconscious fraud on the part of Valiantine? If unconscious fraud, why was Bradley so upset with Valiantine?

AFTERWORD

So many questions, but nearly a century later there are still no answers beyond what one chooses to believe.

Michael Tymn
July 2022

The End

INDEX

A

Ahlefeldt-Laurvig, Countess, 278, 280-281, 398
American Society for Psychical Research (Journal of), 13, 509
Anchester, Henry, 86
Annesley, Priscilla, Countess, 224-225
Archer, William, 207, 209, 247-248, 323
Ayres, Mrs., 409

B

Baines, Jack, 240, 322
Baldwin, Harold, 349, 404
Baldwin, Oliver, 348-351, 403-404, 406
Baldwin, Stanley, 406
Balfour, Lord, 106
Bannerman, Miss Margaret, 213, 348-350, 364
Barrie, Sir James M., 386
Beaverbrook, Lord, 119-123
Bechard, Mdlle., 242-243
Bendir, Mrs. Arthur, 392-394
Benvenisti, Mrs. E., 215-217
Bethell, the Hon. Mrs. Richard, 245, 344-346
Bethell, the Hon. Richard, 347
Bird, J. Malcolm, 42, 73, 75-81, 85, 86, 88
Birkenhead, Lord, 403-404, 406
Bisson, Madame, 252
Boler, E., 359, 361
Bottazi, Professor Filippo, 511
Bottomley, Horatio, 191-192
Bovill, Mrs., 231, 234
Broad, Dr., 240
Brooke, Clifford, 364
Bryant, Charles, 364
Butt, Dame Clara, 270, 296-300, 374

C

Calthrop, Donald, 65, 67-68, 348
Campbell, Herbert, 132
Cannell, T. C., 381-382
Carleton, Miss Billie, 263, 267, 272, 385, 387-389
Carson, Miss Frances, 65, 67
Cathcart, George, 148

Catholic, 379, 399, 443-444, 468-469, 474, 502, 507
Cernikoff, Vladimir, 348-350
Chevalier, Albert, 310, 312
Chevalier, Mrs. Albert, 309-310, 312
Church of England, 468-469
Clayton, John, 67
Coats, Mrs. Dudley, 362, 364-366
Cohen, Miss Ida, 48, 242, 243
Cohen, Miss Madeline, 47, 48, 119, 207, 283, 286, 299, 330, 332-333, 431
Colley, Major, 224-225
Collier, Miss Constance, 296-300, 392
Collins, Greville, 207-208
Compton, Edward, 263, 266-274, 385-388, 404
Compton, Miss Fay, 263, 266-274, 385-388, 404
Cooper, Miss Gladys, 362-366
Corbett, Lionel, 231, 233-234, 282
Craddock, F. F., 28, 125-127
Craig, Mrs. Gordon, 355, 357
Crandon, Dr. L. R. G., 5-7, 229
Crandon, Mrs. L. R. G. ("aka Margery'), 4-7, 229, 508, 510
Crawford, Dr William J., 252, 509-510
Crookes, Sir William, 508-509
Crosland, T. W. H., 157-159
Curzon, of Kedleston, Lady, 404, 406
Curzon, of Kedleston, Lord, 403, 413-414, 431-432

D

Dewar, Lord, 472, 478, 480, 483, 485-488, 490-491, 493, 506, 514
Dharwar, Mr., 245
Dick, John M., 129, 131-136

Dingwall, E. J. 94, 254-255, 275-276, 279, 368-371, 475
Doyle, Lady, 309-310, 505-506
Doyle, Sir Arthur Conan, 6, 101-102, 119, 167, 285, 309, 437, 454, 456, 458, 472, 478, 480-486, 490-491, 506, 514
Doyle, Adrian, 505-506
Doyle, Kingsley, 309-310

E

Ectoplasm, 78, 80, 247, 252, 418, 421, 495, 509-511
Ellis, Mrs. M. I., 221-222
Engster, Miss, 215-217
Evans, Caradoc, 25, 27, 33, 78
Evans, Mrs. Caradoc, 32-33, 35
Everidge, Dr. John, 414, 431-432
Eyles, F. A. H., 131-132, 134
Eyles, Mrs. F. A. H., 131

F

Fender, P. H. G., 393-394
Florence, P. Sargent, 241
Flower, Newman, 317
Forest, John De, 157
Fry, Edward, 25, 68
Fry, Gertrude, 25, 62

G

Gainsmore, L. D., 242-243
Galsworthy, John, 226, 364
Gardiner, Miss Margaret, 240
Garvice, Charles, 283-284
Geley, Dr. Gustave, 252, 338, 342
George, D. Lloyd, 130, 472, 485, 487, 491
Glynne, Miss Mary, 403-405
Goligher, Kathleen, 509-510
Goodson, Miss Kate, 208-209

INDEX

Graham, Mrs. Robert, 204, 318, 416
Graham, Winifred, 25, 29, 40, 44, 204, 218-219, 283, 380, 391, 416
Grenfell, Lord, 193, 453
Grinling, Denis, 317, 403-406
Grinling, Mrs. Gibbons, 317, 403-404
Gruber, Dr. Karl, 509

H

Hall, Miss Radcliffe, 256-257, 289-291, 301-305, 313, 316, 325, 343, 368, 462
Hall, Sir Edward Marshall, 167, 372
Hammerstein, Oscar, 393, 395
Hannen, Mrs., 393-395
Harrison, Austin, 247-248, 250-252
Hawker, Harry, 133
Henderson, Admiral Wilfred, 231, 233
Heretics' Society, 240-241
Hewitt, E. P., K.C., 344-345
Hewlett, Maurice, 408
Hicks, Captain Ben, 73, 83, 86, 88
Hornung, E. W., 309-310
Hunt, George, 69, 233, 243
Hunt, Mrs. George, 183, 242
Huntley, Alec, 131, 145, 150, 359
Huntley, Mrs., 359
Husk, Cecil, 98, 134, 150-152, 176, 184, 193, 197, 453
Home, D.D., 508
Huskinson, Edward,

I

Imperator, 514

J

Jaquin, Noel, 27, 32-34, 399-401, 409-410, 416-418, 420, 425-426, 428, 441, 461, 475-476, 479-482, 484-486, 488-497, 502, 506, 514

Johnson, Alfred, 381, 383
Johnstone, Mrs. W. Y., 242-243
Joicey, Edward, 322-324
Jones, Kennedy, 179

K

Kakucs, The Baroness, 192, 452
Kardec, Allan, 513
Keith, Sir Arthur, 437-438, 442
Kennedy, Mrs. 179, 226, 247-248
King, John, 98, 150, 511-512, 176, 184
Kinloch, Mrs., 215-216
Komai, Gonnoské, 278, 280-281, 294, 309, 311

L

Laurence, W. W., 240, 322
Laurie, T. Werner, 171, 473
Law, Bonar, 119, 122-124
Leno, Dan, 129, 131-132, 193, 453
Leonard, Mr. Osborne, 30, 31
Leonard, Mrs. Osborne, 17, 21, 24, 30, 32, 39, 53, 71, 113, 123, 153, 168, 176-177, 183, 237, 260, 271, 284, 290, 292, 313, 316, 317, 439
Lodge, Raymond, 231-232, 344-345
Lodge, Sir Oliver, 1, 13, 42, 231-235, 238, 263, 287, 313, 345, 512
Loraine, Miss Violet, 321-323
Lupino, Stanley, 132
Lycett, Joan, 321
Lycett, Randolph, 321
Lynn, Miss Olga, 364-366

M

Maberley, Captain C. J. Astley, 211-212, 282, 299
Mallory, George Herbert Lee, 145-146

Malmesbury, Susan, Countess of, 355, 357-358
Marlowe, Christopher, M.A., 130, 416-417, 419, 422-423
Maskelyne, Captain Clive, 229-230
Maugham, Mrs. Somerset, 365
Maugham, W. Somerset, 362, 364-366
McKenna, Justine, 395
McKenna, Mrs. Theodore, 393-395
McKenna, Reginald, 393
McKenzie, Mrs. D. F., 396
Miller, Allan, 83-84, 86, 355-356
Molesworth, Viscountess, 344-345
Monkman, Phyllis, 207, 209, 405
Moore, the Sisters, 28, 109-111, 328, 330, 334, 337
Morris, Alfred, 283-285, 288
Morris, Frederick, 272
Moseley, Sydney, 130, 452, 455-456, 458
Munnings, F. T., 129-133, 135-136, 145-147, 152, 165, 176, 183-184, 191-194, 451-459, 503
Murray, Professor Gilbert, 106
Murry, John Middleton, 248
Myers, F. W. H., 235

N

Neilson-Terry, Dennis, 263, 265-269, 403-405
Nichols, Beverley, 344, 346
North, H., 359
Northcliffe, Viscount/Lord, 43, 53-61, 63, 121-123, 168-176, 228
Novello, Ivor, 296-299, 363, 392

O

O'Donnell, Dr. T. Moore, 328, 330-334, 336-341,

O'Donnell, Mrs., 339
Oeitiongham, the Countess Tyong, 226-227
Owen, Louise, 43, 47-48, 50, 54, 56, 120-121, 167, 169, 170, 172-174, 176-184, 208, 283, 285-287, 372-375, 431
Owen, the Rev. Vale, 167

P

Palladino, Eusapia, 510-512
Peebles, Dr., 338-340
Pelissier, Harry, 263, 266-267, 271-272, 385, 387, 389, 404-405
Philipson, Hilton, 296-299
Philipson, Mrs. Hilton, M.P., 296-297
Pinero, Sir Arthur W., 364
Playfair, Arthur, 207, 209, 405
Powell, Dr. Ellis, 131, 133, 298
Powell, Mrs. Ellis, 372, 373
Powell, Evan, 28, 119-121, 123, 282, 285
Price, Harry, 372, 373, 475, 495
Prins, George, 322-323
Prinsep, Anthony, 213
Probyn, Major Dighton, 215-216
Probyn, Mrs. Dighton, 215-216
Purefoy, W. B., 392

Q

Quartermaine, Leon, 274, 385-387, 404

R

Ransome, Dr. Herbert Fullerton, 145, 148-150, 152, 176
Reynolds, Mrs., 226, 228
Richet, Dr. Charles, 510-512
Richards, I. A., 240

INDEX

Rodems, Mrs. Grace, 83, 355
Roman Catholic Church, 443-444, 468-469

S

Sargeant, Mrs. Gaston, 113-116, 118, 161-162
Saunders, R. H., 205, 454, 456, 458
Scales, Mrs. M., 113-114, 116, 126, 161-162, 164, 214
Scarpa, Professor Oscar, 511
Schneider, Rudi, 4-5, 508-510
Schrenck Notzing, Baron von, 252
Scientific American, the, 76
Scott, Mrs. Dawson, 263, 265, 268-270, 272, 274
Scott-Nelson, Mrs., 215-216
Seamans, Mr., 86-87
Sevening, Miss Nina, 364
Shackleton, Sir Ernest, 221-222
Shalders, Julian, 70-71
Shaw, George Bernard, 445
Smith, Mrs. Travers, 137-141, 143
Society for Psychical Research (SPR), 13, 62, 88, 93, 94, 98, 104, 106, 192, 234-236, 238, 253-258, 262, 282, 289-291, 299, 303, 313, 343, 370-371, 452, 462, 509
Spender, J. A., 143
Stanhope, the Hon. Mrs. Fitzroy, 278, 280-281, 307-308
Stainton Moses, William, 514
Stead, Estelle, 109
Stead, William, 120
Swaffer, Hannen, 43, 47, 53, 55-60, 65, 121, 123, 134-135, 139, 141-142, 169-176, 248
Swaffer, Mrs. Hannen, 393, 395
Sykes, Charles, 25, 213, 381-382, 416-418, 422, 424, 427, 429, 441, 475-476, 480-481, 484-485, 488, 490-492, 496-497
Sykes, Jessica, 381

T

Terry, Ellen, 355
Tristram, Lieut.-Colonel Miles, 215
Tristram, Miss, 215-216
Troubridge, Una, Lady, 256-257, 289-291, 301-304, 313-314, 316-317, 325-326, 343, 368, 462-463

U

Uzielli, Mrs. Theo, 396

V

Vlasto, Mrs. Erato, 372-373, 376-377

W

Walbrook, Lilian, 372-377
Walker, Miss, 313-314
Walker, Mrs., 359-360
Wallace, Dr. Abraham, 125-126, 328, 330, 334-335, 337-341, 454, 458, 476
Washburn, W. Ives, 82, 84
West, Rebecca, 355, 357-358
Whaddia, N. P., 245-246
White, Mrs. Helen, 211
Whittet, Mrs. H. I., 242-243
Wilde, Oscar, 5, 137, 141, 402
Wimbury, Harold, 78, 317
Withall, Henry, 150
Wodehouse, Miss Leonora, 192, 385-386, 452
Wodehouse, P. G., 65-66, 68, 192, 385-386, 452
Woolley, Dr. V. J., 192-193, 228, 255-257, 276-277, 279, 287, 289, 291, 301-305, 314-315, 368-369, 452-453

Woolley, Mrs., 314-315
Worrall, Harry, 407
Worrall, Miss Maud, 407
Worrall, Bobby, 202, 211, 218-219, 232, 264, 280, 296-297, 308-309, 318, 339, 358-359, 361, 386, 388, 407, 411, 413, 431
Wyckoff, J. De., 8, 10, 18, 39-40, 42-43, 73-76, 80-88, 95, 103, 110, 355-356
Wynn, the Rev. Walter, 372-373, 376-377

www.ingramcontent.com/pod-product-compliance
Lightning Source LLC
Chambersburg PA
CBHW021137160426
43194CB00007B/612